My Ego Screwed My Acting Career

Jason Croot

MY EGO SCREWED MY ACTING CAREER

STRUGGLERS GLORY BOOKS

Copyright © 2024 Jason Croot

All rights reserved.

ISBN: 978-1-0687911-0-9

INTRODUCTION

'I appreciate you proofreading my book. Can you take a butcher's at my introduction?'

'Sure fire away!'

'Okay, here it goes...We're born not knowing where life will lead. We continue through life's journey, with some planned and unplanned aspects of life...None of us can ever be 100% certain where life will lead...apart from that, ultimately, we will all eventually near the end of our summers...'

'Hmm, it's too cryptic...sorry Jay!'

'Uh huh...hmm...okay, no, that's okay. Let me work on it, and I'll call you soon with a new one.'

'Looking forward to it!'

111+ Cups of coffee Later
'This took me ages to do, but I think it's good...quite chuffed with myself in fact. See if you like this.'

'Right Jay...I'm ready...'

'Okay, fingers crossed...take two...My mind holds onto numerous memories... some happy and blissful, others perhaps the substance full of nightmares...Then there are those thoughts I have surreptitiously pushed away, hidden in a locked box and thrown away the key, pretending the negative things never happened....Now my box has been smashed open, and almost all of my untold secrets will be revealed for the very first time in this book...It's a book that goes deep inside my heart, mind and soul...feedback?'

'Hmm...well, don't get me wrong, it's good...but it's...uh...um...it's just not you! Maybe work on it a bit more? Get to the grit of Jason Croot. Get to what your story is trying to convey...the heart...the essence...you know what I mean?'

'Um...I think so...okay!'

11 Episodes of Curb Your Enthusiasm later
'I think this is what you're talking about...I think I've managed to make it more me.'

'I'm all ears Jay...fire away...'

'Okay...here it goes...I've spent what felt like ages stuck in this limbo...life-wise, relationship-wise, and career-wise...and still haven't fully grasped what was actually missing. I've always been striving to do more, to have more, to say more. I've made the kind of rash and not-so-wise decisions that most probably will make you wince.

Like acting and filmmaking, writing has been a journey for me. It has been frustrating and enlightening. There have been times when words would just flow onto my computer screen, make me smile, make me cringe and make my heart break, sometimes all at once.

I was robbed and almost arrested in Mexico, kidnapped and nearly locked up in Greece, lured in by a pimp in Italy AND stalked in England... So what d'you think?'

'Um it's better Jay...but...'

'BUT?!?!'

'It's just that you're missing that *je ne sais quoi*. Perhaps it's the tone...it's kind of different from the whole tone of your book...D'you get what I mean?... '

'Okay, let me get on it...'

8 Supermarket shops later
'I've changed the intro; let me know what you think...'
'Will do, Jay; ahem, apart from the intro, have you thought about the early years stuff? I mean after proofreading your book, I got thinking about the early years section. Not everyone wants to read about that stuff in autobiographies, you know!'
'Like I mentioned before, it's more than an autobiography...Anyway, the early years stuff is about the period that made, moulded and shaped me, you know. It's about the times that created the person I am today.'
'I know but...'
'...Look, I'm finding this a little disparaging! What d'you want me to do? Change it?'
'No...edit Jay, edit...Maybe you can put...'
'...Look! If the reader wants to read the racy stuff, they can go to chapter 11 or later on in the book and read about the parts with the wild partying and debauchery, you know? It's their prerogative. What I'm trying to say is that they can skip the early years bit if they want, but I figure some will like the childhood Fandango..'
'...Listen, Jay...I have to take my dog out before it decides to do *hari-cari.*'
'Okay, no worries. Thanks for your advice anyway. Speak soon!'

88 Cat Naps Later
Still holding on to the last thread of patience I have left...
'... Say it as it is Jason...say it as it is...SAY IT AS IT IS...'

'Thanks for taking the time again, I appreciate it...Are you ready? I hope this is good enough! Because this introduction will be the death of me...'
'I'm ready Jay...'
'Right here it goes...They say you shouldn't make the same mistakes twice, but I've made the same mistakes thousands of times...Making mistake after mistake after mistake has been the story of my life. So why not write about it, I thought?
I'd like to think this book is not just about my life and acting career; it's also about my journey to discover the meaning of life, but I'm still trying to figure that one out.
I can categorically say this is not a how-to book; on the contrary, it's more about how-not-to. So for all new upcoming or established actors looking for a how-to, this isn't the book for you! And to all

non-actors out there, I have thousands of, reasons for you not to buy this book, which include and are not limited to the following:

You feel uncomfortable about things that make you feel uncomfortable.
You get highly offended by descriptions of an intimate nature; xxx.
You're not interested in the story behind the story of an actor.
You never mess up in life, and can't relate to my fuck ups.
You've got better things to do than read this book.
You don't like reading about conflict.
You don't want to read about my travel adventures.
You are looking to read a book that is grammatically perfekt..
You don't know me, and you're not interested in knowing any more.
You do know me, and you are not interested in knowing any more.
You've read this intro and realised I'm not as profound as Shakespeare.

This book is definitely not for most, if not all. So people, if you choose to buy it, do so at your own peril. Be warned that the story you have been crazy-mad enough to embark on is my point of view, my side of the story. I'm pretty sure some of my former teachers, lovers, friends, etc. will have their sides too.

This book is BASED on my side, my life story. I'm capitalising BASED because I've had to change some things to protect the identity of people, places, events, establishments etc. I've also had to change some names of people and productions I've acted in.

For all who are mentioned in the book, the conversations are not exact, but the essence still remains very much as it was, because to be frank, my memory is great, but not that great, to actually remember everything word for word.

For all the smart Alecs out there, you will find some grammar errors. For those who don't like to read anything smaller than a 9-point font, stop right here. For all the prudish amongst you, look away, turn away and close the book right now or forever hold your peace, because from here on in this book is glittered or littered (depending on what your viewpoint is) with lots of colourful language, stories of sex and debauchery...So? Yeah? Good?'

'Not bad, Jay, not bad at all! I hope folk leave you some honest reviews!'

'Me too. Thanks again. Let's print it. Otherwise, I'll be here for the next twenty years writing this damn thing!!!'

1 MAMA MIA

'Why?...Why?...But whyyyyyyyyy?...Pleeeeeeeeeeeeeassse. Me!!! It's not fair!!!'

I was in the midst of a fairytale when my four-year-old heart was hacked into a billion pieces.

Salty droplets soaked through my yellow *Basil Brush* jumper.

Shards of my heart sprawled across the floor next to Mum's Dolci's leather handbag. Through blurry eyes, I watched all the other children perform alongside the stars of the show on the magnificent stage. Then, the whole auditorium burst into a rendition of Happy Birthday. This, of course, made me well up even more. I had tried every way I knew to beg and to plead with all my might.

My four-year-old tears seemed to have no effect as Mum yanked me back down to my seat by my jumper.

Going to the theatre should've been a wonderfully rewarding and exciting time. However, this wasn't entirely the case this particular weekend when I went with Mum to watch *Goldilocks and the Three Bears* at the Alhambra Theatre in Bradford, Yorkshire.

I had been in awe as soon as I stepped foot into the breathtaking and divinely decorated playhouse. During the performance, I was mesmerised by all of the actors, especially Anne Aston, who was playing Goldilocks. She seemed to glide like a newly hatched butterfly when she moved and her wide smile lit up the whole auditorium. I was as keen as mustard when Goldilocks asked the audience if it was anybody's birthday.

'Hello, little bears! Are there any special birthday boys or girls amongst us today?'

One eager bear was sitting at the front near the stage. His enthusiasm was loud and clear for all to hear; his hand shot up in the air as he called out to Goldilocks.

'It's mine! It's mine! It's mine!'

The adult-sized, true-to-life Goldilocks then welcomed him warmly.

'Oh my, we've got an eager birthday star! Come and join me on stage, my dear and let us make this magical day even brighter. What's your name, little bear?' she enchanted.

'It's Timmy,' the beaming boy replied.

'How wonderful! Let's give Timmy a big round of applause, everyone! Now, are there any other little bears ready to join in the fun? Don't be shy. Come and join us!'

I was aware that I only had a fox's chance to convince Mum that I should be up on the stage too. I dared anyway.

'Me, Mum, me, me, me, pleeeeeassse, Mum,' I begged as I tugged away at her heavy winter cardigan.

'Jason, I'm sorry, Luv, ye can't; it's not yer birthday today. Next year, ye can...I promise.'

Goldilocks invited more birthday children to join Timmy on stage. Eagerly, my hand shot up in the air, and Mum quickly pushed it down. I put it back up, desperate for Goldilocks to know it was my birthday, even though technically it wasn't. Me putting my hand up and Mum putting it back down continued until Goldilocks had all the willing children on stage apart from me; she was no longer calling for anyone else to come up. My heart was like Baby Bear's chair: Well and truly broken.

The experience stays with me and is still as vivid as if it happened yesterday.

It was only later on in life that I realised the significance of that day. I was meant to be in front of an audience. I was meant to perform.

2 LITTLE SHOP OF HORRORS

'This is crap, crap, crap,' I hollered.

The red-faced waitress hurriedly removed the disappointing food from the café's table. I had made it very obvious that the plate of food without chips and ketchup she had dared to serve me was absolutely, in my four-year-old world, NOT to my taste!

'Jason, behave yourself, will ye? Or I'll wash yer mouth out with soap and water.'

'Leave him be, Alice Luv.'

'But, Dad, I'm worried that he'll swear when he starts school.'

'He'll be fine,' Gan Gan reassured

'Aye, he'll be fine, Alice Luv,' Nana echoed.

In my early years, my colourful language and free-spirited attitude were never met with scolds, harsh words or even looks of disapproval from Gan Gan and Nana, who always showed their love and acceptance of my unique and lively nature.

Mum, on the other hand, had a different stance on my colourful language. She was worried I would continue to use such distasteful vocabulary when I started school; so, in a bid to prepare me for the institution of school, Nana and Gan Gan were told by Mum to make sure that I followed her strict instruction, NOT to swear anymore.

When I was eventually called up to start school at Saint Medard's, Allerton, at age five, it didn't take long for me to realise that it wasn't for me. Born out of boredom and frustration, my shadow always trailed behind me in the shape of mischief and always seemed to land me in trouble.

One teacher who always had his eye on me and my questionable ways was the infamous Mr Charles, our strict headmaster and sports teacher. He had a deep scar on his left cheek that spanned from the corner of his lazy eye to his cheekbone, which gave us mere mortal children, the heebie-jeebies. Rumours had it he got his scar from wrestling a crocodile whilst on safari in Africa.

Tuesdays were our mixed gymnastics lesson when we had the pleasure of being taught by Mr Charles, whose short fuse snapped one such Tuesday due to my horsing around with the other pea from the same pod as me, Stephen Farrell (Ste). As soon as we met, Ste and I bonded as best chums through playground rhymes, penny sweets, and plenty of poorly thought-out pranks that would span the course of our friendship.

I was putting on my pumps, which were two sizes too big, when Ste came to me with a panicked plea.

'Jay, Jay, you got any spare shorts? I've forgotten my kit.'

Ste was petrified, like all the other children, to face Mr Charles's wrath.

'What's it worth, Ste, a lolly?'

'But, I only have one left.'

'Do you want the shorts or not?'

'....Arghhh...okay...okay...go on then...I'll give it to you...I swear...'

So, luckily for Ste, in exchange for the promise of a Drumstick lollipop, I kind of...sort of...hmmm well almost, saved the day and his behind, by loaning him the spare pair of clean shorts that I had in my gym bag.

During the gymnastics class, the lofty Mr Charles stood in his tighter-than-tight and shorter-than-short shorts, his whistle, which he used like a weapon, dangled on a cord around his neck. Hardly any of the children dared to breathe in the wrong way or step out of line with Mr Charles in charge. Today was no exception as he instructed us about the task of running and then jumping over the school's pommel horse, one by one; each kid took their turn proud as punch when they landed correctly as Mr Charles ordered. When it was Ste's turn, he ran, then jumped, and before landing on the mat, the shorts and his shame fell down and landed around his ankles. His bright red Y-fronts matched the colour of his face as he stood fixed to the gym mat, mortified even more by the giggles of the mixed sports class of children. I stood behind the group of children and was the one who laughed the hardest of all, till my belly literally ached. I had known, without a shadow of a doubt, that when I lent Ste my shorts, they had very loose elastic on them!

Mouths twisted to the side as the children's mumbles soon turned into hysteria, causing an almighty disruption to our lesson. Mr Charles was none too pleased. He blew his whistle so hard I'm sure I could feel my eardrums vibrate. He thrashed his aggravation towards us unrelentingly.

'Crooooot and Farrrrrelllll, it's the likes of you two boys who spoil it for the rest of the class. Well, if you're going to act like infants, you can sit with the infants. Does anybody else want to join them?'

As Mr Charles threw out that threat, a blanket of silence fell over the rest of the class. Ste and I were marched towards the nursery and shoehorned into their miniature world. Here, we had to sit uncomfortably in a corner of the nursery, hands on our heads, crossed-legged on the floor, facing the wall while the oblivious three-year-olds played around us.

'This is your fault, you twonk!' Ste jibed as we sat, staring at the crumbling magnolia paint. I retaliated with.

'You're a bigger twonk. Where's my lolly?'

Although few and far between, there were times I managed to contain the excitement of mischief and not let it take over, for example, when the starring role of *Good King Wenceslas* in the school play was bestowed upon me. I didn't want to put a foot wrong and risk Mrs Thompson, the music teacher, taking the prestigious role away. I managed to stay angelic right up to a few days before the big performance, but as irony would have it, it was my bad tonsils rather than my bad behaviour that ultimately lost me my starring role. Two days before the performance, tonsillitis struck, coupled with a high fever, but even though I was so unwell, I desperately wanted to perform in the play. I begged and pleaded with Nana and Gan Gan, but Mum told them to keep me home. I was devastatingly close, but the chance for my big stage debut once again was scuppered. Mrs Thompson had no option but to give the role of *Good King Wenceslas* to another of my school chums, Steve McAleavy, who jumped at the promotion, and just like that, he was set to STAR alongside the other reason why I was desperate to keep the part, one of the prettiest girls in the class, Justine Holliday.

Not so sweet
'No custard for me, please.'

The sight of the bright yellow substance and the sickly sweet smell made me gip, and it was the one and only thing I detested about school dinners.

Other than custard, contrary to the reputation of British school dinners, the lunches at St. Medard's were actually quite nice, though still pale in comparison to Nana's homemade meals. Kids would queue up willingly, eager to get a portion of the amazing cheese flan and yummy rhubarb crumble. I'd often eat quickly so that I could get a chance to get a second helping of pudding if there was any left. I once tried my luck at going up for thirds, only to be met with a mardy response from an eagled-eyed dinner lady.

'Have ye got a tapeworm or summat? You're eating far too quickly!'

Maybe it was the smell OR the playground rhyme which had recently spread around children like a rumour, that had put me off custard for absolute life. Whichever it was, I couldn't shake off the image of yellow belly custard and green snot pie mixed together with a dead dog's eye. So, when the dinner ladies routinely ladled the custard over children's puddings without even asking, my belly curdled. I often tried swerving my bowl away from the sickly, thick, yellow-belly substance when it came to my turn.

'No custard for me, please,' I said sweetly on one occasion when I went up for a second helping of steaming Jam Roly Poly pudding.

'I'm allergic,' I lied as if offering her this information would win her over.

However, the dinner lady's suspicions arose, and she proceeded to quiz me as if I were on trial.

'Ye drink milk, don't ye, sonny?'

'Yeah, I do,' I murmured realising only after that that I had slipped up.

'Hmm, well, ye can't be allergic to custard then,' she replied as she rested her case and proceeded to plop the steaming custard over my pudding anyway as if it was a compulsory medicine. My initial excitement about having a second slice of Jam Roly Poly pudding drowned in my custard that dinnertime! Utterly disappointed. I had no other option but to give it to my chum Robert Coulson (Coulsy), who ate anything and everything.

Many adults at school at that time shared attitudes similar to that of the dinner ladies. It was either their way or no way, which was very frustrating for me. One exception, though, was Mrs Aubrey, our class teacher, who had the patience to give any saint a run for their money. She bestowed the responsibility of being the class snack monitors to Ste and me. We couldn't believe it, seeing as our behaviour wasn't always the best. Being a class monitor for a day was a great privilege and one that Mum was very proud of when I told her. The monitors were entrusted with the prized big jar of sweets and a massive box of crisps, which they sold for pennies each break time to other hungry children.

It would be most children's delight to be amongst an array of wonderful goodies. Snacks like these would be limited for many children at home, and I was pretty sure no one would have access to the amount we had, from bags and bags of pickled onion Monster Munch, smoky bacon Wheat Crunchies, and roast beef-flavoured Seabrook crisps to multiple packets of brightly coloured sweet and sugary treats: Rainbow Drops, Refreshers, Flying Saucers, Space Dust popping candy and my favourite type of soft chewy nougat on sticks, Drumsticks.

When it was our day to be the monitors, our jealous mates looked on. With our halos polished, Ste and I held the snacks like the Crown Jewels as we made our way to the school playground. We placed the snacks on our makeshift stall, and in exchange for the tasty packets filled with e-numbers, we collected the children's money to take back to the school secretary.

Once we'd finished, Ste and I headed up the staircase towards the school office. However, before we got there, we made an executive decision. In a moment of calculated madness, we decided to go to the boys' toilets and tuck into a few sneaky sweets. No adults would catch us there, as the smell was too putrid. We knew we had to be quick.

Despite the air in the room being invaded by the stench of urine, we held our noses and began unwrapping a few mouth-watering sweets. But one sweet became two sweets, two sweets became four, and before we knew it, we had eaten around eight packets between us. The hard evidence was strewn across the floor in the form of multiple sweet wrappers. Ste had just filled his mouth with an entire packet of popping candy, and I was tucking into another Drumstick lollipop when the door of the boys' toilet flung open. It was Mr Charles, our strict headmaster. He launched into the toilet, his scarily lazy eye honed in on us sitting on the floor. Our mouths were still full of sticky sweets. In a roar that I was sure made the rickety door of one of the cubicles shake, Mr Charles bellowed in a tone sharper than the cheap tracing paper that pupils used for bog roll.

'What the devil is going on here? You boys, up to my office, NOW!!!'

I dropped my half-eaten Drumstick lollipop on the floor and obeyed Mr Charles; Ste followed, and in the silence, I could hear candy remnants still popping from Ste. We left the evidence of half-eaten packets of sweets on the cold concrete floor. Boy, were we in trouble!'

Milk, milk, lemonade around the corner, our chocolate was made.

Guilty as sin, our heads bowed low as we dragged our feet and trailed behind the furious headmaster. He marched towards his intimidating desk and stealthy chair. It was as if we were walking our last walk towards the gallows. I felt like the sickly yellow-greenish colour of the unkempt grass that covered our school grounds. Ste and I both stood silently, awaiting our fate. A picture of Jesus on the cross was hanging behind the head of the angry Mr Charles, who tapped his knee, indicating he wanted one of us to volunteer to be the first to repent. Ste, with Rainbow Drops guiltily hanging from his school jumper, nudged me forward, so I walked over to Mr Charles's desk. The open bible on it suggested that he was going to read us a moral passage from it, so I innocently sat on his knee as he had indicated by his tap. As it turned out, I had got the wrong end of the stick, and Mr Charles interpreted this as me being belligerent. He pushed me off and barked.

'No, boy! BEND over my knee.'

I was now going to be crucified. Mr Charles proceeded to give me six hard slaps on my backside, or "six of the best," as they were known. I started to cry, which made Ste cry, and he hadn't even had his six spanks yet!

3 THE GOOD OLD DAYS

It was 1971, the same year that CUPNOODLES were invented. The first small Starbucks store also opened up its doors on the cobbled streets of Seattle. And *Imagine*, the best-selling single of John Lennon's solo career, was released.

It was Thursday the 4th, and the day the biggest postal strike in the UK for five decades ended, with workers set to resume their deliveries; another major delivery happened in the labour ward of the Bradford Royal Infirmary.

It was March and only a few weeks before Tom Jones's single *She's a Lady* went gold, the lady of the moment, Alice Croot, gave birth to me, another rising star.

'I've seen him, Alice. He's beautiful, he looks like a movie star,' Dad chimed.

My parents, Alice (Mum) Croot and Dennis (Dad) Croot wanted to name me Matthew after the saint, but that wasn't to be. Instead, I was named after a famous playboy author who had a sideline as a detective. He was a character named *Jason King* from the hit 70s TV show with the same name.

Martin's afternoon of enjoying his favourite TV programme, *Jason King*, was interrupted by Mum and Dad, who had brought me to their home at Rosedale Avenue and formally introduced me to him.

'Meet Matthew, your new baby brother.'

But instead of welcoming me with open arms, Martin threw an almighty tantrum. In between his yells, kicks and screams, he shouted.

'No! No! No! you have to call him Jason...*Jason King!*'

He went on and on and Ariston about it, and eventually, he won.

So, I was baptised Jason Matthew six months later, named after the iconic legend *Jason King*. Ironically, it then followed quite naturally that as I got older, I became an actor, author, and playboy! Although my penchant for being a detective has yet to surface!

Martin lived on the opposite side of the city with Mum and Dad on Rosedale Avenue, while Gan Gan (William Banks) and Nana (Eileen Banks) raised me in their Bradford home on Sewell Road until I was six years old.

Our humble two-bedroom red brick council house sat on a cobbled street. A wooden cart was parked in the front yard for Harry, Gan Gan's trusty workmate, a beautiful black and white shire horse.

Harry, who was just as hardworking and dependable, dutifully tugged Gan Gan's oak wooden cart to and from Wakefield Road Market every day, where Gan Gan worked hard as a hawker, hawking fruit and vegetables to local shopkeepers to make ends meet.

From age three, I accompanied Gan Gan when he and Harry went to work, and I loved the twenty-minute morning rides to the busy local fruit and vegetable market. I often sat proudly high up on the cart when Gan Gan guided Harry. Sometimes, we would pass other horses and carts with their equally hardworking owners trying to make ends meet, including a local seller whose work involved collecting anything and everything that people in their homes were willing to give away or sell. As his own old horse trotted along the Bradford roads, he shouted.

'Rag and bone, any old Rag and bone.'

When Harry overtook the other horses, tugging their carts, I felt like my favourite comic character, *Asterix*. Children seated at the back of their parents' cars would stare up at me in awe when Harry stopped at the traffic lights. They most probably wished that they were in my place, on top of the world, as Harry trotted towards the Wakefield Road Market.

The market was jam-packed with flat-capped hawkers whose boots click-clocked as they foxtrotted around; their shoes with their Blackey's metal segs sounded very much like those of Harry and Gan Gan's when they walked. The hawkers would buy from very vocal vendors who cast out their spiels to reel in eager buyers.

'Ey up lads, come and get yer bananas and tomatoes, freshest in all of town.'

Their vendors' tables were packed full of big heads of cauliflowers, newly plucked King Edward potatoes, sticks of Yorkshire rhubarb, marbled Ribston Pippin's apples and bunches of sunny-smelling bananas from a world beyond Bradford. I often helped Gan Gan by handing him the stray fruit and vegetables that had rolled off his cart.

'Gan Gan, one more time pleeeeeassse Gan Gan.'

'Okay, Jay lad, climb up t' dancers again. Be careful, lad, t' steps are wet.'

The thrill of my day was when Gan Gan let me slide down the market's potato shoot. It was better than any playground I knew.

After a long day's work selling the fruit and vegetables that we'd bought in the morning, we'd often finish the day with Gan Gan carrying me on his shoulders into the Bedford Arms pub, a pub that belonged to my charming Uncle Peter, Gan Gan's son.

The Bedford Arms was a smoky place with a buzzing atmosphere, which was always packed with flat-capped Yorkshiremen, typical of their generation. They had been born and bred in the same city and likely had never set foot out of the confines of Yorkshire. They refused to spend a penny more than they had to on most things apart from pints of Yorkshire Tetley's bitter and tobacco. They would gather daily and share stories of new and old whilst swearing, drinking and putting the world to rights.

I felt like one of the men when Gan Gan and Uncle Peter would allow me tiny glugs of stout beer in my blue sipper cup, unbeknownst to Mum, who would often visit me at Sewell Road on weekends.

One Saturday evening, I overheard Mum's hair curling when she caught a strong whiff of stout beer after opening the lid of my blue sipper cup whilst I pretended to be conked out on the sofa.

'Dad, he's not drunk, is he? Is he okay?'

'Aye lass, don't worry luv, he's as reet as rain... isn't he Eileen?' Gan Gan said, looking to Nana for backup.

'Aye Alice, he's as good as gold...he's just jiggered from going t' market, that's all; he'll be going up t' hairy mountains to bed soon,' Nana reassured Mum calmly.

I treasured Nana's calm presence, especially during moments of panic that would overwhelm most people, including myself.

One afternoon, after eagerly awaiting her return from work on the steps of our old house, I rushed inside to tell Gan Gan when I spotted her. However, I tripped on a step and crashed onto the cold concrete floor, banging my mouth. Horrified, I saw blood gushing from my mouth onto my bright yellow *Basil Brush* T-shirt. It was Nana who soothed both my distress and my wounds. As always, her words were like a comforting ointment.

'You'll soon be as reet as rain Luv... and then ye can have yer favourite apple pie.'

Nana's culinary creations were another source of comfort that I cherished deeply. After working all day in the local wool mill, she'd come back to our home, which she kept like a palace. Using some of the unsold fresh produce that Gan Gan and I brought home, she'd conjure up the heartiest of meals. Her specialities included mouthwatering beef and carrot stew, corned beef hash, and my favourite, her silky apple pie. Each dish was prepared and served with a generous sprinkle of love. Each and every dish she made in her kitchen was fit for lords and emperors.

When cooking was all done, she'd often say.

'Aye, it's reet good to get off mi feet for a bit. Mi feet are burnin' like Roman candles.'

Then, she'd join Gan Gan and me in the toasty living room around the open fire, and we'd watch our favourite episodes of *Laurel & Hardy* on our 16-inch black-and-white TV. All the while, the sweet and savoury scents of Nana's culinary creations wafted from the kitchen and made all of our mouths water in anticipation.

Nana's Apple pie wasn't the only pie I loved. When the spirits moved him, Gan Gan would often serve me up his very own speciality: chin pie, which always made me giggle when he rubbed his whiskers on my baby face. After supper, Gan Gan, satisfied with his appetite, often drank his bottles of Guinness while lying on our ageing three-seater sofa. He also gave us an additional helping of warm, comforting pudding through his storytelling—something Gan Gan had a real flair for. Then he'd pop some music onto his vintage record player, including one of my favourite records, *Take Me Back To My Dear Old Blighty*. He and Nana would often join Florrie Forde and sing their rendition just to me.

Take me back to dear old Blighty! Put me on the train for London town, take me over there, drop me anywhere, Birmingham, Leeds or Manchester, well, I don't care! (Whoa!) Tiddley-iddley-ighty. Hurry me back to Blighty. Blighty is the place for me!

Those were doozy moments which warmed me up like Nana's comforting apple pie. Those days were splendiferous. Those were the good old days.

4 HERO

'You'll keep your eye on him, Dad, won't ye? Blackpool's so busy this time of year, ye know.'

'Don't worry, Alice Luv, he'll be all reet, won't he, Eileen?'

'Aye, Alice, don't worry, Luv, he'll be all reet.'

On occasion, Nana, Gan Gan, and I would step out of the comfort of Sewell Road and venture on day trips together, relishing in the delights that dear old Blighty had to offer. Blackpool was one of our favourite places.

Here, we'd venture to the top of the world and look down from Blackpool Tower at the busy tourists that packed out the Golden Mile, and when our feet were firmly back on the ground, we'd be drawn in by the tunes coming from every nook and cranny of the promenade. Nana, Gan Gan and I would trot our way to join the eager amusement arcade worshippers who were feeding the two penny slot machine Gods, all hoping they would grant them a line of tickets so they could claim any of the heavenly prizes from key rings to playing cards and whoopie cushions to baseball caps.

Of course, like most who enjoyed the arcades, we'd leave without the prizes we'd hoped for, but I never felt I'd lost out on anything.

It was while bathing in Blackpool's magic that Gan Gan showed me another magic trick he pulled out of his own tartan hat. He conjured up a tartan flat cap and a new pair of ankle boots with Blackey's segs just for me. I was excited that I could now look and sound just like him. But to my dismay, when I tried them on, we found that the highly anticipated new ankle boots were far too tight. However, Gan Gan promised to work his magic, saying that by the morning, they'd get much bigger.

At five years old, I was more than willing to embrace his fairy-tale promise, and why not? Gan Gan always kept to his word.

Lo and behold, when I awoke the next morning, I was much like Jack when he discovered a random beanstalk growing outside of his window: I found two big sprouting King Edward potatoes inside my new ankle boots.

'Yer new boots are magic. They grow tatties, Jay lad.'

'Nooooooo, Gan Gan, they don't, do they? Nana?' I said, latching onto the raconteur's fantastical tale.

'Aye, Jay, yer Gan Gan gets all his tatties from yer boots.'

Wouldn't you know, when I tried them on, unlike the day before AND just like magic, my new ankle boots were a perfect fit!

Life up to that point had always had a happily-ever-after-ending, and I hadn't realised that there was any other kind.

'He'll forget me when I'm gone, Alice Luv.'

'He won't. Dad. Jason will always remember ye, and yer not going anywhere!'

I had heard the loud whispering whilst sitting outside Gan Gan's bedroom. I wondered what was happening and where my beloved Gan Gan was going.

He stopped working as a hawker, he stopped going out, and in front of my eyes, my towering, strong hero became fragile, became delicate and eventually became bedridden.

I thought that Gan Gan would get better. I thought that there would be more times when he would take me on his cart and more times he would allow me to be free and slide down the potato shoot. And I thought there would be more times he'd say to me:

'Okay, Jay lad, climb up t' dancers again. Be careful, lad, t' steps are wet.'

I thought everything would be okay again. Reality hit home hard when tears and agony took over Sewell Road. The home, the treasured island that I knew to be the one of smiles and joy, had been wrecked with sorrow and invaded with pain.

On the 2nd of March, two days before my 6th birthday, Gan Gan eventually passed away from his short illness of cancer. No one had prepared the almost six-year-old me for having to say goodbye forever to someone I loved with every part of me.

It was difficult for me to comprehend that Gan Gan, my hero, was actually gone because, before this, I believed that all heroes and all good guys lived forever, like in the movies and fairy tales.

'Jason, I'm sorry, Luv, ye can't go.'

Through her intention of trying to protect me, Mum decided I shouldn't attend Gan Gan's funeral. So, while my family shared their grief and fond memories of Gan Gan and said their goodbyes, Mum's neighbour, Mrs Gibson, sat in with me, and, while she did her knitting, she turned on *Jackanory* for me to watch. But that day, I was in no mood for fairy tales. R.I.P Gan Gan.

5 FIELD OF DREAMS

It was the year the world's king of pop, Elvis Presley, died at the age of 42, and supersonic speed was set to take the life of humble aeroplanes to a different league altogether with the commercial introduction of Concorde. 1977 was also the year when I lost the hero of my own world, and the course of my life changed at Concorde speed.

A wildfire of questions still littered my once innocent and carefree child world, but no one was able to answer the questions that I wanted to hear: When would he give me chin pie again? When would he take me out with Harry again? And when, oh when, would Gan Gan be coming back again? It seemed that Gan Gan had taken the answers to my questions up to heaven with him.

After the loss of Gan Gan, I also lost being in the warmth and security of the home I had known since I was one year old. I had to leave Nana all alone when Mum decided it was best for me to move back to Rosedale Avenue to live with her, Dad, and Martin.

Rosedale Avenue was a cul-de-sac located in Allerton, which was a village at the edge of the city, 15 minutes from Haworth, home of The Brontë Sisters. Even though Rosedale was suburban, it was more like the countryside. We were surrounded by acres and acres of green fields.

Mum and Dad's Yorkshire stone-built semi-detached house was different to that of Sewell Road in more ways than one, including the fact it had an inside toilet.

'You farted our kid?'

'You smelt it. You dealt it, Martin!'

When Martin and I opened the bedroom window, the slightly sour and pungent smell of manure wafted in from the cows and horses that grazed in the field opposite us. At night, When Martin reached the land of nod before me, I would sit at the edge of my space (the bottom bunk of Martin's bed) and look outside, sometimes spotting opportunistic foxes trespassing in the fields in search of their evening meal.

'Jimmy, Jimmy, why did you kill me, why did you kill me? You killed me, Jimmy!'

As I held my spud gun and kept one eye open, I let out a dying groan and collapsed dramatically into an over-exaggerated heap on the floor.

'Don't be daft, our kid. Think about it. You wouldn't be able to talk if I'd killed you, you twonk?' Martin (AKA Jimmy Dean) reminded me, big-brother-style, just before our bellies which had been riddled with imaginary bullets, ached from laughing so hard.

One of the benefits of now sharing a home and a childhood with my older brother was having someone closer in years to me to bounce my vivid imagination off of. Martin and I would play our days away, imitating TV and story characters that made an impression on us, from cops and gangsters to cowboys and villains.

Every month, we'd spot one villain ("Rentman") as he scuttled up Rosedale Avenue and hurried down our gravelled front drive. He would come to collect the monthly mortgage payments for the bank and would often invade the Croot headquarters. Martin and I were always on full alert, and after spotting the enemy Rentman, heading towards our front door, we would race each other towards Mum in the kitchen, where she would be cooking. Then we'd tugged on Mum's apron.

'Rentman!' 'Rentman!' 'Rentman!'

We'd say in a loud whisper, trying to beat each other to say it first.

Mum would turn off the hob, quickly move the pan away from the hot stove and stop what she was doing. Then we'd all crawl under the large pine kitchen table as the invader tried to find another way in. As the intruder knocked on the back door, we saw his silhouette through the frosted PVC door glass, and we stayed deadly silent. My heart always pounded as fast as gigantic stallions caught up in a cowboy chase as I tried to swallow my breath. My giggles and my fear were all squashed into one great big ball. To me and Martin, it was like a game. To Mum, however, it was no laughing matter.

Once we heard Rentman scuttling away on our gravel, Mum would release her stress on the undercooked potatoes or whatever meal was on the stove that afternoon.

Though there was nothing *Cordon Bleu* in our house, Mum's rustic, hearty grub always did its best to try to comfort us. Mum always tried to make sure we always had a hot meal for supper, like steaming beans on toast with chips, bubble and squeak or piping corned beef hash, usually served on a Thursday, which would last until Monday. When money was short, and the invader got his claws on the housekeeping money, Mum would make sure our bellies were still filled by slicing pieces of sweet banana on buttered, thick, crusty white bread.

To keep Rentman away from the door, Dad worked all the hours God sent as a textile labourer at Taylor & Turner's textile mill. Weekends were his only free time, and then he was able to live out his passion for football.

'Come on lad, get yer ball,' Dad would sometimes say to me early on weekend mornings.

I'd rush to my bedroom, put on my hand-me-down shorts, footy boots and bright orange Johan Cruijff no.14 Netherlands football jersey. The metal studs on my oversized boots click-clocked as I bounce, bounce, bounced, my leather football on the pavement on the walk up the steep hill to Prune Park.

Martin preferred playing kerby and wasn't as keen on football as Dad and I were, which was fine by me as it left just me and Dad to spend hours playing footy together on the earthy-smelling pitch. More often than not, Dad was the goalkeeper, and I was the striker. Dad was a top-notch quality player, and I was well aware that I was never a match for him. Dad would keep me on my toes, saving more goals than I would score, although I knew that sometimes he allowed my goals to go in, and when they did, I'd celebrate *George Best style*.

One weekend, after playing football, we crossed the field in between the pitch and home. Dad lifted me over a fence without telling me why. Leaving just me and a perplexed Billy goat in the field, with the lone goat giving me the daggers with his goaty eye. The Billy goat's horns were big and pronounced, serving as a warning for me not to approach it. Dad, however, who within a minute, had climbed into the field with me, was a towering and strong man and wasn't scared at all; in fact, he ran towards the Billy goat and proceeded to kiss the startled goat on his snout before it promptly ran away.

'I Luv ye, goat,' he laughed, and I joined him laughing so hard as we fell into the wet mud.

'Why did you do that, Dad?'

'Well, yer Mum's always saying I'm acting the goat.'

Our boots were unrecognisable with mud, our whiter-than-white shorts were stained with grass, and we were both drenched in sweat. And by the time we got back to the pristine surroundings of Rosedale Avenue, I felt both bedraggled and exhilarated, having spent quality one-on-one time with Dad.

'Ye better take yer muddy boots off, lad before Mum plays pop,' Dad whispered.

Dad's warning came too late, though, when Mum opened the door to two mud monsters. Mum (just like Dad had predicted), of course, played pop.

'Look at the state of him, Dennis... Jason, yer hacky, and yer boots are black bright.'

The sight of me made Mum wince—so much so that before I stepped foot off the front door mat, she made me strip down to my Y-fronts and sent me upstairs to have a fresh, new, hot, soapy bath.

'Does anyone want the bath water?' I called out as soon as I finished.

I heard Martin (who'd been skateboarding) rebuke my offer.

'Mum, don't make me get in there. Have you seen the colour of the water, and the twonk has probably peed in it?'

In our household, to save money on the immersion heater, we often shared the bath water. These muddy days however, were the rare occasion when I wasn't the second or third one in the tub. Dad usually went first.

Dennis Croot Bags A Hat Trick Again.

Dad wasn't unfamiliar with having his name in the headlines of our local newspaper, The *Telegraph & Argus*. I would often be the one wanting to relish the bubbles of Dad's football glories when seeing his name and picture in print. When Dad wasn't playing amateur footy with me, he would play out his passion as a semi-professional footballer for Slingsby United in the Yorkshire County League.

Dad's amazing skills as a footballer caught the attention of a professional football scout after one of Dad's matches. Consequently, the scout invited him to a trial to play for Blackpool F.C. in the top professional league. I would have loved Dad to have said yes and to have had a Dennis Croot Star Soccer football card to show my school chums. If Dad had got into the professional league, it would've meant him moving away to Blackpool, but Mum decided it best that we all stay in Bradford, so Dad had to give up his dream and turn down the offer. Later, Dad became the manager of the Slingsby United team.

MY EGO SCREWED MY ACTING CAREER

Dennis Croot, top left with the Slingsby United team. Courtesy of the Telegraph & Argus Bradford.

6 DREADED DENTIST

'Where is he? The dinner is ruined! Every Sunday is the same. He comes back from the pub drunk as a lord,' Mum huffed and puffed whilst she yanked the burnt roast pork out of the oven.

Sundays were Dad's days to soak in his Ambrosia—Tetley's Beer. He would go to Allerton Working Men's Club for a few pints after we'd all been to Sunday mass, and Mum, Martin and I would walk home.

Dad could easily guzzle eight pints with his teammates after celebrating a Slingsby United victory. It wasn't uncommon for him to turn up home on a Sunday, later than expected, and jovially drunk. However, Mum was not so jovial on such occasions, having spent hours in the kitchen preparing the family Sunday dinner—*The Dinner of Champions*.

One Sunday, a few hours after Dad went AWOL, Mum decided to serve dinner anyway. The food had already been kept warm in the oven for several hours, more than desired. Silently, Mum laid the table to please her two ravenous children. By the look on Mum's face, Martin and I could tell she was in no mood for pleasantries, so we did not dare complain about the pork being dry as a bone, the Yorkshire puddings being as hard as nails, and the sprouts being like bullets. We both quietly and considerately worked our way through Sunday lunch and were careful not to step into the fire of Mum's wrath. As I shovelled another spoonful of cremated sprouts and something that slightly resembled crackling into my mouth, I felt my front tooth crack and saw my yellow temporary crown fall into my plate of burnt offerings.

'Mum looooooookkkkk,' I mumbled innocently now with a lisp,

holding out my crown. Martin, who was opposite me, I could tell, was trying not to laugh, so he was looking down at his plate, fiddling around with his pieces of dry pork and then putting pieces in his mouth. The hilarity of the situation (for him, anyway) was far too much for him to stay quiet.

'At least you won't be able to sprout off like you normally do! Get it? SPROUT off?' Martin laughed open-mouthed, revealing the pieces of dry pork that had refused to be swallowed.

'Shut your cakehole you berk!' I launched at him with not just my words but also a firm chunk of overcooked sprout from my spud gun, which made direct contact with his head.

'You wait til later, you Nobhead. I'm going to bray you,' Martin threatened in a loud whisper.

'Pack it in the pair of ye; I'm going to have to call the dentist tomorrow now!' Mum barked tersely as she took her frustration out on the dishes and leftover food that she was starting to tidy away.

'No, Mum, nooo please, nooooo, not the dentist,' I begged.
Mum was not hearing my desperate pleas as she scraped the last of the dinner into the bin.

'What time is he going to the dentist, Mum? Tooth-hurty? Quipped Martin as he burst out laughing once again at his own joke. Mum didn't hear the joke, and I kicked Martin hard under the table. I was just about to well up when Mum said.

'Don't worry, Luv, I will go to school and tell off anyone who makes fun of ye.' Of course, this made me feel a bajillion times worse!!!

'Can I have some apple crumble, Mum?'

'I can't do everything, Martin. I've only got one pair of hands... where's yer Dad? Where is he?' Mum hollered, almost blowing the house down.

When we heard keys fumbling at the door, Mum said to Martin.

'Let yer Dad in, will ye, take the Chubb lock off!'

When Dad stumbled into the house as drunk as a coot, it was apparent he was in hot water as Mum let off all the steam that she had reserved for him.

'What time do ye call this, Dennis, eh? You're drinking too much again!'

'Aye, but it's the weekend, Alice Luv.'

Mum's eyeballs rolled towards the ceiling.

'Don't ye Luv me, Dennis Croot. It's always the weekend for ye; yer dinner's in the bin!'

Dad got no dinner and a proper roasting from Mum, and the

argument simmered on, just like Mum's pan of corned beef hash on the hob for tomorrow's tea.

The following morning, Mum had booked a 9:30am dentist appointment for me before she left for her part-time sales assistant job at Dolcis, a chain shoe shop in the city centre. Reliable as always, Nana came to Rosedale Avenue to take over the childcare reins. Nana would be taking me to the dreaded dentist while Martin was due to be dropped off at Mrs Gibson's, our retired fuddy-duddy next-door neighbour whose house was like a Roman archaeological site because it hadn't changed in 2000 years. Martin begged and pleaded with Nana to take him with us because he didn't want to stay with Mrs Gibson. On previous stays, Mrs Gibson would make Martin practise the skilful art of cookery and plough him with his own dreaded nemesis: fig biscuits.

Mrs Gibson was a full-figured woman with salt and pepper coloured hair and thick-rimmed NHS glasses. She had an air of seriousness about her. She was a former volunteer classroom helper at St Medard's who, because she'd worked in a school, had adopted the strict attitude of many teachers. She didn't have any children of her own. She also did a lot for the community, including running cookery clubs for the local children, which Martin was forced to attend and despised.

'Are ye ready lads? We're going to be late,' Nana chimed as she looked at our rusty clock on the fireplace, which seemed to have stopped.

'Nana, pleasaassseee, can I not go to the dentist?' I lisped.

'Don't worry, our kid, I'll look after ya. Nana, I will help you take our kid to the dentist as long as I don't have to go to Mrs Gibson's.'

I could always rely on my brother to back me up, NOT! Our attempts to play on Nana's soft spot fell on deaf ears. She was under strict instruction from Mum, so she stood her ground.

'Get yer coats on, lads; we'll miss the bus,' Nana said as she double-checked her watch for the correct time.

Whilst she was looking down. Martin nudged me, raised his clasped hands together and made a champion gesture, thinking he'd got one over on Nana and me. To Martin's dismay, Nana dropped Martin off at the dreaded Mrs Gibson's. As he walked down her long path with his head looking to the ground. I loud lisped.

'Can you make me some fig biscuits?'

As he turned, he raised his fist. I raised my clasped hands together and made a champion gesture. Although neither one of us were champions that morning.

Nana and I walked to the end of our street and waited 30 minutes for the two-tone green and cream, 616 double-decker bus. Reluctantly, I hopped on the bus with Nana when it arrived and headed for the upper deck, where the air was thick with stale yellow smoke. I normally loved riding high and feeling like I was on top of the world, looking down at the ant-like army of people on the pavements, but this wasn't one of those days.

Eventually, we arrived at our stop and got off the bus. I dragged my feet and slowed my pace down as I begrudgingly walked to the dentist's clinic. The exterior of the clinic was a cold, grey, stone-clad building, and each step towards the entrance felt like I was walking towards my impending doom; the only thing missing was the tune of Chopin's *Funeral March*. Before I knew it, we arrived at the clinically coloured front door. My dislike for dentists stemmed from the time I cracked my tooth when I tripped on the step in Sewell Road. Following that traumatic day, my front pearly white incisor was replaced with an ugly custard yellow crown! The perpetrator was the dreaded family dentist, Dr. Hamilton. On returning to the grounds of my archnemesis, I was shaking like a leaf when Nana pressed the door buzzer. Seeing that I was nervous Nana hugged me like a Mama Bear.

When Mum booked the appointment, she'd been offered a choice of anaesthetic, an injection or gas to temporarily numb the impending pain. Mum usually chose the injection, but this time, the dreaded dentist had convinced Mum that I should have the gas.

In Dr.Dread's lair, I sat helplessly in the intimidating grips of the blue leather dentist chair to which I'd been summoned.

'Open wide, say ahhhhh.'

Dr. Dread proceeded to prod and scrape. The gas was beginning to kick in, and rather than focusing on pain, I was distracted by the intimidating pieces of silver weaponry placed beside me and felt anxious about which one would be used next.

'There you go. All done. Mission complete. Well done, you've been a brave soldier,' Dr. Dread declared.

He then proceeded to brand me by sticking a sticker of a smiling, toothy bunny on my Yellow *Basil Brush* T-shirt.

On the way home, Nana and I sat on the top deck of the 616 bus again, and both of us were quiet for a while. Nana then tried to make light of the situation.

'That horse over yonder looks like Harry,' Nana heartened as she pointed to a horse in a field we were passing.

'Who's Harry?' I responded crossly as I looked out of the window.

I was still slightly annoyed that I'd been made to go to the dentist. So I acted like I'd lost my memory by pretending I didn't have a clue what Nana was saying, but she became worried and made an enormous fuss over me.

'I'm going to cut ye a big slice of yer favourite apple pie when we get home.'

'Apple pie? What's apple pie?' I pretended whilst stumbling off the bus.

Nana called in at Mrs Gibson's house, explained the emergency and asked if Martin could stay overnight. As we walked away from the house, I saw Martin in an oversized striped apron looking at us from the window, trying to figure out what was happening.

As I trailed behind Nana as she opened the front gate to leave, I looked back at Martin and teased him by thumbing my nose. He responded by raising his fist up to me furiously behind Mrs Gibson's newly polished glass windows. I cupped my ear, which infuriated him even further.

By the time we returned home, Nana had become increasingly worried. I enjoyed her undivided attention as she waited on me and showered me with her concern, so I relished in the soapy lather and kept up the act. Nana waited nervously, hoping that my memory would return before Mum did.

When Mum arrived, she and Nana piled on the questions. Secretly, I was enjoying the buzz I got from convincing them both I'd lost my memory. They were like putty in my hands. As they flapped and flustered, they continued to ask questions, to which I responded impressively. 'I'm not sure. I'm not sure. Who am I? Where am I? What am I doing here?' I tried my best to look bemused and not give myself away. I kept up this pretence for about an hour. Mum's panic was becoming increasingly frenzied as I continued my stellar performance, even as Mum picked up the phone to call Dr Dread. Mum asked me to sit next to her. She was getting flustered at mis-dialling the dentist's number for the third time on our rotary phone. As her fingers were spinning the dial, a knot was forming in the pit of my belly. But there was no turning back now.

'My son, Jason, has just had gas and lost his memory!' Mum spat her furious rage at the startled receptionist when she answered. Perplexed, the receptionist sputtered.

'Oh dear, I'm sorry to hear that! Let me have Dr Hamilton call you back.'

However, Mum was in no mood to wait and thundered like a howling typhoon.

'I need to speak to him NOW!!!'

By this time, I was cacking my pants.

'Hello, Mrs Croot, how can I help you?' The oblivious dentist greeted Mum ornately.

Oh Crap! Crap! Crap! Dr Dread was now on the other end of the phone, my ears were pricked, and I waited with bated breath. I knew then I'd bitten off more than I could chew, and the anticipated outcome would be much worse than Mum's cremated sprouts and a loose custard-coloured crown! Mum told my symptoms to Dr Dread, and I could hear the utter panic in his voice from where I sat.

'This is unusual! We've never encountered anything like this before with patients under gas,' his tone was tainted with urgency as he pleaded with Mum.

'Mrs Croot, please bring Jason back to the clinic immediately. We need to evaluate the situation.'

The uneasiness in his voice matched the growing unease in our living room, and it was unmistakable that my act was now pushing the frontiers of believability.

7 SNOTTY COWBOY

Angry at Dr. Dread, Mum refused to take me back to his clinic and hung up the phone on him. She thought that calling an ambulance would be a better option. That's when Nana came from the kitchen. She was as cool as the apple pie filling that was framed in Nana's renowned golden pastry, as it sparkled like the crown jewels. She presented this treasure to me on a saucer and asked me.

'So ye want a piece of apple pie?'

The temptation was too great to resist, and forgetting to stay in role, I replied far too eagerly and far too quickly.

'Yes, please, Nana.'

My memory of my pretend amnesia had slipped momentarily. It was at that moment that the penny dropped for Mum and Nana, that they'd been well and truly hoodwinked. Unfortunately, the end of my performance was not preceded by an encore and rapturous applause. In fact, the only clap I got that night was the one from Mum, around my ear! As a consequence, I was sent up the dancers to bed without supper and, of course, no apple pie!

Apologies, Dr. Dread (Hamilton), if you read this!

'I'm sorry... I'm sorry...I said I'm sorry!!!' I screamed as Martin bent my twisted arm up my back when he realised that without telling him, I'd scoffed an entire packet of his Maltesers from what he thought was his secret stash.

'Scoff my sweets, will ya? I'm going to knock your block off.'

Apart from fighting with Martin, the summer holidays were like a whole summer of Saturdays. Six blissful weeks without school meant the freedom to do what I loved most: having fun and doing my own thing.

In the kitchen, I spent part of the day creating culinary delights like sugar sandwiches and half-frozen golden top milk with Cadbury's Flakes and Mars bars. My brother and I also amused ourselves by competing to see how many cream crackers we could eat in a minute without drinking any water.

'Can we have some bubble gum balls, please, mister?'

Hearing the tinny tune of *Match of The Day* outside was a favourite part of both our days. It meant Mr Whippy was in town! The melody beckoned the neighbourhood children to spend their parents' spare change on sweet treats from the ice cream man. Martin and I would run outside with our empty 5-litre margarine tub, asking him to fill it with soft vanilla ice cream topped with strawberry juice and sprinkles. Then we'd spoil our appetites with fluffy frozen rainbows and sweet bubble gum balls.

The rest of the holidays were spent watching TV, playing video games, laking football, hanging out with friends, riding bikes, collecting Soccer Star football cards, and reading *Beano, Asterix,* and *Dandy* comics. *Desperate Dan* was one of my favourite characters; he always ate Cow Pie, which looked golden like Nana's.

While our parents worked, Nana took care of Martin and me for a few weeks. She'd journey across the city from Sewell Road, filling the house on Rosedale Avenue with the wonderful aroma of her home cooking, including her silky apple pie.

From age six, my parents, brother, and I enjoyed traditional British holidays by the coast every year. We'd spend many days on the beach, and my parents would join the other British adults hoping to get their money's worth by catching the sun, which would make a welcome appearance for a few weeks of the year. British summers were always unpredictable, and sometimes it rained buckets, even in August, which would disappoint the adults who had been aiming for an ultimate holiday tan.

Our regular holiday destination was the seaside town of Bridlington on the East Coast of Yorkshire. Its broad, golden sandy beaches spread for miles, making enough space for eager tourists. On sunny mornings, families would rise early to find the best spots on the shore to set up their armfuls of rented seaside equipment. It was a common sight to see dads of the families hammering their sturdy windbreakers into the sand and positioning their deckchairs for the day so that their clans could ultimately have a fantastic view of the sparkling, murky grey North Sea.

Bridlington was a fishing town and an English paradise for escapism. During the summer, it buzzed with young and old, who were drawn to the video game arcades, jetty boat rides and bouncy castles for children. Adults would enjoy its nightly variety shows and heaving disco bars and pubs.

'I Luv Brid. Have ye lived here all yer life, Albert?'

'Well, not yet, Dennis!'

'Did ye think about it, Albert?'

'As long as yer kids don't mess about Dennis, they can walk mi donkeys!'

'Cheers, Albert, another pint of Tetley's?'

Over copious pints of Tetley's Yorkshire beer in the Half Moon pub. Dad negotiated our terms of employment with Albert Tablock. He had landed us our first jobs as Donkey boys.

While Dad and Albert knocked back the pints, Mum hummed to *Save All Your Kisses For Me,* which pumped through the jukebox. Martin and I, Bridlington's newly recruited donkey boys, dined on Seabrook's beefy crisps and lemonade in the kids' room whilst being robbed of our shekels as we surreptitiously played Tic-Tac-Toe on the pub's one-armed bandit, (which was strictly prohibited for over 18s).

My parents got to know Bridlington Beach's very own tycoon, Albert Tablock, during our visits to Bridlington Sunday mass at Our Lady and St Peter's Church. Tablock was one of the prized parishioners who distributed the holy communion. And this, of course, put Tablock in Mum's trusted good books (on account of him being a churchgoer). Dad was simply happy to have a companion to share a laugh and pint with. The magnate was also the owner of all the donkeys who worked on the beach. He was now mine and my brother's very first employer.

Martin and I were entrusted with the responsibility of each taking care of a donkey and walking them up and down the beach as they carried excited children on their backs for a cheap as chips 50 pence ride.

My donkey was Beulah, a name that connotes intelligence and stubbornness and one whose heart's desire is to be of service to the world. Beulah and I became inseparable, and between us grew a mutual friendship in which I would always have her back, and she would have mine.

After several summers of working, I'd become an expert donkey boy thanks to my loyal and trusty sidekick, Beulah. Martin and I were paid very little after we finished our job for the day, but one staff perk was being allowed to ride the donkeys for the 25-minute ride from the beach into the old town of Bridlington to take the donkeys home. For me, this was the best perk of the job.

'Frame yourselves, we're going to be late!' Mum spouted whilst putting the suitcases near the front door at Rosedale Avenue.

'But I can't find my ball,' I moaned, hoping Mum would know where it was, and she had simply tidied it away.

'Your ball? I took it to school, and it got stuck on the chuffing roof... remember you said I could borrow it?'

'I didn't, Martin, you twonk!'

'Mum, Jay seems to have lost his memory again!'

'You berk Martin!' I said as I popped my strawberry chewing gum bubble with my teeth to make me look tougher before I dug back at my brother.

I was utterly annoyed at how *blasé* he was about losing MY ball. My voice raised as I turned to my flustered Mum.

'Mum, Mum, Mum, Martin lost my ball.'

Mum was too busy fussing over the suitcases and didn't see Martin pull my *A-TEAM* T-shirt and give me a brotherly warning.

'Listen, our kid, if ya tell on me one more time, I'm going to put your lights out and kick your head in.'

'You and whose army?'

My reply stirred up Martin as he gave me a friendly but not friendly hard slap on my back, causing me to swallow my chewing gum. Rather than turn the other cheek, I did what any younger brother during a spat would do! I jumped on my brother's back and tried to choke him. He swung me around until I felt drop-dizzy and fell onto the sofa with stars in my eyes. Flashed in front of me was the surreal possibility that my ball of chewing gum would be stuck in my gut for eight years on account of my meat-head brother.

'For crying out loud. Pack it in the pair of ye; what are ye trying to do? Torture me to bloody death, eh? We're LATE, we're going to miss our coach...and why's yer dad not back from the shop? I bet he's gone to the chuffing bookies again!'

'Mum...I don't feel well...I feel sick...'

On a stifling hot coach from Bradford to Bridlington, we were heading to another one of our family breaks on a journey that took around two and a half hours. I hated these trips because I suffered severely from travel sickness. And this journey, which was no exception, was even worse because we were stuck in a chuffing traffic jam that was so backed up that you could have lost *King Kong* in it. The Coaches vent window let in no breeze, and some plonker farted, which smelt like rotten eggs. This resulted in me vomiting up the morning breakfast into a plastic supermarket bag that Mum had come prepared with. Whilst travel sickness wreaked havoc, Martin made coarse jokes in between listening to Ska music on a borrowed Walkman while playing *Donkey Kong* on my Nintendo handheld game and watch. Mum made a fuss about not getting vomit on my shorts and catastrophising the situation, and Dad made the most of the holiday atmosphere by drinking cans of beer and joining the other happier-than-life holidaymakers as they sang the *Walking On Sunshine*-type sing-along songs to pass the time away. In my sickly state, I still thought about the piece of chewing gum stuck in my gut.

On arrival, we stayed at our usual self-catering Belgrave Road Holiday Rooms, which wasn't anything fancy. Our musty-smelling, compact open-plan room, which was just enough for the four of us, consisted of a kitchenette equipped with a chip pan, an old fridge-freezer, a kettle and a small hob. A double bed and a bunk bed took up most of one side of the room. Martin, being the oldest, always managed to bag the top bunk whilst I was left with the bottom bunk. The one and only time I tried my luck to bagsy the top bunk Martin warned me off.

'Do you really want me to chuck you off the top bunk, our kid? It's a long way down, you know.'

'You're such a crybaby just because you're losing.'

Martin said whilst vigorously rubbing his index finger on his bottom lip, making a sound like *Daffy Duck* on helium.

'Martin, you cheater, Dad, look, he's twisting me again; he's got a card up his shirt. I'm not playing with him anymore.'

I was more than annoyed that my brother was about to win YET again from unscrupulous tactics as he hid his grin behind his hand of cards.

'Come on lads, play fair.'

The voice of Dad's firm but fair reasoning would often calm the stormy situation between Martin and me, especially when we'd play cards, Crossfire or Monopoly (which would always end up in a fight.) Whilst we'd be playing, Mum would mostly be pottering around, cleaning, cooking, writing postcards, and preparing grub for her clan, which included Spam sandwiches on buttered white Hovis bread, which Martin and I would insist she cut into triangles because they tasted miles better than squares. Mum would not find it as easy to completely let go and enjoy herself, but these holidays were a welcomed break for her.

Our Belgrave holiday room was a stone's throw away from local amusement arcades, a stone's throw away from the beach and a stone's throw away from the Bridlington beach donkeys —including Beulah.

As Beulah and I returned back from her third ride of the morning, under the scorching sun, I caught wind of Albert Tablock's son, Geoff, yammering about the donkeys to his brother Liam (they too both worked as donkey boys).

'If ye chuck a pebble from t' beach in a tin can and give it a good rattle up and down, t' donkeys will scarper like there's no tomorrow.'

In the heat, Beulah remained placid and not as agitated as I was. She was ready for the next customer in line: A snotty-nosed boy who was much bigger and heavier than me plonked himself on Beulah. Dutifully, Beulah began to carry him across the beach, but unsatisfied with her speed, the snotty-nosed boy started to kick Beulah as if she were a toy horse. I took that very personally.

The snotty-nosed mulish boy demanded.

'Faster, faster, make it go faster.'

As he gave her another kick to her side with his heel.

'Oi, knock it off, will you, don't do that. You can't kick my donkey,' I fumed and tugged on Beulah's reins.

'Why has the stupid thing stopped?' The snotty-nosed cowboy oinked.

Beulah was in no way having any of the abuse and demonstrated her smartness and stubbornness by refusing to move a step further.

'Make it move, will you, donkey boy!' the snotty-nosed cowboy demanded.

In the corner of my eye, I spotted an empty 7-UP can on the sand. I picked it up and scooped up some pebbles. I could see that Beulah was exhausted, but I needed to show the snotty-nosed cowboy he couldn't lasso me or my donkey with his unreasonable demands. Not really knowing what to expect, I let go of Beulah's reins, and I dropped a pebble into the can and shook it up and down a few times like I'd overheard Albert's sons talking about. Then, that's when shit hit the can!

Beulah bolted off like a thoroughbred racehorse, galloping down the beach with the snotty-nosed cowboy hanging on for dear life to Beulah's reins.

'Mummmmmy! Mummmmmy! Mummmmmy!' His cries were loud enough for all of Bridlington and probably the man on the moon to hear. I stood donkeyless and speechless with only the pop can in my hand. I hadn't really expected that Beulah would or even could move like that. As I stood gaping at Beulah running, the snotty-nosed cowboy's bum sprung up and down on Beulah's leather saddle.

I didn't feel at all guilty, apart from making poor Beulah run in the heat. But as a consequence of my donkeying around, I was fired, and my brother Martin resigned as a sign of camaraderie because the snotty-nosed cowboy's mummy wedged an official complaint with Albert Tablock.

Martin on Tiny, Albert Tablock, our ex-boss, and me on Beulah.

8 WHO LET THE DOGS OUT

'I bet he's at the pub again!'

Puffed Mum as she sawed through the over-cooked joint of roast beef.

Dad's time remaining in Mum's good books had lapsed; he was late again for Sunday dinner, hence the near-cremated joint.

Back home in Bradford, things were back to normal again, but "normal" was just about to change when we heard an unexpected noise at the door. Before Martin and I could get up from the dinner table, an out-of-control black and white fur ball shot in from the hallway. It consequently sent one of Mum's Lladró angel figurines flying headlong into the carpet from the coffee table. Obliviously, it continued to follow its snout and the higgledy-piggledy trail of unfamiliar smells. The fur ball was followed by Dad.

'Hello Alice Luv. What's for tea?'

'Eh, you what, eh? Are you daft or what? what have ye done now, Dennis?' Mum asked, holding a plate of roast beef. Her face, which was stern at first, seemed to melt at the sight of the black and white cross-bred cocker spaniel who rocketed like a firecracker around the kitchen like there was no tomorrow. The ball of cuteness was curious about the smells of the slightly charred aroma of roasted meat.

To compensate for getting fired and the heartbreak of not being able to work with my beloved donkey Beulah anymore, Dad had responded to an advert in the *Telegraph & Argus* and bought a cross-bred cocker spaniel puppy and even found the time to get her new name engraved on her dog tag: Beulah.

Beulah was my first real pet. Sure, I'd had a few goldfish from summer fairs, but they never lasted long. Unbeknownst to Mum, I kept a few spiders in matchboxes under my bed, but they didn't fare any better as pets.

So having my very own dog was heavenly. Beulah was a playful, adorable furball of crazy. I loved taking her out for runs, and her energy bounced all over the place like a bouncy ball. At night, she would settle down after tiring herself out and she would keep my feet warm when she curled up in her spot at the bottom of my bunk bed.

'Mrs Croot, we haven't allowed any dogs to stay here in the past. Can ye assure me that yer dog is well-behaved?' asked a reluctant Mrs Brown (the Belgrave Road Holiday Rooms landlady).

'She's as good as gold, Mrs Brown,' Mum replied convincingly during a phone call to Belgrave Road Holiday Rooms. As it went, Mrs Brown agreed to allow Beulah to stay.

I was chuffed to take my new friend on our return to Bridlington for another family breakaway with Mum, Dad, Martin and, of course, Beulah, where we were to stay at our usual holiday room that we had been accustomed to staying in on Belgrave Road.

'Can ye make sure ye wipe her paws if ye take her on the beach? I don't want my carpets ruined,' a serious-faced Mrs Brown stated, whilst crossing her arms and shielding herself from being won over by the charms of the playful spaniel, who was sniffing at her pink fluffy slippers. She unfolded her arms momentarily and stepped over the underfoot spaniel to reach over for our room key that dangled behind the front desk and handed it to my parents.

'Oh, by the way, there was a mix-up with the bookings due to a double booking error. It will mean the first week you'll be in room no.10, and the second week...you'll have to spend the second week on a different floor in room no.15. Sorry about that. Enjoy yer stay.'

Week one went without a hitch; Martin and I took Beulah out for long walks until she was one pooped pooch, and she loved it as much as we did. As Mrs Brown had ordered, each time we returned, we wiped Beulah's feet at the door with a beach towel just for her. On the second week, during one of the days, the idyllic serenity was chaotically interrupted. As usual, Martin and I took Beulah for a walk on Bridlington's beach. As usual, her nose led her everywhere, including to places where she had not been formally invited, which that day was the shell of a snoozing hermit crab and some unsuspecting sandworms, which she startled with her playful bark and sandy white paws. As usual, after a final dip in the murky sea, her wet, soft black and white fur was covered in sand, and we headed back to the holiday rooms.

On our return to the B&B, the front door became jammed when

Martin and I tried to shut it. I let go of Beulah's lead as Martin and I turned our attention to the troublesome jammed door, not thinking that our troublesome cocker spaniel would speed off, but she did! Before we could stop her, she bolted up the stairs, most likely in search of Mum and Dad. Martin and I tried to catch up with her, but she was faster than a Formula One car.

'You gormless berk, why did you drop the lead?' insulted Martin, who was puffing like an out-of-breath marathon runner.

Martin and I followed the track of wet dog paw prints on the thick pile lime-green-carpeted stairs, and as we ran up another flight, we looked at each other in abject horror when we heard 'ahhhhhhhhhhhhh!!!' an almighty scream.

'You're in the crap now, you twonk!' Martin said, stating the bleeding obvious.

'Stop talking wet MARTIN, you berk!!!'

Our gut instinct told us that the panicked shrieks that followed must've had something to do with Beulah.

We followed where the sounds of fussing and screaming were coming from, which led us to room no.10 — the room that we'd stayed in on the first week. Beulah, the furry intruder, must've used her huge snout to push her way into the unlocked room, then jumped on the bed and clambered underneath the blankets. The sodding wet, sandy spaniel was oblivious that this wasn't our room anymore. She'd woken a stunned mother and young daughter, dressed in their pyjamas, from their catnap. Beulah, in her craziness, must have gotten confused and sniffed our lingering scents. Martin and I were at a loss for words, glued to the spot temporarily, not knowing whether to laugh, cry or what! But what we were sure of was that we were in deep dog poop! With wet sand and seawater still clinging on to Beulah's fur for dear life, she obliviously continued to bounce all over the beds. She saw the mother's and daughter's flapping and fussing as one big game! When she noticed Martin and me appear at the door, Beulah, still on one of the beds on all fours, did a last defiant shake. All the remnants from our damp sandy dog's fur flew towards the mother and daughter. With her tail wagging like a helicopter propeller ready to fly, Beulah launched off the bed and trotted innocently back to us like butter wouldn't melt.

Mum and Dad were among the other B&B guests who came to the room, along with Mrs Brown, who was in her curlers and cupcake pink fluffy slippers, wondering what all the screaming and kerfuffle was about.

Mrs Brown exclaimed.

'Oh my goodness, flippin eck, what's happening here, huh? Is everyone alright?'

I was embarrassed, but I knew I had to apologise.

'I'm so sorry, Mrs Brown, our dog Beulah got a bit confused.'

The landlady barked.

'Well, we can't have that, can we? It's a good thing no one got hurt.'

Jumping to Beulah's defence, Mum barked back.

'Beulah would never hurt anyone…she's as daft as a brush! Look at her.' Mum pointed at the adorable, doe-eyed spaniel, who had no clue of the saga she had just caused.

Beulah's looks of innocence weren't washing with the aggravated landlady, as she said in a tone that was both stern and sarcastic.

'Well, I'm afraid I'll have to ask ye to find another place to stay. Beulah doesn't seem to be as well-behaved as ye described Mrs Croot. I can't have her causing any more disturbances and upsetting the other guests.'

Mum was fiercely protective over her brood, including Beulah. She didn't like to hear any strangers saying a bad word about any of us. So, following the spaniel saga, we cut our holiday short and left Bridlington the following day.

Sadly, Beulah was no longer allowed on family holidays with us. Without her darting around like a loose pinball in the midst of a game, holidays were never quite the same.

Beulah's madcap ways were part and parcel of who she was, wherever she was, and whoever she was with, as Andrew Drapier, my school chum, found out.

Andrew and I both supported Liverpool F.C. and shared my interest in video games. Mum used to allow him to sleep over sometimes, and we'd spend the evening trying to beat each other by playing car racing games on my Atari.

One Saturday morning, Andrew had slept over at our house at Rosedale Avenue. We woke up to the smell of Mum cooking an English breakfast but were still feeling pretty groggy after staying up until 4:00am playing Formula One. Bog-eyed and hungry, we left the bunk bed unmade as the aroma of smoked, crispy bacon met our nostrils, tempting us out of bed. Andrew was first to the stairs, and I closely followed behind him. He was half asleep, and I noticed he hadn't pulled his socks up properly. As he dragged his feet down the stairs towards the kitchen, his socks hung lethargically from his toes. Blurry-eyed, he was not yet quite alert, but the over-energetic Beulah was! As Andrew's socks wriggled slowly on the stair carpet, they were too much of an irresistible tease for the mischievous spaniel who was standing at the bottom of the stairs, wagging her tail excitedly. When Andrew reached the hallway, Beulah started to pull playfully at Andrew's socks as she barked. Startled, he fell on his backside, but Beulah saw this as an even wider invitation for her to continue with her own tug-of-war game, so she just kept tugging. I had to hold my aching belly from laughing too hard as I watched Andrew plead with the out-of-control spaniel.

'Buely, Buely, stop it. Crooty tell her to give up.'

Mum came from the kitchen, put a stop to Beulah's antics, and demoted her for a while in the backyard so she could do some doggy time out. Needless to say, Andrew remembered to pull his socks up from then on in, which is more than I could say for myself.

Andrew wasn't the only school chum with whom I had a laugh in light of canine capers. Another classmate, Scott Berry, who lived near Rosedale Avenue, got his taste of doggy drama too, but this time, it was a rare occasion where Beulah's antics were not to blame.

Often, my walk home from school was with Scott. Every day, we'd make our way home routinely up the steep Allerton Road, passing the renowned Yorkshire Seabrook's crisps factory. Its strong medley of crisp flavours peppered the air, which made our mouths water and our hungry tummies rumble. At the top of Allerton Road stood a row of cottages called Stoneybank. It was here we would go our separate ways, me to Rosedale Avenue and Scott to the bottom of Prune Park Lane.

Scott had been sick with German Measles for a few weeks, and I'd missed his company, having to walk home every day alone. It had been pretty boring every day he was gone apart from one afternoon outside no.11 Stoneybank Cottages. I was eager to share my tale with Scott when he had recovered and returned to St. Medard's.

The day Scott returned to school, I couldn't walk home with him as Mum was picking me up to take me to buy a new pair of school shoes. So before we finished our classes, I wanted to tell Scott what I'd seen when he was off school. In the playground, I collared my chum and deadpanned.

'Scotty, you know what, when you were off, I saw a cute Yorkshire terrier dog that looked like *E.T!!!!*'

'Yeah, right! I believe you, Crooty, but thousands wouldn't.'

'AND, Scotty, it can do the moonwalk. I'm not kidding.'

'Where, Crooty? Where? Tell me.'

'I'll tell you if you give me one of your Ace Star Soccer cards?'

Scott went to his pocket, sifted through the football cards and begrudgingly gave me his Liverpool, Kenny Dalglish Ace Star Soccer card.

Even though it had a tear in the left corner. I was over the moon to bagsy this rare card as I supported Liverpool, I added it to my collection. I then told Scott where to find the dog at no.11 Stoneybank Cottages and told him that he should go to the gate and shout Sheeba loudly so that it would come out of the cottage, and then he could see it do the moonwalk. I left it at that.

In the school playground the next day, I spotted a mardy-looking Scott who was heading right for me like a speeding arrow. He nudged my shoulder with the palm of his hand, not too hard but with definite intention. I momentarily lost my balance as he raised his voice, which he rarely ever did.

'Friggin *E.T?* You berk! GIZ me back MY Kenny Daglish card! You wazzock, it wasn't the dog playing tricks. It was you, Crooty! You twonk. You're such an arse. Where's my Daglish card?'

He continued to call me all the curse names that we knew. I kept my serious face on as best as I could as I tried not to fall to the ground in a hysterical fit of laughter.

When Scott had been away, what actually happened was that I was walking home from school alone and was about to walk past Stoneybank cottages as I was tucking into a half-eaten hotdog sarnie that I'd sneaked in my bag from school dinners. I wasn't sure if it was the strong, meaty scent of the orange-coloured processed sausage or the rustling of the wrapper, but as I took another bite, a huge and menacing German shepherd dog suddenly ran out of no.11 and made me jump as it stood on its hind legs and stuck its huge head over the creaky wooden gate, barking, snarling and growling intimidatingly. It scared the living daylights out of me. On top of that, I dropped my half-eaten hotdog on the floor, which then landed near the creaky gate. I was already cacking myself from the size of the enormous dog and was not about to pick up my half-eaten hot dog. Momentarily, I was frozen to the spot, fearing that I was about to be the German shepherd's afternoon meal. An unfamiliar elderly lady, who, like the dog I hadn't seen before and presumably was the dog's owner, ran out and shouted.

'What's up with ye, Sheeba?'

The elderly lady's voice had no effect as she continued to growl.

'Sheeba, what are ye playing at? Get in t' house NOW,' she hollered this time with the sternness of a sergeant major. The dog obeyed the command, headed back into the house, looked back at me one last time, and gave a bark as if to say.

'I'll be back!'

It was probably peeved at having to leave my juicy-looking hotdog on the floor. As the German shepherd disappeared back into the house, I ran the rest of the way home in shock, trying not to cry.

In the playground, the fuming Scott explained he'd gone to the gate of no.11 like I told him and shouted for Sheeba. Then he came face to face, not with a cute *E.T.* moonwalking Yorkshire terrier that I'd described but a big, angry, snarling German shepherd. He told me he nearly dolloped in his kegs and ran the rest of the way home when he realised that the creaky gate looked like it was going to give way.

At that point, I couldn't hold in my laughter any longer, and I held my stomach as it ached from laughing so hard. After a few seconds, Scott seemed to see the funny side of it, and I sweetened him up by giving him my last Drumstick lollipop. I traded some Star Soccer football cards with my chum Steve McAleavy and then split them with Scott to help make up for the doggy drama. Fortunately, it did. If only it was always as easy to get out of life's scrapes with a lollipop and a couple of Star Soccer football cards.

9 FRIENDS

'Oh, my sainted aunt, what are ye larkin' at lad, eh? Spinning about like that. Av ye no schoolwork to do? Look, you've ruined my chuffing self-raising. AND does yer Mum know that yer wearing her high heels?' hollered Mrs Gibson, who seemed to be in a tiz-woz.

I had been spinning around on Rosedale Avenue, in Mum's shoes, when I bumped into Mrs Gibson, who was about to open her front gate. She was carrying two bags of shopping. As a result of the collision, one of her packets of self-raising flour fell and split open, leaving a haze of flour in the air rising from the pavement.

The collision happened during a 'Spintastic' reenactment of my favourite weekly TV series called *Fame*. The series was set in a New York Performing Arts School. The show's premise followed the striving and struggling students of the school. They aspired to achieve their dreams of making it as big as musicians, dancers, and actors. I watched the programme avidly every week, and the catchy, upbeat theme tune earwormed its way into my mind. The programme opened with a group of zestful actors running out of the performing arts school onto the New York streets and breaking out into dance on the roads and on top of car roofs as the music blasted out from the students' ghettoblaster.

Each week, when the *Fame* theme song came on at the beginning of the TV show, I'd run out of my front door onto the street, imitating the characters' moves, dancing, spinning and feeling wondrous. As I emulated their freedom, I didn't realise then that the same dream to perform was also alive in me waiting to be discovered. The neighbours must have thought that I was looney. For me, they were my audience, and they had no idea I was mimicking the actors on the show.

Getting lost in the world of television was one of my much-loved pastimes. Once the school day had finished, after parting ways with Scott Berry, I would often rush the rest of the way home to watch my favourite TV shows. Whilst my friends were learning about life from *Tom and Jerry, Scooby Doo* and *Dangermouse*. I enjoyed being immersed in the world of film, including the black and white movies with *Laurel & Hardy, Harold Lloyd* and *Charlie Chaplin*. Mum often would try to prise me away from the TV, often catastrophising with a standard warning.

'Jason, ye know watching too much television is bad for yer eyes...you'll end up with glasses and square eyes when you're older.'

St. Eugene's

After bidding a see ya to St. Medard's at 11, I left behind the days of six-of-the-best spanks, knee-length shorts, and woolly jumpers, along with paying marbles and the egg-and-spoon races. St. Eugene's, Allerton, middle school ushered in a new era: rugby, boxing, smart baggy trousers, school blazers, and the dreaded cane, which was lashed over naughty boys' fingertips for very little reason, including running in the corridors. Despite my resolve to stay strong, a sickening anticipation churned in my stomach at the prospect of changing schools. The older students at St. Eugene's seemed enormous and were rumoured to give new kids wedgies, dead legs, nipple twists and Chinese burns. Thankfully, I had a tight-knit circle of friends; almost all had made the transition with me from our previous school.

In our bid to look and sound tough, we deepened our unbroken voices. We walked with broadened shoulders. And we fed our pre-teenage egos with the nicknames we had awarded ourselves: Stephen Farrell, AKA Ste (The Body Popper); Martin Canning, AKA Paddy (The Striker); and Robert Coulson, AKA Coulsy (The Kung Fu Master); I was known as Crooty (The Joker). The newcomer to our gang was Rupert Lyttleton, AKA Rups (The Smiler). Rups and I first met on the bus to school over shared packets of Spangle sweets and some ad hoc lessons in Jamaican Patois; we became instant friends.

Our gang were from an eclectic mix of backgrounds. Ste and Paddy were the Irish rebels of the gang who got their kicks from breakdancing and footy. Ste was picked to be in a Bradford body-popping crew whilst Paddy rose to the ranks of being a member of the school football team; I, however, was a terrible dancer and tried to make it in the school footy team but failed miserably, not even coming close to living up to Dad's skills as a footballer.

Rups was Jamaican, and Coulsy's parents were from a Greek Cypriot background. Rups and Coulsy were much calmer characters than the rest of us and kept themselves out of trouble. They got their kicks from their computer games and racing remote-controlled cars. Some days, after school, I used to go back to Coulsy's Yorkshire stone-built house, which was five minutes away from our school, and sometimes, we watched poorly dubbed kung fu and karate films and imitated the Bruce Lee-esque moves in his mum's living room whilst ensuring we didn't knock over her best China ornaments. Coulsy was lucky to own many of the latest gadgets that most of us didn't have, like his Commodore 64 home computer and his cool Kyosho petrol remote-controlled car. Occasionally, we'd play *Donkey Kong* and Night Driver on his Commodore 64 computer, which was so much better than my second-hand Zx Spectrum. Whilst we gamed, Coulsy's mum would bring us melt-in-the-mouth shortcake biscuits that she had baked herself and cups of freezer-cool fizzy pop. On other days, we played outdoors on the dirt track at the back of his house, racing his awesome petrol remote-controlled car. I always wished I could have the same one, but my parents didn't have much money for luxuries. Eventually, after a barrage of pleas from me, Mum, bless her, bought me a remote-controlled car from Bradford Market, but it was only a slow battery-operated one. So it wasn't surprising that my car WAS LEFT FOR DUST when I raced it against Coulsy's car!

Just like in my previous school, St. Medard's, I tested many teachers' patience in my new school. However, One teacher who saw the potential in me was Miss Sullivan, my English teacher. In my first year of middle school, she boosted my confidence in my writing after reading one of my stories. The short story homework on the theme of friends and friendship was only meant to be four pages long. My story ended up being twenty-nine pages long, which I eagerly wrote in one evening. The following day, Miss Sullivan kept me back after my English lesson.

'Jason, your story was excellent. You have such a vivid imagination...so natural...it was sad, it was happy, and it was so emotional. You really showed how able you are to take your story in many directions.'

It turned out that that very story took me to receive my first A+.

Mrs Sullivan's feedback was encouraging, inspiring me to write more and more until, unfortunately, I had a different English teacher the following year. Mr Bryan.

'Elbows OFF the table, Croot!'

'STOP staring out of the window, Croot!'

'It's your own time that you're wasting, NOT mine, Croot!

Mr Bryan, or Mental Bryany, as many kids thoughtlessly named him, was a sharply dressed man who sported tailored suits and thick-rimmed glasses. He walked with a slight limp. No one knew exactly why he had a limp but rumours had it that he had a wooden leg. He had a volcanic temper and would regularly fly off the handle for no valid reason, although one morning, I gave him one.

Most of my classes consisted mainly of English students, and Mr Bryan's class was no exception, apart from one Punjabi classmate called Balminder Singh.

This particular morning, Mr Bryan called the register just like he did every day. From Anderson to Berry and Coulson to Croot, he continued right throughout the register in alphabetic order. We, just like we did every day, responded to our surnames as he hollered them out; everyone apart from Balminder Singh, that is. When Mr Bryan called out Singh, I knew Singh was absent that day, but I didn't tell Mr Bryan. Mr Bryan repeated louder this time.

'Singh? Singh? Singh?'

The opportunity to capture an audience once again was too tempting, and I couldn't help myself. I did as Mr Bryan had inadvertently directed.

I broke into the Musical Youth song, *Pass the Dutchie*. A roar of loud laughter took over the class, but Mr Bryan was livid. He pulled me outside by my arm whilst barking at me.

'You Boy, I will not stand for such insolence, so you want to act like a fool, do you?' he asked me rhetorically.

He then demanded that I stand on a chair in the corridor and wear a cone-shaped paper hat with a D written on it, which stood for Dunce, a name that connotes a person who is slow at learning, a stupid person. Mr Bryan hadn't finished there as he yelled.

'Stand up straight, Croot. Have you no respect?'

Oh boy! It took all I had inside of me to swallow the retaliation that was bursting to jump out of my mouth, namely the words of the great Joe Dolce song *Shaddap Your Face!*

The mutual dislike between myself and many of my teachers, like Mr Bryan, was slowly chipping away at my motivation to learn and work hard in the subjects they taught. Their constant criticism bounced off me like raindrops on a duck's back. My focus became less and less on the lessons and turned more towards a new subject interest: Girls.

My teenage testosterone was playing havoc and driving my

attention more and more to the many pretty girls in my classes. One of my crushes was on Zara Gil, who was a near-spitting image of the pop sensation Madonna. Zara Gil sat near me in Mr Pascal's French lessons. Zara's beauty mark on her face and wildly permed hair made her exude star quality in my teenage eyes. I was desperately seeking Zara's attention, which was reflected in my multiple attempts to pass notes to her, usually invitations to meet me at "The Underground" at lunchtime. But just like a superstar, Zara was always out of reach, and my gallant efforts were never ever reciprocated.

It wasn't all doom and gloom, though, because although I had my fair share of fall-flat-on-my-face rejections on the teen dating front, I'd often get chatting with other girls at the back of our school in an area that was aptly named by the students "The Underground." Here, some kids, like novices, would spend their break times puffing on forbidden cigarettes that they had pinched. I would venture to "The Underground" but not to smoke. Hell no! Not me. I had been permanently put off smoking when I was eight years old. Nana had asked me to fetch her burning filterless Woodbine cigarette, and I did as I was told, partly. But before I got back to Nana, my curiosity got the better of me, and I tried it. Consequently, I nearly vomited my insides out and nearly choked to death.

While most kids puffed their brains out, my taboo interest in "The Underground" was to catch a sneaky snog with any girl who also was keen to step beyond the school boundaries into the forbidden. One of them was Tonia Lockwood, who I also knew from Mr Pascal's French class. As I dusted off my school jumper from the multiple rebukes of Zara Gil. My fleeting teenage romance developed with Tonia after she let me copy her French homework one morning, which ultimately saved me from detention with Mr Pascal. Tonia often came into school with her skirt's length just below the knee; by lunchtime, she had rolled it up so high above her knee that it was nearly like a micro mini skirt, and by her next lesson after lunch, it was adjusted to the length her Mum had intended for it to be. We'd often meet in "The Underground," find a quiet spot in the covered concrete area and spend many-a-lunchtime canoodling. The group of rule-flouting, don't-give-a-damn students who were regular visitors to "The Underground," including me, weren't best pleased when teachers arrived and caught them in acts that definitely defied the school rules, and I'd been caught a few times.

It turned out that I was to pay the price for focusing on French kissing rather than French lessons as we neared our final classes and had to sit exams for upper school. The short-term fling with Tonia was overshadowed by the arrival of a new attractive and very busty French teacher named Mrs Caron. Again, my concentration on French vocabulary was marred somewhat by my major teenage crush on Mrs Caron, who had a sexy French accent.

During our French entrance exam, I sat next to my best friend, Paddy. A few weeks later, we got the results: I got 98%, and Paddy got 99%.... *Mais...*

Our outstanding exam scores were NOT because we'd knuckled down on our French; in fact, we were both terrible at the subject. Our outstanding results were due to the fact that Paddy had managed to swap the exam answer paper for two rare Star Soccer football cards with Scott Berry. Berry had pinched the paper from Mrs Caron's desk but was smart enough not to use them himself. However, just like Paddy, I copied them from the piece of paper we had hidden under our desk.

10 KARATE KID

'*Bonjour,* class 7, settle down! Let's begin,' chirped *Mademoiselle* Vera.

I opened up my *Tricolore* book, which had a sketch of a penis and breasts on the inner page. I showed it to Paddy, who started giggling.

'What is so funny? Come on, share with the rest of the class,' *Mademoiselle* Vera said.

I could hardly tell her that we were laughing at a drawing of a dick and a pair of titties which most probably had been drawn by a former pupil of French, who, like Paddy and I, was just as disengaged with their French lesson as we were and had alleviated their boredom through the art of the human form! Our slightly flushed faces signalled to *Mademoiselle* Vera that her threat of exposing the *Les tétons* and *Le pénis* artwork was enough to make us stop giggling. So, she continued her lesson and proceeded to play a French cassette for us.

'*Répétez, s'il vous plaît,*' she invited the advanced-level students between pauses to echo what they'd heard. Paddy glanced at me, and I glanced at Paddy AND *Merde! Je ne sais pas!* We were completely and utterly lost.

Paddy and I had used some chicanery in our French entrance exam test! However, after a couple of weeks, it became painfully evident to *Mademoiselle* Vera that Paddy and I were utterly adrift. Consequently, our undeserved ascent to the top quickly crumbled, and we were demoted to the lowest-level French class within our year group at St. Balthasar's, an all-boys grammar school.

The older I became, the more I lost interest in most subjects. Most teachers already labelled me a troublemaker and rapscallion, so expectations were low, and incidents of being in trouble were plenty. I often found myself in detention after school, which was usually held in Mr Hindle's science lab.

On my way to one detention, an open classroom door caught my eye. I stopped for a moment to peer in and caught a glimpse of a student on stage who appeared to be performing. His fellow classmates and teacher watched from their chairs. A makeshift sign on the door indicated that this was a drama club. I had to prise myself away from the allure of the stage, realising I'd be late for detention.

Seeing my new friend Gary Carlson sitting in detention was a welcomed sight. He had cheated during the school's cross-country race. He'd hopped on a bus on Haworth Road but got spotted by a snake-eyed sixth former who grassed him up when he got off near the checkpoint at the school gates. I had double detention because my crime was much bigger! I had inadvertently rang the silver altar bell during school mass, like *Quasimodo*, making all the boys in our year laugh hysterically, and the priest furious. He preached after the mass.

'CROOT, Boy, you will NEVER-EVER be an altar boy AGAIN!'

I'm not sure why Paddy and I were chosen as altar boys in the first place, but we were. During mass, I'd forgotten when to ring the bell and just tried to wing it. Well, actually, Paddy nudged me when to ring it, but he purposely gave me all the wrong times. I never grassed him up, so he didn't get in trouble.

In detention mine and Gary's punishment was to write lines over and over again. Gary was looking the other way out of the classroom window when I pelted a scrunched-up spitball his way. There were a few desks between Gary and me, but once I had his undivided attention after a spitball bounced off his hand, I whispered.

'I think I want to sign up for drama club!'

I was thinking that, like me, he'd think it was pretty cool. Unfortunately, he didn't and jokingly limped his wrist; his implied perception of drama somehow being associated with being gay was made as clear as glass. His reaction was sharp and cutting, but I brushed it off and convinced myself that it, of course, was a ridiculous idea anyway, but in the back of my mind, I was still intrigued by how it would feel to perform on stage. I didn't want to be ousted out by my friends just because I signed up for a drama club. Gary convinced me to sign up for the boxing club with him instead, so that's what I did.

Mum reluctantly bought me a £3 gum shield that was so big it could have fit a racehorse and, although nothing fancy, some yellow boxing gloves for £5 from Bradford Market. I could have sworn that they were both left-handed gloves when I tried them on.

The night before my first boxing class, I needed some inspiration and found it in the classic boxing film *Rocky III*, which blasted out of Mum and Dad's bedroom as I watched the VHS film on my parents' 20-inch TV. After watching it for 15 minutes, I put on my big yellow gloves and tried to emulate Rocky's boxing moves, step-step-jab-jab, back, envisioning myself in a ring as a champion boxer until...

'Jason, yer supper's ready, come on, it's going cold...no boxing for ye tomorrow if ye don't come down,' Mum warned shouting from downstairs.

Dun, Dun, Dun, Dun, Dun, Dun, Dun, Dun, Dun...as the iconic *Rocky III* theme tune belted out, I begrudgingly had to switch the film off just as it was nearing another pivotal moment. I threw in the towel, flung my boxing gloves against Martin's Madness pop poster and stomped downstairs to the stew and dumplings waiting for me at the table.

'You're boxing tomorrow, our kid?' Martin enquired whilst pulling out a piece of beef gristle from his teeth.

'Yeah, I can't wait.'

'Why you berk? you'll be knocked out...YOU couldn't fight your way out of a paper bag,' he voiced discouragingly, raising his two fists towards me.

I was about to swing for him but then realised Mum would put the *kibosh* on my boxing dream if I did, so I didn't.

The eye of the tiger

As I walked into the school gym in my white vest, long white shorts and big red boxing gloves, my other classmates shouted. 'Crooty, Crooty, Crooty.'

The Rocky theme song was playing in my head: Dun, Dun, Dun, Dun, Dun, Dun. I was buzzing as I climbed into the large grey canvas ring and put in my gum shield. Mr Saxon, the slender sports teacher with a whistle around his neck, donning a tight black tracksuit, strode into the gym. Behind him, I could see the heavy and serious stomps of the biggest boy in our class and the Cock of our year, Fred Hill (Hilly), who appeared by the way he was shadowboxing to know more about what he was doing than I ever could. Shit, I thought to myself as Hilly climbed into the ring. He looked like a hungry tiger ready to rip off the head of its prey. Mr Saxon climbed in and asked us both to come in the middle.

'No biting, No spitting and No hitting below the belt. I want a clean, good fight,' he announced as if he had rehearsed lines from a boxing movie and as if we were heavyweight contenders.

Hilly was staring at me, and I looked down at my unfastened black canvas boots, but before I could tell Mr Saxon that I needed to fasten them, he rang the bell, and Hilly and I faced each other.

'Crooty! Crooty! Crooty!' The class sang in an out-of-tune and not-so-harmonious chant which ricocheted off the gym walls.

I lifted my hands and swung my right glove to Hilly's chin. Bang! I missed, AND Hilly lamped me. With one punch, I was out, sparko, on the deck.

Hilly had walloped me so hard that my gum shield flew out of my mouth, and my teeth were killing me. I was done, done, done. As I lay on the canvas, I saw bright white rings flashing in front of my eyes, and then, the further kick to my teeth came in the form of echoes of my loyal classmates' chanting.

'Hilly! Hilly! Hilly!'

Mr Saxon threw some water on my face and asked me to count his fingers. I obviously miscounted because he took me straight away to be checked over by Mrs Barber, the school nurse. I'd taken a dislike for school nurses since having an unnerving 'Cough and Drop' procedure performed by one of them in my previous school. As part of the WEIRDEST school medical examination I'd ever gone through, one by one, I and all the other boys had to go into the sick room and drop our trousers. Then, after being asked to cough, the school nurse briefly inspected our balls.

Fortunately, Mrs Barber's examination of me wasn't so intrusive, but her phone call to Mum ensured my boxing future lasted as long as the lifespan of a fruit fly; she never let me participate in boxing ever again!

Karate Club

Mum had softened up somewhat when I persuaded her to let me join the Karate Club a couple of weeks later. I managed to convince her that it would not be as violent as boxing. To my surprise, she agreed. She signed my permission slip and gave me £2 to hire a karate outfit from the school office.

'You tramp Crooty, wearing Spencers... you can't afford Farah's like me!!!'

'Says you with your tramp Trutex blouse.'

'Tramp? At least my mum doesn't get her clothes from Oxfam like yours does!'

'Shut it, you numpty.'

Have you keffed Crooty?'

'Nah, Gary, you bellend it's your breath. You smelt it, you dealt it!'

Before our first karate session, Gary Carlson and I trash-talked each other in the changing rooms. As we slammed each other's outfits and fell to the ground in hysterical laughter, we'd lost track of time. Gary and I went into the school gym to join the intermediate-level class, but we were late. As we walked in, the stench of stale teenage sweat hit us both. Fifteen shoeless boys who were kitted out in their outfits were already sparring. Mr Saxon was barefoot and donning his white suit with a black belt; we could tell from his hard stare that he wasn't impressed by our tardiness.

'Carlson and Croot, you boys are late!... Karate is about discipline...punctuality equals discipline...the next time you are late for my lesson, you can sit on the bench,' Mr Saxon warned.

'Sorry, sir,' Gary said.

'Sorry, sir,' I echoed.

'Call me Sensei, NOT sir. In this class, you refer to me as Sensei!'

After he taught us the basic moves, it was time to pair up and bust some moves. I had watched plenty of karate and kung fu movies with Coulsy. How hard could it be? I figured I knew what I was doing. What could go wrong? I was partnered with a bigger-framed boy called Clive Richards, who I squared up to. With matching karate-esque movements, the words.

'Ai-Aya, Ai-Aya, Ai-Aya, Ai-Aya,' jumped out of my mouth as I emulated the unnatural and comical dubbed martial arts movies. All eyes turned to me.

My antics had interrupted the serious reverence of the class, and by the looks on Mr Saxon's face, he was not amused. The students, however, seemed to be feeling quite the opposite. Their efforts to suppress their hysteria were given away by their shoulders jiggling up and down and spurts of laughter trying to escape their mouths through their sweaty palms. Clive was smirking. I was secretly loving the attention on me and hearing the giggles that my antics were causing. Mr Saxon came over, wagging his finger and barking at me.

'Croot! Stop being infantile, boy!'

As we set up again, I did what I thought was the best thing to do. I did it again!

'Ai-Aya, Ai-Aya, Ai-Aya.'

Most found hilarity at my tomfoolery apart from Mr Saxon that is, who stomped over.

'It's the likes of you, Croot, who spoil it for the rest of the class,' he barked.

(I seemed to have heard that said to me before!) He grabbed me by my belt and pulled me across the gym.

'And wipe that stupid smirk off your face before I wipe it off for you.'

'Sorry sir....'

'Sensai!' he corrected.

Mr Saxon's nostrils flared as he ordered me to sit on the bench for the remainder of the lesson. At least I avoided receiving the standard punishment: the bamboo stick over the fingertips, which, let me tell you, flipping hurt.

Cookery Club

As Mum and Dad had to work, Mum felt more reassured that I was safe if I was in a club after school instead of hanging around on the streets. I was chopped from karate lessons, I was knocked out of my boxing class, and drama club remained an elusive dream. What next? Chuffing Cookery Club at Saint Medard's Kitchen, that's what! Mum's choice, not mine, of course!

My brother Martin had already paid his dues and graduated from the Cookery Club, and now it was my turn. Mum reminded me not to forget my apron before I went to school. Martin made a jesting dig at me.

'What's cooking, good looking?'

'Shut up, Martin! You Pillock!' I replied whilst elbowing Martin in his side.

Martin wasn't the only one from whom I got some stick. Ste, Paddy, and Gary had their fair share of digs for me when they found out about my new extracurricular activity.

'Crooty, baking? You pansy!'

'Shut it, Gary, you Nobhead.'

While my friends were practising how to become champion footballers or renowned breakdancers, I was trying to master the act of looking like I was interested in becoming the next Mr Kipling. It wasn't all exceedingly bad, though.

'Crooty ya jammy get!' Gary said when he found out that I was the ONLY boy in the cookery club amongst eighteen girls.

11 SMELLS LIKE TEEN SPIRIT

Punk-style hair, Atari home game consoles, and acid-washed ripped jeans were part of the raging trends of the 80s—arguably the coolest decade ever!!! Duran Duran, R.E.M. Culture Club, Prince, and Michael Jackson tracks played in every club, bar and house. Gigantic ghettoblasters blasted out the cooler-than-cool tunes in parks and on every street corner. And while Madonna, the Queen of Pop, was *Desperately Seeking Susan* in the movies, my friends and I desperately sought to find out where we belonged in life.

Ste, Paddy, Gary, and I contemplated forming a boy band, but we soon gave up those thoughts when we realised that we couldn't even play the triangle or a recorder between us. We modelled ourselves on our movie heroes, *The Wanderers,* who, like us, exuded camaraderie, oozed bravado, and formed tighter-than-tight bonds.

We kept up our rebellious pretences, which were influenced in different ways by being continually misunderstood. We found acceptance with each other, which was often lacking for each of us in the outside world. We had each other's backs in the face of the types of teenage adversity, conflict, and any strife that we may have faced.

We were slaves to fashion and as cool as ice (in our world anyway) as we donned our bright-coloured Le Shark polo shirts and acid-washed, flared, ripped jeans, which we found hard not to trip over when our Dunlop Green Flash trainers kicked the inside hems of our flares. Our £3 haircuts were from the same barber, Gerado, who styled our hair in exactly the same way, side-parted and short back and sides, which were all paid for from our own pocket money. Our image brought us as near as dammit as we could be to the style of the idols we wanted to emulate. The symbol of our misplaced teen aspirations: *The Wanderers*—a gang from the 80s cult movie.

In place of *The Wanderers'* cool 1949 Buick Super 51 car, we had our own mode of transport: bicycles. The acrylic bomber jackets that our mums' bought us for £10 from Bradford Market were a substitute for the cool satin baseball jackets donned by the characters in the movie.

On weekends, those of us who dared. Namely, Gary and I chartered into unknown territories. We were only 14, but we'd often hit on 16 and 17-year-olds as we walked into women's clothes shops and tried out the techniques of our movie idols. The "elbow tit move" was a technique (though highly inappropriate) that we'd seen in *The Wanderers* movie. A technique which involved walking past girls and then placing our elbows on their breasts. We were lucky to never be landed with a slap and a severe telling-off, but what we did land instead were several dates.

One such weekend, Gary and I tried this manoeuvre on two girls. One of whom was half blushing before I even had a chance to finish my chat-up line. We ended up copping off with the girls and taking them to the local cinema to watch *Weird Science*. We'd discovered that we could get in without paying by sneaking through the cinema's fire exit door. Having snuck into the darkened cinema successfully, Gary and I, along with the two girls, Lizzy and Sam, sat in the only available seats in the front row. The movie had already started. I sat next to Sam, and Gary sat next to Lizzy. I put my arm around Sam, who moved up closer to me. Soon enough, Sam and I started tonsil tennis, and then we went hell for leather, moving quickly from bra-fumbling second to the third set, but before I could get to match point. Gary gave me a kick as the loud grunts Sam and I were making awkwardly, caught the attention of a fuddy-duddy usher, who consequently ushered all of us out of the cinema in a rather embarrassing fashion. Gary and I went back to watch the movie the following day because we both had a crush on Kelly LeBrock.

Films and TV gave youths like me a connection to a world where teens were very often misunderstood and unheard, especially when it came to questions about taboo topics. Much of our gang's misaligned awareness about the "birds and the bees" came from programmes like *The Young Ones* (with Bradfordian Adrian Edmondson as the crazy Vyvyan). And our testosterone was fuelled by 18-rated flicks like *Porky's, Screwballs, The Wanderers,* and *Lemon Popsicle,* which, during sleepovers, we'd watch secretly behind bedroom doors which were shut to disapproving adults.

Hanging out together, out of school (whether at sleepovers,

cinemas, parks, or shopping centres), was a much-needed vitamin to our teen years. As a group of friends united in our distaste for school, we loved any excuse for time away from lessons and teachers. Teachers' strikes were becoming very common as teachers fought for better salaries. Students, much to the dismay of their parents, relished in their teachers' battles for one reason and one reason only: because it meant time off from school!

Not long after the cinema saga, several Bradford schools closed due to strikes. On that day, Gary, Ste, and I decided to head to Bradford town centre without a plan. Allerton was about an hour's walk, so taking the bus was our best option. *Ker-ching* Saver Strip bus tickets, costing £1.50 for 12 rides, were the cheapest choice but still ate into our pocket money, which we preferred to spend on Wimpy meals. So, we resorted to some chicanery.

Plan A: The first person would *Ker-ching* our one and only ticket and distract the driver while the other two sneaked on. This didn't always work, so if we got caught, we'd try Plan B: Claim we had no money. Being under 16, the drivers, who often lectured us, legally had to let us on. They'd ask us to jot down our names and addresses, which we provided—fake, of course.

'Telegraph, get yer Telegraph!' yelled the newspaper seller at the bottom of Sunbridge Road, where we got off.

We cruised through the Arndale shopping centre, hoping to catch the eye of any female teens enjoying the day off due to the teachers' strike. Instead, we caught the eye of the shopping centre's security guard, who, following his rather large snout, trailed not far behind us as we innocently loitered in and out of the shops. However, our ducking and diving into various shops to shake the pitbull security guard off our tails were not working, and relentless in his pursuit, he eventually managed to catch up with our gang. The pitbull security guard proceeded to sink his teeth into us.

'So why are you not in school then?' he growled as if to assert his manhood.

'School teacher strikes,' I replied, trying to keep as cool as the banana milkshake in my slightly trembling hand.

'Mmmmm...which school is that then?' he latched on to my response, hoping to rip my story apart and reveal untruths.

'St. Balthasar's!' Gary said with conviction, adding with his response a few spoonfuls of attitude.

'Are you a member of "The Ointment?"' the guard snarled, unphased by Gary's efforts at a fierce teen attitude.

'Don't be silly!' Gary served back, refusing to lower his screen of teenage bravado, which then resulted in the pitbull guard taking his mission to the next level (literally) as he roared ferociously.

'Right! You lot, come with me!!!'

Sheepishly, we followed him out of the shop as he marched us across the shopping centre; as we rode up the escalator, Captain Sensible's *Happy Talk* played through the shopping centre's speakers. Before we knew it, we were on the next level where, besides the public toilets, next to what appeared to be a cleaning cupboard was his office. The pitbull security guard slammed the door open, almost knocking it off its hinges. We all stood in a row, and now, in the confines of his office, he thought it appropriate to crouch down to place his huge adult snout in line with our 14-year-old faces in order to break our wall of steel and tear our story to shreds.

'I'll ask you again, are you in "The Ointment?"' Spat the pitbull guard.

"The Ointment" was a football hooligan gang that would go to matches and often get involved in football violence and consequently get arrested. Now more sheepish, Gary bleated.

'No, I'm not.'

'Right, sonny, so is your school on strike?'

Gary replied.

'Yes, it is.'

Then the pitbull put his face in mine so close I thought we might end up snogging and he hollered.

'Is your school on strike?'

'Yes, it is,' I replied. Finally, he went to Ste, who had been unusually quiet during this time.

'You, is your school on strike?'

'Yes, it is,' Ste replied.

'Right, I'm going to call your school, and if they tell me that they are not on strike, you're all in BIG trouble. BIG, BIG trouble.'

I looked at Gary and Ste, and their expressions said it all. We were in BIG trouble because our school was one of the few schools that, unlike several in the area, was NOT on strike, and we were actually bunking off school (as he'd sniffed out from the offset)! The pitbull guard took his place at his desk and took out the phonebook to look for our school number. The masochistic meathead guard then started to dial; however, he only keyed in four numbers; all Bradford numbers had six numbers. Trying to *Shanghai* us, he snarled.

'It's your last chance to fess up. Last chance, do you understand?'

He placed down the phone receiver on the desk with a stance as aggressive as an American movie cop chomping at the bit for a confession. Now, with a dot of white foam starting to form at the corner of his mouth, he came into our faces again.

'Are you lying?' growled the guard.

'No!' Gary said.

Next was my turn.

'Are you lying?' he barked.

'No!' I said, still holding my now melted banana milkshake and not wanting to slip up.

Finally, he got right in Ste's face.

'Are you lying?' He spat in utter disgust because he was failing at breaking our wall.

'No,' replied a shaky Ste.

As the pitbull guard turned and walked back to the desk...

Ste hollered and pressed the panic button.

'Yeah, yeah, yeah, we ARE lying!'

I looked at Gary, and Gary looked at me; sweet doodle fuck! As a result of Ste caving in at the last second, We all ended up getting in BIG trouble not only with our school, where we had to attend a week's detention but we also all found ourselves grounded for two weeks by our parents. So it was double the trouble.

After our two-week period of confinement, we paid our dues, and we continued our defiant ways to show the world that we belonged. On days we weren't exercising our machismo in town by chatting up the local girls or getting into hot water playing truant from school, we started to venture into another area that was off-limits to us: Alcohol.

A few of our gang would often hang out in Prune Park. When we were not playing footy, we'd drink small bottles of Smirnoff vodka and some Diamond White cider that Gary sneaked out from his dad's secret stash. Gary's dad was a strict prison warden, and Gary rebelled against his father's discipline.

Sometimes, this meant pinching his dad's alcohol and disguising it in a bottle of fizzy pop. We'd congregate in the park and share the forbidden bottle of vodka or cider, believing that with each bitter glug, we were becoming more accepted into our own gang's definition of cool.

One afternoon, our gang had gathered in Prune Park. Gary had managed to ask his older brother to buy him a six-bottle pack of Diamond White cider, but unfortunately, we couldn't get the metal lids open. That's when Gary revealed a small silver camping knife, and with this, he showed us what he had obviously learnt from somewhere: how to pierce the metal lids of the bottles so that the cider's gas didn't escape. Apparently, this would make us get drunk quicker. So Gary pierced his lid first with the camping knife, and monkey see, monkey do, we all followed suit. Gary had brought enough cider for each of us to have a bottle each. We got drunk very quickly and started to chant:

'Everywhere We Go, People Wanna Know...' Over and over again.

After a while of glugging down the cider, which none of us admitted was ghastly tasting, my head spun like tumbleweed. The sickly cider taste gathered like a ball which rose up to my throat, and I tried to hold it back by swallowing, but trying to swallow the sickness down appeared to make this worse as it began to shoot back up again with an angrier vengeance this time.

'Never! Never! Never again!' I muttered as the ground spun underneath my feet.

'What's up Crooty? Why are you beefin'?' an unsteady Gary slurred.

No sooner had he thrown the cider-infused question my way than I caught the stench of cider clinging to his stale sweat, and before I had a chance to throw a drunken response his way, the sickly cider feeling I'd tried so hard to contain rocketed up out of my mouth and presented itself as manky orange-coloured vomit in front of my gang and over my Dunlop Green Flash trainers. Gary threw out an untimely, drunken insult.

'Crooty! You Arse! That reeks! It smells like VOMITVILLE!!!' With my cool boy image temporarily depleted and my Ego dented, the gang stood around howling with laughter like a pack of hyenas, and I had to walk home on my own with my tail between my legs and vomit-stained shoes.

12 EASY RIDER

'Jason, they're like moving death traps. Absolutely not! ye cannot have one!' Mum vehemently insisted.

Inspired by watching the cult movie *Easy Rider* cruising the roads on their cool chopper motorbikes, I revved up my attempts to nag, badger and pester Mum and wear down her refusal to buy me a chopper, but my efforts were like spinning wheels of a fallen motorbike; they were going nowhere. So there was no way, shape, or form that my motorbike dream was happening; not til that was when I got placed in motor mechanics studies and got the chance to ride like the wind.

I had been put in Motor Mechanic studies alongside other students who had issues with their behaviour. Like me, they prided themselves on being the rebels of the school; teachers, however, saw us as unruly teenage tearaways. We were no teachers' pets; we were more like teachers' pests!

One of those so-called teachers was a Motor Mechanics teacher, Mr Khidasheli, who was on the wrong side of 50, and we were warned not to get on the wrong side of him. The Georgian teacher had a militant and authoritarian approach and a reputation for being very cruel. He had an unorthodox disciplinary right-hand partner: the long-as-an-arm-bamboo-stick! Students knew never to cross his path because he, to put it lightly, had the patience of a maniac.

His punishment of choice for a student talking during class was once throwing a chalk rubber at his head. For a small misdemeanour like having chewing gum in class, he'd hold up his bamboo stick threateningly, climb on a stool to get more elevation to jump, and then fly off the chair and hit the student in question over their trembling fingers with his trusty bamboo stick using his almighty force. No one knew exactly why he was so cruel. Rumours had it that his dad, Levan Khidasheli, was an executioner in the 60s.

At the end of our Friday lessons, the tearaways would be granted the chance to ride on a red 50cc moped belonging to the school. It was on one wet and windy autumn Friday. We all were revved up as we waited to take turns driving the school moped. We were to ride the short distance. We were to ride on the concrete ground to the brick wall and large wooden green school gates. We were to then turn around and ride straight back. This was EXACTLY what Mr Khidasheli had directed us to do.

As I watched and waited for the others, the three-minute ride for me didn't seem long enough. I wanted more. I wanted to be like one of the actors from *Easy Rider,* but dressed in my V-neck green acrylic school jumper and grey skinny cotton trousers, I was never going to look like an *Easy Rider* character. With no girl in sight, just ten boys dressed in the same uniform as me, I really had no one to impress. But, like always, I wanted to be different. One by one, the class took turns to put the helmet on and drive up to the gate and back to the starting point, and then it was my turn. I put on the white helmet and revved up the 50 ccs red moped beside Gary Carlson, who was standing amongst a group of boys waiting for his turn. Using a chat-up line from *The Wanderers,* I pouted my lips, and in a camp voice to Gary, I delivered.

"Hey there, Gary baby, do you believe in love at first sight, or should I ride by again?"

Recognising the movie line instantly and wound up by my rendition, Gary raised his fist at me in anger, blurting out.

'Say that again, Crooty, and I'll smash your head in.'

'As IF!!!'

All the other boys jeered and shouted.

'FIGHT! FIGHT! FIGHT!'

'Be quiet. Any more nonsense and I will stop da lesson and take da bike inside,' yelled Khidasheli.

I hopped on the moped helmeted-up and left Gary and the rest for dust. I then proceeded to break every rule that Mr Khidasheli had set out as quickly as the dial on the speed gauge went from 0-30 mph. I sped up to the gates as fast as I could, and then, instead of making a U-turn at the gates as instructed, I made an executive decision to make a detour around the trees and onto the grass—the very wet grass. It had been raining, and the wet grass was making the ride trickier, which caused me to ultimately lose control of the moped, AND like *Humpty Dumpty,* I came crashing to the ground. With the bike that came tumbling after...

Out of the corner of my eye, I saw an infuriated Khidasheli, who was not running to put me together again; quite the opposite, there was no doubt in my mind that he was going to rip me apart and that I was in for something very painful. Even though I was flat on the ground, I thought on my feet. So I started groaning and holding my leg as if it was broken. Khidasheli bent down so close I could see a small yellow-reddish angry pimple ready to burst on the corner of his long, slightly bent nose. He grabbed me and pulled me up by the scruff of the neck, shouting through his clenched teeth with a robust Georgian inflexion.

'Da bike, da bike, da bike. I will kill you, BOY. Look at da bike.'

I could see the venom and anger in his eyes. So I carried on acting. 'My leg, ahhh my leg, my leg ahhhh...I think I've broken my leg!' I screamed, hoping that I'd crack his iceberg compassion.

It seemed to work, or so I figured. When Khidasheli thought I'd actually damaged my leg, he dropped me on the ground. I let out another loud fake scream, and Khidasheli looked frightened, thinking he'd caused more damage by dropping me. I was rolling around on the floor like a South American football player pretending that he'd been fouled when he really hadn't. Khidasheli picked up the dented bike, wheeled it back and left me on the floor writhing in pretend pain. What's more, he ordered everybody apart from me back to the classroom.

'Crooty, you tosser! I didn't even get my turn,' moaned Gary Carlson.

I continued rolling around on the floor, and eventually, I got to my feet and pretended to limp back, trying my best to make it look realistic by remembering to hobble on the same leg with the feigned injury. When I got back to class, I continued rubbing my leg and trying to look like I was in terrible agony.

I escaped the wrath of Mr Khidasheli's right-hand partner, the bamboo stick, and I was granted my stay of execution. Instead, I was given an hour's detention in Mr Khidasheli's class after school had finished. With my motorbike dream dampened and my Ego slightly bruised, I spent the hour in detention writing one hundred lines of the same sentence in my best handwriting: I MUST FOLLOW INSTRUCTIONS FROM MY TEACHER, followed by another hundred lines saying: I WILL BE RESPONSIBLE FOR MY ACTIONS. What a waste of paper! How environmentally friendly, NOT!

13 ANOTHER BRICK IN THE WALL

'Your academic achievements have been exceptional. You've been an outstanding student, a real credit to your parents. Your dedication and hard work have set you apart, and you have an incredible future ahead of you. If you keep pushing boundaries, you'll achieve remarkable things: an engineer, a doctor, or a pilot, maybe. The sky's the limit for you.'

After taking a moment to bask in Mr Hindle's rays of praise, Robert Coulson stood up from the desk and spotted me as he started to walk away. Grinning like a Cheshire cat, he gave me a wink and a thumbs-up as I sat waiting to be called.

'Good luck, Crooty,' Coulsy whispered.

It was my turn next, and I had arrived almost an hour late as I had lost track of time while having a kickabout with my chums Paddy, Gary, Ste and Rups.

'Can you throw that out! You know we don't allow chewing gum in this school! Right, let's see,' Mr Hindle, the deputy head teacher, said distastefully while his eyes turned to the papers inside a folder with my name on it. Scanning through the papers with his fingers, he appeared to be searching for some of my highlights.

'Jason Croot, where do we start?' clearing his throat, Mr Hindle commenced.

'You showed no dedication, no decorum and certainly no discipline. Your class clown antics may have got you some laughs, but what can you do with them now?'

Holding my piece of chewing gum between my fingers, I stared down at my Dunlop's as he continued.

'Clearly, you have no prospects and are heading nowhere fast. A shelf stacker, fruit picker or, at best, a security guard. Mark my words, Croot, you will not go far, and you will end up in a dead-end job. Thank heavens you are leaving this school.'

This was my very last day, and this was my career advice assessment. I totally pooh-poohed his pontificating feedback. This was utterly motivating. NOT!

I left, but not before sticking the now stale chewing gum under Hindle's desk. On the way down the empty corridor, I had one thing left to do before I left this jailhouse. I looked around to see the coast was clear. I picked up the small 3-inch hammer on the wall and smashed the red fire alarm. As I walked out of the prison gates for the last time, I saw prison wardens Hindle, Khidasheli and the other militant teachers standing in the playground, trying to sort out the unruly 200 pupils as the alarm bells rang out.

A few things made my school days often feel like being in San Quentin State Prison, including being punished multiple times with bamboo sticks, being humiliated with dunce caps, being detained after school for more times and more reasons than I can even remember and having to endure the school's torture tactics of writing mind-numbing lines. Despite this, there was something quite special about seeing my friends every day, sharing stories, sharing the camaraderie and sharing the support we gave inadvertently to each other when teachers made us feel so small after we'd driven them to their ultimate limits. The trouble I found myself in and often improvised my way out of was undoubtedly character-building. But not for any longer. I had served my sentence after 11 years of the institution of school, and no longer would I have to wear *Baggy Trousers,* no longer would I have to go through this *Madness.* I was finally free. I was now in the big bad world. And this was bloody scary stuff. I had flunked my exams, and however much I tried to shake off the labels Hindle had branded into my conscience, I couldn't. I wanted to prove doubters like him wrong. I wanted to be the rogue bull that escaped from the herd headed for the slaughterhouse. I wanted to charge toward the red rag Hindle had waved in front of me and find a job better than what he had said I was only good enough for.

I'd been up all night with my video games and my fantasies, which were stuck on Madonna like the blue tack that held her to the ceiling alluringly.

'Jason, get up. It's 2 O'clock, ye know, ye can't sleep all day...'

Snap, Crackle, Pop. I had responded to Mum's abrupt 85th call. I got up and flushed away my popadom-like tissues. Sat googly-eyed at the kitchen table and proceeded to pour some Kellogs into a bowl. Breakfasts were relatively quiet compared to the days I would eat and bicker alongside Martin. He had surprised everyone by responding to a calling of his own: To become a monk. He was away in the Bonnie Isles of Scotland, making Mum very proud that he was following a religious path.

Groggy and annoyed at Mum, who was jumping on my habits, I sat at the breakfast table, and my alertness felt like it was drowning in the semi-skimmed milk that I was pouring over my bowl of Rice Krispies. My eyes were filled with images of UFOs and aliens from hours of playing *Space Invaders,* and my aching video game thumbs accidentally lost grip of the carton of milk, which I managed to spill on the table, adding fuel to Mum's fire. There was no time to cry about it, though, as Mum proceeded with her lecture as she wiped away the spilt milk. My yawn refused to stay put in my throat, which tipped Mum over the edge as she put the milk back in the fridge and went upstairs.

'Jason, are ye trying to torture me, eh? Why have ye left the hot water on again? Money doesn't grow on trees, yer know! And open yer bedroom window, will ye? Yer room needs some fresh air.' Mum shouted down.

Mum was still a part-time employee at Dolcis, and Dad worked at Taylor & Turner. No sooner had I left school than Mum was pushing with all her might to get me into the world of work.

'Jason, ye can't sleep your life away; ye need to find a job. Yer cousin Peter has a joinery company. Can ye call him?'

'Yes, Mum, I can call him.'

'I'm sure he'll give ye a job...or have ye not thought about doing what Martin's doing?'

'Mum, there is NO WAY I'm going to be a monk!'

Mum stopped in the middle of sweeping the kitchen floor as if I just announced the world was going to end.

'Well, Jason, you'll have to do something; ye can't sleep yer life away. Have ye had a shower this week? Make sure ye wash up yer bowl, won't ye?'

Every day, I stayed up for hours on end playing video games and watching TV. Every day, Mum went on and on about this job, that job, and the other job. Every day, my teenage hormones continue to bounce all over the place. But unlike my brother, I wasn't interested in living like a monk. My interest in dating the opposite sex, however, was hindered somewhat by a lack of money. So, for now, my relationship with my right hand and my Madonna poster would have to do.

'It was running without its head; I almost puked up; I couldn't work there anymore,' Gary Carlson clucked while we were hanging out drinking cans of Carlsberg in Prune Park. He, too, had flunked his exams and ended up working in a chicken abattoir, but after a week, he quit.

'Lad, it's not great pay, but a job is a job,' Dad said over a fish n' chip supper.

Monk, Chicken Murderer or Textile Apprentice were my three options; maybe I should have paid attention in school after all.

14 TROUBLE AT MILL

'Come on, lad, you don't want to be late for yer first day, and if yer late, they'll dock yer pay. You don't want yer Mum to play pop at ye lad do ye?'

'What, er, what time is it? Five minutes, give us five minutes more, Dad.'

Dad had woken me up at an ungodly hour, a time of day I'd only have seen if I'd been playing video games all night. After about a minute of refusing to accept that I had to get up, I knew I had no choice, and I didn't want to let Dad down, so I swallowed up my Catholic guilt and powered forward with eight Lucozade Energy tablets.

Dad had helped me get my first job as an apprentice at his workplace, Taylor & Turner textile mill where most employees were middle-aged or set to retire. But at 16, from day one, I knew this wasn't going to be a job for life. With the pay being £50 per week for forty long gruelling hours, I knew I certainly wouldn't be driving past Mr Hindle on the streets in my top-down Ferrari any time soon.

The mill was filled with steam billowing from the antiquated, loud metal machinery, spinning and clanking away dutifully. It was a hive of activity where loyal workers, including Dad, guided the machinery along on a daily basis to churn out textiles and rubber to sell to major foreign clothing companies. The pungent stench of burnt rubber and fumes would often clench the inside of my hair, my skin, and my nostrils—it was a stench that didn't come off until I got home, removed my rubber-infused clothing and showered.

Working at Taylor & Turner bored the pants off of me. I spent my days trying to make my laborious role working on the windowless factory floor winding cords on a steel machine go quicker. To make things a little more entertaining for me, I often played my favourite 80s Bros single, *When Will I Be Famous,* over and over again on my portable tape recorder, and, to the further annoyance of my co-workers. The boss, Narky Bernard, played pop at me about my 80s music one day as he cleared his throat loudly and purposefully, and in a tone not authoritarian enough for me to take notice, he yelled.

'What ye playing at, huh? Stop the chelping racket! Show some respect!'

He then disappeared into his office for the rest of the day, but a few days later, when I started playing my music again, he called me into his cave.

'Look, lad, I'm going to have to give ye a warning. There have been too many complaints about ye pratting about. Buck up yer ideas, will ye? Yer poor old dad is getting some stick for it. If ye don't stop yer shenanigans, I'm going to have to let ye go,' he muttered, feeling awkward and uncomfortable as the words struggled to leave his mouth as he wrestled with a strand of his comb-over which fell on his face.

As I returned from Narky Bernard's office, the co-workers' dislike for my 80s tunes was demonstrated by my Bros cassette tape mysteriously ending up in a bucket of Taylor and Turner's specialist glue.

One colleague, more on my wavelength, was Anthony Jowett, whose father Jeff was a local stand-up comedian, whose claim to fame was that he'd been on the TV show *Bullseye,* and he almost won the star prize, a speedboat. Anthony was only two years older than me, and he had a wicked sense of humour. And, like me, he loved playing practical jokes. One morning before the masses arrived, Anthony dared me to put some of the factory's dark blue ink on the staff toilet seat. Given my impetuous nature, I did.

We watched and waited. Another colleague named Kevin Brylcreeme Boocock, a semi-professional basketball player and a huge mountain of a man almost seven feet tall went into the toilets. It was 20 minutes later before he came out, but judging from his face, he didn't seem to be annoyed by anything, or so we thought.

The following day, Kevin came into work and marched angrily towards us. He bailed Anthony and me up in the corner, shouting. 'You pair of pillocks, my wife Tara spent five hours last night in the shower trying to scrub blue stains off of my bloody arse. A little birdie told me you two schoolboys may have had something to do with it.'

For me, the urge to laugh was enormous, but I was conscious

about what Kevin might do to me. He was absolutely livid and, by now, as blue in the face, as I assumed his ink-stained arse was.

'I'm going to kill the pair of you! You bloody dickheads!' he threatened. I tried to look as sympathetic as I could, and without a kernel of truth, I proclaimed.

'It wasn't us! It was Little Richard!'

'Richard, another dickhead, I'll swing for him; where is the stupid git, huh?'

'Ummm... he's...ah...running late...yeah, he's running late, Kev.'

My words cautiously stumbled out, but I was pretty impressed at my response nonetheless.

Little Richard was another one of our colleagues, and my attempt to divert the attention of our heads being knocked off our shoulders appeared to work. Kevin's malice seemed to ease temporarily. I knew full well that the scapegoat, Little Richard, was away on a fortnight's holiday in Skegness with his family.

Over the fortnight, the blue-arsed brute Kevin, appeared to be biding his time while Anthony and I laid low, hoping that by the time Little Richard returned, Kevin's anger, along with the ink stains on his arse, would have worn off.

On the day Little Richard returned to work, looking as red as a lobster after sunbathing in Skegness, he didn't know what was about to hit him. He soon found out, though, when the blue-arsed brute approached him, barking.

'Come here, you bastard. Like to do ink jokes, do you?'

The pink-faced Little Richard was a skinny, short guy who hadn't the foggiest idea what the brute Kevin was talking about and was shocked, to say the least; he proceeded to be manhandled by the scruff of his T-shirt and pleaded.

'What's wrong with you? What are you talking about? I was in chuffing Skegness! It wasn't me, Kev! It wasn't me! It wasn't...arrrghhhh!'

These were Little Richard's last words for the day before he received a hard thump to his sunburnt stomach.

Little Richard was bundled up, holding his belly in pain. The blue-arsed brute walked away, and Anthony and I, who had been watching the whole incident whilst hiding behind a stack of pallets, felt both relieved and guilty.

After Kevin Boocock, the blue-arsed Brylcreemed brute got fired for hitting Little Richard, Narky Bernard did an investigation, which resulted in Anthony and I being called into his office and given our marching orders. So, after six months at Taylor & Turner, the fate that now faced me was signing the *UB40* and being counted as one of the country's millions of unemployed. However, at £28.05 per week, I wasn't going to get rich fast.

'It's okay, son, these things are sent to try us, but ye should try and find another job before yer mother gets on yer case, unless we win the pools this week, of course,' Dad's words were reassuring, but I could see the disappointment in his eyes.

I didn't want Dad to feel the reverberations from others about me being the black sheep of the family, and the horrid catholic guilt washed all over me; this spurred me on to look for another job.

'Put some more coal in t' fire, Jay Luv, it's freezing out.'

'Will do Nana. Do you want another cup of tea or anything to eat?'

'Aye, ta, Luv, why don't ye warm some of my apple pie so we can share it? Another brew would be lovely. I can't seem to get warm; it's so parky today.'

I was staying over at Sewell Road for a few days to keep Nana company and mainly to get away from being underfoot at Rosedale Avenue. As I shovelled more coal onto the warm, open fire, Nana who was once a contributor to Bradford becoming the wool capital of the world, mentioned a wool mill near her that was looking for workers.

'T'll keep yer mother happy for now, Jay, while ye think about what it is ye really want to do, but it's up to ye Luv.'

Nana and I sat and watched *Laurel & Hardy's The Music Box*. We nearly cried laughing at their attempts to move a piano up a long flight of steps. Their final mishap with an ink-spraying pen brought the reality of the job I'd just lost due to my own ink misdemeanour back to mind. The world of *Laurel & Hardy* certainly seemed more exciting than the one in front of me.

As I hugged Nana, left Sewell Road, and walked to the bus stop, I noticed Trisha Brannan, who lived with her dad, Walter, at the bottom of Sewell Road. I smiled and said hello. At the time, I never knew that her son, Zayn Malik of One Direction, would be a future SUPERSTAR. Well, at least someone from Sewell Road, had made it to the BIGTIME. In my world, the ceiling was the limit!

A couple of months after being fired, I landed a new job as a forklift truck driver at the Watson & York wool mill. As soon as I entered, the strong smell of wool was reminiscent of the comforting aroma Nana brought when she came home to Gan Gan and me in the good old days. It was the same smell that had always weaved its way into her thick, warm cardigan, the soft wool cardigan that I would bury my face in when I bear-hugged her tight on her return home.

Watson & York Wool Mill provided stable employment to around

200 employees, who punched the mill's clocking-in machine at 7:00 every working morning. The workers were a mix of males and females from England, Pakistan, and Eastern Europe, and they mainly operated the machines that spun the wool.

One of the employees was Margaret Metcalfe, an expert secretary who had started work on the factory floor of Watson & York alongside her mum and two aunts as soon as she had left school. Margaret Metcalfe rose from the ranks of working on the factory floor operating the machines, to the dizzy heights of working upstairs in the small office, typing, answering calls and being on hand for whatever Harold Watson, the often grumpy and demanding factory boss, needed. The wagging tongues of many of the workers seemed to be drawn to the talk of the factory: Margaret Metcalfe's legs. This small-mindedness occurred mostly at break times when she made her routine walk down the 23 steps from her executive position in the office, across the factory floor, towards the staff canteen vending machine, and her long, slender assets emerged beneath the very, very modest hemlines of her skirts. Knowing she had a daily club of adoring spectators, she'd playfully wink at her admirers when she caught them gawking at her. At the vending machine, she'd bend over slowly and pick out her snacks from the machine's bottom drawer, each time revealing an ever so sneaky peek of her underwear, which peeped out from beneath her short skirt. Her allure appealed to and excited many employees, including myself; however, with my troublesome teenage acne and a tad of adolescent insecurity, Margaret Metcalfe was way, way, way out of my league.

Margaret Metcalfe's legs broke up the monotony of my day because, at its best, my role as a forklift driver was as exciting as the wooden pallets that I was loading and unloading.

I certainly wasn't the best forklift driver, nor did I aspire to be one, and I definitely wasn't on the shortlist of Watson & York's Forklift Driver of the Year. On a hot summer morning, I was operating the forklift, unloading a lorry for delivery of spindles, when Margaret Metcalfe walked past. Momentarily distracted, I took my eyes off where I was going and dropped the pallet, but as I did this, one of the boxes split open. It unexpectedly revealed not the delivery of spindles but items labelled as massagers, otherwise known as vibrators.

'Do you need a hand,' asked Margaret, genuinely concerned. A quick one-liner flashed in my head, but instead, I was sensible.

'Nah, you're alright. I'll sort it out,' I replied, cool as a cucumber. As I was taping the boxes up, I had an idea.

I went to the canteen and then headed to the vending machine. It was a temperamental vending machine that would often eat up coins from the unsuspecting worker and would get its kicks out of stubbornly refusing to release snacks that the worker had been craving for all morning. After driving its hungry workers to despair, the machine would often succumb to being shaken or banged, hit or kicked, but still did not stir. Then, along would come another worker whom the machine would favour, and after making their snack selection, they'd get double what they'd expected.

It was a few minutes before Margaret Metcalfe was due to come into the canteen for her routine snack. But instead of watching Margaret Metcalfe swan down the 23 steps, I made it to the canteen before her, switched on a vibrator that I'd taken from the delivery, and then proceeded to plant it in the bottom drawer of the machine. Hidden only by a metal flap, the excitable contraption produced an unfamiliar humming noise as it bounced around. I sat down at one of the small tables with a couple of my just as excitable workmates, Ali and Snowy. They curiously looked up from their matching Pot Noodles, and they had witnessed what I had done, and we waited. Right on time, Margaret Metcalfe walked in, smiled at her admirers, and enquired about the buzzing noise.

'Is the vending machine broken?'

'No, it's working, Margaret; you can still get snacks.' Holding my poker face.

Margaret Metcalfe proceeded to feed the machine her coins, chose a chocolate bar, bent down to the drawer, and opened the flap to retrieve her snack. When she touched the moving six-inch rubber vibrator, she screamed, giggled and turned rosy red with embarrassment and then left with her chocolate bar, leaving the noisy vibrator bouncing around in the machine.

15 BIG BERTHA

'Sorry Jason, I'm going to have to let you go; my hands are tied. It's just that...well...I've had too many complaints about you from other staff. I'll make sure you get your pay, including any holiday days due.'

'Okay, Harold.'

I didn't argue with my now former boss because, to be honest, there was no love lost with my forklift driver role at all, just as there wasn't with the socially awkward Harold Watson himself! My antics at Watson & York hadn't gone unnoticed. I didn't take heed of the warnings from various people, including my boss. So, after working for 12 weeks lifting and moving boxes of deliveries, Harold gave me my marching orders, and once again, I was fired! I was back again on the dole, filling out my *UB40!*

Although I walked out of Watson & York with my head held up high, it was becoming obvious that I needed to lay low after Mum found out that I was fired once again. Needing to keep out of Mum's hair, I didn't wait to let the grass grow under my feet, and a few weeks later, I started working at Green Road Petrol Station based on the outskirts of Bradford. It was another of many jobs that I loathed. Day in and day out, I served the various customers who would pull onto the forecourt with their vehicles to make use of the petrol station's self-service pumps or jet wash machines, which, for £1, gave customers three minutes to wash their cars.

'What's up with ye jet wash? Is it broken or what?' yelled a miffed cab driver trying to get to grips with the temperamental machine.

'One pound for three minutes! What a sodding racket!' exclaimed a suited man who emerged from an expensive mini campervan, aggravated at the pumped-up price of water to wash his 20k+ vehicle.

'My car's still hacky. I want a refund!' complained a gum-chewing, spotty 18-year-old who came to the till and also paid for a packet of condoms.

Though the customers were mardy and these comments aggravated me, I simply nodded and apologised. I was aware if I told them what I really thought of them, it would do nothing but add fuel to their fire. These types of comments were a day-to-day occurrence. My only temporary escapism from the boredom and ridiculousness was flicking through the pages of the latest glossy magazines that I'd taken from the petrol station's shelves. I got a glimpse into the opulent lives and glamour of the red carpet celebrities, which sparked the wonder within me about the bigger and wider world beyond the confines of Green Road Petrol Station, Bradford.

'Hello, Jay, Luv. Come sit here; tell me about yer day,' Nana said as I returned home from work.

Mum had decided to up sticks and sell the house on Rosedale Avenue. Our new home was now on Sewell Road: the home of my childhood, the home I had shared with Gan Gan and Nana and the home which, now having moved back, was bringing back a mix of memories for me.

While living with us, Nana had adopted the affectionate nickname that I gave her, *Big Bertha,* after the much-loved 80s children's TV animation. Some of the theme tune's words reflected Nana to a T, particularly about people always being able to depend on her, particularly me.

After taking the time to listen to how frustrating work had been, Big Bertha would say.

'Jay, Luv, there is always something. When ye have a problem, even if ye fix that problem, a new one is waiting for ye around t' corner...Can ye make us that cuppa now, Luv? I'm parched...'

'Here you go, Big Bertha. Do you want me to see what's on telly for you?'

'Aye, Luv, see what time *Prisoner Cell Block H* is on.'

'I'll check for you.'

'Ta, Luv. Can ye turn t' lamp on? I can't see a hole in a ladder. Oh, and can ye pass me mi pills and mi Crunchie Luv.'

Big Bertha had lost her teeth a few years back, but she would still often suck on a Crunchie bar whilst watching her favourite Australian soap on her 22-inch TV whilst sitting in her old armchair in front of the new gas fire that Mum had bought to replace her old coal one.

While she was watching TV, I would often sneak up behind Big Bertha, ruffle her hair, and pull her armchair back. Her legs would dangle in the air, and she would waggle her fluffy grey Damart slippers and say.

'Jay, pack it in Luv, stop yer larkin'.'

Then we'd both burst out laughing before I'd put the chair back on all fours and wrapped Big Bertha around my big bear hug.

Once strong, Big Bertha's frame had transformed in my eyes; she was now more delicate and fragile than before.

Heartache

'Jay lad, it's me, Dad. Can ye come to the hospital?'

This call I received at work was about Big Bertha, and it was a call I'd never forget. She'd had an angina attack, and her serious and sudden turn for the worse had meant she was rushed to the hospital. Though she never complained about her health, Big Bertha had been relying on her medication for the angina she'd been suffering from for a few years.

'Is my mother going to pull through, Doctor?'

'We are trying our utmost best, Mrs Croot.'

Hours went by, and the whole family rushed to the Bradford Royal Infirmary hospital. My uncles, aunts, and cousins all stood around suffocated by the grey mood that hung over us. Waiting and waiting and waiting.

As I sat with Mum, Dad and Martin in the waiting room, the doctor came in; his expression and body language said it all…the news that none of us wanted to hear. My Nana, My Big Bertha, had lost her fight and passed away. Big Bertha, who was my world, had left, but memories of her last words remained etched inside of me.

'Jay, wherever I go, I will never be far, and you'll always find me again.'

I wiped away the tears with my jumper sleeve as thoughts of my childhood with Gan Gan and Nana flooded back. A waterfall of tears bled from deep inside the core of my heart as it cried for Big Bertha. I felt like I had been yanked out of reality and dropped into another, more surreal world.

As I was shielded from Gan Gan's funeral on account of me being too young to understand, Big Bertha's family funeral at St Peter's Church was the first funeral I had attended. It was a time when the surreal reality of a permanent goodbye hit me hard. Every part of my body ached, and I had no control over my volcano of tears and feelings of despair. My cousins, Andy and Marco, tried to comfort me with big bear hugs, but what I longed for was a bear hug from my Big Bertha.

After the funeral, work at the petrol station resumed. Shifting my schedule to work nights helped fill the months of sleepless nights I'd been enduring. My daytimes were spent sleeping as I attempted to shut out the world around me. Quiet night shifts lacked customers for hours, allowing thoughts to drown me deeper and deeper. At 18, I was in the darkest place I'd ever known. It was the first time in my life I contemplated ending it all.

16 SERENADE

The intensity of my depression came in ebbs and flows. I couldn't pinpoint at the time what it was exactly that I needed. I wanted something different. I wanted more than I had. I wanted change.

I quit my job at Green Road Petrol Station and looked for a way out of what was now my norm. A hotel junior concierge job in Penzance, Cornwall that I'd seen advertised at the Job Centre in town piqued my interest. And made my contemplation of a life outside of Bradford seem almost a possible reality. Penzance was eight hours away from Bradford by train, the same time it would take to fly to New York. Though the English coastal town wasn't quite the Big Apple, to me, it would be practically like living abroad!

A few weeks later, the contents of a brown envelope confirmed that my thoughts of a new venture had, of course, bit the dust.

I did manage to venture somewhere I hadn't reached before, though: The TTJ & Bros Construction Limited football team.

I eventually landed a new labourer job at TTJ & Bros Construction Limited, but it wasn't much different from any of the other jobs I'd had before. Other than that they had a football team that played in the Bradford Sunday Alliance Football League. And what blew me down with a feather is that I ACTUALLY was picked to be a striker as part of the company's team. Okay, they only had eleven male employees under the age of 55 (including me) who actually wanted to be in the team. However, it felt good to focus on something other than watching cement dry, literally and figuratively speaking.

My Dad almost played pro football for Blackpool F.C. My uncle Alan Horne had an England under-21 football cap, and his son and my cousin Peter had played professional football for Huddersfield

Town.

So, was being on a football team in my genes? And were all these years of dreaming about playing on a football team, all it was cracked up to be? It was, if you called, failing to score, being battered and bruised and losing every single one of our first ten games, being all it was cracked up to be.

I could have blamed the terrible football pitches, which had more craters than the moon, and on my acne face. I could have blamed our manager, who was quieter than *Mr Bean*. I could have blamed my tighter-than-tight Gola faux leather football boots, BUT I had to face it. Though a workman should never blame his tools, I did. I, including myself, was in a team of tools who didn't appear to know their arse from their elbow when it came to kicking arse in Sunday league football. But in the words of Yazz, *The Only Way Is Up!* So down, but not yet out, with our egos and morale fried like crispy bacon, we tried to make it up, wherever that was.

We were in The Bradford Sunday League Division 3, which was for the Wannabes but would never-be pro players like me. The pitch served as a stage where all the pent-up aggressions of many of those who played were let loose, and what I discovered was that this wasn't like the football I had in mind at all. It was more like a wrestling-boxing-football combo. And more and more, I realised how downright dirty the game at Wannabe but would-never-be pro level really was.

'You FUCKING cheating, WOP.'

Hollered a meathead opposing right winger as he kicked me to the muddy ground.

It was my eleventh game, and I'll never forget it because I actually scored my first goal—well, kind of.

It was a wet, freezing cold November, and the 80-degree pitch was more like a watershoot than a footy pitch. Our opponents, Regency Club Rovers, were as hard and hollow as walnut shells with peanuts for brains. They all seemed like they'd been spawned from the likes of *Giant Haystacks, Big Daddy* and *Hulk Hogan*. They were much wider than they were taller and had the bulldog facial aggression to match. They were from the high-flying world of nightclub bouncers, apparently!

We were twenty minutes into what so far was a 0-0 game when the 70-year-old referee, who was slower than *Slowpoke Rodriguez*, was on his last legs as he pootled around the waterlogged pitch like a snail. He was as successful at keeping up with the game as I had been at scoring goals.

'Pass it here, Maggot!' I screamed to one of my teammates, who awkwardly crossed the ball over to me where I was standing about three feet from the goal. I had one eye on the meathead goalie, who seemed to be having as great a day as the referee, as he slipped on the mud onto his huge butt.

With the ball at my feet, I went for it and toe-poked it into the open goal, YES, YES, YES...but no...It seemed I sang prematurely as, by the great law of bloody sod, the ball got stuck in the mud on the bloody goal line and, like a hyena, the guffing defender pounced on the ball and cleared it off the line.

The dawdling referee was near the halfway line and nowhere near me, so of course, I did the most sensible thing I thought at the time and lifted up my hand to celebrate *George Best style,* knowing that I hadn't actually scored a goal.

As luck would have it at that time, the referee, whose mind had probably already made its way halfway home heading towards a steak and kidney pudding dinner, blew his whistle, and ALLOWED MY GOAL!!! Halle-bloody-llujah! The decision left my team, the 11 meatheads' on the opposing team, and me open-mouthed. Despite the big lie, I rolled with the pretend victory anyway. I felt like Maradona when he scored the 'Hand of God' goal for Argentina in the 86 World Cup against England, and I celebrated *George Best style*.

The meatheads' protested. The referee ignored them. My goal stood.

If the other team had been as quick and fast at scoring goals as they were at calling me all the names under the sun once the game resumed again, then the story would've been different. But as the story went, for the first time, our team was winning, and I wasn't going to fess up to the referee for anybody!

'If that was a goal, I'll stand the drop of York,' a mud-splattered Maggot said at halftime. The score was still 1-0. We were all buzzing, eating our muddy slices of sour oranges and discussing the contentious no-goal. My team laughed loudly at the ridiculous but greater position than we'd ever been in our team's history.

This laughter, however, seemed to fan the meatheads' flames, and I could smell the chargrilled barbeque of our teams' flesh they were envisioning for their supper.

'If you win the match, you are all FUCKING dead. Do you dig what I'm saying, you cheating twats?' mumbled one of the meatheads' whose front teeth were like *Shergar* the racehorse. MISSING!

The other owners of their shared three brain cells amongst them, also threw out their threats, like shrivelling sausages on a grill. Their small-minded remarks matched their shrunken steroid penises.

Did we defy the meatheads'? Did we heck! With the meatheads' threats frightening the bollocks out of us, alongside a baron of two-footed-late-stud-up-sliding-reckless-tackles, which lamed me and most of my team. We waved the white flag and resigned to letting the other team win.

The referee blew the final whistle, and the game ended: TTJ & Bros United, 1, Regency Club Rovers, 13. Yep. We lost 13-1.

The pitch wasn't the only place I would often fail to score; this was often also the case on my nights out to the Bradford bars and nightclubs on the weekends with Ste and Rups.

In a smoky, noisy Yorkshire nightclub called Dukes and Silks, a regular club of ours, I stood at the bar waiting to order drinks whilst Ste and Rups were tearing up the dancefloor to Inner City's track *Big Fun*. I seized the opportunity to break the ice with an attractive blonde by asking her.

'Is your father a thief? Or did he steal the stars from the sky and put them in your eyes?.... Don't arrest me for saying that!'

'Arrest you?'

'Yeah, you're Detective Cagney, aren't you?'

My cheesy chat-up lines made Cassie, a local hairdresser, giggle. She looked like Detective Christine Cagney from the hit American TV show *Cagney and Lacey*. I was enamoured by her outer beauty, and within a few months, we went from dating to a full-on romance—Cassie and I, that is, not Cagney and me!

I picked Cassie up in my £250 two-tone beige and burgundy Ford Fiesta MK1 banger, Delilah. Though Delilah was certainly not a car that I thought would impress the ladies, it was a reliable and trustworthy vehicle.

I had reserved a table for an evening meal for Cassie and me at Alberto's, which was situated on a hill with wonderful views of Bradford. At that time of the night, the lights from the local households glittered the landscape. It was a view that had been sometimes likened to the glamorous Monaco. The Italian violin players enhanced the romantic restaurant setting, decorating the atmosphere with their tunes of amore.

Cassie's face glittered as brightly as the single English rose placed on our table. Her cheeks were slightly flushed from the white wine she'd been sipping, and her brown eyes were longing and soaking in the attention I was lavishing on her. She'd dressed to the nines for our date. She'd got herself primped and trimmed, polished and plucked and was dressed in the sleeveless silky blue dress she reserved only for special occasions. She looked spectacular. I, however, was a stark contrast. I was bronzed after renting a sunbed to get rid of my spots, dressed in my frayed jeans, baseball boots, and my favourite Amber and Maroon striped Bradford City football top underneath an oversized navy blue blazer that I'd borrowed from my brother, and I was clearly not showing any decorum.

My romantic efforts, when I really tried, were always deep and meaningful, but they had been few and far between.

'Jason, why are you so edgy, huh?' Cassie asked, perplexed as I slung a deaf un and mopped up the remains of my *carbonara* sauce. I then flagged the waiter for the bill, and without asking Cassie, who had been longing for the *tiramisu,* I told the waiter that we didn't want dessert!

'Would you like to come in, Jason?'

'I'm a bit zonked; I'll take a raincheck if you don't mind.'

Cassie seemed somewhat narked off about not being able to have the *tiramisu,* and even more so when I turned down her offer to stay the night. When we pulled up outside her parent's house, I didn't even offer to walk her to the door.

'Are you sure, Jason?'

'Well, to be honest, Cassie, City are playing tonight, and I want to catch the football highlights on *Match of the Day,* and I've got a game tomorrow morning.'

Cassie's aggravation escalated to anger. She stormed off, slamming the car door without so much as giving me a peck on the cheek.

What Cassie hadn't realised is that earlier, I'd secretly spoken to her parents.

After watching Cassie go off in a huff, I drove off. I parked the car out of sight of her house and waited for about half an hour. From where I was, I could see her bedroom light go off.

As quietly as possible, I walked to her parents' unlocked garage, as I had pre-arranged with them earlier. I grabbed the guitar and the ladder that I had borrowed from my neighbour, Tawi, and had stored there.

I propped up the ladder leading towards Cassie's window. This wasn't easy as I had to hold Tawi's guitar still with one hand and keep my balance on the ladder with my other whilst not making a noise as I slowly climbed up each rung. Obviously, no one was at the bottom of the ladder to hold it steady, so I hoped I wouldn't have a dizzy spell. It was 11:00pm and dark, with the only light coming from a window next door. A moth flew by my face. I swotted it away, trying to keep my balance, and then the next couple of steps up was Cassie's window. Reflecting on this, I see that it was a brave and bold move, considering that I got dizzy even when stepping on the bathroom scales!

Although my guitar skills were as good as a cat trying to play chess with mittens on! I began plucking the strings anyway. The terrible strums accompanied my improvised rendition of the classic song, *Every Breath You Take*. It didn't take long for the sight of me to take a beaming Cassie's breath away when she opened her window and realised my attempts at a romantic and surprise serenade.

Before I did myself any serious injury, I climbed down the ladder to her front door and was met by Cassie in a mint green dressing gown. It was then I bent down on one knee on her parents' bristly wipe-your-feet doormat and proposed. She accepted, and I stood up and wiped the tears of joy away from the corner of Cassie's eye.

'I knew something was up with you,' she chimed with a smile so big it could have lit up Monaco.

Only a few weeks after, we had an engagement party, started a sandwich business, got a mortgage and moved into a two-bedroom Yorkshire stone-built cottage overlooking a canal.

Not long after we moved in together, we took a trip to Cornwall on the South Coast of England. We sampled some of the famous Cornish scones topped with jam and clotted cream, but though the cream was sweet, we both knew the whirlwind relationship was showing signs of turning sour.

We spent a week trying to enjoy the golden beach, the weather and the warm sea, but as waves collided against the rocks, we both knew the inevitable was nigh. The trip away was our attempt to make things work, but the rows between us, even over the smallest of things, were becoming ever more frequent. A couple of weeks later, some life-changing news knocked us for six.

17 ONLY IN MEXICO

Ellie, swimming with dolphins in Cancun, Mexico.

'Cancun? Mexico? Really?'

We left Yorkshire, got in a taxi, and took the M62 to Manchester airport. Her initial thoughts were that she was flying from Manchester to London for a short trip, but when we arrived at the airport, I gave her the flight number and sent her to check the flight board. When she discovered our actual destination, she returned with a smile so big it could have lit up a Christmas tree.

'Dad...Oh my gosh...Dad! Really?'

The surprise news Cassie had delivered to me on our trip to Cornwall brought rushing emotions at the time, and then again when, nine months later, she delivered our beautiful daughter Ellie. During

Cassie's labour, the excitement and surreal atmosphere, along with the queasiness brought on by the sight of blood and the emotional memories that hospitals brought, had caused me to faint in the delivery room, much to Cassie's dismay!

After Ellie was born, her presence brought so much joy to my life, but it was difficult for both Cassie and me to ignore that our relationship was just not working out. The bickering and arguing continued and intensified, and one year after Ellie was born, Cassie and I called time on our relationship and Ellie stayed with Cassie.

Ellie and I went on many trips together, just the two of us, sometimes to places in the UK and other times, we'd venture even further afield. One year, I surprised her with a trip we'd both never forget.

When we landed in Mexico after our gruelling 11-hour overnight flight, we disembarked the plane, collected our bags from the conveyor belt, and stepped out of the cool airport into the scorching Cancun heat.

Our minibus made different stops to drop various tourists at their hotels, some of which were grand and opulent and surrounded by tropical palm trees; all the while, Ellie's eyes dazzled with excitement, but as we were on a budget, I knew our humble lodging wouldn't compete with such luxury. As the minibus pulled up, the exterior of our hotel didn't boast any frills, but I could tell by Ellie's face that she was still just as excited to actually be in the land of *Speedy Gonzales* as I was.

As we entered our *hacienda*-style lodging, the hotel's sign, Hotel El Centro, dangled precariously from the exterior wall. The interior decor, although modest, was surprisingly of a reasonable standard.

Bright and bold Mexican paintings hung from its pastel-coloured walls. A paunchy Mexican man in his mid-40s, in a cheap polyester suit, with close-set greedy eyes and premature wrinkles, was sitting at a front desk. However, this was no Frida Kahlo painting; this was Alejandro, the hotel's assistant manager.

'Good afternoon, Sir. Let me check you in. Your names and passports, please?' he said with a Spanish inflexion.

Attempting my phrasebook Spanish, I replied.

'*Buenas Tardes.*'

His cheap, citrusy aftershave delivered a headache-inducing and pungent scent as I neared closer to him to hand over the required documents as we engaged in small talk. Receipts from the hotel's red guest book were handed to me, and we secured our basic room.

The lift was out of order, so Ellie and I had to trawl our heavy suitcases up the spiral staircase to the third floor until we got to our small white-walled room. The ensuite room itself was laid out in terracotta-coloured tiles, and the two single Mexican pine beds were a welcome sight for our exhausted feet. Ellie dropped the suitcase she held to jump on the bed while I hung up my jacket in the small wardrobe, and I changed from my jeans into my shorts before they melted into my thighs.

Ellie and I were shattered after our 11-hour flight, but we were as keen as *Jalapeños* to check out the local area. After unpacking our suitcases, we took a quick shower, left our hotel, and went to the lively downtown area of El Centro.

Mariachi music played on every street corner as we looked around the local shops, which sold vibrant arts, Taxco-made silverware, Mayan jewellery, and, of course, giant sombreros.

Ellie had spotted a shop where a girl was having her hair weaved.

'Can I have that, Dad?' She asked as she pulled me into the shop.

The Mexican woman indicated by wagging her finger that the customer whom she was already weaving her magic on was to be her last one before she closed for the traditional *siesta*.

'Lo siento Señor...mañana, mañana,' she voiced, as she kindly shooed us away.

Ellie's disappointment was quickly forgotten when she pulled me towards a street seller who was trying to offload the last of his colourful bandanas.

The temperature outside, which was over 90 degrees, was sweltering, and when we arrived back at the hotel, the room felt like a summer greenhouse. There was a slow and lethargic propeller ceiling fan that had clocked on that it was *siesta* time and hardly did anything to cool down the intense heat trapped in the small room. The tiny window, left open, offered a slight and welcomed breeze. As the night drew in, the open window was an invitation for the high-pitched crepitating locusts, scurrying lizards and hungry mosquitoes in search of some fresh English tourist blood. They managed to get what they were looking for and left their big red, itchy calling card on my neck as I didn't use the hotel mosquito net like Ellie had smartly done.

The next days were packed with trips, shopping, and sampling the local food, which we found way too spicy for our English palates. We spent most of the holiday eating like teenagers, much to Ellie's delight, as we dined on fried snacks and fast food. We planned to relax and snack at the beach for the last few days, so after breakfast at our hotel, we headed to the local *supermercado* to stock up on some food supplies.

'Hold on El...I think...I think I've forgotten my wallet,' I said, patting myself down, hoping to find that this wasn't so.

'You mean the wallet you put in your jacket? The one in the wardrobe?' she asked, zooming in on my reaction with the camcorder in her hand that she had been using to shoot an amateur movie.

'That's the one. Come on, Robert Rodriguez! Let's go!' I joked as we did an about-turn to go and get it.

Once we arrived back in the room, I headed for the wardrobe but was surprised to find the wallet, the money, and the rest of its contents weren't there. Our carefree morning had also done an about-turn and was heading down the hill of panic.

We both turned the entire room upside down, but we had no joy. The wallet was gone. With no other option, we went to the reception and were greeted by Alejandro, and I explained to him that we'd been robbed. His broad face smile dropped, and his demeanour seemed to change.

'Are you sure? Have you checked your room? You may have misplaced your wallet outside, no? Nothing like this has ever happened in this hotel before...I will call Junita, the chambermaid and ask her if she has seen your wallet.'

Alejandro turned away from me and headed to the reception's back room. He was still in my view as he picked up the telephone and dialled. I spotted that he had his finger on the phone's receiver, which meant he had ended the call or not even made one in the first place, but he still had the phone to his ear.

'*Hola,* Junita!'

That is all I could comprehend amongst the mumbo jumbo of words he appeared to be speaking.

Alejandro returned to the front desk.

'Unfortunately, Sir, Junita has not seen your wallet. I will do an inquiry,' he said as if this was some sort of comfort.

Somehow, his explanation didn't ring true. Frustrated, I responded.

'I'll have to call the police if my wallet isn't found!'

Without a further word, Ellie and I left the front desk.

Ellie was flicking through the Mexican television stations as quickly as the various thoughts and scenarios were flicking through my racing mind when there was a knock on the door. It was Alejandro who came into the room and asked permission to do his own inspection, which resulted in absolutely *nada*. Before he left the room, he turned around to me and suggested for a second time.

'Perhaps, Sir, you HAVE lost the wallet outside?'

It was raining heavily with Alejandro bathing in his lies, but I didn't need an umbrella; I needed answers.

The following day, still frustrated, I felt the need to speak to a higher authority when I went to the reception and saw Alejandro.

'Can I speak with Pedro?' I asked.

Pedro was the hotel manager. A jovial man with a rounded belly who looked like he'd consumed copious amounts of Corona's and *churros* over the years.

'Pedro is not working until this evening,' said Alejandro, whose response seemed suspiciously rehearsed.

'Can I be of any assistance to you, *Señor* Croot?' He said as I turned around and walked away.

I ignored him and went back to my room. I didn't want the memories of our trip marred by what'd happened. I'd managed to salvage a few *pesos* that I'd found stuffed in my shirt pockets, so I took Ellie to the local downtown shopping area to do the last thing she hadn't ticked off on her to-do list: hair braiding. As the budget was very tight, I successfully bartered with the Mexican hairdresser on the price of the braids, which now left us with a few spare *pesos* (about £3) for the rest of the trip.

As we left the hairdresser's, the sun was beating down, and we were both sweating cobs. As Ellie loved fruit-flavoured iced drinks, we looked for an ice drink bar. We found one, and with a quick glance at the prices on the Spanish menu, it looked like I had just enough coins to buy a drink.

'That one, Dad, that one, that red one,' Ellie said as she pointed to her tipple of choice on the photo menu, thinking it was strawberry or maybe something a little more exotic like *guava*. We waited patiently as the sales girl poured it into the cup along with two straws. Ellie and I were both parched, and the icy beverage was a welcomed treat, or so we thought. We both took a sip of the fruity drink only to realise that it wasn't a delicious quenching fruit-flavoured drink after all.

'Yucky, Dad, what's this?... it tastes like medicine.'

Ay caramba! Ellie was right. It was more like a fiery *habanero* chilli drink than the delightful sweet treat we had anticipated. To reassure her taste buds that they were not wrong in ringing the alarm bells of sheer disgust, Ellie took one more sip before pushing the cup away, grabbing a tissue and wiping away the spicy red residue from her tongue.

'I can't drink any more of that. Dad, that's rank!'

Ellie looked toward me, hoping that her refusal to drink was okay with me. As I took a swig, my eyebrows almost frazzled.

'Neither can I, El. It's pretty disgusting, isn't it?' I wasn't as brave as Ellie to take another sip.

'Can we get another one, Dad? I'll choose that one that the little girl has got over there...that blue one...can we?'

I dug deep inside my pocket, hoping that I may, by some miracle, find enough coins to grant Ellie's simple wish.

'Sorry, El, I can't. We've only got enough money left for the bus fare to get to the airport tomorrow.'

'That's okay, Dad,' she said as her voice dipped, twirling one of her new braids around her index finger to hide her disappointment. However, I saw the disappointment in my daughter's eyes because I couldn't afford to buy another drink, and it shot through my heart like an arrow. I refused to just let the situation beat us, so I resorted to asking tourists for small change, just like a beggar. I felt desperate as I begged and as Ellie watched people walk past without sharing so much as a *peso*. Exhausted from our day in the Mexican heat, Ellie and I headed back to our hotel and stepped into the lobby, where we were intercepted by an overly enthusiastic Alejandro.

'Good evening, *Señor* Croot!'

'It may be for you!' I replied sternly, as I was in no mood for small talk and pleasantries with a man who was as dishonest as the night was dark.

'Señor Croot, wait!' Alejandro made it apparent he had something more to say and stopped us in our attempt to make a beeline for the stairs.

'Unfortunately, *Señor* Croot, due to a hotel system error, there has been a situation where your room has been double booked. A party of guests has been booked on the entire third floor, and that includes your room.'

Alejandro's smile was as straight as a coiled rattlesnake, and he must have noticed my face starting to bubble like a volcano, so he was quick to offer a solution.

'I've sorted a room for you both at our sister hotel, Vista Haven. It's not far. It won't cost you, don't you worry.'

I was so angry. I really wanted to twist Alejando's alligator pears, but he probably didn't have a pair. With no money or credit cards, and much like the filling in a *tortilla*, Ellie and I had no option but to roll with it and pack our bags. So Alejandro took us on foot to the new accommodation for our final night's stay in Mexico.

We fell asleep under the blankets while the giant mosquitoes lay in wait on the wall for an English feast, and judging by the sore mound on my back in the morning, they looked like they had had one.

We had a few hours before we had to catch the bus to the airport. We went down to the lobby of our new hotel, and I asked the receptionist if she could keep her eye on Ellie for a few minutes. She agreed. I walked around to Hotel El Centro. I wanted to tell Pedro about my missing wallet and give Alejandro a piece of my mind.

As I entered the lobby and approached our original hotel's front desk, Pedro greeted me. Swerving the small talk, I got straight to the point.

'*Buenos dias,* Pedro. Is Alejandro not here Today?'

'*Buenos dias,* today, Alejandro is not here.'

'So there's no news about my MONEY? My WALLET? the one that was STOLEN?' My frustration heightened with each and every word that came out of my mouth.

'Money? Wallet? I'm sorry. I'm not understanding,' he replied in a gruff Spanish accent and broken English.

I was so aggravated that there'd been no further news on my wallet AND that Pedro appeared that he didn't have the foggiest idea what I was talking about. There had been no follow-up on what Alejandro said he would do to investigate. There was no closure. And now, with our flight leaving in just a few hours, I had no time to get the police involved.

Pedro looked me up and down and said.

'Please wait here.'

Pedro marched up the stairs and came puffing back down again after a few minutes and proceeded to lock the hotel's double doors. I wasn't sure what was happening, but by the looks of Pedro's body language, it didn't feel good. As he walked around the desk, he pulled out the hotel red receipt book, which Alejandro used at check-in. Pedro went down the list of rooms in the book with his index finger. He looked up and into my eyes with anger. And in another twist to this Rubik's cube of a story, Pedro retorted.

'You, not pay, you not pay.'

I was bewildered because I HAD paid Alejandro at check-in!

By the look on Pedro's face, he must have seen that my room was empty; he must've sensed that something was not quite right; he must have thought that I was trying to run off without paying. It was becoming more apparent that Alejandro, *The Cucaracha! The hijo de perra! The Diablo*...was dodgy! It was becoming more apparent that I may have been screwed over. It was becoming more apparent that I was in quite a predicament as Pedro's voice raised and became more demanding.

'You must pay NOW for room!'

Pedro pushed for the *pesos* again. I tried to keep my cool and told him that I'd already paid. Pedro picked up the phone and dialled, retorting something in Spanish. I didn't have a clue what he was saying, but the one word I did recognise was *Policia!*

Holy Guacamole! I had read before my trip that the Mexican *hacienda* law is different to many parts of the world. In Mexico, you are guilty until proven innocent. *¡Dios mío!* I was possibly going to jail. I didn't need Detective *Columbo* to work this out.

With so many emotions running through my mind, I wondered if I should try and run. But then I'd look guilty, and I wasn't. I stood my ground while worrying about Ellie, who I knew would be worrying about me. I'd been locked in the hotel for almost an hour. Ellie had my mobile, so I couldn't contact her or the other accommodation.

The arrival of the armed Mexican *Policia* made my heart pound as fast as a flamenco guitarist's strum. The three strapping officers looked me up and down, and then Pedro conversed with the officers in Spanish. The Mexican standoff seemed to last an eternity.

As time ticked by, rationality began to drip back into my thoughts. It was at that moment that I realised that I'd always put my receipts in my "johnny pocket" (the small pocket in men's trousers designed for men's rubber contraceptives --johnnies).

As luck would have it, I was wearing my only pair of trousers, the same ones that I'd been wearing at the time I'd checked in with Alejandro 11 days earlier. I wore them only for the journey going to Mexico and was planning to wear them for returning to the much colder England. God was looking down on me. I found the folded payment receipt. The "johnny pocket" commonly used to keep contraception that covers men's parts had covered my arse, Big Time! I showed it to the scowling Pedro sitting behind the lobby desk. His demeanour changed to one that was over-apologetic. He realised not only was I telling the truth but that his colleague Alejandro had made a questionably suspicious error. The hotel's booking system did not note or indicate that the room had been paid for in full.

Alejandro's lies appeared to be coming apart, like his cheap, fraying polyester suit. Now, he was the one who would have to answer to the Mexican *Policia!* My relief eventually gave word to my lungs that I could breathe as Pedro conversed with the officers in Spanish and I was allowed to leave.

The last hour of nearly getting locked up by the Mexican armed *Policia,* of course, dented our schedule somewhat. We'd missed the bus to the airport, and I was worried that now we'd miss our flight.

Down but not out, I was determined that we'd get home. I did as the old Yorkshire saying goes: If you don't ask, you don't get. I told the English-speaking officer my dilemma. I was with my daughter, and we had no money to get a taxi. He told me to follow him, so I accompanied him to his flatbed police van and hopped in the back as I was directed. I was relieved that this time, I was on the right side of the law and heading in the direction of the other hotel and not a Mexican prison.

Lieutenant Rodrigo told me to get Ellie and my bags. With so much that'd happened, I'd forgotten that Ellie had been oblivious to the dramatic events of the last hour, so when Ellie walked out, she almost cried when she saw the police van and the heavily armed police officers. She thought we'd both been arrested. I quickly explained that we had a lift to the airport. Her fear was then overtaken by excitement and her thoughts about how cool it was. She ran to the van quicker than *Speedy Gonzales* and said.

'Can we film it, Dad?'

'Let's not push our luck, El, eh.'

Thirty minutes later, we arrived at Cancun airport just like delinquents and notorious gangsters. Nobody but Ellie and I knew we were really English tourists hoping to get the next flight back home to Yorkshire, ready to leave the drama and beauty of Mexico behind.

18 YORKSHIRE GIGOLO

Mexico was magical, and the more I ventured out of Bradford, the more I felt I could breathe. Thoughts of travelling the world, however, met the ground with a bump when an accident whilst working at TTJ & Bros Construction Limited resulted in a severe injury to my ribs. Though I sued the company for negligence and won, I felt like no champion. After being diagnosed with Clicking Rib Syndrome, which continued to cause me debilitating pain, I was put on the waiting list for a rib operation.

'Take four tablets a day.'

'Thanks, Doctor.'

'They may make you feel drowsy though…Don't forget your sick note. I'll put six months on here for now.'

Unable to work, I was signed off with a bank balance healthier than I was after receiving a significant compensation payout and obviously, my goal of becoming a star player in Bradford's Sunday Alliance Football League Division 1 had been squashed. Boredom was starting to kick in as I spent many days alone at home, so I did the most sensible thing I could think of: I bought myself a new white sports car.

Cleopatra was my new Ford XR3i, which cost me a whopping £1850! It was a flashier, more glamorous and alluring sister of my former car, Delilah, my two-toned, beige-burgundy, clapped-out Ford Fiesta banger, which, sadly, I had to get scrapped after a succession of mechanical problems.

While looking through the classifieds one morning searching for some sporty car seat covers, I found an advert that caught my eye. I rang the agency on my new Nokia 2110 phone and arranged a meeting with them the same day for a new job.

'Heartbreak again for Bradford City fans, with City finishing in 7th position, just one place from the playoffs. It was a tough blow, especially after their huge "nearly season." Let's hope they can get it right next season. This is Pennine Radio 107.9FM. I'm your host, Paul Jonas. Now let's add some flavour to your commute this breezy spring morning,' chimed the radio announcer before seamlessly transitioning into the Bee Gees *Win Again* tune.

At the same time, I pulled into a car park not far from where my appointment at the agency was.

The agency was a small office above an Arabic store called Mahal in downtown Huddersfield. The store sold everything from fresh mangoes and bananas to halal meats and mobile phone cards. I was due to meet an agent called Rita Hornik, who buzzed me in and told me to come up to the second floor. The creaking narrow staircase led me to a barely furnished office. The smell of overripe fruit and Middle Eastern spices from the store downstairs had permeated into the room.

The fruity, cinnamon-sweet scent of Rita Hornik's perfume hit me as soon as she approached to shake my hand. Rita Hornik was a middle-aged Czech woman whose armour of makeup gave nothing away about her.

'Sit here, please, Jason,' she asserted, looking down at her paper while her short, red, chipped fingernails pointed to a cheap, fraying navy blue chair where she wanted me to sit. Rita sat opposite me on her swivel leopard print patterned chair, matching her tight leopard skin jumpsuit. Her eyeballs scanned my body whilst I took a seat, and then her eyes honed in on my face and hair.

'So Jason, you're from Bradford, right? cigarette?' Rita said, offering me one out of a nearly full gold packet of cigarettes.

'No thanks, I don't smoke. I want to stay beautiful.'

Rita didn't react, so I tried my humour again.

'I'm trying to protect my soprano voice.'

'Ah, so, you sing, huh?' Rita asked like this prospect somehow excited her.

'No, that was just my sense of humour,' I said, only then realising that she was finding me as funny as the butts in her ashtray. Rita raised her eyebrows as she took a puff of a new cigarette that she had placed in a *James Bond*-esque silver metal holder.

'So, let's talk about the job Jason. You understand fully what this line of work involves, right? And that discretion, client confidentiality, and, of course, customer satisfaction are key in this line of work, right?'

I nodded as Rita lowered her voice slightly.

'Now, here's something important. We like to use aliases when dealing with clients. It adds an extra layer of privacy, you know?' After a few minutes of toing and froing over potential names, Rita decided on one.

Pleased with her discovery, Rita leaned back, her fingers tapping the desk thoughtfully.

'Roberto Verado. I like it. It's mmmmm...how do you say it?....intriguing!'

As she found the word she sought, she asked me to stand up, turn around, and lift my jacket up, which I did, revealing my Levi 501s. I stood facing the wall for 30 seconds before she invited me to sit back down.

'Welcome onboard, Jason.'

I took a deep breath, feeling a surge of weirdly nervous excitement.

The job caught my eye because it involved meeting women who wanted a short-term companion, and I'd be paid for it. The position I'd just landed: Male Escort—*Gigolo.*

Rita went on to explain that the clients were mainly older women looking to meet younger men.

'Your pay rate, Jason, after agency fees will be £80 for the night...Anything extra from the client would be a tip for you. How does this sound?'

After signing on the dotted line, I said.

'I won't let you down, Rita.'

I left the agency office, popped into Mahal Stores and bought a couple of lamb *samosas.*

I waited for the calls to come in. A few months passed, and nothing had materialised.

One afternoon, while waxing Cleopatra, I felt a vibration in my 501's. It was Rita from the agency.

'Jason, good news, I've got work for you, but I need to know if you own a tuxedo?'

I didn't, but I was eager to take on work, so I replied impulsively.

'Yes, Rita, I do.'

My heart began to race as Rita stressed her instructions: The place: Bagley Hotel, Huddersfield, room 38. The date: Friday the 23rd, The time: 7:30pm and The client: Mrs T.

'Go there, dressed in your tuxedo. You'll be there, right?'

'Definitely, Rita, I'll be there.'

As we ended the call, thoughts entered my mind about where the fuck I'd get a tuxedo from by Friday.

With two days to find a tuxedo, I went into Bradford and found Suits You Sir, a menswear store in the shopping centre that rented tuxedos out for £100. The cost of the suit would outweigh my fee of £80. I left the store empty-handed. I then remembered a local theatre playhouse that rented out cheap costumes.

'Can you tell me where the Costumes are?'

'Over there, Luv,' said an elderly lady reading a TV magazine and sipping tea from a polystyrene cup.

She directed me to the theatre playhouse costumes, where a small collection of outfits was hanging on a rail. As I looked through them, I could see that the musty, mothball-scented garments weren't what I was expecting. The only one in my size was a Spanish *Matador* costume that smelt of onions, but I was running out of options. Peering up from her magazine, the lady shouted over to me over her bifocals.

'That one's only £20 for three days if you want it, Luv.'

Friday arrived, and I got a text confirming everything. I showered and shaved carefully, making sure not to nick my face. Wanting to look and smell good, I put on my best aftershave, *Kouros,* a strong French cologne. I swapped the fancy *Matador* shirt for my own white one and added a black dickie bow tie I found in Martin's drawer. Originally, I planned to take the bus so that I could drink and avoid expensive parking. But it was already 7:00pm, too late for a bus to Huddersfield. So, after some *Dutch courage,* I called a cab instead.

'Where to Lad?'

'Bagley Hotel, Huddersfield, please.'

Either the car was way too hot, or I had put the dickie bow tie on too tightly, but whatever it was, I was feeling a little suffocated. To top it all off, the cab's air conditioner was blowing out warm air as it became entangled with the sickly aroma of the pine-scented air freshener, battling with my onion-scented tuxedo. I was starting to feel queasy, so I rolled down the window.

The middle-aged Asian driver was chatty and in broken English, he commented.

'You look very smart, no? You look like a handsome tailor's dummy, no? You're going to a wedding, right?'

So, rather than overcomplicating things and telling him about my new job, I replied.

'Yeah, a mate's wedding reception.'

He looked through his rearview mirror with a warm smile on his face.

'Ah, weddings are lovely occasions, I tell you, summat, right? I've seen my fair share of people in this taxi going and coming from weddings and celebrations...and a lot of bloody vomit.'

As I stepped into the hotel lobby, I began having second thoughts about how potentially risky the situation could be. What if the client was an unhinged man or woman? What if the client was somebody I knew? What if I got robbed? The £20 note and jingle money I had in my wallet and my plastic blue Swatch watch worth £30 were not even worth stealing. 'Fuck it.' I said to myself.

My heart was pounding as I knocked on the door...

The door opened to reveal the dimly lit room. A lady in her late 50s answered and asked me if I was Roberto. I smiled and nodded, so she let me in. I closed the door behind me.

Mrs T was a buxom lady with thinning, shoulder-length, bleached blonde hair with black and grey sprouting roots. She had wrinkled skin like she smoked or had hammered the sun when she was younger. She was casually dressed in white jeans and a Fila sports vest top. I wondered why on earth I was asked to wear a tuxedo. Clearly, I was overdressed.

In the room was a double bed with creased sheets in a bed that looked unmade, almost like it had been the chambermaid's day off. One of my nemeses (a bottle of Diamond White Cider) sat on the chest of drawers, goading me as Mrs T poured two glasses of the sickly drink for both of us and then proceeded to sit on the king-size double bed, all the while saying nothing whilst she sat next to me.

After drinking a couple of mouthfuls of the cheap-tasting plonk, Mrs T went to the bathroom, and I was left sipping the cider whilst trying not to gag. Ten minutes later, she appeared standing like a Madam in black lingerie, stockings and suspenders. I froze for a second, thinking how surreal this was. She sat next to me on the bed, stroked my inner thigh and asked if I needed to refresh. I didn't want to kill the mood by saying I needed a piss, so I just nodded and went to the loo, splashed water on my face and washed my other bits. Whilst I was checking myself out in the mirror, Mrs T shouted.

'Are you okay in there?'

'I'm just adjusting my dickie,' I replied, giggling to myself.

I entered the room, and Mrs T was already under the blankets.

I undressed and got into bed.

BUT...

I really don't know what came over me.

Well actually...I did.

It was me!

Yes, after 15 seconds...I shot my load.

I certainly wasn't a Yorkshire *Gigolo* that night. Mrs T was far from pleased and asked if she could call me a cab. Just like that, cold as fuck and, of course, no tip.

19 DOCTOR DOCTOR

I tried my luck. 'Will you go down anymore?'

'Feel how SPECTACULAR it is... go on feel it...feel it...silky, smooth...you see? this is not rug...you ask why it is this price...I tell you why...like velvet...like real silk...real pearls...look...feel, it's cushty!'

This wasn't another client wanting my services as an escort. It was Sharif, an Egyptian owner of Sharif's Classics, who had seen me coming.

During a trip to town earlier that day, whilst browsing on the high street, he had managed to charm me into buying what he said was a one-of-a-kind, velvet and silk purple shirt with pearl buttons (that were apparently real pearls) and as I got carried away by his *spiel*. I agreed with the boutique owner that I looked spectacular and then spent a whopping £80 on the shirt.

That evening, Ste, Rups, and I went on a night out and planned to drink the town dry. I had done my best to put my short-lived Huddersfield escapade as a Yorkshire *Gigolo* to the back of my mind.

We were in a swanky nightclub in Bradford: Cloud Nine. Ste, Rups and I were all suited and booted in our best glad rags, as Cloud Nine only permitted guests dressed in smart attire. The prestigious high-end club was as flashy as its neon-lit decorated bar. Good-looking and scantily clad Tequila hosts were tempting yuppie revellers to spend their money on the expensive array of shots they were promoting, cocktails with names that were as risque as their drinkers: *Sex In The Town, Screw Me Slowly,* and *Hard Up Against The Wall,* to name a few.

As Ste busted some dance moves to MC Hammer's *U Can't Touch*

This under the giant crystal disco ball, he picked up his empty Budweiser beer bottle and peered with one eye inside it to indicate it was my round.

I stepped off the dance floor and over Ste, who was now impressing onlookers by doing the 'Windmill' move to Ollie And Jerry's—*There's No Stopping Us*. As I made my way to the bar, I was caught up in the dense mist billowing from the club's smoke machine. As my vision became clearer, I couldn't help but notice a tall guy with a skinhead staring in my direction. I wasn't sure who he was, why he was looking at me, or if he wanted a fight. He strutted over towards me, and he got closer.

'Where, what, Eh?' he hollered over the loud music and chatter whilst pointing to his one-of-a-kind velvet shirt.

After chatting to him briefly, we figured out that we'd both been the daft fuckers who'd fallen for the Egyptian boutique owner's spiel as our one-of-a-kind shirts were both completely and utterly identical!

I ordered three beers at the bar and sat waiting for my drinks. The 90s pop music blasted out from the enormous speakers. A middle-aged buxom brunette with a lightly weathered face wearing a short fitted velvet blue dress leaned over where my arms were stretched out on the bar. The alluring stranger reached for the drink that the bartender had brought her. As she did this, her breast brushed against my arm, and she smiled innocently. She looked at me, held up her shot glass of amaretto topped with Irish cream, and toasted me.

'Cheers, honey.'

I picked up an American twang and commented on how good her drink looked. She inched closer to me like a wild cat, closing in on its prey.

'It's called a *Blowjob,* what's your pleasure?'

'I drink everything, but I've not tried that one.'

'Try it! Honey, you might like it!'

A sucker for beauty, I followed her lead, and when the bartender came our way, I signalled to him.

 'Can I have a *Blowjob*, mate!'

'Coming right up!' replied the barman.

As the American stranger sipped her second *Blowjob,* I observed her full red lips as she introduced herself and offered me her hand.

'I'm Kirstyn. Mind if I join you, honey?'

The sultry woman had a strong New York nasal accent.

'So what's an American doing in a city like Bradford? I asked, genuinely intrigued to know.

'Well...my life is like a cocktail, and I'm here to mix.'

She remained as cool as the ice cubes in her drink, and her mysterious aura was intriguing.

I must've lost track of time because Ste and Rups came off the dancefloor over to the bar, wondering where their drinks were. They could see I was preoccupied.

Ste whispered to me loudly over the pulsating beats of Salt-N-Pepa's *Push It*.

'You never told me it was Grab a Cougar Night!'

Ste and Rups laughed as they took their beers off the bar and walked away. I didn't think that Kirstyn had heard Ste's joke, or if she had, she hadn't been affected by it because under the bar and out of sight, her firm hand started stroking my inner thigh as we talked and flirted. One thing led to another, and Kirstyn and I started kissing. Things were becoming hot and steamy very quickly. Kirstyn's seductive tone broke through the lively chatter of the bar.

'I think we'd be better off finding a quieter spot. Don't you, huh?' she suggested with a playful glint in her eye.

'How about we grab some fresh air?'

Her suggestive tone was getting me aroused. I gestured to Ste and Rups that I would see them later.

Kirstyn and I left Cloud Nine club, and a rowdy stag party clamoured on the pavement outside as we walked around looking for a quiet spot but couldn't find one anywhere. It was summertime, so it was pretty warm. Eventually, we found a place at the back of the nightclub, a metal fire escape.

It wasn't perfect, but it was quiet, apart from the odd shouting and cheering from the drunken revellers below. We started kissing wildly, and our hands explored every part of each other's clothed bodies. After a few minutes, Kirstyn undressed me and ripped the top few buttons of my £80 velvet shirt, and then I heard the mother-of-pearl buttons as they bounced off the metal steps into the abyss. Caught up in the moment, I tried to ignore how painful that was! She hitched up her velvet dress, revealing her knickerless and shaven velvet underground. I placed my hands on the shaven haven, and she assertively pushed my shoulders down until I was on my knees. It didn't take long before I pleasured her. I stood up, and then she unzipped my leather trousers whilst we were kissing. She pulled me tightly towards her, and up against the hard brick wall of the fire escape, we had sex until we climaxed.

Kirstyn pulled her dress back down as I zipped up again and

fastened the only two buttons left at the bottom of my £80 velvet shirt. We made our way down the steps of the fire escape. While I was walking her to the taxi rank, Kirstyn told me she'd be leaving Yorkshire in a couple of weeks and wrote her number on a piece of tissue with red lipstick from her handbag.

I kissed her before she got into a waiting cab. She blew me an air kiss as the cab drove away. I saw Ste and Rups coming out of Cloud Nine and I shouted over for them to hang on. When I crossed the road, Ste looked at my bare chest and couldn't help but quip in true Ste-style.

'What's with the open shirt, Crooty mate, eh? Have you been in a fight or what? And where's your aunty?'

I just slung a deaf un as we followed our noses and appetite for spice and *ghee* to Nawaab Restaurant, where the smell of garlic and Asian spices floated in the Friday night air from a mile away. And where the curries, especially after a few beers, were absolute DYNAMITE.

'Why didn't you just pop one on, kid?'

'I don't know Ste...I wasn't thinking...look, I'll catch you later!'

A couple of days later, I noticed an itchy red rash starting to appear around my lower extremities and other parts of my body.

Needless to say, I was getting a little fraught and even more so when I looked through a medical book that Mum kept on the living room shelf, hoping that I'd find the cause of the rash. I did. My symptoms matched venereal disease, an infection transmitted sexually. I felt faint at the thought of it, so I called my doctor immediately and made an appointment for the next day.

I wasn't sure if the rapidly spreading and even itchier rash was psychosomatic, but what I was sure of was the relief that I was actually getting to see the doctor.

The doctor listened to my ailments and my concerns about having a venereal disease after having unprotected sex a few days ago. After asking me to strip down to my underwear and examining my rash with his rubber-gloved hand the doctor gave his diagnosis: Chickenpox! *Peñis Colada!!!*

MY EGO SCREWED MY ACTING CAREER

Ste, Tina Turner, Me and Rups.
Courtesy of Madame Tussauds Amsterdam.
"What Happened in Amsterdam Remains in Amsterdam!"

20 LIKE A FISH OUT OF WATER

'Shit, shit, shit, it's everywhere!!!' Rups shrieked from the bathroom.

'The toilet paper...the toilet paper...it won't go down, the water is coming up and going everywhere...help me out, will you, Crooty?'

'Have you had a dump?' I said as I pinched my nose and entered the bathroom with caution.

'Rups! You put the bog roll in the toilet...I told you to put it in the bin...look at the side of the bog! You plonker! Remember? Bog roll doesn't flush in Greece! Remember?' I said, now with my t-shirt over my nose.

It turned out Rups hadn't remembered.

Minus this toilet saga. Rups and I were having a ball. He had accompanied me to Corfu for what was to be a short break for him and a longer one for me in my attempt to break away from the norm.

Corfu was a beautiful Greek island with breathtaking scenery. The French Venetian architecture was sublime. However, our joint holiday plans were not as cultivated as the surroundings. Our hotel, Sun Beach, in Kavos, was situated in the southern part of the island, an area known to be a wild haven for party revellers. Each street was filled with expensive tourist trap restaurants, noisy bars offering cheap cocktails and rowdy nightclubs, which disturbed the peeved locals on a daily basis.

The sweltering sun cast its midday glow as *Only Fools and Horses* episodes played on the bar's TV. Rups and I were sat outdoors at a restaurant table, drinking our ice-cold Budweisers. I had jogged Rups's memory about a PlayStation palaver that I'd dragged us both into back in the day.

'...You fool Crooty. How could I forget?'

'Rups, I told you the laser gun was faulty, I told you. Remember? I told you not to play it night and day because of the dodgy laser?... But you didn't listen; you thought you were *Dirty Harry* or something!... Then you wanted a refund because it stopped working!'

'Yeah... that's when shit hit the fan with my mum...with your grand plan, Crooty, you fool!'

'I told you I'd find a buyer, didn't I?'

'Yeah, but you really landed me in it Crooty, by putting out the ad...Mum was like...ROOOOOPERT, ROOOOOPERT, why yuh sellin' a GUN! Ya mad?' Rups said as he mimicked his mum's Jamaican accent, reliving the moment when she hit the roof of their semi-detached house.

'Mum thought it was something hinky...we were getting calls in the early hours of the morning...our phone was ringing off the hook...my mum's never quite forgiven you for that!' Rups laughed. He shook his head at the memory as he remembered the aftermath of my hasty decision to sell the PlayStation with the gun for £35 without informing Rups or his mum that I had put an ad in a local newspaper. AND his phone became like a hotline.

'You fool Crooty!' Rups said, laughing

By now, Rups was downing his fifth Budweiser. Our heads and hearts were light from the beer and nostalgia.

'I'm starving...are you?...looking forward to this curry, aren't you, Crooty?'

Rups was a real creature of habit. He hadn't been too impressed with the Greek scran; for him, it was miss and miss; he had been longing for a curry similar to the ones we would regularly have back in Bradford.

'I think I'll skip this,' I said, pointing to the bizarre menu, which had obviously been incorrectly translated into English.

Butter chicken—Murder of the chicken, roasted in the tandoor, served with smooth tomatoes.

This wasn't the first time during our trip that we'd seen baffling menu errors of dishes that had been incorrectly translated into English and inadvertently gave the description a whole new and often horrific meaning. Other errors included: *lamb shops* instead of lamb chops, *boiled children* instead of boiled chicken, and *Cock* instead of Coke.

'Two more ice-cold býres, *parakaló*,' I said to the Greek waitress as we continued to wait in anticipation for the two chicken *tikka masalas* and *naan bread* we'd ordered.

The restaurant's clientele sitting at the small wooden tables appeared to be mainly British tourists. The expensive, dull menu shouted out TOURIST TRAP. Rups and I were expecting the fantastical smells that we were used to when we would order from our favourite local curry house, Nawaab Restaurant in Bradford, but the smells of sumptuous spices and fried curry leaves were far and distant or rather non-existent. The only smells that were knocking on our nostrils' doors were those from the sewage running under the streets of Kavos. When the waitress returned with our beers, she offered an apology.

'Sorry, guys. We don't have *naan bread*. The chef said he was missing the special ingredients.'

Rups and I looked at each other.

'Can't believe they have *naan*, man! Get it? Have *naan?*...'

'*Naan* man, you fool Crooty,' Rups said, laughing at me, laughing at myself cracking my poor *naan* joke.

'Let's *aller mouche*...'

With our appetites unsatisfied and still craving the taste of home we longed for, we instead headed to a nearby kebab shop, swerving over some drunken revellers who were outside a bar on the floor doing The Gap Band's—*Oops Upside Your Head*.

'Crooty, are you going to be cool on your own?'

For no longer than a fraction of a millisecond, Rups's question jolted *Oops Upside my Head* for the first time. God's honest truth was that I didn't know if I was going to be cool on my own or whether I was doing the right thing.

The next day Rups left the island and flew back to the UK. This was the first time I was going to be away, alone, for a long while, from the city and the people I knew. Rups's absence that first night after he left to return to Yorkshire made my new, lone Greek adventure all the more real. Ready or not, it was time for me to go it alone.

While in Greece, my main priority was recuperating from my recent rib surgery. But there was also the side of me that wanted to truly venture into a life different from what I knew through new adventures, living like the locals and attempting to look and sound like one.

My plan was to spend a few months travelling around various Greek islands. Before I left England, I photocopied the ferry timetable from an 80s travel book of Greece.

I reached the Corfu ferry terminal at 8:30am. Despite my limited Greek vocabulary, I decided to pose as a local. Alongside the port, I spotted a small white wooden kiosk with a sign reading *Aktoploïká*

Eisitíria: Ferry Tickets. Attempting to speak in Greek, I ordered a ticket.

'*Kalimera, um.. éna eisitírio gia to.. um... Irákleio parakaló.*'

While fishing for his thoughts, the ticket master stroked his beard and responded in a thick Greek accent.

'Apologies, but the Heraklion ferry won't arrive for another two days. You'll have to make your way to Syvota and then catch a coach to Athena.'

Clearly, my Greek required some work but the ticket master's silver tongue could've convinced Plato to buy a philosophy book. He convinced me that my best bet would be to buy a much cheaper ticket for the Zorbas, a boat that departed for Syvota at 9:25am.

An hour went by, and eventually, I saw the Zorbas boat pull into the harbour. It was a tiny wooden vessel painted blue, red and yellow with a Greek flag waving on the bow. Zorbas was spelt out and hand-painted in white on the body of the boat and the clear glass windows. I double-checked my ticket; there was no mistaking that this was the boat I would get on. No passengers got off, and none were queuing to get on. I was wondering if there was more than one boat called the Zorbas. A burly, bearded Greek man wearing a yellow smock placed a wooden plank from the boat to the harbour floor. It seemed that I was expected to walk the plank, which was less than a meter wide and about five metres long. Reluctant but with no other option, I fastened my heavy yellow rucksack tightly, so I wouldn't end up like an anchor in the sea. The last thing I wanted was to join the Greek sardines by falling into the salty brine of the Mediterranean Sea. Plus, I was a terrible swimmer. As I boarded the boat, I saw an overweight grey-haired Greek man dressed in a black turtle neck jumper, orange plastic trousers, and black Wellington boots. He smelt like a mixture of pungent cigarettes and fish guts. He retorted something to me in Greek. However, I couldn't understand a word. I showed him my ticket, and he smirked and directed me to the wooden seat. As I looked on the floor, I saw a few stray silvery fish entangled in a net. Some of their tails were still flapping, and some were taking their last gulps of air. It was then I realised that I appeared to be the only non-fisherman on the boat. Nevertheless, the boat set off with me sticking out like a septic thumb.

The rocky, choppy waves took two hours to bounce the boat to the next port. The motion of rough bullying waves and the aggressive stench of fish guts made my stomach jump off the side of the boat and swim home. It was a fortunate miracle that I didn't vomit.

Glad for my feet to be on solid ground. I arrived at the port in

Syvota at 11:30am, where I had to catch a coach to Piraeus in Athens. I had an hour to kill before my coach arrived, so of course, I explored Syvota. The pretty town looked like a picture on a postcard with its pastel-coloured houses. Though it didn't have much to offer the tourists, it suited me just fine. I wanted to blend in with the surroundings as much as I could.

There wasn't a postcard in sight as I browsed through some of the small quaint shops that sold handmade clothes, leather belts, and a variety of books. As I flicked through its small collection of texts, I was drawn to the stunning photo on the front cover of one book, of a beautiful Greek naked goddess emerging from the crystal clear sea. The book was titled *Αφροδίτη*, and even though it was all Greek to me, I bought it anyway.

I parked myself up for the remainder of the time, and a much-needed drink was in order. After my coffee, I attempted my smattering of Greek to buy a coach ticket.

'*Eisitírio gia Athína parakaló.*'

And whad'ya Know? TA-DA! I proudly managed to pull it off.

21 THE GREAT ESCAPE

'*Athína, eisitíria parakaló...Athína,* tickets please,' bellowed the bus driver with an air of exaggerated authority as his unruly beard flapped in the mountainous breeze. It was as if he were the gatekeeper to Hades rather than a bus driver heading to Athens.

The granite-haired driver had stepped off the bus, holding a cigarette in one hand as he proceeded to open the luggage flap with the other. I showed my ticket to the driver and placed my heavy yellow rucksack in the hold.

The passengers boarded the Athena-bound two-toned white and blue bus. Judging by their attire, I presumed the rest of the forty or so passengers in the queue were locals. When I got onto the bus, I took a window seat at the front, positioning myself behind the smokey driver's seat. I settled in, put my head down, not wanting to stick out as a tourist and started to flick through my new book. A young Greek man sat next to me. He made himself comfy and put a small burgundy travel pillow behind his head.

'*Kalispera,*' he said, looking at me. I was somewhat chuffed that he assumed I was a fellow native. Maybe it was my new hairstyle that made me look Greek? Inspired by Keanu Reeves's cool longhaired look in the final scene of *Point Break*, I had grown mine too.

'*Kalispera!*' I returned the Greek greeting, wishing him good afternoon as we left Syvota behind.

The journey to Athena was due to last almost eleven hours, and less than halfway there, it had already been testing, to say the least. I was experiencing the inevitable: travel sickness. The stench of the bus toilet was overpowering, but I couldn't open the vent window, and the air conditioning was non-existent. I was also trying to avoid overthinking about the mountainous (but petrifying) views from my window.

The bus driver's driving was risky and erratic rather than calm and sensible. He was more like a rally driver as he failed to slow down around the winding twists of the mountain's edge. It was a 300-foot drop! Needless to say, this made my anxiety shoot sky-high.

I tried to distract myself from the death-defying drop with the bit of comfort I got from clinging to my new Greek book and listening to Blur's *The Great Escape* album on my MP3.

A few hours back, we'd stopped to let some passengers on and off, including the man sitting next to me. Three men dressed in winter coats and hats (which I thought was pretty strange given it was roasting outside). They boarded and headed straight for the seats at the bus's rear.

All seemed pretty calm as we were driving into a local town when, out of nowhere, sirens rang loudly from two police cars and three police vans, which overtook us. Officers from the speeding police car signalled to the bamboozled bus driver to pull over. The driver did as ordered, opened his doors and let some armed police officers storm onto the bus of stunned travellers. One of the officers looked seriously pissed off. His gravel face and strained brow added to his fierce demeanour. I was still sitting behind the driver near the front of the coach as the police officers asked each passenger questions in Greek. The serious-looking officer, who I assumed was the Lieutenant-General by the different badge on his shirt, hollered something in Greek at me. Obviously, I didn't understand, but I welcomed the opportunity to use my smattering of the local lingo and quietly mumbled.

'Signomi, then milow elenica.'

The Lieutenant-General aggressively waved his hand and ordered me off. I soon found out that the bus had been unsuspectingly harbouring three criminals, the men at the back of the bus, who were also promptly ordered off. Like the other men, I followed the police officer's impatient gesticulations to stand in a line.

A group of locals had gathered. Morbidly curious, they pointed at us and stared. One of the locals accompanied another jeering spectator; his donkey started to bray, 'Hee-haw, hee-haw, hee-haw.' Then it dolloped on the ground; I guess it got there before I did.

The scorching sun was beating down on my body whilst the cold fright was beating the crap out of me inside. The other passengers gawked at us from their seats as if we were goldfish in a bowl. The presumed convicts, including myself, stayed powerless with nowhere to go.

The furious lieutenant-general, who seemed to have the patience of a maniac, started interrogating the suspected criminals, and, one by one, they were handcuffed and pushed into the van. The crowd taunted while I mumbled to myself.

'Oh, crap! Oh crap! Oh crap! I'm about to be slammed up abroad. Oh CRAP!'

I had the lieutenant-general's red face so close to my face that droplets of his saliva sprayed on my cheek as he shouted unintelligibly.

'Ahem, sorry, I'm um, English,' I responded in a hushed and shaken native voice as I continued.

'I don't understand what you're saying, officer.'

My whole body shook like a leaf in autumn, not knowing what to expect next. I trembled, sweated, and, to be honest, nearly shit myself. The officer, in broken English, responded.

'So why? Why, you say to me, *Signomi, then milow elenica?* Why you not tell me…you are Englishman?'

A veil of sweat was now covering my whole body. Scared out of my wits, the words:

'Um, I'm sorry, I was, um, practising my Greek…' tumbled out of my mouth.

This apt *Epictetus* quote came to the forefront of my mind:

"We have two ears and one mouth so that we can listen twice as much as we speak."

I should never have spoken Greek to that police officer. What was I thinking? What a fool I had been.

Why did I say *Signomi, then milow elenica?* Which meant SORRY I DON'T SPEAK GREEK. Why the heck did I say in Greek that I DON'T SPEAK GREEK? What WAS I thinking, man? You fool Crooty!!!

Now, I wasn't sure if I'd inadvertently implicated myself in a crime I clearly didn't commit. My attempts to fit in like a Greek local might've been about to land me in hot water as a suspected criminal! I felt fear right to the souls of my feet.

With no sign of his face softening nor a hint of compassion, he yelled.

'DOCUMENTS!'

The sun glistened down, which reflected on the Lieutenant-General's handcuffs, which he swirled around his sausage right fingers. Without thinking, I went into my pocket for the passport but was abruptly ordered to HALT! He then shoved his hand into my pocket and dragged out the passport himself. He flicked through it, first checking the photo, then the itinerary and the date. He shoved the passport back into my sweaty palms, retorted something in Greek, gave me a sharp, steely stare and ordered me to get back onto the bus. I guess he had bigger fish to fry. A sense of relief washed over me as I headed towards the bus at Usain Bolt speed, but just before I could board, the lieutenant-general shouted something in Greek (but WTF do I know?) My immediate reaction was to raise both my hands in the air, just like you see criminals do in episodes of *Starsky and Hutch*; I slowly turned my head like a sedated owl, relieved to see that Lieutenant-General wasn't actually talking to me!

22 DRAMA

After the trials and tribulations of a bus journey that would've pushed Hercules himself to his limit, it was almost midnight when I arrived and stepped off the bus in pitch-black Athens, unsure of where to go or what to do. My run-in with the Greek Police scuppered my plans and meant that I'd run out of time to roll with my original plan, which was to take the ferry down to Crete the same day. Obviously, I had missed the ferry departure, and obviously, I had time to kill before I could sort out another departure time in the morning.

After I got lost in the labyrinth of Athen's streets, I stumbled upon a late-night café called Parthenon Kafeneío on the corner of

Apollonos Street. It was packed to the brim with people. Seeing a café still open during those early hours was rare. Many were sitting outside underneath the café's blue canopy on wooden chairs, chatting, smoking and munching on the Greek savoury snacks they'd purchased. The fuel keeping them going was evident from the tables, each scattered with several cups of strong coffee and half-drunk glasses of wine. I found an empty seat and took off my heavy yellow rucksack. The lady at the table next to me was snacking on a tasty chargrilled meat skewer, which was making my mouth water. Both starving and parched, I browsed the menu and ordered a small plate of grilled pork meatballs smothered with a tasty *tsalafouti* cheese sauce. When I saw another waitress carry out a few platefuls of thinly cut, crisp golden fries, I couldn't resist. I strayed away from the alcohol for now and opted instead for a coffee to quench my thirst.

I soaked up the ambience like a sponge, glad to have my feet on the ground, glad to have relatively fresh air and glad to no longer be cooped up on the bus like a piece of meat on a kebab skewer. I watched the locals chowing and drinking and listened to their Greek conversations tumble from all different corners of the café. In the corner of my eye, however, I spotted a small group of four men who seemed more out of place than me as they suspiciously loitered on the corner of the dimly lit street. Maybe it was my paranoia, but I thought they were giving me the eye, or eight eyes, to be exact, and the tense atmosphere left me a little unnerved.

The waitress brought over my order, but rather than enjoying the delicious-looking food, I hardly tasted the balls of meat and fries and hurriedly guzzled them down, wanting to do my best to move from the intimidating eyeballing of the gang on the other side of the street.

It was confirmed that I was actually the target of their stares when, brazenly, one of the gang walked over from the corner, looked me up and down, and then returned to his gang without so much as a word to me.

I asked for the bill and paid the waitress, making sure not to pull out my wallet in the gang's eye view. My radar was on high alert, and rightly so, because as soon as I stood up to leave the café, the back street boys followed me down a dimly lit, unfamiliar street. As I upped my tempo, they, too, increased their speed.

God or the universe must have been looking down on me on that night because walking directly ahead of me was a police officer. I looked back towards the gang. They, too, must've clocked the proximity of the policeman, because they had disappeared. I followed the officer, thinking logically that he would be heading to the local police station, and fortunately, the police station was where we ended up. He, without him knowing it, had been my protection.

It was now 1:30am, and the beginning of my Greek adventure was already a bloody nightmare. Feeling lost and lonely, I yearned for the very thing I was trying to take a break from; I yearned for familiarity.

After pressing the intercom button at the Hellenic police station entrance, a Greek-speaking officer answered. I couldn't make head or tail of what he was saying. An irrational thought crossed my mind that I would run into the irate lieutenant general from my bus drama. It took a while before they found an English-speaking officer, and that was when a huge sense of relief washed over me.

The intercom's audio was crackly, though I could just make out what the Greek-accented officer was saying.

'Hello, Sir, can I help you?'

'Yes, I'd like to report an attempted robbery...' I blurted out.

The release of my words was coupled with the relief that I had a listening ear with authority who could offer some sort of reassurance that they would take action.

'Sorry to hear that... when was this?' said the officer, the concern in his voice apparent.

'Just now.'

'...And where did this happen?'

'Well, I'm not sure of the street name...'

'Did they take anything from you, sir?'

'Well, um, no, they didn't actually take anything,' I said, and by now, I was feeling less optimistic as the words escaped me. The officer appeared to pause.

'So you are saying that no crime has been committed?'

'Well, in a word, no...'

My flickering hopes of any action by the police were halted just like that.

'Well, sir, there's little we can do,' the officer replied with a dwindling concern in his voice.

'If you have no hotel to go to I suggest you head to the nearby local café...it's called Athena Kafeneío...if you look to your left, you will see it... it'll open in a few hours...just sit outside there, and you should be safe...many of our officers pass by that café on their way to work, *kalinihta*.'

The metal shutters of the Athena Kafeneío were down, and its canopy was rolled up. The graffiti tags sprayed on the closed shutters did little to make me feel at ease. I sat on the edge, on one of the café's hard wooden chairs, waiting for it to open, feeling like a little lost lamb. Then something surreal happened. I was totally caught off guard or caught at the leeks, as they say in Greece.

The start of my journey in this country couldn't have been more bizarre, and it was about to get even more so.

A barefooted guy in his late 40s who donned a white tattered suit and a long black beard, looking very much like the saviour Jesus, jumped over a wall on the opposite side of the road. He jogged over to me, offering me a red apple as he sat beside me. He seemed to be as high as Mount Olympus when he greeted me in various languages to determine my nationality.

'*Geia sou milás Ellinika?*'
 '*Hal tatahadath Alearabia?*'
'*Hola, ¿Hablas Español?*'
 '*Bonjour, tu parles Français?*'
'Hello, do you speak English?'

Open Sesame. His pursuit paid off. Now, we could converse in English, which ignited a spark that, in that instant, connected us both. Weirdly for me, this high-as-a-kite loner's knowledge of English made me feel a tad more secure. I finally found someone who could actually understand me, someone who wasn't trying to rob me, and someone who had a mutual wanderlust.

The stranger started regaling me in English with a mild Greek accent about his travel tales. Initially, I was very reluctant to speak to him or take the apple he was offering, which he was still holding towards me in his olive-skinned hand with dirty yellow fingernails.

He introduced himself as Jona, and he seemed fascinated with my English accent and name when I shared it with him.

 '...Jason...you know in Greek we say Yason? You know this? Yason, like the mythological character, you know, the leader of the *Argonauts* on the quest for the *Golden Fleece?*...'

Jona had a type of wrinkled face like an antiquated map that told a thousand tales, and he had a vivid mind to match. I spent the next few hours in the comforting company of this weirdly wonderful stranger sharing just as weirdly wonderful stories from his vibrant travels around Greece and Europe.

As time passed with stories, the sun woke up and gradually shone its light into Athens; she, too, was beginning to wake up. Before I knew it, the tranquillity of dawn was overtaken by traffic noise that became so loud it hurt my ears. Passing by were swarms of speeding mopeds with helmetless riders and women passengers who clung tightly for dear life as they sat side-saddled behind their manically speeding male companions. These moped drivers bent low over the handlebars and seemed intent on manoeuvring through the traffic madness with speed.

Athena Kafeneío opened its doors, and I decided to treat Jona and myself to a much-needed strong Greek coffee.

Jona took a sip of his coffee but looked perplexed before examining the dispenser he had picked up from the table.

'Even salt looks like sugar.'

'I concur and couldn't agree with you more, Jona.'

After loading up on our rocket fuel, our paths became uncrossed as we launched ourselves in separate directions towards what Greece had in her hands for us.

23 SLEAZY RIDER

Sitting on the Blue Star ferry deck journeying to Crete, memories of days gone by flooded my thoughts. Seven years before this lone Greek adventure, I visited the island of Crete on holiday at the breathtaking resort of Rethymno. I was 18, and I wasn't alone. I was with my parents and my school pal Ste Farrell.

Ste and I had hired motorbikes and decided to venture into the mountains. The rough terrain was hard going, the cliff edges were death-defying, and manoeuvring around the winding, steep drops and multiple hairpin bends was as dangerous as hell but thrilling to explore, especially on our motorbikes, especially to our young and naive eyes. Ste and I were in our element.

Tucked into the bends of many hills we sped past were candle-lit shrines left in the memories of lost loved ones who had died tragically in collisions or accidents, reinforcing the dangerous nature of driving on these treacherous infernal roads. This was a danger we chose to ignore. At 18 years old, Ste and I felt somewhat indestructible. We wouldn't have ever admitted to each other that the clear evidence of multiple vehicle accidents scared us. So we kept up the bravado.

Ste's motorbike rental had a bigger engine than mine, and as he was a more skilled rider than me, he was getting bored as I trailed behind him.

'Crooty, you're riding like a big girl's blouse. Meet me back at the hotel. See ya, kid,' Ste yelled before he sped off, leaving me in the dust.

During our ride, I had not kept an eye on my petrol gauge, and suddenly, the motorbike came to a halt. My fuel gauge was now empty, and I was stranded in unchartered territory. The hotel was about 20 km away.

Ste and I had dowsed ourselves in factor fuck-all coconut-smelling suntan lotion, and we'd gone out topless, as the weather had been scorching that morning. I was wearing only extremely tight denim shorts, and I was without a mobile phone. A thousand miles from nowhere, 100 in the shade and there was no shade. With barely a breath of wind, and no vehicle in site I had no alternative but to start walking down the steep, hairy roads that didn't have any pavements.

Not much later, a camper van pulled over, and a middle-aged, grey-haired, pale-faced man poked his head out.

'Is that your motorbike, back there?' he enquired in a foreign accent.

I thought to myself no shit Sherlock. I'm hardly going to be in the middle of what was like a desert, walking down a baron mountain just for the fun of it. I nodded but remained suspicious of him.

'I thought I'd check if you needed a ride. You look like you could use one,' he said, pointing out the bleeding obvious.

I stared at the pale-faced man, checking him over to see whether he was a killer on the loose and assumed that because he didn't look like the mass murderers I'd seen on TV, he was safe, so I climbed in.

'Thanks, I need to get to the nearest petrol station.'

The stranger introduced himself as Joost from Rotterdam. Not long into the journey, he began to share his life story as if he had known me longer than all of ten minutes. I began to switch off to what he was saying. I was hot, stressed, and more concerned about finding a petrol station to fill up a jerry can and return to my motorbike.

We drove into the first town, which was more like a ghost town with no soul in sight. I thought the Dutch stranger had seen the Esso petrol station ahead, so I was expecting him to pull into it, but he didn't. I was now feeling worried because we had driven past yet another petrol station. Then, five minutes later, we passed another.

'You must be tired from all that walking. Why not take a snooze?' Joost said, glancing at my sweating legs and bare chest.

Is he kidding? No way am I napping! Only then did the thought of me being in danger strike home. Only then did I think I might actually be being KIDNAPPED. Only then did my mind rev up a gear and started to work a bajillion miles a minute. Peering over my seat towards the back, my eyes latched onto a walking stick. The plan was to jump over and grab it and hit the Dutchman if events took a turn for the worse and if he tried anything sinister. As the camper van careened around the corner, the speed dramatically increased, as did my heart rate. I had to do something.

A few minutes later, we approached an EKO petrol station. 'Drop me here!' I demanded.

His eyes were still fixated on my bare chest.

'Oh, I'd love to invite you over to my place for a cup of coffee, and afterwards, we could return to where your motorbike is parked,' his reply was concerning as I hadn't agreed to go back to his apartment for a coffee. Freaked out by this and aware that I needed to get out as soon as possible, I shouted at the top of my voice.

'STOP!!!'

The Dutchman slammed on the brakes, and as the van stopped dead, he acted as if nothing had happened and asked.

'Is everything okay?'

Which, of fucking course, it wasn't okay! I flung open the van door, jumped out, and, as a consequence, was almost knocked over by an oncoming speeding motorbike while running into the petrol station. Shaking like a leaf, I stopped to compose myself. I then bought a jerry can, filled it, and began the long trek back to my motorbike. I was glad to have had my wits about me that day...After filling the motorbike with petrol, I drove back slowly to the hotel to strangle Ste.

24 ALTER EGO

On arrival at Heraklion port on the island of Crete, it was 8:30pm. The eight-hour Blue Star ferry crossing went smoothly and without any incidents. I was relieved as I already had had my fair share of drama!

As I walked down the ferry ramp, I was hit with a strong smell of fresh fish in the air. It was coming from the vicinity of the moored fishing boats bobbing up and down on the crystal blue Cretan Sea, waiting for the next day's fishing trip.

My initial plan was to venture around the island, but given the strange turn of events of the last day and a half, I had second thoughts. So when a bus destined for Malia stopped in front of me, I hopped on without hesitation and took the short journey to the seaside resort.

As I exited the bus in Malia, my big yellow rucksack, which screamed that I was a backpacking tourist, caught the attention of a middle-aged, overweight Greek man with a thick handlebar moustache. He was sitting on his white motorbike, which was parked conveniently in front of the bus stop. He introduced himself as Manos and asked me if I was looking for somewhere to stay. I told him I was, and in broken English, he said.

'Ah, you're lucky today, my friend. I've got a cheap room, it's cosy...it's nice... it's in the old town... it's a quiet place, peaceful, not far, er just ten minutes from party street. What do you think, my friend?'

He made the offer for the room in his home that he shared with his wife and daughter sound more appealing when he explained that his price was much cheaper than most Malia hotels. The bargain price of a few hundred *Drachmas*, approximately £200 per month, is what sealed the deal for me.

My first-floor room was small and cosy, and it was directly above Manos's bedroom. However, the one and only rule was that I wasn't allowed to bring women back to his home.

A power snooze in my new non-air-conditioned room recharged my batteries, and I was ready to explore. Even though Malia had many temptations I reminded myself that I had to remain disciplined, remain refrained and remain serious about ignoring my overwhelming urge to be part of the cracking party atmosphere. So I explored Malia's harbours, its mountains and its architecture and found temporary comfort in the peace, tranquillity and solitude. However, after several consecutive dog days, living like a saint and getting to know this serene cultivated side of Malia, I became bored! I needed noise and action! I needed fun and wildness, and I needed them now!

The other side of Malia was pumping out from the centre of the coastal town, which was a hot spot for young, adventurous party-goers. At night, the strips of nightclubs and bars lit up the town with their luminous lights and their razzle-dazzle as they pumped out loud club tunes that could be heard far and wide.

Now in my mid-20s, I was in my prime and drawn in by the club scene, the lights, and the action, I hit the bars! But what hit me instantly was that it wasn't what I'd expected. I began to understand the saying that a bar is the loneliest place in the world if you're alone, and believe me, it was true. I was feeling it.

A cocktail sign flashed on the external wall in hot pink neon lights, and a printed poster advertising Happy Hour from 7:00pm to 8:00pm caught my eye as I walked into another bar. This time, it was the Green Ocean Bar, and this time I was alone again.

'Are you looking for work, fella?' Gregg, a friendly Australian bartender, asked as he served me a pint.

We got chatting about how we ended up in Greece, and in no time, it felt as if we'd known each other for years.

Gregg Mitchell was a laid-back fashion design student from Sydney who was on a gap year and living life to the fullest in Greece. He was like most of the young long-term visitors in Greece who were likely seeking to create distance between themselves and their problems back home.

The thought of working in Greece hadn't entered my mind. Still, I was intrigued by what he was laying before me as he described a potential job opportunity as a nightlife promoter touting outside the

Green Ocean Bar to attract new customers.

'You're a good-looking fella, you know,' asserted Gregg, not realising that his smooth, silky Australian accent was somewhat flattering to my Ego.

'You'll reel the chicks in for sure.'

With that line, Gregg had sold me on the idea. After I had downed my last glug of beer, he took a break to show me around and introduce me to a local Greek family.

A waitress had brought a tray of hot coffee beverages to the family sitting outside on the deck. They were the Papadopoulos family, the owners of the Green Ocean Bar. They were chatting amongst themselves when Gregg and I arrived at their table. The head of the family, Angelo Papadopoulos, a balding guy in his 50s, greeted me with.

'*Yassas.*'

He shook my hand. He was sitting next to his much younger wife, Georgina. After a short introduction from Gregg, my gift of the gab and Yorkshire charm seemed to appeal to Angelo. He hired me on the spot as a bar promoter. The pay was 35 Greek *Drachmas*, around £10 a night, including free food and drinks. The offer was too tempting to turn down.

The following day, I was picking up some groceries from the small local supermarket opposite Manos's. My shopping basket accidentally collided with that of an attractive woman in a long, white summer dress. I looked up to see the long, flame-haired, blue-eyed beauty give me a sweet smile.

'*Scusa Bella,*' I apologised for our accidental colliding baskets.

'*Nessun problema,*' she replied with a hint of flirtation.

Her response, however, threw me a curve ball as my Italian vocabulary, just like my Greek, was limited. Needless to say, I was relieved when she added in nearly perfect English.

'So what part of Italy are you from?... I love the accent.'

She appeared to be in just as playful a mood as I was, so I joined in.

'From Sicilia, Bella, my-a name is Roberto Verado, and-a you-a?'

The beauty introduced herself as Sara from Austria, and I kept up the game as Roberto Verado. After chatting and picking up our essentials at the supermarket, we found ourselves heading towards a nearby bar, and the teetotal Sara ordered us two ice-cold lemonades. Time flew by as we chatted at the virtually empty bar, which was playing the iconic *Zorba Dance* music.

My English-Italian accent jumped around like a flea on a dog and would be enough to make any Italian wince, but Sara appeared to be enjoying my efforts. Like my accent, the topics of our conversation bounced everywhere. One place it landed on was my six-inch deep rib scar from my operation due to my injury at work in TTJ & Bros Limited, Bradford. I showed her my injury as I framed the description of my battle wound in my newly acquired Italian accent.

'You see this-a scar right-a here?'

Sara leant in, her curiosity piqued.

'That looks serious…what happened?'

'It's not-a something I talk-a about often…but I was-a…in Sicily and was-a stabbed by a member of-a…Mafioso gang.'

As I fixed my Steven Seagal-esque ponytail Sara's eyes widened as she played surprised.

'Wow…you were stabbed by the Mafia in Sicily?'

'*Si, si Bella*, it was pretty-a intense…you see, I used to be part of the Mafioso.'

'You were in THE MAFIA?' she wowed with a dramatic tone to match.

I was excited that she was interested, and she was rolling with my tale, so I continued.

'I was-a…but I had-a to get out-a…now, they're trying to find-a me…but I can't say-a anymore.'

I put my finger to my lip and then to hers, lowered my voice and whispered.

'It's a *Cosa Nostra* secret!'

Our connection appeared to deepen as I shared my tale.

'You have quite the past, don't you?…you're quite the Italian Stallion!'

She flirted, and she appeared to love every exciting syllable of what I was saying.

Sober as judges, we flirted, and we both became overly amorous. It was apparent between the two of us that one thing was going to lead to another and another, so we walked to Manos's house nearby. Manos's motorbike was parked outside the house, and his bedroom curtains were drawn, indicating he was home and settled in for the evening. With Manos out of sight, I told her we could sneak back into my room, but we needed to be quiet. After a few minutes of riskily kissing and fondling wildly, there was only the sound of our lips meeting together. I opened the front door quietly and carried her up the stairs, her long legs wrapped around my body, her lips nuzzled on my neck. I was concentrating on trying not to make a sound as I carried her towards my room. When we got to the bedroom, I placed my hand behind her head and put her on the bed. All the while, Sara's legs stayed draped around me. Her legs detached from being wrapped from me as I bent over to unbutton her white dress. Her nipples were protruding through her white silk bra. I unclipped it. As I began getting on top of her, she lowered my shoulders. I slowly removed her silk ivory panties with my teeth and looked up at her to see her delicate rose-coloured lips smiling back at me. I started to massage the back of her legs with my hands as I gently kissed her from her ankles, slowly making my way up the inside of her long legs towards her inner thighs. When I got there, I squeezed her pert buttocks and buried my head into the place she wanted me to explore. Her hands pushed the back of my head, guiding me to her sweet spot, which I proceeded to tease with my tongue. My head was squeezed between her thighs, which blocked my hearing. When I realised, she was moaning with pleasure a bit too loudly, I became more conscious of the fact that Manos and his wife were sleeping in the room directly below mine. The creaks from my bed became louder and faster as Sara moved and moaned in delight.

'Roberto! Yes, Roberto! Oh, don't stop Roberto!' She moaned.

I was sweating, but not in a good way, so I stopped. I was slightly worried, hoping Manos wouldn't wake up, wondering who the fuck Roberto was!

25 FIGHT-OR-FLIGHT

I put my hand gently over Sara's mouth as her body shuddered to a climax. We fell asleep for a while and then waited for Manos to leave on his motorbike before walking back to Sara's hotel. Then we parted ways.

'Good evening, ladies and gentlemen. I hope you are having a good holiday. Can I tempt you into the Green Ocean Bar? We've got a hunky Australian barman called Gregg and some delightful cocktails.'

That night, I was touting outside the Green Ocean Bar during Happy Hour. It was our busiest time because we were encouraged to sell 2-for-1 cocktails. I was trying to entice party revellers inside. I was back to being a Yorkshireman and pitching people with my native Yorkshire accent.

As crowds and crowds of drunken party-revellers roamed up and down the high street. I hadn't realised that Sara was walking past, looking right at me, perplexed about how my jumbled Italian accent had somehow morphed into a sharp, gruff Yorkshire one, screaming my roots. I literally was lost for words, and so was she as she stormed off. I never saw Sara again.

'Plenty of fish in the sea, fella, don't worry!' Gregg quipped as he watched Sara take the understandably large chip on her shoulder with her as she went off in a huff.

'I'll show you how to party,' Gregg chimed.

After our shift, true to his word, he did.

As I waited for him to get ready back at his place: a small apartment on the high street. Gregg called out.

'Nearly ready, fella!'

Then, he came into the living room with just the white sheet of his bed wrapped around his bronzed body as if it were a toga.

'Are you game?' he asked as if to dare me.

'I'm game, Gregg!'

We went into his flatmate's empty bedroom to use his sheets. When in Greece, I thought to myself!

After a few shots of robust Greek *Ouzo*, we left Gregg's apartment and walked down the busy high street donned in nothing else but our makeshift togas.

"Friends, Romans, countrymen, lend me your ears," we yelled, reciting from Shakespeare's *Julius Caesar*, which drew in even more stares from passers-by.

Greg and I carried on regardless, without a worry or a care in the world, making our way through the droves of more conventionally dressed party-goers.

'Wae aye man, do you have anything under that toga pet? You look like you are a party waiting to happen,' a buxom brunette quipped.

Her forwardness caught me off guard.

The buxom orange-tanned brunette woman in her mid-30s was part of a group of rowdy Geordie women dressed in short lycra Union Jack dresses and long red PVC platform boots to match. The group were enjoying a hen party and it looked and sounded like they were searching for a good time, as they sang along to the *It's Raining Men* song that pumped out of nearby bar speakers.

'This way, girls, let's follow the Roman Gladiators,' the buxom woman called out to her troops.

The group did an about-turn. Gregg seemed to be in his element, getting gobbled up by the gaggle of women trying to pull off his makeshift toga. The brunette and I led in front.

How about it then, pet?' She inquired, linking my arm; her laughter lines were trying to beat their way through her deep bronze makeup.

'How about what?'

I knew what she meant but was excited by what she was suggesting.

'I want to see if I've won the bet that I had with myself that you're wearing nothing under that toga. I bet what you have under there is a real Bobby Dazzler. Come on, Tarzan, let me take a peek!'

She cheekily lifted up the part of the sheet that covered my behind. Seconds later, she pulled me toward the beach.

Gregg, who had his arm around two women, now had only his lower regions covered by his white bedsheet. As he headed in the same direction as the other excitable hens, he called out to me.

'I will see you tomorrow sport, and bring my bed sheet...oh and hey Jay...I told you, fella, didn't I?'

Plenty more fish indeed, I thought as the Geordie and I walked down the road leading us to the sea. But we didn't quite get there because the orange-tanned brunette stopped at a taverna doorway that had already shut for business.

The crashing waves, cricket chirps, and party revellers were the only distant sounds in the air as we engaged in some steamy *alfresco* fondling and kissing in the taverna doorway. The brunette untied my makeshift toga, which fell to the floor, and she looked down.

'I knew it, you beefcake,' she said as she leaned towards me with a stare that made me feel even more naked than I already was. I pulled up her tight dress, and she slipped off her red thong. After unclipping her bra, her large, bouncy, rounded right breast, paler than the rest of her orange body, welcomed me to nibble it playfully, and I did. She appeared to like this and shoved the left breast in my mouth for a turn. My hands then squeezed her bare, meaty backside, and now I was erect. We both slid down to the floor of the taverna doorway. Laid down on Gregg's flatmate's bedsheet, we fumbled around exploring each other's lower regions, and finally, she mounted me and started to ride me bouncing up and down like a rodeo cowgirl riding a bucking horse. Meanwhile, I felt a sharp pain in my injured rib area, which was getting more and more intense and causing me to scream in agony. It seemed she mistook my noise for pleasure. The more I screamed, the harder she bounced. We both climaxed and then she dismounted. She passed me a tissue, and sore and aching, I wiped myself. I'd be lying if I said I wasn't relieved that it was over. She picked up her thong, and whilst I tried to figure out how to put the sheet back on me, I asked for her name and what hotel she was staying at.

'Sorry, Tarzan, you're cute and all and almost worth sticking around for, but I'm getting married next week.'

It was now mid-August, and the height of the season had attracted more revellers. I was juggling between roles as a waiter and a promoter. It was an ordinary, busy evening at the Green Ocean Bar, and I was touting to get new punters in when a car speedily drove towards me, almost knocking me over. Instinctively, I dived out of the way like a stuntman, falling on the floor to safety. The speeding car had then stopped, so I got up and ran over to it. What I hadn't envisaged was the huge seven-foot man who got out of the car and towered threateningly over my six-foot frame. He was built like a brick shithouse. I, on the other hand (inside), was shitting bricks. The giant waved his colossal fist at me and yelled wanker wanker in Greek.

'Malaka, Malaka!'

His face set in anger. His eyes were nearly popping out of his sockets as he shot me a steely stare. He looked like he was ready to tear out my windpipe. It was surreal. What on earth had I done? How on earth was I in this situation? Why on earth did I desert my senses to square up to a guy who looked like he belonged in the French Foreign Legion? But what choice did I have but to square up to the brute; after all, he'd nearly run me down.

Then, a giant bolt of lightning seemed to flash in the darkening sky. For a moment, it was as if I was channelling the might of Zeus himself. My holding back of the giant lizard's iron chest seemed to have worked, and his aggressive demeanour had appeared to subside. It was like I had the power and magic of Zeus when he confronted the ancient threat that once attacked Crete, protecting those around him with a quiet, divine authority. Well, in reality, it wasn't quite like that and more like...

'Malaka, Malaka!' the brute roared.

'Daxi, daxi, daxi,' Angelo said, trying to calm the situation down. Angelo, who always seemed so unassuming, stood firm. After hearing all the ruckus, Angelo, who was a much smaller five-foot man, ran out from the bar and tried with all his might to push me and the grunting giant apart. Of course, I was glad that he was there amongst the bedlam, but I didn't know for how long he could hold off this hulk of a man.

After a furiously quick and heated exchange in Greek between Angelo and the giant brute, all seemed to calm down until...

'Calm the fuck down!'

Gregg shouted as he, too, had joined the brouhaha.

'BACK TO THE BAR NOW!' Angelo ordered Gregg and me to get back to business, but I really didn't want to work. My hands were trembling, and on top of this, I felt my ribs were aching even more from the fall. I sat at an empty table.

'Down this, fella,' Gregg voiced, handing me a shot of straight whisky.

'Are you Okay?' Angelo said as he walked over to me and put his hand on my shoulder. At that moment, I saw in Angelo's eyes the spirit of *Zeus*. I was grateful that he had been my protector in my time of need. However, it wasn't enough to save me and my own now shaken and stirred spirit. Without telling a soul, I packed my bags that evening and left Crete and Greece for good.

26 COOK ME UP SOME LOVE

Reader, are you still with me? How is it going? Chapter 26, and you haven't jumped ship! Mustard! Cheers for that. I know all too well myself that finishing off a book isn't easy. I'm glad you've stayed with me through the backstory of me trying to find myself. You've got here and reached a turning point, as do I. Hang in there to find out how losing a competition in front of millions set me on a course of my life which was never to be the same again. It would be great if you could follow my journey, keep reading and stand by me.

Friendship, life's ups and downs, and liberated chats about taboo subjects were addressed in programmes like *Sex in the City, This Life, Seinfeld,* and *Friends,* all of which hit our TV screens in a big way. Television had evolved from millions of viewers taking an interest in the likes of the rich and the beautiful, such as *Dallas and Dynasty.* TV now had tantalised the taste buds of viewers with hopes, dreams, people and lives they could actually connect with.

Tupac released *Changes,* Radiohead released *Creep,* and Oasis released *Wonderwall.* Hot news centred around the theme of going down, including the blockbuster *Titanic* and a former American President's mistress. We were nearing the end of the 90s. Meanwhile, this was a time when I was still trying to find my own meaningful connection with life itself. This was the decade I too, needed changes.

I hungered for something more than what I had but had little idea about what that was. I had tasted what a freer life could be like in the world outside of Bradford, but now, after returning home from my Greek adventure, I was feeling down. Mum never told me until I returned home that Dad had become sick while I was away, which added to my gloom.

Driven by my frustration, my thoughts culminated in doing something drastic, so I applied to be on a dating-cooking show called *Cook Me Up Some Love.*

'Get in there, back of the net,' I yelled as I busted a few jubilation moves on the kitchen floor.

'Have ye been gambling again, Jason?' Mum shouted downstairs.

The reason for my elation wasn't a winning football accumulator bet; it was because I'd received a letter, an invitation to attend an audition in the neighbouring Yorkshire town of Huddersfield.

Buzzing from the excitement, I hoped that *Cook Me Up Some Love* would cook me up some type of opportunity that my heart was yearning for, whatever that may have been.

'Mum, do we have any feta cheese, houmous and olives? I'm testing a new recipe.'

'What did ye say, eh? Cheese? We have some crumbly Lancashire in the fridge! And some Costco Farmer's Boy ham. No olives, though.'

'Fresh houmous, Mum! Not processed packet ham! Oh, never mind...'

'Don't make a mess, Jason, and clean up after ye have done, will ye?'

'No Mum! Yes Mum!'

'Why are ye cooking anyway? I've made some corned beef hash.'

'I'm preparing for a TV Dating cooking competition!'

'Eh, a what? What ye doing that for? Dating? What happened to that lovely girl you were courting, ye know the one from church? What was she called, hmm, Ann? Or even that lovely Italian girl ye was seeing before ye took yerself off to Greece?'

'What? Mirella?'

'That's her; why don't ye call Mirella?'

A few weeks later

'Bananarama, what the friggin hell was that?' I yelled.

A loud bang startled me when I turned Cleopatra's ignition and dropped her handbrake. I leapt out of the car to investigate. The culprit? SHIT, it was my flask, which I'd inadvertently put on my roof and had forgotten about. I was pressed for time and needed to press on despite being desperate for a caffeine fix to give me the pizzazz I needed after a fitful night's sleep with pre-audition jitters. If I wanted to make it to the audition on time, I had to leave what was now a small, steaming puddle of Nescafé on the pavement. As the radio crackled to life, the host's voice broke through.

'...some delays expected due to ongoing roadworks on M62 near Junction 24...that wraps up your traffic updates for the hour...stay tuned...this is Pennine Radio 107.9FM. I'm your host, Paul Jonas. Still to come this hour are the classics, Police's, *Walking on the Moon,* Curiosity Killed the Cat's, *Down to Earth,* Swing Out Sister's, *Breakout.* And for now let's add some smooth tones to your commute on this wonderfully sunny morning with *Sleeping Satellite,* by Bradford's very own star, Tasmin Archer.'

I had just enough time to swerve past the M62 Junction 24 traffic jam. If I just sped up a tad I'd make it. But oh how wrong I was!

'Do you know how fast you were going, sonny?'

'Hmm, 85, I think, officer.'

'And, do you know the national speed limit?'

'Hmm, 70, but I heard you give 15 % leniency.'

'70 miles an hour is the limit, sonny, AND 15% of 70 is not 85!' the mardy traffic cop stated before he proceeded to write me a ticket.

After receiving a chapter and verse about traffic laws, I arrived at downtown Huddersfield twenty minutes late for the audition. As I entered, it was like Wannabeville, packed full of hopeful males, including me. Fortunately, I snuck in without anyone noticing my lateness.

The other contestants and I had to demonstrate our culinary skills in a small kitchen and produce a complete dish in front of a panel of judges. I had to dig deep. My only cooking experience, however, was limited to what I did in Mrs Gibson's cookery club and helping Nana in the kitchen back in the good old days.

Each contestant was directed by Gabby, the production assistant, to take a seat in the Green Room, which fortunately had coffee on tap. Some of the potential contestants were nervously hanging out on the rows of blue cotton chairs, weighing up their fellow competitors.

All 32 contestants were given a number; mine was number seven. The first small group of hopefuls were called into the kitchen area, and after conjuring up their dishes, they returned. Then, it was the next group, which included me. Gabby delivered the brief instructions.

'Contestants, you have fifteen minutes to make and name your dish, and you can choose five ingredients from the food baskets. Happy cooking, and good luck! Go.'

I briskly walked over to the baskets, and some bananas, bread, hazelnuts, squirty cream and cooking chocolate made up my selection. I had no idea what to cobble together from my ingredients or what to name it, but after some quick thinking, I conjured up my creation: Love on Toast.

'Bloody awful, chuffing 'eck, I think I'll name mine Pigs Ear,' moaned a roundish-bellied guy next to me. He'd created an indescribable mishmash of ingredients that looked like a real mess. At least mine was better than that.

Gabby took our plates to the judges to taste and deliberate over the culinary creations whilst my group returned to the green room to await our fate.

After all the contestants had finished, we all sat waiting nervously. Gabby came in and called out numbers one, five, and twenty-nine. She'd also called number seven. Top Banana. I made it!

We were now face-to-face with the judges. Each judge fired multiple questions at us. One of the guys seemed to falter when put on the spot, and his efforts came across as flat as a pancake. But the heat in the kitchen wasn't getting to me. After a few minutes, the judges asked number five and number twenty-nine to leave, leaving another guy, number one, and me to do the final task.

'Alright, contestants, imagine the audience is ready, the show is about to start, and it's time to shine! Get out there and give it your all. Make us laugh, make us dance, and make us believe that your party piece is the best!' Gabby cheered.

Again, I had to think quickly. The other contestant went first, and he recited some poetry, which seemed to impress the judges. Stumped about how I could match his sonnet, I just winged it and started busting some obscure dance moves, moving my left hand in a slapping motion as if I was doing this to someone's bottom, my so-called potential love interest.

I think I nearly made one judge choke on his coffee as he watched my crazy moves. The middle judge was writing notes on her clipboard, and Gabby was pink in the face, trying to hold back her giggles. The other contestant and I were told to take a quick break, so I went to get a drink. Twerking was thirsty work.

27 COOKING ON GAS

Did I cut the mustard at the *Cook Me Up Some Love* auditions? It wasn't until three months later that I found out.

On a soggy April morning after returning from the betting shop, I met a soaking postman heading for my door who handed me the day's letters, and there was one that stood out amongst the handful of bills. The franked letter indicated it was from GOFS TV Studios, London. Holy mother of fuck! I ripped the letter open.

'Tea, coffee, sandwiches,' oinked a surly attendant with a turned-up snout as he pushed his food and drinks trolley down the aisle.

'An Americano, no sugar, please...oh, and do you have any corned beef pasties?' I asked.

A few months after receiving the letter from GOFS TV Studios, I had confirmed my acceptance to be part of the *Cook Me Up Some Love* prime-time TV show. I was on the way up and going down to London on the train whilst the rhythm of Jamiroquai's *Travelling Without Moving* album filled my ears with *Virtual Insanity*.

Before I knew it, it was 3:00pm when I arrived at London Kings Cross, where I was met by a TV production driver called Tim. He was a middle-aged Cockney who, on the twenty-minute drive to the studios, shared his thoughts on the bright lights of London.

'How's it living in London?' I enquired.

'Pfft, London! London ain't what she used to be. Everybody wants something from someone. Spent my whole bleedin' life in the heart of the east end, but now, it's all gone pear-shaped. It's enough to drive you bananas...'

He looked at me through his rearview mirror and continued.

'Can't blame a bloke for wantin' to pack up and leave, can you.'

It was as if I'd opened up a huge can of worms, and it made me wish I'd never asked. I thought exactly the opposite of Tim, who had obviously fallen out of love with London. For me, the idea of living in a city that held a huge pot of various opportunities excited me, and if I had the chance to stay in the smoke, I was certain that I wouldn't ever get tired of the vibe of London.

'Good luck, geezer,' Tim said as he pulled in front of GOFS TV studios overlooking the picturesque River Thames.

Nerves knotted my stomach as I approached the reception.

'Good afternoon. I'm here for the *Cook Me Up Some Love* show,' I said, trying to keep the nerves from strangling my voice.

The receptionist quickly located my name badge. It was one of many neatly arranged on the marble counter in front of her.

'Here you go, Sir. If you'd like to take a seat over there, I'll let them know you're here.'

I sat on one of the shiny leather chairs and looked down to see that I hadn't brushed away the golden flecks of pastry from my corned beef pasty. While wiping the crumbs away from the front of my V-neck jumper, I thought about looking for a toilet to pee and check if I had any other remnants of pastry in my teeth.

'Jason?'

Before getting up, a slim guy in his early 30s dressed in a grey shirt and pinstripe trousers, with an aftershave that smelled strongly of citrus fruits, offered me his hand as he introduced himself as Nick. He was the assistant director.

'How are you doing? Good journey?'

'Not too bad,' I responded as I followed him to the lift.

I'd heard that small talk was big in the more conservative South, which was proved straight away in my conversation with Nick. After exchanging more small talk about my journey and the weather, we stopped on the 10th floor, left the small talk in the lift and joined the other contestants, Jim and Andre.

It wasn't long before we had to get our teeth sunk into rehearsals. We had been directed to put on our *Cook Me Up Some Love* aprons and position ourselves on the purpose-built kitchen-style set while Nick instructed us on what to do and what not to do. Jim, Andre, and I took two rounds of practising our dishes. My Rarebit Tomatoes with Dijon mustard dish was hardly *Raymond Blanc style*, but I knew I could smash this, and as we all geed ourselves up, I wasn't backward in coming forward in sharing banter about this with the others either.

We were on a tight time frame, and once rehearsals were done, we were called straight into costume and makeup to get tarted up.

'I thought you were Al Pacino when I first saw you!' said Kelly, a makeup artist, as she picked up her foundation sponge.

Her gothic makeup looked like it rebelled against the conventional, and she again directed her flattery towards me.

'Sasha, don't you think he looks like Al Pacino? Dishy, ain't he?.... Sash, don't you think, huh?' she said as she placed enough foundation on me to sink a battleship and bounced the suggestion again over to her hairstylist friend Sasha.

'Damn, where's the hairspray? Sorry, what was that, Kelly? Who's hot? Al or him?... Sorry, I don't know your name, darlin',' Sasha apologised whilst stepping back, eyeing me up and down and giving me her own evaluation.

'...Hmmm, nah, he looks more like Andy Garcia, I reckon Kel. Do you know where I put the bloody hairspray?'

Before Kelly or I could respond, Nick came in and called.

'Five minutes to set!'

As I sat in the chair, being over-styled like a *Crufts* canine contestant, I felt sick to my stomach. In just a matter of minutes, the cameras were about to roll for real.

All dolled up, Jim, Andre and I were directed to wait until we got our cue to enter the stage.

A large flashing blue light sign read: TV Studio Kitchen — *Cook Me Up Some Love*. The stage was set, the cameras were rolling, and the audience was hyped up.

An audience of 1,000 people was already seated as we walked onto the set and into their applause.

With my nerves left in the makeup room backstage, the lights, the cameras and the action made me feel like a sizzling *Cordon Bleu* dish ready to amaze an eager palate. Rarebit tomatoes, here we go!

As the audience continued their rapturous applause. My energy buzzed, my soul sang, and my mind flashed back to my four-year-old self when my dreams of being in front of an audience were abruptly dashed. This was my moment. Now, I was in control.

The show's hosts, Joan Barnarde and Harry Woodland, were both celebrity chefs. Joan and Harry were smartly dressed in an attire and style that would not have looked out of place if they were on a Paris catwalk. They both stood facing the audience. The first host read the autocue.

'Welcome to the *Cook Me Up Some Love* folks! I'm your host, Joan Barnarde, and I'm here with the one and only Harry Woodland.'

The signal for the second host to speak was given.

'Thanks, Joan. We've got a sizzling episode lined up today, and we're joined by three cracking chefs, Jim, Andre and Jason, who are aiming to dazzle their potential love interest Monica, who is hidden from them behind that screen.'

The audience's claps were loud and alive as they were given their cue by the floor producer.

Joan waited for the audience's applause to subside as a signal to hype them up again. Then she looked at me.

'You know, Harry, I'm intrigued about one of our contestants. Rumour has it that Bradford's answer to Keith Floyd and Cassanova believes his ingredients will create the winning masterpiece.'

Like a cheesy TV shopping host, Harry winked and then gave the audience the bait for their laughter.

'I've heard that too, Joan. The question is, will it be a masterpiece or a recipe for disaster?'

The members of the audience were reeled in, and their laughter lit up the studio. I, however, wasn't impressed by their jibe directed at me. I wasn't going to take the bait. The floor production manager signalled the audience to simmer down their laughter.

I took it upon myself to use the pause between the hosts' scripted lines as a signal for me to give the audience the bait rather than be the bait. I didn't mince my words and needed no autocue for my line.

'Well, we'll just have to wait and see what I whip up, won't we?'

A slightly bemused-looking Joan was thrown off course; obviously, improvisation wasn't her forte, so she returned back to her scripted prompts.

'Jason, we're all about unique flavours here on *Cook Me Up Some Love*...'

And Harry, finishing off his co-host's sentence, tried to deliver another punchline.

'Yes, Jason, what is it about your unique dish that can win over our mystery contestant's heart?'

The cheese oozed off Harry's gleaming, wide-tooth smile. Harry and Joan both grinned in solidarity as he put his arm around Joan. Their hairy jibes were well and truly spoiling my butter! But not wanting them both to get the last laugh, I honed in on this as I scooped out my beef tomato.

'Well, like this dish, Harry, I'm hot and juicy, much like you and your rarebit Joan.'

My off-the-cuff responses got a thumbs-up from Nick, the assistant director, who sat in the front row. I had the audience eating out of my hands as the room was electric with laughter, and I loved it. However, the hosts were becoming slightly agitated as I'd interrupted their scripted one-liners with my unscripted wit.

The cooking challenge was timed; however, I was getting so caught up with the cameras, the audience and my responses to the hosts that I was now way behind time.

My no-trouble dish was starting to become trouble. I realised I'd added way too much mustard into the filling, and as I was squeezed for time, there was nothing I could do about it before I had to put the rarebits into the oven. When I opened the oven door, it took more than a bit of persuasion to convince the charred rarebit tomatoes to leave the baking tray. Luckily, with just a few seconds remaining on the clock, I managed to prise the once-juicy tomatoes off the tray and present them so that they would be somewhat identifiable. The screen rolled back, and the blindfolded potential love interest Monica was then asked to taste three dishes. Andre's *Lobster Thermidor* looked like a car crash. As for mine, by Monica's several gulps of water following the tasting of my dish, I could tell straight away that burnt Dijon-filled tomatoes weren't her thing either.

Harry poured on the praise.

'Jim, your dish looks like a party waiting to happen.'

Joan added another dash of compliments to Jim's exquisite-looking *bœuf bourguignon*.

'I couldn't agree more, Harry; it certainly looks and smells like Jim's dish is fit for a queen.'

Monica also agreed as she pointed to Jim's dish.

So it turned out that Andre and I were beaten hands down by the *bœuf bourguignon*, but nevertheless, Nick, the assistant director, was full of praise for me after the show had ended.

'Jason, you had the audience lapping it up; you were wonderful.'

'Shame my rarebit tomatoes went to pot though, eh Nick?'

'Don't worry about that; your ability to entertain is just what caught the producer's eye about you, and you didn't let us down.'

I felt ready to burst, knowing that even though I wasn't directed to be funny, my sense of humour shone brightly under those studio lights.

Despite not winning *Cook Me Up Some Love*, the date with the contestant Monica, or the holiday to the Balearic Islands. I won a bigger and probably the most valuable prize I'd ever had by being on that show, and they weren't just the *Cook Me Up Some Love* aprons I got to keep. I NOW knew what I had been hungry for for so long. It was a doozy moment, and my soul felt like warm apple pie.

28 FAME

'Tickets, Tickets please!' asked the mardy inspector on the train from London to Yorkshire.

'Hold on, mate,' I muttered, fumbling around in my jacket pocket for my return ticket. I found it, pulled it out and with it fell a small piece of paper. Handwritten on the paper: **Hey Pacino, Call me. Kelly 0181*****56 xxx.**

On arrival back in Bradford, the highs of my London adventures soon wore off. I felt like the walls were closing in on me, just like in an *Indiana Jones* adventure movie scene. However, I didn't feel like a hero. In fact, I felt pretty low. A life-changing event for me had come and gone, and another was unravelling at home. I remained under the covers until past 1:00pm on most days. I didn't want to get out of bed, and I listened over and over again to the songs on George Michael's album *Older,* hoping to lose myself in its comforting melodies. Dad had received a diagnosis: Cancer.

'Hurry up, Jason Luv, you're going to miss it,' Mum shouted.

'Come on, Jay lad, it's starting,' Dad shouted.

Mum and Dad couldn't contain their excitement as they sat together in front of the 32-inch TV. In between the adverts for Colgate and Milk Tray, I was making the tea, psyching myself up for my big screen debut, the *Cook Me Up Some Love* show, which in those next few minutes was due to be broadcast on prime-time television.

17 million viewers, each sat in their homes, just like Mum, Dad, Ellie and I. They, like us, were all ready to watch the show.

'Dad, look, look, look... you're on TV...oh my gosh... you're on TV!' Ellie said with her excitement nearly matching what I was feeling inside.

'Jason, those trousers are so tight. It looks like you're going to burst.' Mum's comment hit briefly like a hailstone to an eyeball as she, of course, questioned my choice of attire, silk shirt, skinny jeans and hightop trainers that I wore on the show, while I tried to soak in my big moment. In between her ooooohhs and aaaaahhhs, Mum continued to comment on how I could've worn the black brogues she bought me to wear to midnight mass last Christmas. I thought to myself, Mum, I had my First Holy Communion 20 years ago!

'Well done, lad,' he said as he laughed timely at my TV show punchlines.

Dad's eyes showed me how proud as punch he was of me.

'You've remembered to press record on the video haven't ye lad? You'll want to remember that moment?'

I definitely wanted to remember that moment, and watching it for real was the recognition that I felt that I needed.

'I know you from somewhere, don't I?' asked a guy with a zebra-patterned shirt.

'Yeah, it's that cooking guy,' added his female companion.

On my night out at The Haçienda Club Manchester with Ste and Rups, I purposely wore the same clothes that I'd worn during the filming of *Cook Me Up Some Love*, hoping that I might get recognised. A bubbly couple who were living it up in the club that night had recognised my face from the show, and another woman who was amongst a small group of women at a table we had gatecrashed jokingly suggested that I could cook her up some love anytime!

After weeks of going on nights out in Bradford, Birmingham, Manchester, Leeds and Newcastle, my Ego was well and truly being fuelled by the attention. But the more weeks that passed following the shows airing, the less I was recognised, and my tank was soon running empty. This was a hard blow to take.

'Jason, why did ye pick this wonky-wheeled supermarket trolley, eh?' Moaned Mum, who was irritated that I'd happened to pick a trolley at Costco that had a reluctance to go straight and was hindering her mission of getting the weekly shop done on time, getting home and getting the dinner on before she went to her evening prayer meeting at Saint Peter's.

To appease Mum, I went and got another trolley for her. At the same time, she searched for a tin of Quality Streets. The second trolley was just like the one before: as useful as a chocolate fireguard with an orange creme centre.

'Jason...Jason? You're away with the fairies...what's up with ye today, eh? This trolley's just as bad as the first...didn't ye see?'

The truth was that my wandering mind was far from wonky trolley wheels and assorted chocolates. I managed to tame the wayward trolley enough to get it to its final destination, the checkout tills, without crushing anyone's toes. Mum was getting flustered because she had to wait for a replacement and price check to be done on a packet of Mattessons sausages that had refused to be recognised.

'You need another one anyway, love...these ones are out of date!' the cashier said to Mum, who wasn't best pleased. The mature cashier turned her attention to me as she waited and did a double-take before saying.

'I know YOU... you're off the telly!...hang on, wait...do you mind signing this?' piped the autograph-hunting cougar cashier as she waited for the supermarket runner to return with the bangers.

The out-of-breath, pimple-faced runner came back a minute later with the same packet of sausages he left with.

'I can't seem to find them, Sandra...there should be more than just these!' he said, holding the packet of sausages up to the cougar at the till whilst Mum huffed and puffed impatiently.

The supermarket runner was right; there should be more than this! While he was thinking along the lines of out-of-date sausages, I was thinking more along the lines of my life in general.

I perused the small collection of books in the autobiography section during a visit to Bradford Library. I picked out a few books about prominent Hollywood actors, and I settled into a tucked-away corner of the library and became engrossed. The early days of these famous actors all started with a common thread between them. They started with the basics. They started with education. I was inspired to do the same. This time, my willingness to be part of education was driven by my want to learn everything I could to be an ACTOR.

29 AN ACTOR PREPARES

'Gather around everyone. Tonight, we're jumping into the deep end. Students, buckle up because I'm about to serve you some reality about acting. Acting isn't a stroll through the park, you know. It's more like climbing Everest blindfolded. So, if any of you have visions of sparkling fame, endless riches, and a lifelong, glorious acting career, I'm here to pop that bubble. Pop!' Beverley Kaldwin, delivered in a tone like sandpaper!

A few soft, unsure chortles rippled through the room, but I wasn't so amused. Beverley's tough but candid introduction continued as she clicked her fingers.

'Don't get me wrong, the notion of being a household name and having your face plastered everywhere is a tempting daydream, you know. But let's wake up and smell the coffee, shall we? The journey isn't paved with red carpets; it's paved with hard work. Acting... well, acting it's the trickiest gig you'll ever know.

You will be constantly trying to be the best amongst millions who also want the same dream and the same opportunity as you and have the same thoughts that they, too, are the best. There will be plenty of times you won't make it, you won't get a role, or you won't land auditions. There is no doubt you'll face a shed load of rejections, a shed load of heartache and a shed load of self-doubt,' Beverley Kaldwin said all of this without a glimmer of sympathy.

Her honesty was already trampling the dreams of the class of hopeful wannabe actors.

Students were gathered on the cold, hard floor during my first class at the rundown Boardwalk Theatre, Bradford. I had signed up for a one-year diploma in acting at Yorkshire Performing Arts

MY EGO SCREWED MY ACTING CAREER

College.

My tutor, Beverley Kaldwin, was in her mid-30s. She was a straight-talking, no-nonsense former deputy headteacher who worked for the local theatre running drama classes. Her stern vibe reflected Beverley to a tee. Beverley Kaldwin was a woman who meant business. As shown by her introductory welcome speech to us.

Whilst the expressions of my fellow acting class students looked disheartened, I saw it as a challenge. I hadn't come to this class having finally found my calling, only to have my hopes dashed at the first hurdle. I disagreed with her comments. I wanted to prove Beverley Kaldwin wrong, and I became very motivated to do so.

During our performances on the stage of the Boardwalk Theatre, rain dripped in through the cracks in the ceilings, and floorboards creaked as we moved across the stage. While the old theatre was seeing its last days, I felt reborn and had never in my life felt more alive than when I was acting on stage. Unfortunately, the old theatre was condemned in the middle of the course.

A new venue was found where we could finish the remainder of our classes, but the building was a corporate one, which lacked the *je ne sais quoi* and soul of the old theatre.

'Wooaaaahhh Jason, you smashed that! You act like a real pro!'

The positive feedback from fellow thespians I received about my acting was feeding something inside of me.

'Rrrrrrrrrrrrrrrrrrroar!!!' being on all fours, in a lion position, was somewhat surreal to me and a role that I hadn't envisaged myself playing. However, I didn't care what I was directed to do; I just wanted to do it—I just wanted to act!

'You're really good, Jason, you know, you should really think about doing acting full time,' praised my fellow classmate Davey Wardall in a comment that obviously then fed my Egotistical monster.

The more it was fed, the hungrier it became. The compliments about my talent made me buzz, but I was getting frustrated by the lack of stage time, so I demanded more. This ultimately resulted in Beverley Kaldwin and I coming to loggerheads in front of the other students, as she told me in no uncertain terms before the curtains drew on our class.

'Jason, this class is for all, not just for one!'

Beverley then concluded our session, addressing us all.

'...You will receive harsh comments THROUGHOUT your acting career. Next week, I will be observing and critiquing your monologues. Bring your rhino skin with you.'

I seemed to upset Beverly again the following week, not by my ever-growing Ego but this time by my choice of attire. She commented on my Puma trainers, Fila jogging bottoms, and blue and white striped Sheffield Wednesday football shirt with CARBONE 8 printed on the back.

As I was about to leave class Beverley put in her two penn'orth which she'd been holding back.

'Jason, remember to wear something a little more conservative next acting class and try to refrain from dragging yourself in here looking like you've come back from a day out watching football at Wembley!'

As the weeks went by in our theory classes, we explored the works of Shakespeare, touched on Stanislavski and Brecht and read about the history of theatre and romanticism. We covered playwrights such as the brilliant Bradfordian J.B Priestley and the American greats Arthur Miller, Tennessee Williams and Eugene O'Neill. The more time went on, the more interested I became and the more I wanted to discover the journey of influential figures in my new field—the acting world.

An Actor Prepares

Our preparations for our final performances symbolised how near the end of the course was. Each student was set to perform a classical and contemporary piece at Russell University, Bradford. The performance counted as part of the final exam. I rehearsed diligently in my bedroom, kitchen, car, you name it, I rehearsed in it. As the weeks whizzed by, I still didn't feel I was truly ready. I just wanted to get the characters in both plays spot-on.

My characters were Demetrius from Shakespeare's *Midsummer Night's Dream* for my classic performance and for the contemporary piece Edmund Tyrone from *Long Day's Journey into Night*. It was with Eugene O'Neill's work that I connected and found a real affinity with his downtrodden character, Edmund Tyronne.

The big evening had arrived, my nerves were jangling, and the other actors' nervous energy filled the air of the university's small theatre room. The audience of about a hundred people was mainly made up of the actors' families and friends, who filled the theatre chairs. I didn't invite anyone.

Though it wasn't amazing, my Shakespearian performance went well, though I didn't believe I nailed it. I could tell that the applause following this was more kind than emphatic. BUT it was in the second performance as the lead protagonist, Edmund Tyrone, that I was living the character. I WAS Edmund Tyrone. My heart was pounding as I crossed the stage and delivered my soliloquy. I felt the room fall silent when, in a fit of rage, I told my father, James Tyrone, that I wouldn't go to any state hospital to combat Tuberculosis, the illness that I was dying of. While I was delivering the lines, it pulled back a curtain in my mind. The feeling around Dad's terminal cancer unleashed from within me a beast of repressed emotion and pain.

Receiving the rapturous applause from the audience felt sublime. I felt honoured to receive the rare golden nugget of Beverley Kaldwin's praise.

'Jason, your performance was full of pathos; you got it 99.9% right.'

I have never forgotten those words. I passed with a distinction. I felt on top of the world.

I needed that boost in confidence. I needed more of this euphoric feeling, and I needed to be an actor. I knew I had a long way to go from Bradford to Hollywood, but I was determined to make it happen.

30 MY LEFT SHOULDER

'Jason, if you want to burst through that industry door, you should totally dive into TV extra work!' explained a caffeine-hyped Mohsan Qureshi, who appeared as excited as I was about my potential to be Bradford's answer to Al Pacino.

After my drama course ended, my mind worked overtime, and I thought about what I should do next in my pursuit of being a full-time actor. From my conversations with Davey Wardall, one of my fellow students, during my drama course, I learned that TV background artist work may be a good way to be seen. So, to get my foot lodged well and truly in the industry door, this is what I did.

I rang a local background artist agency, Coloring Book Casting, and after an initial meeting with the agency, I signed on to their books. My eager agent was Mohsan Qureshi, who was just as hungry for work and success as I was.

'You look great darling, very 80s,' complimented Wendy Davenport, a costume designer, as she kitted me out in a silk shirt and flared jeans.

The attire was for my debut role as a professional in the acting world in a northern sitcom called *It's Rough Up North*, which was one of my most memorable appearances. I was paid £75 to play a partygoer at a Bradford nightclub. I put my all into standing out and being noticed by the camera and got stuck into pretending to be having a wild time in an 80s club scene. We filmed for five hours, and as I performed near the main actors, I was excited that I would be on TV.

After filming, I phoned my friends and family and announced my big news about my *It's Rough Up North* performance.

'Hey lads, I'm going to be on TV,' I voiced over Chumbawamba's *Tubthumping* that blasted out of the jukebox.

'What show? *Crimewatch?*' joked owt for nowt Tezzo, one of the locals, who threw out his comment after aiming his dart, which consequently missed the board and made a hole in the wall.

Though I expected the types of beratings I would receive from the pub crowd over pints and pies, I couldn't help but gasconade to the locals at The Dog and Goose about my upcoming TV appearance. In my excitement, I even texted Kelly from *Cook Me Up Some Love* and asked her to tune in.

Several months after filming *It's Rough Up North*, the time had arrived for my second big primetime TV appearance. I called my friends to remind them of the time it was on, and they promised to tune in.

My brother, Martin, had given up the idea of becoming a monk and was now running his own haulage company. He joined the clan to gather around the box. Mum remembered to get the popcorn in for the big night, and our impatience was calmed by our handfuls of popcorn, glugs of tea and fizzy bottles of Babycham as we sat through each and every advert and every scene before my appearance.

'What's it about? Mum enquired. I've told Aunty Eileen and Aunty Mary you're going to be on TV.'

The anticipation fizzed as erratically as the bottle of fizzy Babycham I'd just opened, knowing that my stunning performance was in the next few minutes. The thoughts of stardom were like racing pigeons in my mind. And there it was, lo and behold, I appeared on the screen, or rather my left shoulder did!

I didn't realise when I was filming that when the cameras were rolling, they were not actually pointing at me but instead pointing at the stars of the show. It was disheartening, to say the least.

'Can I have your autograph, our kid?'

'Shut it, Martin...You monk!' I replied as I pushed away the popcorn. I switched off my Nokia before I was mocked by my mates and walked out the door before Mum bombarded me with questions. Hearing Dad's attempt to divert Mum's attention, as he said.

'I think whatever's on the hob is burning, Alice, Luv.'

'Don't forget to pick up these olives,' an assistant director instructed me. Down but not out, I had picked myself up from the embarrassment of that night and picked up the olives as the assistant director directed. I'd landed a featured walk-on role in *Yorkshire Nights*, a TV drama series, playing Sevi, a Spanish waiter who worked at a restaurant called Tapas Delights.

'Your timing is exceptional. What's your name again?' the director asked.

His comment made me feel like the explosive fizz in the bottle of champagne that my character Sevi had just popped open as part of the scene. I was looking forward to watching my performance when it aired, but having been bitten by the humiliation of having my shoulder as the star of my last TV appearance; I kept the details about the *Yorkshire Nights* episode pretty hush-hush.

Four 'Corned Beef Hash Thursdays' later, I was sat on the sofa laughing my bollocks off at the *Knowing Me, Knowing You with Alan Partridge,* and tuned into the *Yorkshire Nights* series whilst Mum cooked another Thursday dinner.

I moved closer to the TV, I was hoping for some screen time, and my eyes almost popped out of their sockets because this time, the camera caught my face, not just my shoulder, in a range of close-up shots. At the time, there was no rewind or pause for live television, so I hollered to Mum in the kitchen when my face appeared on our new 38-inch TV screen.

'Mum, it's me, it's me, come quick Mum look it's me!'

Mum wasn't too impressed when my excitement made her jump and drop the pan of corned beef hash on the floor. Mum didn't leave her priority of salvaging the corned beef hash and consequently missed my big moment.

'Jason, what did ye do that for, eh? Ye made me jump out of my skin. The dinner is a right shambles! I'll have to make bubble and squeak, now!'

'Crapping heck!'

Steam billowed out from Cleopatra's head gasket which had blown, so it was just as well that Express Deliveries Ltd., the courier company that I worked for as a sideline to TV background work supplied a small van: Gertrude.

Driving long hours gave me plenty of time to think and think and think.

After *Yorkshire Nights* aired, a few people at The Dog and Goose told me they'd seen me on TV, which I had mixed feelings about. Being a TV background artist gave me a taster of what the professional acting world was like, but I wanted more than walk-on roles. I wanted to be more than a police officer, a barman, a partygoer and a waiter. Though I was grateful for getting my foot in the industry door as a background artist, I wanted more. The more I worked alongside established actors, the more I realised that being in the background wasn't quite cutting the mustard for me. Although it wasn't all doom and gloom, I did manage to land a walk-on role as a schoolteacher in a Granada TV series called *Blood Strangers*. I had one line of dialogue to deliver to Paul McGann from the cult classic film *Withnail and I* (which also starred Richard E. Grant).

While I was driving back from my deliveries in the Bonnie Isles of Scotland to Bradford, a novel idea came to me about how I could become more recognised. I drove into Gretna Green to take the first step of action that might kick-start my future. I pulled in at the first service station and bought a packet of coloured biros, which cost a whopping £6, but it would all be worth it, I hoped.

When I got home, I searched high and low for some writing paper and envelopes and went to my room, ensuring I locked the door behind me. I proceeded to write around 20 fan mail letters in different handwriting and pen colours. I highlighted Sevi from *Yorkshire Nights*, praising him to the high heavens in each letter and begging to know when he'd be on TV again.

Appletreewick, Oswaldtwistle, Mytholmroyd and Accrington were some of the towns I stopped at to post the fan letters that I'd written about Sevi to the *Yorkshire Nights* production company, hoping that someone influential would be impressed by the adoring fan letters about Sevi and offer me a more prominent role.

31 PULP FRICTION

I managed to pull it off! Sevi's adoring fan letters somehow landed in the lap of someone from the same production company as *Yorkshire Nights*, and as a consequence, I landed an audition with a well-known Manchester casting director, Samantha Scheffer. The role-playing another waiter, Turkish this time, for a big-budget TV movie, *Güle Güle Istanbul*.

I received a call from Samantha's assistant, Darius, who told me I would receive the script for my scene in the post, along with all the audition information attached. There was one sticky point: the dialogue had to be delivered using some Turkish words and a convincing Turkish accent. Darius added that the successful actor would be filming in Istanbul and would be credited on the TV movie.

'I guess you like Turkish food then?... I went to Bodrum with the girls once...but that's as far as my Turkish goes...' said Sandra, the autograph-hunting cougar cashier who had called me after I left her my autograph and number whilst waiting for a price check on Mattessons sausages at Costco.

The date was the second opportunity I had taken to eat at Sultan Grills Turkish restaurant in downtown Huddersfield, and as Sandra yabbered away, my mind was elsewhere observing the movements of the waiting staff who were rushed off their feet serving köfte, shish and tasty-looking *meze* platters.

When I addressed the waiter who had approached our table, my *Get By in Turkish* phrasebook-acquired words stumbled out of my mouth and felt as hard as the olive pip that Sandra had just picked out of hers.

'*Merhaba...um...iyi...um...akşa mlar.*'

My greeting, naively, had come out in the shape of a broken foreign-type accent in the thought he'd understand me better.

'...Uh..sorry pal...I'm not Turkish...I'm from Scarborough...' replied the tanned-looking waiter with dark features and a broad East Yorkshire accent as he quickly changed the subject to our orders.

'What can I get you?'

'Can I have a small meze platter...and a...*halloumi* wrap... I'm just practising for an audition...I just wanted to get the accent down, you see?'

I shared in an attempt to smooth over the embarrassment and keep my cred in front of the waiter and the autograph-hunting cougar.

'Ah, I see...what can I get you, sir?' said the half-convinced waiter, smiling awkwardly as he finished taking my order and then continued to take Sandra's order of an eye-watering pricey plate of *Karides Tava!*

'What about the library...have you tried language cassettes?' suggested Sandra.

Her suggestion to improve my Turkish language was food for thought.

In no time, our sizzling food arrived.

'It's the first time I've been here. The reviews I read were right; the food is great...Mmmm, this is delicious. Are you sure you don't want one?' asked Sandra as she sucked on the head of a chargrilled prawn.

Any hopes of future dates with Sandra after that night were as *Baba* as the *Ganoush* that had been served to us. The hopes of me learning the accent from eating at this Turkish restaurant felt pretty much the same.

In the morning, I headed from Sandra's Huddersfield pad to the centre of Bradford having left her in bed snoring like *Old McDonald's* tractor. At Bradford Library, I managed to borrow a dusty version of Start Speaking Today Turkish Language Cassette Course that had last been checked out a couple of years ago.

Two weeks later, the day of the big audition had arrived, and I was cutting it fine with time. After getting ready in my Turkish waiter-ish ironed white shirt, black trousers and black brogue shoes, I added some £2 Bradford Market fake bronze tan, which I hurriedly caked over my face and neck for the final touch. As I washed the tan remnants of my hands in the kitchen sink just before I was about to leave, I goggled at what I hoped wouldn't be the reason I would be late, which was parked in Mum's yard. I yelled as loudly as I could.

'Martin, can you come down and move your bloody tipper wagon? I can't get my van out. I'm going to be late... I've got an audition!!!'

Now, I was panicking and muttering under my breath at how stupidly my brother had decided to park and consequently block me in. I could hear him shuffling on the top landing as he hollered.

'What's up with you....I was on the crapper...hold your horses, our kid...hold your horses!'

As my mardy brother entered the kitchen, I looked through the mirror and saw him searching for his Havaianas. Flip flops on, tipper truck keys in his hand, he headed to the door and did a double take at my newly acquired bottled-tan look.

'Bloody hell, our kid, have you been *Tangoed* or what? Martin squashed.

Before I retaliated with an expletive, Mum had come to the doorway where I was slicking my hair down and saw that I was nearly ready to leave. She dashed a drop of Lourdes holy water on my forehead.

'...what time will ye be back?...can you call me when you get there.?' Mum asked in mum-like timing.

'...I don't know yet, Mum; I'm only going to Manchester, not Marrakesh, ' I snipped whilst checking that I had everything that I needed and then doing one last check in the mirror.

'Looks like you've been to the equator, our kid...'

'...Very funny monk, can I cage £20 for some fuel.'

'Absolute chaos on the roads today, there are major delays expected on the M62 westbound, between Junction 16 and 11...that wraps up your traffic updates for the hour...stay tuned...this is Pennine Radio 107.9FM. I'm your host, Paul Jonas. Now let's add some heat to your commute on this glorious summer morning,' he announced, seamlessly transitioning into Billy Idol's *Hot in the City*.

My work van, Gertrude, was crawling across the congested M62 motorway and stuck behind a police-escorted wide-loaded truck. It was scorching and cracking the flags; I was feeling as hot and bothered as I assumed everyone else who was stuck in the traffic would be. I felt as overheated as one of Mum's Sunday roasts in our oven whilst I sat inside Gertrude. It didn't help that her air conditioning was about as effective as Mum's overdone meat would've been for a pensioner with false teeth. Somehow, in the nick of time, Gertrude and I had made it.

I arrived at Canal Studios, took a last look at the script, and touched my face up with the remaining drops of warmed false tan from the (now nearly melted) bottle I'd brought with me.

Donned in my white shirt and waiter attire. I walked into the studios to see a row of seated hopeful actors with scripts in their hands, all checking each other out.

After around fifteen minutes, I was called into the stiflingly hot audition room by the casting assistant, Darius, a guy in his early 30s dressed in jeans and a pink striped shirt that looked like it had been painted onto his chest. He introduced me to Samantha Scheffer, the casting director, a forty-something who looked as sharp as the pencil that was being held in place by her neat and perfect hair bun.

She was sitting on a leather chair with a notepad and another sharp pencil in her hand, ready to take down some notes. After exchanging pleasantries, Darius, who was operating the camera, directed me to stand on the X on the floor. Samantha Scheffer would read the customer's lines back to me. She called. *'Action.'*

"*Merhaba*, madam. May I take your order, please?" I delivered.

"Good evening. May I please have the seafood platter and a pot of Earl Grey," Samantha replied.

Still looking down, I noticed odd drips of brown had appeared on my script and also on my white shirt. I initially thought I was bleeding, which I wasn't, but my false tan was. In my eyes, I looked like I'd been shot, and my white cotton shirt was now as noticeable as a piece of Jackson Pollock art! Fuck!

'Okay, thank you, Jason. That's very good. We'll be in touch,' Samantha said tentatively.

What a plonker I was. What on earth must Samantha Scheffer have thought? What on earth was I thinking about when I literally iced my face with fake tan? What on earth would this mean for my big opportunity, my big chance to be in a big-budget TV movie and my big time to shine with a renowned casting director? I wish I could've said my tantalising streak of luck was as strong as the streaks of my fake tan, but I couldn't! I didn't get the job, and it certainly wasn't *Kismet!*

MY EGO SCREWED MY ACTING CAREER

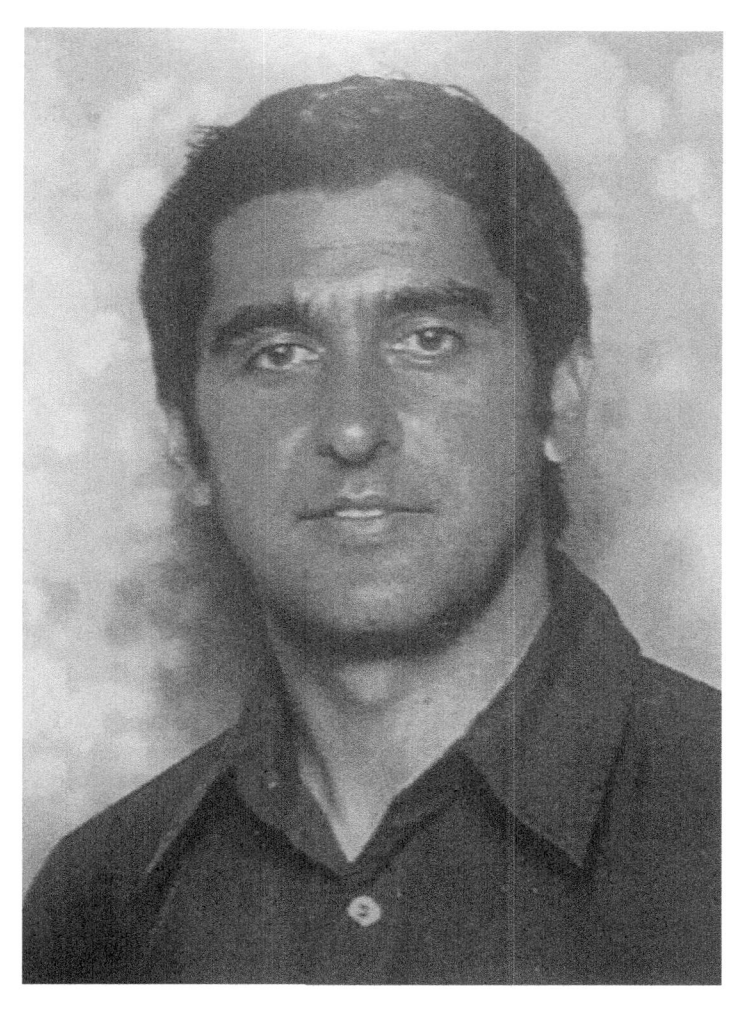

Me after 'Tango-ing' myself with fake tan.

32 TWO FACED

'Hi there, err, we've never met, err, and you might think this is a bit, err, cheeky, BUT I've written a script, and, err, I'd LOVE you to be in my FILM.'

'Well....'

'...I loved you in *This Life*.'

'Thanks for that! Look, send the script to my agent, and we'll take it from there,' said the smiling TV star trying to be heard over the din in the bar, and The Nightcrawlers' track *Push the Feeling*, which pumped out of the club's speakers.

This was an impromptu conversation I had while I was out boozing at Revolution nightclub with Ste and Rups. I had noticed a familiar face: Steve John Shepherd. We'd never met before but I recognised him as one of the actors who appeared in one of my favourite TV shows, *This Life*.

AND as the Yorkshire saying goes, *If you don't ask, you don't get*, and this is what I did: I asked but alas, I never got!

Plans were bubbling in the pipeline to make my very own debut short film with the help of the enthusiastic Mohsan Qureshi.

After asking around for background artists with previous acting experience, we got a cast of 15 actors. After Mohsan asked around among his contacts at the local film college, we got a free camera and free sound equipment. After asking a local businessman, Big George Taylor, whether he'd be interested in loaning us his bar, The Golden Horse, as a filming location, we got it! For one day only, in return for the promotion of the bar and a cameo role in the film for Big George. Moshan and I reached out and asked a mutual contact of ours, Rick Sendo, about lighting, and we managed to secure it. Rick worked as a lighting technician and agreed to borrow the lights from his local theatre for the film. The one snag with the lights was that I had to collect them and Rick in the early morning, at 6:00am on the day of filming.

Ready for action, filming day had arrived, and I drove to Rick's home in Outwood, Wakefield. The sun hadn't risen yet, and I was soon to realise neither had Rick. I knocked on his brown chipped door and pressed the jarred doorbell, first once, but after a minute and no signs of life, I pushed it forcefully several times more. The shrill noise jarred on my nerves, but after another few minutes of no one coming to the door, I continued to push it in the hope that somebody would answer. My frustration continued to tick like a time bomb of irritation.

Tick! Tick! Tick! Mohsan could tell I was on the cusp of exploding.

'What's Rick playing at?... there's still all the bloody...prep work to do!' I said, spouting off to Mohsan over the phone, who sounded just as concerned as I was.

'I know, Jay, but what else can we do?... I'll try calling him again,' Mohsan said, hoping that this time Rick would pick up and that this would then deactivate the mounting pressure.

My stress heightened even more when Mohsan called me back apologetically.

'Sorry, Jay...he's not answering.'

'It's going to take about three hours to set up the lights, Mohsan...to get it spot on...you know...Lighting can be the difference between the making or breaking of a film...' I said, getting even more aggravated the more I thought about it.

A further 15 minutes was spent by Mohsan continuing to ring Rick's phone only to be met by Rick's voicemail and by me knocking and knocking and knocking on Rick's door.

Of all the Toms, Dicks and Harrys we could've got to lend us the lighting. It was typical, just typical we got neither a Tom nor a Harry but the other!

'Do you mean the big hairy man, huh?' she asked in a high-pitched voice that belonged in a cartoon.

Aggravated at her fatuous question. I replied.

'Yes, Rick, is he in?'

I had nearly reached the end of my tether when a woman looking worse for wear, with dishevelled hair and smudged mascara, opened the door. One strap of her dull white bra was hanging from her shoulder, and her bottom half was covered only by her red polka-dot knickers. Without a further word, she went upstairs, leaving me standing by the opened door.

A couple of minutes later, Rick came downstairs, looking as if he'd just woken up, dressed in only his boxers. He could barely open his eyes wide enough to see how furious I was.

Rick was a night owl, and it was obvious he'd been out partying hard the night before. What I wanted was for Rick to get his arse into gear, get the lighting equipment and get in the car. What Rick wanted was different.

'Want a coffee, man?..... I make a badass bacon butty; want one, huh?' Rick enquired, oblivious that my frustration matched his whistling kettle that was about to reach its boiling point.

My patience was running thin. He first insisted on having breakfast and then a shower whilst I waited, and waited, and waited for what seemed like an eternity. Although I was highly aggravated, I was powerless to say anything because we were getting the lighting and his expertise for free, and we didn't have another backup. Rick's body and mental capacity moved with the inertness of a sloth. Time was ticking. There were still no lights and no bloody action!

Where are you guys???

The text was from Mohsan who had been waiting patiently and reassuring all the cast and crew at the filming location. He was obviously now feeling the wrath of everyone's impatience.

It wasn't until two hours later than planned that Rick, me and the lights turned up at the film set. The cast of actors and the rest of the crew who'd all turned up on time were clearly not happy. It didn't look good at all that I, the film's co-creator, had turned up so late.

We were way behind time, and it took over three hours to set up the lights. Mohsan was getting edgy but trying to remain professional, as we only had one day to film.

Rick the prick had really screwed things up good and proper. To top it all off, it was getting too warm and too clammy in the tiny bar, but we couldn't put the air conditioning on because of the noise it made. With all the cast, crew, lights, wires, props and cameras, it felt like we were in the Black Hole of Calcutta. People were getting irritable, some were getting impatient, some were starting to argue, and one frustrated twenty-something called Clark yelled.

'This is bloody awful! I'm outta here!'

Clark (who was the sound guy) then walked off-set and left us in the heat of his fuming steam.

Fortunately, the actors and the rest of the crew stuck it out, and once real filming got underway, it seemed the palaver of the morning was all forgotten. As Moshan called. *'Action.'*

One of the characters, Rob Wainwright, walked across the crowded bar, approached a glamorous single lady (Vanessa Pound), and blurted out the character's best chat-up line.

"Hi, I'm Rob, I love surfing!"

"Surfing? There's no beach around here, Luv, but you can get me a Sex On The Beach at the bar if you want."

Moshan called. 'Cut.'

Scene by scene was shot, and slowly but surely, I was seeing a way out of the lion's den I had fallen into when I arrived on set. I was also pretty chuffed that I was able to bag myself the lion's share of the screen time. I had written myself in as the film's lead character, an arrogant double-glazing salesman called Rob Wainwright.

Now, I had a credit for a leading role as an actor in the film, which I named *Two Faced*. Only once filming was wrapped up and I watched the film back did I notice that most of our efforts had been in vain. The peeved sound guy Clark had unplugged the microphone when he left, and most of the film's audio had been lost. Boom, boom, boom, shake the room. Needless to say, it was a disaster. *Floppero*.

Me, as Rob Wainwright on the set of my debut short film, Two Faced with two actors.

33 TEARS IN HEAVEN

Dear Filmmaker,
Thank you for submitting Two Faced to our film festival. After careful consideration by our selection committee, we regret to inform you that your film has not been selected for inclusion in this year's program.

A typed letter from Yorkshire Screen and Film Festival Director Jack Barrow concreted to Mohsan and me what we already feared. After trying our best to salvage what we could from the shambolic sound of our film *Two Faced*, the letter in print confirmed to us that it probably wasn't wise to send it off to any further film festivals because of these issues. Despite being able to salvage some sound, it was destined to be a straight-to-shelf VHS, my shelf, that is. At the very least, what I did have was a VHS copy to show potential film directors.

I was looking at ways to move to London to pursue my acting dream, but I had no contacts other than some of my Granddad Croot's wealthy relatives who lived in the opulent Hampstead North West London, but Dad nor any of the family were in contact with any of them, so I could hardly jump on a coach or train, turn up at their houses and say.

'Hello, I'm Jason Croot, your estranged second nephew. Can I come and stay with you?'

Dad's physical health was deteriorating, but his spirits remained high; his wish was for us all to have a family holiday. He chose the destination of the vibrant British seaside town of Skegness for a family break that differed from our previous intimate family trips. Aunties, uncles, cousins and children from Mum's and Dad's sides of the family were amongst the troop of 30 people who packed their suitcases to join us for the four-day trip at a holiday park in the sunny climes of the East Coast of Lincolnshire. Our family cars arrived together at the Butlins holiday park, and then each of our clans dispersed as we checked into our self-contained chalet huts.

The sun smiled on us all during the whole four days in Skegness. Daytimes were chilled and spent relaxing together on the red and white beach deckchairs. The older adults in the group fell asleep while they baked like crabs under the sun. The children built sandcastles and paddled in the warm sea under the watchful eye of parents who were soaking in the tranquil atmosphere. It reminded me very much of my childhood days in Bridlington with just Mum, Dad, Martin, and me.

Now older, Martin and I sat among the men in the family, including Dad, and spent our days emptying the coolers that'd been packed with beers as the women sat by their husbands dutifully to ensure they didn't overdo it with the alcohol.

In the late afternoons, we'd trundle back into our chalets and refresh ourselves with a quick shower before heading out to the holiday resort's various entertainment rooms, where the livelier evening activities were taking place.

On the final evening, before we left, a showtime extravaganza was held in the main entertainment foyer. We all attended and watched the entertainers perform a range of acts on stage. In between the one-liners and glitzy cabaret tunes, the relaxed men of the family continued to enjoy the rest of the night with even more pints of beer whilst Mum and most of my aunties sipped sensibly on their glasses of chilled white wine. Dad's free and convivial spirit shone as bright as ever as he wanted to be part of the entertainment. He tugged at Mum's arm as he got up to run on stage. After having had a few wines at this stage, Mum was subdued but not enough to completely let go of herself, so Dad's sister, Aunty Lynn, joined him on stage instead. Aunty Lynn put on one of the performers' black wigs, and Dad removed his denim shirt and wrapped his tie around his forehead as they danced and leapt around like spring lambs while everyone else sang to The Monkees' hit *I'm a Believer*. Laughter and smiles flowed aplenty that night.

We returned to Bradford with our hearts etched with happy and unforgettable memories of those four days. Dad's declining health had meant he had to stop working nights. On the old three-piece suite in our small living room, while my mum and brother slept, Dad and I spent time together studying racehorse and jockey form, enjoying sneaky beers and reminiscing for hours about years gone by.

'Of course, it's Georgie Best Lad, there's no contest!'

'How can you say that? Kenny Dagleish wins hands down, Dad!'

One night, after I took out my Star Soccer playing cards from the cupboard drawer, we debated over who we thought were the best players in their heyday. This was followed by talk about Dad's own heyday as a Slingsby United striker, his rise to become the manager of the team and his elation when his team won the County Cup.

'Let me tell you, lad, it was one of the best moments of my life to hold up the County Cup.'

We reminisced about how Martin and I then reenacted the momentous triumph of the trophy win as if we were famous football players when Dad brought the Yorkshire County Cup home. The players would hold the FA Cup high in the air for all to see and run around with the trophy euphorically on the Wembley stadium pitch after their big wins. Holding our Dad's victory as high as we possibly could, Martin and I ran down Allerton Road boldly and proudly, shining as brightly as the silver trophy itself. Disaster struck when Martin dropped it, but I took one for the team and accepted the blame for the dented cup.

'I know you lads were just playing, but I had your mother playing pop at me about how on earth I was going to go back and tell the team that I dented the cup. It was all alright in the end though Lad... like it always is...it's always alright in the end.'

Dad and I continued to connect through our own tapestry as we reminisced and weaved through memories that we hadn't even known had stood the test of time until we spoke about them; memories I hadn't realised were lodged deep inside Dad's heart as they were in mine. We spoke about his deal with Albert Tablock to land my brother and me our first jobs as donkey boys and his consequent temporary fallout with Tablock when we got fired, which was then smoothed over with a pint of Tetley's beer. We talked about how our beloved spaniel Beulah, had been the inadvertent reason for Dad finally managing to take the family to travel abroad, after being banished from our much-loved regular holiday flats in Belgrave Road, Bridlington. We laughed hard about the fence that he'd jumped over to kiss a startled Billy Goat in a field and revealed that his reason for doing this was to detract my attention from a bull that I hadn't seen, which had somehow lost its way and was heading towards us.

Although Dad's cancer was weakening him physically with every day that passed, his spirit and his zest remained our tower of strength and reason to stay upbeat and positive. When visitors came to see Dad, he didn't want to see any tears.

'Tears belong in heaven,' he said

Anyone who started to cry was ordered out. He wanted to treasure memories of joy and smiles, and the rest of us had to follow suit for Dad's sake; while inside, all our hearts were quietly but painfully breaking, and we prayed for a miracle. At home with Mum, Martin and I by his side, Dad eventually lost his fight against cancer.

Mum held tighter than ever onto her faith with the belief that one sunny day, we would all be reunited in heaven. Dad's wishes for us to keep on smiling extended to his funeral. Each person who came was asked to wear a smiley face badge :) And adhere to the dress code that Dad had expressed: Smiles No Tears. My Brother Martin, my cousins Andy and Marco and I were pallbearers, and we carried Dad's coffin that day as hundreds of people attended his funeral. A deep, painful sadness was shared amongst us all in St Peter's Church that morning as we mourned the loss of a loyal friend, a devoted husband and a good father. He was a great and happy man. He was a legend in his own right.

The grounds of Bowling Cemetery were littered with dried autumn leaves, the signs of a harsh November. The wilted, decayed branches of its oak trees shaded lost loved ones, including Nana, Gan Gan and now Dad.

My tear barrels were nearly dry as I wiped away one of the last of my tears on my jacket sleeve. The pain, the loss and the void littered my heart as it literally bled. I was in a very, very, very dark place.

It was six weeks until Christmas, and while the majority of the country was preparing to gear up for jubilation and all things merry, our family was bracing ourselves for the harshest December ever: Our first Christmas without Dad, our own shining star. R.I.P. Dad.

Dad and Mum at a family wedding.

34 FAREWELL TO THE FAMILIAR

Following the loss of Dad, numbness and void once again became part and parcel of my very being, and my temporary comfort and escapism were nestled in copious drinking, excessive clubbing, and numerous one-night stands.

One woman I met in a Harrogate nightclub seemed different to most of the other women I'd been with before. She walked with a certain air of confidence and radiated the magnetism of a Hollywood movie star with skin like smooth satin, full and inviting lips and deep and soulful green eyes.

'You have everything else. All I need is your name,' my best repartee broke the ice on our first encounter.

She smiled, and her face lit up as she replied.

'So, Yorkshiremen can be charming when the spirits move them. I hoped you'd notice me....my name's Charlotte, by the way. Another red wine?'

We had a mutual connection, a mutual admiration, and a mutual attraction. Each time we met, I became more smitten by her charming nature and her curiosity.

Charlotte Beaumont-Lloyd was a Bradford-born law student who was studying in Durham; she had an Audrey-Hepburn-esque haircut that would only suit the brave and selected few women, and she was also my new girlfriend, who would often ply me with questions about what I wanted to do in my life. We were inseparable while she was home in Bradford before she returned to Durham, and we would talk on the phone every day and night. She'd sometimes come back home to Bradford to visit her family and me, and sometimes, I'd travel up to her studio flat in Durham.

We were a desirable contradiction. Charlotte was from the well-to-do area of Oxenhope, Bradford, and came from a bourgeois family, so her standards greatly contrasted with mine and my working-class family background.

I enjoyed traditional Yorkshire scran and simple, hearty rustic foods that I grew up knowing and loving. Charlotte enjoyed fine wine, exotic flavours and dining on cordon bleu dishes that I had never heard of. I enjoyed nights out clubbing that ended with curries from the local takeaways and conversations about football, women and our good old days. Charlotte enjoyed nights out with her classmates from university, which ended with party games and conversations about world affairs and politics. I used to enjoy family holidays swimming with a £1 snorkel alongside my dog Beulah in the murky North Sea in beautiful Bridlington. Charlotte used to enjoy family holidays that involved scuba diving and swimming with dolphins in places like the Blue Hole in Hawaii.

What we did share was our physical attraction for each other and our insatiable appetites for sex. Our time spent together consisted of eating out, drinking red wine and connecting with each other through sex anywhere and everywhere. I felt differently about her than I did with others because I was in love, and Charlotte was a new lease of life.

Charlotte invited me to stay at her parent's place while they were on holiday in Marrakech and suggested that we make a long weekend of it and visit the nearby Haworth. I agreed and set out to venture for a weekend away from my own familiarity.

I drove to Charlotte's in my trusty van Gertrude and arrived outside Charlotte's family country house in Oxenhope. She emerged dressed in a long white embroidered summer dress and brown gladiator-style sandals.

'You must have sore feet Charlotte?'

'Sore feet?' Charlotte asked, perplexed.

'Yeah, because you look like a Goddess who's just fallen from heaven! Get it? Sore feet because you've just fallen from heaven?'

Charlotte looked confused so I tried to salvage the joke.

'...Because you look like a Goddess...'

Charlotte and I burst out laughing, me laughing even more so at the timing of my own funny joke.

'Flattery will get you everywhere!'

True to Charlotte's word, my flattery led to us kissing passionately in the front seat of my old van before we made the short journey to the neighbouring Haworth.

'Cheese, cheese, cheese.'

'*Kono shōnen-tachi wa daredesuka, karera o shitte imasu ka?*'

Back in the day, Gary Carlson and I used to get our kicks in Haworth from photobombing Asian tourists long before it became a phenomenon.

We used to take the bus there in our matching colourful jumpers and shoes—maybe we were more hip than we realised. We'd go birding it there but failed miserably due to the fact that the local posh totty was more educated and cultivated than us. It was quite ironic that I ended up with a local.

'Yes, just up there, it's free parking, my Dad always parks there.'

I parked Gertrude, and we explored Haworth village, set in Brontë Country. The cobbled streets were filled with shops selling souvenirs and vintage bric-a-brac and with sightseeing visitors, including Charlotte and me.

We walked hand in hand and browsed the array of quaint shops, most of which had only enough room to swing a very curious cat. Charlotte bought me some sunglasses from one pricey vintage shop before we headed to find shade of our own. Eventually, we found ourselves in a small café selling very proper English cream and jam scones, which had tea served on china porcelain saucers and cups with handles so small that I had to hold them with only my index finger and thumb. Though it was painfully pricey, we enjoyed every bite and slurp of the sweet afternoon treat anyway.

Due to me doing the driving, I wasn't able to drink alcohol, but Charlotte had convinced me to leave Gertrude parked in Haworth so we could drink as much as our hearts desired, and I'd pick up the van the next day.

We ended our day in a local wine bar, where she splashed out on some pricey vino before we took a cab back to her parent's home. Charlotte and I had already drunk (several x several) glasses of red wine and that equated to the both of us feeling highly aroused. As she opened the front door, I unbuttoned her blouse from behind before putting my hands underneath her bra and followed her lead as she led my hands to her nipples. She removed her silk scarf so I could kiss her neck whilst she pushed the door open with her foot. We kissed wildly whilst we headed up the stairs to the bedroom.

'Why don't you wear the new sunglasses I bought you?'

We started on Charlotte's parents' four-poster bed, and between the vigorous stroking and touching, we undressed each other until we were completely naked, apart from my sunglasses. We moaned with delight as I stood behind Charlotte and made love to her, and we both moaned loudly as she held onto the frame of the open bedroom window with only the nighttime view of beautiful Yorkshire in front of us.

A few months went by, and en route to Lincolnshire, during a delivery job, I had to pull over to take a phone call.

'Jason, I have some news.'

At this point, we were still only dating and not living together.

'I've just been offered a job as a legal secretary in London.'

35 LONDON'S CALLING

On the relatively empty train from Leeds to London, we kissed and fondled before pulling in at Kings Cross station. Charlotte was over the moon about her new job role, and I was in my element because I never imagined that I would be upping sticks and moving to London. I was armed with my acting diploma and a VHS copy of my short film *Two Faced*. I was ready to break into the acting industry in a big way. I was ready for the bright lights of London; this was it.

We arrived at our new four-storey, five-bedroom home on Hyde Vale in Greenwich, South East London, an opulent historic district next to the River Thames. Charlotte started her job as a Legal Secretary the day after we arrived. As for me, I had no job, no real plan and hardly any money. But I was in London, and the roads were paved with gold, or so I thought.

A week after moving in, the novelty of the new adventure soon wore off. The idyllic set-up of Charlotte and me living together was interrupted by the arrival of our new housemates, some of Charlotte's Durham University friends who had also landed jobs in London and who Charlotte called "The Troop."

Every evening (like millions of others), "The Troop" would leave the rat race behind until the following day and make their way to the place I had called home before they moved in. On most evenings, it was obvious that I was always the outsider looking in, or more like the outsider looking for a way out. While we all lived under the same roof, false pretences continued to hang in the air, along with the mutual dislike that "The Troop" and I had for each other, which was often highlighted over dinner.

'How's the acting world, Jason? are you finding lots of work?'

Inquired Monica, a stuffy-nosed, junior estate agent who was one of "The Troop."

'This chicken is great, Charlotte,' I said, purposely ignoring Monica's question (because, in all honesty, the chicken was horrible).

If I had lots of acting work, I could've replied, but I had *nada,* and I was pretty damn sure Monica, knew this!

For every day that I wasn't acting, my self-esteem was dwindling away, so this question was like a subtle kick in the front teeth that nobody blinked an eyelid at as they continued to gnaw away at their dry chicken. When "The Troop" eventually dispersed to their own quarters, Charlotte and I were left alone in the kitchen, where the air was so thick you could've cut it with a knife.

'The subtleties speak the loudest, Jason.'

'And what is that supposed to mean, Charlotte?'

'I saw the way you ignored my friend Monica at the dining table.'

'There you go, Charlotte.'

'And what is that supposed to mean, huh?'

'YOUR friend, NOT MY friend!'

'MY friends are helping pay the rent; how do you think that we could afford this five-bedroom house in Greenwich?'

'It always boils down to one thing: Money! well, Charlotte, there is more to life than bloody money!' I countered her response in retaliation to her jibe, but I also knew it would rattle Charlotte just as she had rattled me...and it did.

'How rude! How bloody rude! This has nothing at all to do with money; it's about how you are with my friends.'

'Never fails, does it? Be frank, and somebody calls you rude or mean!'

'You always want to get the last word, don't you, Jason... Always!'

There was a touch of irony in her words, as we both knew all too well that she, too, in fact, always needed to have the final say.

After Charlotte finished tidying the dishes, the unresolved tension hung in the atmosphere like a cheap air freshener.

Charlotte went to bed, and whisky came to the rescue. I was sitting on the hard oak kitchen chair when I was interrupted by Monica, who came to put her plate in the sink.

'Drowning your sorrows, Jason?'

'No, Monica, I'm teaching them the breaststroke!' I snapped before leaving a gobsmacked Monica alone in the kitchen.

I was so pissed off, and generally when the going got tough, the tough would go to the pub, but it was late, and I was skint.

I didn't fancy sleeping on the sofa, so I crossed enemy lines and risked going through the barricades into the bedroom. I got into a bunk next to Charlotte. I waved my white flag, hoping for a ceasefire.

'Are your guns away?' Charlotte ignored me, leant over to the bedside table, picked up a law magazine from the chest of drawers beside her, turned her back away from me and flicked through, taking out her frustration on the pages whilst I stared hard at the signs of a faint crack in the ceiling. This wasn't going well at all.

36 LESSONS IN LOVE

The noughties pushed privacy into a thing of the past and brought everyday human lives into spectator-ville with the likes of Facebook, iPhones and programmes like *Big Brother* along with the bombardment of several other reality TV programmes, which all exploded onto the scene and placed the exhibitionists to share everything upon everything about themselves in their desperation for the heights of Z-list fame. It also provided platforms for others to play unfiltered judges, jurors and executioners from inside their goldfish bowls.

Then there was the launch of YouTube, a platform where every wannabe and their dog, chimpanzee, gerbil, etc could take a shot at getting to the top. This coincided with the end of the iconic Thursday television show, BBC's *Top of the Pops*, where actual stars shone through their music hits to their millions of adoring viewers each week.

We were also entering an era when a once relatively unknown J.K. Rowling, who'd moved to London from the North and had, during a delayed train journey, come up with a legendary idea about a wizard, whilst grappling with a relationship that hadn't worked out, was NOW seeing the fruits of her creative toil and labour on big cinema screens.

Plus, we were in the midst of a period when two subjects in Greenwich were raising two elephant-in-the-room-type questions. One was the should-they-have or shouldn't-they-have-built-the Millennium Dome. The other was the should-we-have or shouldn't-we-have-carried-it-on relationship between me and Charlotte.

As Charlotte and our housemates were at work, the empty house granted me ample time for reflection. I was questioning my choice of moving to London after realising that this wasn't the London I envisioned, and I was missing Yorkshire. My true purpose in the capital, acting, remained elusive, and I felt lost.

My days passed by avoiding reality TV, wannabes, and thrilling need-to-know information about people's toast and red fingernails. Instead, I preferred to get lost in drinking whisky, reading the same acting books over and over, having a punt on the horses with the shekels I had, or aimlessly wandering around Greenwich.

On one of these dog days, I headed out for another day of almost guaranteed boredom when I spotted a newsstand just outside of Greenwich Park, and a hidden gem was urging me to pick it up. It was a newspaper called *The Stage*, and it was my first time seeing this fortnightly rag. After buying it, I found a quiet café and became engrossed in the various theatre and TV audition acting opportunities, inviting people to apply. I was so engrossed in reading as I sat at the café that I lost track of time, and it was 6:00pm; Charlotte would most probably be home by now.

I rushed home, looking forward to seeing Charlotte and telling her what I had found in *The Stage,* only to come home to a cold, empty house and a message on the answering machine saying that she was going for a drink with "The Troop." She'd be late and that I could come and meet them if I wanted. After sticking a Sainsbury's chicken *jalfrezi* ready meal in the microwave, I poured myself a small glass of whisky, circled the auditions that caught my eye and applied.

After weeks of not receiving responses to my applications, I found myself sinking to new depths of disheartenment. This was followed by trickles of self-doubt that were beginning to soak into my skin like an insect repellent. It was beginning to hit me that maybe I underestimated the difficulty of the mission I was trying to accomplish; maybe my dreams of becoming an actor were like building castles in the sky, and maybe I should just quit.

Frustration hit home; I needed exposure! I Googled how to pirate my own film, *Two Faced,* but surprisingly, after days of researching, it seemed impossible to pirate your own film.

I had read Stanislavski's *An Actors Prepares* for the 85th thousandth time, listened to Level 42's *Lessons in Love* a bajillion times, and downed God-knows-how-much whisky; I was really getting fucked off with everything. And to top things off, I think I had piles from so much sitting on the hard oak kitchen chairs. My pockets were emptying quickly from punting, bills and everyday expenses, and I was fed up to the back of my teeth of relying on Charlotte.

Charlotte had been at home from work no longer than five minutes when things took their usual course between us, where a single comment would spark a sharp response and trigger an avalanche of an argument. As I sat on the hard oak kitchen chair, I flicked through the acting newspaper for what felt like the hundredth time, just to avoid making eye contact with Charlotte. However, she kicked things off.

'I'd be okay with you doing the washing up every now and again, you know!' Charlotte commented in a tone that was as distasteful as the stale dishwater that had been left to fester.

I blanked her, aggravating her even more so.

'Are you going to reply to me, Jason?'

'Do you want an argument or an answer?'

'The dishes won't wash themselves, you know!'

'Hmm, okay Mum! Anyway, half of the dishes aren't even mine!'

'What?... Mum? Jason, your excuses are so lame that they wouldn't even stand up with crutches.'

A catalogue from a retail electronics store was amongst the pile of junk mail on the table.

'Here you go!' I slid it towards her before getting up to leave.

'What's this?'

'If you wanted a personal dishwasher for this house, buy one!' I returned her remark as offensively as if I had thrown a wet sponge towards her.

Then, this led to the inevitable: a blazing row where the hurtful comments and the unnecessary were scattered around like the dirty washing on the worktops. I had rarely let my guard down in front of many, but it appeared that it was the trivial topic of dirty dishes that caused my own pile of mounting pots and pans to come crashing hard as I broke down.

Charlotte had followed me up to our bedroom. She took her tone down a notch, but not enough.

'What happened to you, Jason, huh? What happened to the man I fell in love with? It's as if you've checked out or left the city OR you didn't fully arrive here with me in the first place.'

I remained silent. The feelings that she was batting out left, right, and centre were new and unknown to me, which cut me even deeper. I didn't know SHE had been questioning our relationship, and she went on.

'When I first met you, you ignited a fire within me...Your Ego and unwavering confidence...thrilled me and turned me on... and you had what I had longed for...you know...You had what I passionately hoped to find in a man...Jason? Jason? TYPICAL, look, you're in your own world again, and haven't you noticed, Jason, that nobody wants to join you there!'

She stopped and was miffed why I hadn't said a word. I had been staring at the hideous spiral carpet pattern in our room, trying to persuade my thoughts to enter the land of nothingness, but they refused. Charlotte placed her fingertips underneath my chin to lift up my face and look at her.

'I don't know what's happening, I really don't know. I don't know what I want,' I muttered, trying to pull my face away from her fingertips.

The next day, it was Charlotte's day off. As she was asleep, I took a walk to Greenwich Village.

I needed to get the smell of last night's argument off of me and thought I'd find some fresh perspective on a walk through town. Part of me knew that Charlotte was right in some but not all of the things she had said, and her directness stung. My confidence since coming to London had taken a rapid tumble from where it once was. I knew in my gut that I could hardly make it as an actor like this.

My thoughts were lost in the world of I don't know, when a bohemian-looking charity fundraiser in a short skirt initially stopped me to sign me up for a donation on Greenwich High Street, near the Cutty Sark. In her strong Glaswegian accent, she enlightened me about the charity's work and signed me up for £5 per month. She had managed to talk me into applying for work with them. Maybe this was the start of my new voyage.

No sooner had I sent the application off than I got a call for an interview with two managers, Mary and Satvinder, at the charity's head office in Archway, North London.

'Tell us an interesting fact about you, Jason,' asked Satvinder.

'If you scrabble some of the letters of my first and second name, you get ACTOR!'

The relaxed interview lent itself to me by throwing in a few splashes of Yorkshire charm, and I was sailing. I was hired on the spot.

Charlotte appeared happier, but I was still insatiable. What the regular salary did, at least, was to open up doors to the different acting pathways. This came in the shape of a "Method Acting" short course at the Romeo Theatre, other various short courses in the field of acting as well as a 12-month performing arts course at Brook University (starting the following year). I now had the means to

MY EGO SCREWED MY ACTING CAREER

access the tools to strengthen the craft that I came to London to perfect.

One evening, after beers with my new work colleagues, I returned home to find Charlotte in the kitchen in a long, low-cut black dress. As soon as she saw me, she swelled up Sade's *Your Love Is King*, and as it played in the background, the aroma of one of her pasta specialities, *penne arrabbiata,* floated in the kitchen. She had opened my favourite bottle of French *Côtes du Rhône,* which 99% of the time hinted that an indulgent and intimate passionate dessert was to follow. Our flatmates appeared to be out. I noticed a card on the table and opened it as Charlotte dished out the pasta to only then realise that...shit was about to hit the fan...when I read what it said. HAPPY ANNIVERSARY X

Oh Fuck...I forgot! I had no card, no gift, nothing! Here we go again...

My face says it all.

37 LOVE STREAMS

A tear-stained Charlotte stood at the kitchen doorway. She'd returned to where I'd been sitting in the kitchen after she'd stormed off to the bedroom. Me forgetting our anniversary had really upset her, to say the least, and her fit of rage was evident from the plates of *penne arrabbiata* she'd thrown towards the bin but missed. The broken plates made our kitchen floor look like the aftermath of a Greek wedding celebration.

'Maybe we need a break?'

Charlotte threw the comment in my direction for me to catch.

'Break?' I responded as I looked up from my empty wine glass.

Her comment was one that I was half expecting. I found, however, that I got the completely wrong end of the stick.

'Yes, a break, a breakaway…it would be good for us, don't you think? I was thinking Bali…you, me and "The Troop," Charlotte suggested. It was now me who was angry.

'I would prefer to go to the moon with aliens than go on holiday with "The Troop!"' I yelled in an attempt to permanently cut through the suggestion she dared to put forward to me.

'Aliens, how bloody dare you! How bloody dare you! Why would you talk about our flatmates, our friends, like that, huh? You're never happy with anything, you infuriating Bastard!!!'

'Happy?.... Maybe I just can't stand…what you call being happy…do I actually have to blow clouds all the time?…and YOU have no right to call me anything.'

'I have all the rights to call you everything, you are a wanker!' Charlotte's rage was back. My offhand comment about her friends had obviously touched a nerve.

Charlotte's insults bounced off me like rain off a duck's back. After another steaming row, she realised that it probably wasn't the best idea to talk to me about Bali at that time. It was late, and there was going to be no clear champion of our argument. And I knew that the source of the night's eruption was well and truly down to me forgetting about what meant something to Charlotte. I retreated and looked at her eyes, which were seeking some sort of solace from me.

'A *penne* for your thoughts...Get it? *Penne* for your thoughts?' My unfunny but funny pasta joke broke the ice as we both laughed.

'Who told you that you could speak to me?' Charlotte snipped sarcastically.

'You did with that smile!'

'Charmer, shall we finish this off? she sniffed as she poured what was left of the red wine into two glasses.

After finishing off the wine, our argument that night had been temporarily swept away with the shards of broken plates.

'Are you coming to bed, Jason?'

'No.'

'No? Why not?'

Her face questioned where my mind was at now. And whether this was the start of another fiery argument.

The French wine had made me feel horny. I stood up and walked over to Charlotte, who was standing next to the fridge.

'Because we're staying right here.'

Without any further words, we stared into each other's eyes and were on the same page for the first time that evening. We made another fire of our own and made up by making love standing up against the kitchen fridge.

Following the row, we didn't say anything to each other about that night, but I'd been contemplating how to make up for forgetting our anniversary and refusing to go to Bali.

A few weeks passed, and I was sitting at the side of the stream in Greenwich Park. I had a couple of hours to kill before Charlotte would join me for a picnic. My thoughts were a million miles away, lost in the warm afternoon atmosphere when one thought came back and stormed into my mind like an unexpected guest.

'Good afternoon I.T.A., how can I help?'

'Hello, I'm an actor new to London. I read about your agency in *The Stage*...'

'...We're not taking on new talent; our books are closed.'

Testing out my American accent, I phoned again.

'Can I speak to Jonathan Anderson, the head of casting?'

'I'm sorry, but nobody with that name works here. Bert Shahman heads our casting department.'

Now armed with a lead, I hatched my plan.

'What's this, Jason, a love letter?'

Charlotte had arrived fashionably late. We tucked into the supermarket-bought picnic-type snacks that I had chosen from the reduced food aisle as the sun's rays bounced from Greenwich Park's stream into the miniature bottle of Prosecco I'd forked out for. I had slipped an envelope containing the flight tickets to the land of Cornettos, in a napkin for Charlotte to find. She opened it and looked at me, lost for words.

A few days later

'Can I help you?'

'Yes, I'm here to deliver this to, uh, a, uh, Mr Bert Shahman at I.T.A.'

'Okay, you can leave it with me.'

'But, it needs to be signed in person.'

'You can leave it with me, and I can sign it.

'Hmm, my company needs me to deliver it by hand.'

Beaten down by my persistence, the tired security guard agreed and gave me directions to the I.T.A. office.

Arriving on the twelfth floor, my heart raced.

'Excuse me, could you tell me where I can find Mr Bert Shahman.'

The receptionist pointed me in the direction of the casting agent's desk.

I was armed with a large brown envelope containing my headshots, a copy of *Two Faced* (converted to DVD), and my acting CV.

As I got closer, my nerves were getting the better of me. What on earth was I going to say?

A few deep breaths later, my stomach back in its rightful place, I marched briskly to the beat of my heart thuds against my chest cavity.

'Anything to sign?'

I dropped the envelope on his desk, said nothing, and swiftly walked off, leaving Mr Bert Shahman, Head of Casting, looking well and truly miffed.

In the months leading up to our trip, I was still getting nowhere fast. Nothing came to fruition from my attempts to be signed up by I.T.A. My frustrations walloped me on a daily basis with a big, humongous broomstick. My dwindling hopes of golden acting gigs from London—or, I should say, lack of them—were evaporating.

My so-called love life wasn't going any better either. Charlotte and I would argue over anything and everything. We continued to scratch at all the problems that itched at us in our already inflamed and flaking relationship.

'You're so reticent. It would be fine with me if, from time to time, you shared with me what's bothering you, you know,' Charlotte prodded.

'There's nothing bothering me,' I replied as my phone vibrated.

'Who's that at this time of night?'

'Hmm, a possible acting agent.'

'Sure Jason, sure it is!'

38 FLIMFLAMMER

With a bold gesture, I leant across the table and put my hand on her leg. She paused, looked directly into my eyes and proceeded to pour water over my head, then slapped me hard across the face.

This time, however, it wasn't another argument with Charlotte where she had lost her rag. This was an improvisation scene with Olga Antonov, the tutor of a 12-week "Method Acting" course I had recently embarked upon after seeing it advertised in *The Stage*.

Held twice weekly in the Romeo Theatre in Euston, North London, the class was led by Olga Antonov, a seasoned actor with an indirect link to Stanislavski through her training with Uta Hagen, a former student of the Russian master and creator of "Method Acting" Constantin Stanislavski.

The hard-burning slap from Olga was only one of two times where I had been slapped by a woman for the love of acting, and boy did it feel great!

Our class of ten students included the gifted Tonia Buxton, who, unbeknownst to her at the time, would find culinary fame years later as a celebrity chef on the TV show *My Greek Kitchen*.

While I was on stage with Olga Antonov, all the other students sat in the elevated seating and looked on. I was in the midst of improvising a romantic scene filled with awkward silences and tension. That's when I touched Olga Antonov's leg, to which she responded with a hard-hitting finale across my face.

My course ended, and I entered new territories. In my face also, a door was slammed. This abrupt action, however, was neither from an acting tutor nor Charlotte but by a discombobulated old Italian man who didn't have the foggiest what I was saying.

'*Buonasera, una camera per favore?*' (one room, please).

My Italian request was delivered with an unintentional Yorkshire twang, to which the old man responded in Italian. His words were fast and authentic, and I didn't have a clue about what he was saying. I repeated my request, only louder this time.

'*BUONASERA, UNA CAMERA PER FAVORE... CAPEESH?*'

I learnt that word from Marlon Brando in *The Godfather,* but it didn't seem to work. The old man closed one eye, scratched his tilted head and spouted a response in Italian. Then I repeated my request again, this time with pantomime hand gestures. That's when our exchange ended with the frustrated old man shutting the door like he hated it, leaving us no other option but to find another hotel.

Mine and Charlotte's five-day trip to Italy kicked off in Anzio on the west coast of Italy. On arrival, we needed to regroup; it was early evening, and we hadn't pre-booked our accommodation. After my failed attempts to secure a room with my smattering of Italian, we found a café, shared a *cannoli* and downed two shots of bitter Italian *lungo* coffee as we pondered over our map and Italian travel book, weighing up potential new hotels for the night.

My initial plan was for us to stay in cheap hostel-style accommodation, as I was trying to be as frugal as possible because I was paying for the trip. I hadn't ruled out staying at campsites but never told Charlotte about this. However, once we'd set foot on Italian soil and she'd seen some of the run-down areas, it turned out that hotels were what we ended up looking for.

None of the accommodations in Anzio were within our tight budget or appealed to Charlotte's standards, so we both decided to take the train down to the rustic but charming city of Napoli. After one night there, our next stop would be the opulent Capri and then the Amalfi Coast.

On our late arrival at Napoli Centrale Stazione. Our appearance must've screamed tourists as we hauled our heavy rucksacks through the station and looked for the nearest exit. As we tried to find our way out of the station and make sense of the signs, we didn't notice that we were being watched. A well-dressed, middle-aged man introduced himself as Mario.

'*Buonasera, ti serve una camera?* Do you need a room?'

His words were like welcomed music to my ears. Mario was offering a room for 50 *euros,* which was around £30 for the night, and this was well within budget. His eyes seemed sincere, as did his smile underneath his thick, bushy black handlebar moustache. Exhausted and grateful for the help, Charlotte and I agreed to take

Mario up on his offer, and I gave him the cash.

Charlotte's feet were sore as her new designer holiday Roman sandals had been digging into her ankles. Mario offered to help Charlotte with her heavy rucksack as we walked through a dim alleyway to get to the hotel. Charlotte, who was less streetwise than me, was becoming a little suspicious of where we were heading.

The hotel was located downtown in an unkempt area, which was as cheery as Gotham City. When we reached the hotel, it looked more like a scruffy hostel. The paintwork on the door was crumbling, and the lurid neon-lit sign, Leonne Hotel, added to the tackiness of the building. We noticed several olive-skinned women hanging around the entrance, some wearing tight-cropped tops, figure-hugging skirts and hotpants, their faces heavily covered in makeup and false lashes. They looked up and down at the less-than-happy Charlotte in her favourite long gypsy skirt and flat sandals as we passed them walking towards the reception area. Mario went behind the reception desk to look at which room was vacant, and then he said something in Italian to one of the heavily made-up ladies, who then led us up the creaking stairs. An orgy of thoughts climbed through my mind as the scent of sex wafted through an open door, adding to the seedy atmosphere of the building and adding to what Charlotte and I were both thinking; that this setup wasn't quite *kosher*.

Just before the lady of the night opened the door to our room, Charlotte picked up on the loud moans and creaking bed springs coming from the room that was next door to ours.

'Charlotte…it's just for one night…we'll leave early in the morning…'

My suggestion was met with the fire I should've anticipated. Horrified at my mere suggestion that we should stay one minute more in what was her idea of hell, she turned around without so much of a word and began to make her way down the stairs, making it clear that there was NO WAY that she was staying there.

'… But, Charlotte, I've already paid!' I said as my words attempted in vain to catch up with the aggravated Charlotte. Slightly embarrassed at the situation, I shrugged my shoulders and raised my palms to the lady who was looking on. She raised her eyebrows, rolled her eyes and was obviously oblivious to the reason for Charlotte's distress. I had no choice but to follow Charlotte, but I stopped at the bottom of the stairs whilst Charlotte had continued to march straight towards the exit. A perplexed Mario stood up from where he sat in the reception area and walked towards me.

I was standing near the exit. Charlotte had already made it out of the building, much to the dislike of the frowning Mario. I attempted to soften the blow with Mario (in the hope he would return my 50 e*uros*), and I said.

'Sorry, my friend, but the lady doesn't want to stay the night.'

His muffled brow was softened when a larger-framed, hairy-bodied man wearing a vest and jeans came out of one of the rooms next to the reception, paid Mario a handful of e*uros* and left. At the corner of my eye, the room from which the hairy-bodied man had emerged had its door left ajar. A half-naked woman was getting dressed. Mario retorted something to me in Italian and handed me some cash, which I put in my top shirt pocket, and I left.

By the time I made it outside and looked around for Charlotte, I saw the hairy-bodied man trying to chat up a stunned Charlotte, who was trying to back away from him. I pulled her away in time before she became one of the brothel's commodities.

39 THAT'S AMORE

'I'm absolutely not going back there, Jason!!! What the hell are you thinking?'

We'd left the Leonne Hotel in such a hurry that I didn't even realise that Mario, the flimflammer, had short-changed me. I wanted to go back and get my dosh, but Charlotte stood her ground like a bull in a ring and said in an unladylike fashion that I absolutely, positively must forget about the fucking ten *euros!*

As Charlotte, I, and the dark storm cloud that rained over her head walked towards nowhere, looking for a place to bed minus the madames, I pointed at an opulent-looking hotel, which, in retrospect, I wished I'd never pointed at in the first place. Charlotte latched onto my suggestion.

'You saved me the trouble of suggesting it!'

The overpriced, over-the-top and way over-budget plush 4-star Starhotel cost a painful 240 *euros,* almost £150 a night, but to appease a shaken-up Charlotte, we checked in, I paid, and we stayed.

The next morning, we gathered our belongings, and I stocked up on the hotel's complimentary tea sachets, toiletries and stationery to ensure that I got at least near to getting my money's worth from the stay. I made the most of the hotel's superfast internet to check our planned route online. Before we checked out, I checked my emails, only to find a response from one of the castings I had applied for....we are sorry to inform you...was all I had to read before I logged off. Charlotte, I, and the dark storm cloud now about to chuck it down over my head left the hotel.

As we drove our small Fiat Marea saloon rental car through the bustling streets and historic neighbourhoods, we held our breaths, not just because of the pollution but because we shared the road with some of the crazed drivers of Napoli, who seemed to be honking their horns without purpose. When we joined the coastal road, the calmness and the refreshing sea air were a welcomed delight. The horizon was picturesque, and our life and relationship woes, at least for now, were placed way in the back of our minds.

We marvelled at the glassy day and beautiful surroundings that greeted us when we arrived in the beautiful town of Sorrento, which was much prettier than Napoli. After a couple of hours of browsing the expensive boutique shops and eating pricey but tasteless pasta at a tourist trap ristorante, we left the car in Sorrento and took the ferry to the Isle of Capri.

'I must be the first man you've dated who has shown you a slice of paradise like this...no?' I joked.

'Jason, are you dating me or yourself?' Charlotte returned while she adjusted her loose sandal strap as we sat on the deck of the ferry.

On arrival, we had to take the bus from the port to the Piazzetta situated at the top of the hill, where the main shops and restaurants were located. When the bus arrived, passengers were already squeezed on like a tin of *Cantabrian* anchovies. Charlotte was able to jump on first and wedge herself in between the locals, but before I could get on, the doors shut suddenly, and the bus set off. Leaving me standing there like a prized Amalfi lemon. We didn't have international roaming, so our matching Nokia 6310i phones were completely useless, and there was no way to get in touch with each other.

As the sun beamed down, I waited, and I waited at the bottom of the hill, expecting Charlotte to come back to me on a returning bus. My growing agitation was also being fuelled by suspicious thoughts. The longer I waited with no sign of Charlotte, the more my twisted thoughts were getting out of control. I became frustrated and uneasy with irrational suspicions whirling through my mind. What man might she have met up there? What might she have been doing? Who might she have been doing? While no further buses were going up, a few buses returned from the top of the hill. When the doors of each bus opened, and Charlotte wasn't amongst the passengers who got off, I was perplexed and annoyed at why she hadn't attempted to get a bus back down to me. It wasn't until 30 minutes later that the available bus to get to the top of the hill came. I got on it.

It was midday, and I was het up like a mad dog, and that wasn't from the Mediterranean sun. When I finally saw Charlotte, she had just come out from a souvenir shop, having bought a handful of postcards. She seemed oblivious to what had left me feeling irate. Her cluelessness about why I was upset was reflected by her asking me which postcard she should send back to our housemates, which built up the dander in me even more.

'Is there anything wrong, Jason?'

'No, Charlotte, but there's nothing right either! Why didn't you come back for me?' I said, cutting straight to the point.

With her defence mode on, she responded.

'You're a big boy. Couldn't you make it up here by yourself? I was enjoying Capri. What's wrong with that? Maybe you should lighten up and try to enjoy it yourself too.'

She put her pointed finger into her cheek and pouted her lips. I was even more agitated by Charlotte's words and the scorching heat, and I bit back.

'Don't rub my nose in it!'

'I'm not rubbing your bloody nose in anything, Jason. Can't you say something nice for once, huh?'

'I can't think of anything nice I want to say!'

We continued our volley of rows in the packed Piazzetta. Charlotte couldn't understand where I was coming from. Amid our argument, I began to feel faint, probably from the intense heat and the pent-up anger and frustration that'd been building up. Charlotte could see this. She reigned back her approach and put her hand on my back as we walked to a table at a deli next to where we were standing. I needed to sit down. I didn't have an appetite for anything. Charlotte, however, had a *Caprese* salad with a small bottle of white wine and a small dish of olives. Several glasses of water later, my dizziness had subsided, as had both of our frustrations.

'You haven't touched your olives,' Charlotte said sweetly.

'You're beginning to sound just like my mum; you think eating all my food is a remedy for everything! You'll be feeding me next!'

'Your Mum?' Charlotte was more than aggravated to say the least by my back-handed jibe, but this time, I refrained from any further comments that would've sparked off Mount Vesuvius.

'Have I put my foot in it?'

'Yes, Jason, right up to your upper thigh...why are you so complicated and virtually impossible?'

I realised once again that I had to back down; firefighting volcanic fire was a ridiculous equation, particularly in this backdraft of Mediterranean heat. I took a different approach and changed the narrative.

'So, are you going to eat that tomato or what, beautiful?'

'Oh my God, Jason. You do this all the time. Why does your bloody flattery always seem to do this?... You know, if you weren't so handsome, our arguments would last longer...Okay, I accept your apology.'

Charlotte smiled as she forked the lone tomato and fed it to me. I swallowed this with the response that wanted to come out of my mouth about me not actually apologising.

Charlotte had been mellowed partly by the third glass of *vino* she'd just guzzled down.

While Charlotte left to go to the loo, I binned the postcard that she'd half written to our flatmates saying.

Hi "Troop," we're having a great time... We wish you were...

A few hours later, my capricious mood returned as we left Capri. The short ferry journey back to Sorrento wasn't smooth sailing. On the deck, I caught a glimpse of another passenger smiling at Charlotte, and she reciprocated the smile, which angered me. We hit rocky waters as the over-friendly man stood up to let Charlotte sit down.

'Remember me, huh? I'm the man you are on holiday with,' I said sarcastically, loud enough to be embarrassing.

'What are you talking about...stop your jealousy. He was being a gentleman, that's all, more than I can say for you.'

'Gentleman? What type of gentleman? The type where he'd warm his hands before he put them up your blouse?'

'It's not very sporting of you, you know?'

'Whoever said love is a sport, huh?'

'Who said anything about love, huh? What is wrong with you, Jason, anyway?... The man was making room for me to sit down; he was only trying to be sweet...'

'Sweet? You're not talking about a bloody golden retriever puppy, Charlotte...you are not the only one who can attract the opposite sex, you know.'

Without missing a beat, Charlotte retaliated with an equal hit of sarcasm.

'You are a real contemporary *Don Juan*, aren't you?'

'*Don Juan*, that's the understatement of the year!... *Don Juan* couldn't compete,' I responded, this time backed with a hint of arrogance meant to aggravate Charlotte even more.

'Don't look now, Jason, but your Ego is showing...seeing as you have the answer to everything, maybe you'll have the answer to that too.'

'Here's you, here's me, But where's your point? Cos I can't seem to find it!'

With enough bull-headedness between me and Charlotte to sink the ferry, she and I retreated and she neatly folded her red rag and tucked it away in her handbag whilst I stuffed mine in my pocket. Until.

'I'm hungry. Would you like anything?'

'I'm not surprised, Jason; you might want to try the humble pie; I've heard it's good.'

'Bravo Charlotte bravo, I'm off for a coffee; my big Ego needs perking up.'

'You're so bloody melodramatic Jason. You're unbelievable!'

We collected our rental car from Sorrento to drive to the scenic Amalfi Coast, which was a romantic and serene place. The stupendous views were marred somewhat by the unease in my chest. We took several instant photos of the both of us along the quaint, pretty mountain village of Ravello, which was carpeted in lush green hills and flowers. We posed by the crystal blue Tyrrhenian Sea. We ate fresh *Frutti di mare* pasta and bitter lemon *gelatos* in *alfresco* restaurants. But whilst our holiday snapshots depicted the beauty and grandeur of the Italian surroundings, pain and feelings of uncertainty were hidden behind our picture-perfect smiles.

40 KELLY WTF IS KELLY?

'Kelly? Who the fucking hell is Kelly, huh?' Charlotte yelled indignantly, shaking and waking me.

Half asleep and not ready for the bombardment that I was awoken with. The response that sluggishly came out of my mouth was along the lines of:

'What are you on about now?'

This angered her even more. And like a hormonal banshee, she continued her screaming.

'Kelly from *Cook Me Up Some bloody Love*, apparently! For Fuck's sake, Jason, if you wanted to change your menu, why the fucking, bloody, shitting hell didn't you just tell me?'

Now, sitting upright in bed with my eyes half open, I could think and speak more rationally.

'I don't know anyone named Kelly!'

'What? Do you think I'm some sort of idiot?' Roared Charlotte. Her eyes were like barrels of a loaded machine gun.

Now, in the centre of her firing line, my eyes were wide and awake as I was face to face with those barrels that were ready to shoot. I knew I had nowhere to move, and I couldn't quite figure out how on earth she'd found out about Kelly, let alone that she was from *Cook Me Up Some Love*. In a last-ditch attempt to save my bacon, I blurted out a camouflaged answer, which perhaps was not what she wanted to hear, but it was an answer all the same.

'I don't know; it was a few years ago, and to be honest, the event escapes me.'

I scratched my head and acted confused. My response appeared to give me some sort of lifeline before Charlotte began to storm out of the bedroom.

'Oh wonderful...when the event catches up with you...do me a favour Jason...let me know.'

She slammed the door so hard that the walls shuddered like they were going to cave in.

My newfangled BlackBerry (which I'd stupidly part exchanged for my Nokia 6310i) was proving to be a headache. A flirtatious text message that I thought I'd deleted sparked an enormous row between me and Charlotte after she'd gone through my phone while I was asleep. Foolishly, in my frustration with mine and Charlotte's relationship situation, I reciprocated the coquetry sent in a text from Kelly, a makeup artist I met a few years back from *Cook Me Up Some Love*.

'Charlotte, let's talk this through properly,' I called as I went down to the kitchen to try to explain that it was something and nothing.

'If you've come here to give me your bushwa excuses, you can save your breath.'

'Charlotte...'

'Don't you bloody Charlotte me! For all I care, you can choke on your excuses!'

Her words were directed towards me as hard and fast as the breakfast bowl she threw towards my head. As more tears streamed down her face, Charlotte budged past me and stormed upstairs.

'A million Kellys couldn't compare to you,' I yelled in a last-ditch attempt to soften her.

But Charlotte wasn't having any of it. She could see through me like an X-ray machine. Now late for work, I grabbed my jacket and headed towards the door.

'Good morning,' said one of "The Troop" awkwardly.

'In your world, maybe!!! Go fuck yourself!'

I slammed the door on my way out.

Covent Garden

'Sorry mate, I didn't see you,' apologised a stressed-looking guy whose face was plastered with another layer of irritation as his female companion said.

'I need to buy some concealer...where's that makeup shop?'

The guy was towing handfuls of shopping bags, which looked like they were ready to snap as he continued to trail after his female companion like an enthusiastic slug sliding towards a container of salt. He almost sent me flying as he barged past me carrying more bags than a team of Santa's elves on Christmas Eve.

He probably had visions of kicking back to watch the football and not getting pulled from pillar to post around the shops in the bustling Covent Garden, which happened to be heaving with more crowds of people and more street performers than usual. In my mind, however, the hustle and bustle was about what had happened that morning.

While on my lunch break and a million miles away from Earth, I was brought back to the ground by a vaguely familiar voice.

'Hello, stranger, what a small world. What are you doing in London, darling?'

It was Wendy Davenport, an old friend and set designer I'd met some years earlier while working on the Yorkshire production *It's Rough Up North*, and she was now residing in London.

Wendy took a short pause from her last-minute Christmas shopping to catch up on the years with me. As it was freezing out, we went to a Covent Garden café to do this over a pot of peppermint tea and Mulligatawny soup.

'Mmm, the soup's good...are you still working as a costume designer, Wendy?'

'I am darling, and you, what are you up to these days?'

'I'm an actor, well it's a loose term. I'm trying to become an actor, more like...but I've hit a brick wall; I can't get any auditions, and if I do, I get the same answers: either a big fat NO or, even worse, the "pencil-in." Making my mark down here in London isn't as simple as I thought it would be. It feels like I'm climbing up an escalator that is going down. You know what I mean?'

'Darling, acting is the hardest profession in the world; there's no telling where it may take you; you just have to be patient; you have to persevere.'

The familiarity of speaking to someone from back home in Yorkshire comforted me, as I'd missed talking to random strangers on buses and the streets. I also missed the say-it-as-it-is way of the people up north where, for many, there was no holding back when it came to laying out God's honest truth rather than skirting around it, a more common approach that I had learnt from people in the more conservative south, where if you talk to a stranger on a bus or a street they think you're a madman. Wendy and I went on to discuss the film industry and shared details about our lives in London, but the perceptive Wendy must've seen that there was something more that I wasn't saying. Naturally, my rocky relationship with Charlotte was the next topic of conversation on the menu.

'Is everything okay, darling?' Wendy enquired as I stared out of the small window where sleet was starting to fall from the leaden sky.

'I'd like to say it is...but...I'm having relationship difficulties...I moved to London with my true love, and it's become a drama. Now drama has become my true love.'

Wendy, who was a good 20 years my senior and possessed a wisdom that came with age, remained remarkably level-headed. She leaned in, offering her counsel.

'Listen, darling, sometimes it takes a huge storm to clear things up; you ought to give it your best shot to mend things, but don't let things drag out longer than necessary; life is just too short. You should keep persevering with your acting.'

Before parting, we exchanged numbers.

'...Think about it okay and remember what I said Jason darling; if you know in your heart that your ship has sailed, maybe then it is time to focus on new horizons.'

Long after Wendy left, her words hugged me tighter than I'd felt for a long time and comfortingly remained wrapped around me. Wendy had spoken with such honesty, and I knew that she was right. Charlotte and I couldn't keep the same status quo, and it seemed that if we did, our fragmented relationship would be like the Titanic heading towards an iceberg.

Back in Greenwich, after I had orchestrated my thoughts, I needed to clear the air with Charlotte. However, when I opened the front door, the loud chatter and laughter of "The Troop" and Charlotte travelled from the kitchen alongside the strong aroma of Chinese takeaway. Rather than join them, I slowly walked up the stairs, trying to avoid the steps that creaked so as not to make a sound. It was an hour later that Charlotte came into our room and walked towards me as I sat on the bed.

'Oh, you're here. I didn't hear you come in. We just ate Chinese. Have you eaten?' Charlotte asked as she sat on the bed beside me, her tone now starkly different from the morning. I sensed she was ready to talk rationally, and so was I...until.

'You should have joined us.'

I shot a look towards her through the glass barrier between us.

'Jason, you say more with a look than you realise, you know?' Aggravated at her seeming ignorance about what she said.

I hissed. 'I prefer to be alone.'

'What is it you want, Jason? I just don't get it. I just don't get you,'

'Charlotte, I do love you; believe me, I do, but I need some solitude. I need time for myself...I need a break from us...I need to be on my own, especially over Christmas. I have to figure out what I'm feeling.' Without saying a word, Charlotte left the room.

41 NEW YEARS EVE

It was becoming painfully obvious that Charlotte and I didn't want to see the canary in the coal mine. And now it was becoming clear that we'd reached an impasse.

Charlotte and I went back up to Bradford to spend a week over Christmas separately with our own families. We took the three-hour train journey and hardly said a word to each other.

No sooner had we arrived in Leeds than we both parted ways to get on separate connecting trains. Though Charlotte was only going to Oxenhope and me to Bradford, we might as well have been going to the opposite sides of the Earth. The disconnect and distance between us, even before we headed in our different directions, were blatantly apparent. As we left each other, I felt pained but not crushed.

We'd hardly spoken over Christmas, just briefly on Christmas day, and after our Christmas break, we returned separately to Greenwich before the new year. "The Troop" were still away, so there was an opportunity to address the quandary that we were in.

With a sailor's knot starting to uncontrollably tangle in the pit of my stomach at the thought of facing Charlotte, I knew firstly I needed fortification, which I found through the reliable as-ever swig of my amigo—whisky, which I'd hidden under the kitchen sink. Now fuelled and ready for the unexpected, I walked into our bedroom. I took off my heavy yellow rucksack, took out Oscar Wilde's biography and flicked through it, not to read but to avoid looking at Charlotte. She was unpacking, and I sat beside her on the bed with the book on my lap. The silence was awkward for a few seconds before I broke it.

'Go ahead, say it, Charlotte.'
'Say what, Jason, huh?'

'What you have on your mind.'

'Nothing, absolutely nothing.'

'I think we are talking in circles. What's on your mind, Charlotte?'

'So...Is there... someone else?'

'Do you really think that I'd do that, Charlotte?'

The atmosphere was tense, and the weighing scales were toing and froing as to whether our conversation was about to escalate into a full-blown argument or not.

'What was I supposed to think when I read your Kelly text?'

I scanned the back of the book in my hand, but no words other than Charlotte's were sinking in, though I didn't want her to know that.

'I just can't read you, Jason.'

She placed a pile of her underwear into one of the drawers.

'Ditto... you know that it's not that I don't...love you.'

'Pah! Love me! You have a funny way of showing it. That's the voice of the whisky, I expect.'

'Do you love me?'

'I'm seriously considering it, Jason!'

'Where are those lacy ones?' She fumbled around the drawer and held up her turquoise pair of sheer lacy pants.

'I've always admired your *chutzpah*. Do you want me to put them on?'

A fitful night's sleep later, it was the morning of New Year's Eve. I went down to the kitchen and saw that Charlotte was catching up with "The Troop," who'd returned in the early hours and were still in festive spirits. As they engaged in their conversations about their plans for the new year, I didn't say a word. I was about to head back to our room when Charlotte, in her attempt to get me to join them, called out to me.

'There's some porridge here for you.'

I turned back to appease Charlotte. My pride was as hard to swallow as the cold porridge that Charlotte had just served me, and the ambience in the kitchen wasn't much different. She turned to the chattering "Troop."

'What's this? Did you stir my porridge with your hairbrush or something? There's about ten thousand hairs in it!' I grumbled as I swiped my bowl away.

Charlotte, who'd not heard or noticed what I'd said, had her newly dry-cleaned long black dress draped over her arm and in a transparent garment cover. She was oblivious that I'd put a pan on to fry some eggs and bread in an attempt to make a breakfast for myself that was at least edible. Charlotte was busy multitasking, trying to get her primping gear together, having her own breakfast, and sorting the papers she'd been looking at the night before. She was in a rush to catch her regular train to work. I however, wasn't in the best of moods, having burnt my toast, then my fingers and now had overdone my eggs.

'So I'll see you tonight then?' she said, offering me her reddened and strawberry-glossed lips.

I obliged her with a kiss, and she headed for the door.

'Oh Jason, by the way...the envelope is on the fireplace,' she reminded me before shutting the front door. Then, all I could hear was the fading clicks of her high heels running to get to the train station.

"The Troop" had dispersed, and I sat alone at the kitchen table. My burnt toast looked as unappealing as the overcooked scrambled eggs, so I went over to the cupboard to find something to fill my emptiness. I accidentally trod on the broken eggshell that had fallen from the worktop. I poured myself an early morning shot of my only friend, Talisker whisky. Curious as to what the envelope Charlotte had referred to was, I tore it open. It was a ticket to a New Year bash at Velvet Vines, a swanky wine bar in Covent Garden, the same club that "The Troop" were discussing over breakfast.

It was just after nine at night, after several whisky burns, after wrestling with my thoughts, and after making sure I put my clothes that were sprawled out on the bed into my big yellow rucksack. I picked up my tickets and got on a train, not to the New Year's party to meet Charlotte, but to Wendy Davenport's.

While Charlotte partied hard that night, I had packed all my belongings and left Hyde Vale and my life with Charlotte behind.

When I arrived at Wendy's flat in Herne Hill, she showed me to my new small room, which was furnished with a bunk bed,

I sat on the edge of the bed, looking out of the 5th-floor window. The view of London was clear. As I wiped away my tears, I wished my future was, too.

I placed my few belongings on the top bunk and went downstairs. Wendy had made me a cup of tea, and she could see that I was struggling. My words could only reach out as far as.

'Thank you, Wendy; I really appreciate this.'

Wendy's empathy and welcome were the warmth that I needed at that moment.

'No need to thank me. I hope you will be happy here, just remember me when you become famous...a mention in your autobiography will do!'

'Talking of books, I'm meeting up with my friend Will Self, you know, the author, he's a good friend of mine. I'm going to a New Year's party at my local, The Red Lion, you should come. It will help you take your mind off of things.'

Though Wendy was trying her best to make me feel better, I had to politely decline her invitation. I couldn't face being in company, not just yet.

'If you don't mind, I just need some time by myself.'

Wendy headed out, and I saw New Year's in, alone, on a bunk bed, with a cup of peppermint tea, reading Oscar Wilde's biography.

That night I tried to fathom out what was the fucking point to love anyway, especially the kind that can turn around and rip your heart out.

42 BRIXTON

'Sorry, mate! I forgot to give you the heads-up. I had a proper brain fade there, didn't I? Brixton station is two minutes back there, just round the bend!'

It was about 6:30pm when I boarded a bus to the train station one evening. I was heading to rehearsals for *The Tempest* at the Shakespeare's Globe theatre. After paying my fare, I asked the bus driver to give me a shout when we got to the train station. It was a cold, dark, miserable January night, which was made even more gloomy when the bus driver forgot to tell me where to get off.

Brixton was unfamiliar territory for me, but Wendy had given me the lowdown about its dubious repute for violent crime. Although I had considered myself streetwise whilst in Bradford, I was a novice when it came to the streets of London.

As I stepped off the bus, I didn't have the faintest idea where I was. I tried to ask an Asian-looking woman passing by for help, but she continued walking and put her head down without murmuring so much as a word, only looking back when she crossed the other side of the street.

Somehow, I managed to find the underground subway and mainline station situated above it. I realised I had no cash to buy my train tickets, so I looked around the station in search of an ATM. A middle-aged, scruffily dressed man was the only other person in the queue behind me. The stench of stale cigarettes, stale alcohol and a hint of stale urine wafted from his vicinity. As I punched in my PIN number, the man demanded that I give him money, but I took my £10 from the machine, avoided eye contact and walked past him quickly. The incident made me feel slightly ill and uneasy.

I headed towards the sign for the mainline station to buy a ticket to London Victoria. The vendor's attitude was as sharp as her luminous-coloured, claw-like nails as she flung my tickets and jingle change through the gap underneath her window without so much as a 'have a good day.'

As I walked up the dark, dinghy stairs, I held my breath, trying to avoid the urinal-like stench coming from the staircase and was careful not to tread in any inconspicuous puddles. Two men were huddled in a corner, fixing up with syringes. I walked very quickly past them and only breathed out when I got to platform two.

I searched the board for the time of the train but was pissed off when I realised I was actually on the wrong platform. I knew there was no way I was going back down those stairs again, and I really didn't want to be late for my rehearsals. So, I did the most foolish thing that you could EVER imagine.

I stupidly crossed the tracks to get to the other side. I knew not to stand on the track itself and also knew I was risking my life if I did. I had my heart in my mouth, hoping that a freight train or another express train wouldn't appear at any minute. Luckily, I made it to the other side intact, with my heart racing so fast that it could've won the Grand National.

I clambered up onto platform one, checked the arrival tracker and saw that I only had to wait ten minutes before my train arrived. It was as quiet as a tomb and pitch black, as my heart still pounded away like a good 'un. While I waited for the train, I was stopped cold as I caught sight of a huge guy in the corner of my eye. His arms were folded, and I could feel his hard, stone-cold stare piercing through my back, so I did not dare to look at him. With no other soul in sight, of course, it meant I was scared stiff. The digital clock ticked down: 10, 9, 8, 7 minutes. The guy remained fixed in his position; his stare, from what I could make out from the corner of my eye, remained fixed on me. My mind was like an army of fleas deep in battle. Six minutes, five minutes, four minutes, three minutes, waiting for the train felt like an eternity.

'Come on, come on.' I kept repeating to myself.

The announcement came overhead that the train was delayed by five minutes. The guy still wasn't moving and still staring menacingly at me.

Needless to say, when the train finally arrived, I was more than relieved when I jumped on, and the train door closed behind me. It was only when the train rolled out of Brixton station that I was brave enough to have a proper look at the man from my safe seat on the moving train. I could hardly believe my eyes...The menacing guy who I was shitting bricks over was nothing more than a stone-cold sculpture and not an actual person at all. I laughed myself silly with relief. What a friggin IDIOT!

Brixton Bronze Statue. Courtesy of Sachab.

43 THE NEW YORK FILM ACADEMY

Richard E. Grant, Ethan Hawke, Stephen Fry, Gemma Atherton, and now me. I stood where these great stars once shone, breathing in the air, and absorbing the ambience encapsulated within Shakespeare's Globe Theatre. Okay, so my performance might not have been in front of a packed house; in fact, there were less than 100 people, and some of those were my mates like Tom Spender and Dimitri Pieri, who cheered me on, and okay, I might not have been performing alongside any award-winning star names who headlined the West End, Broadway, Hollywood, or at the star-packed major film festivals that ultimately would bring bums on seats, but to me, being able to tread the same boards as these terrific actors was exhilarating.

Twelve weeks into my Shakespeare course, I was set to play Caliban in The Tempest. But Alas, in keeping with the play's theme, disaster struck for real. I had made the rookie mistake of not doing my voice warm-ups. What a shipwreck. Then my voice, or, should I say, lack of voice, reminded me why this was a daft thing to do because two days before the performance, it went on strike, and I completely lost my voice! Fuck; This hissed me into madness, obviously. I doused my system with more lemons than there were in Italy and more Manuka honey than in New Zealand. And what do you know, two days later, like Prospero's magic, I, as Caliban, performed my heart out.

"Be not afeard; the isle is full of noises, Sounds and sweet airs, that give delight, and hurt not."

During this time, inner turmoil and turbulence seemed to be the theme of my acting endeavours because, after my final performance in *The Tempest,* I went silent. It wasn't that I'd lost my voice again, but because of a new psychological drama film called *The Neighbour*, where I, as the LEAD ACTOR, was required to play a virtually silent role.

The Neighbour was a New York Film Academy (NYFA) film filmed over three gruelling days on a chilly February in the suburbs of West London, using top-notch 16mm cameras and directed by the *avant-garde* Greek filmmaker Stathis Athanasiou. He, the NYFA crew, and I poured our hearts into creating the film. I was blown away by how Stathis directed me throughout the shoot in his wonderfully unorthodox yet remarkably compelling and unique style. Stathis was a genius at weaving light and shade effects to transform the film into his masterpiece. He used analogies and metaphors to help me make my character truly connect with raw emotions and feelings of hatred, nihilism, anxiety, fear and paranoia without using words.

'I think they're annoyed about Bonzo's tipper wagon that yer brother's left in the front yard...It's a right eyesore in front of both our houses...Andy, at number 11, just got a new brown Volvo; he's had it valeted, and he's washing it every day. It's his pride and joy; it's got a private reg with his name on it. It says AND for Andy. He hasn't said owt about Bonzo's tipper, but I could tell it's getting on his wick...What d'ye think, Jason eh?'

'Sorry Mum, can I ring you back?'

While sitting at Wendy's kitchen table, I hung up on Mum to click on a notification alert I received on my BlackBerry. It was an email from Stathis Athanasiou, which, following the production of *The Neighbour,* many of the cast and crew and I received. The email subject line *"la la la la la la"* piqued my curiosity:

Greetings, everyone! I don't usually send out messages to so many people at once, but The Neighbour is set to screen at the following festivals: Drama International Film Festival, Athens International Film Festival, Thessaloniki Festival of Independent Filmmakers, Filmstock International Film Festival, Festival De Cine Internacional De Barcelona, Festival Du Cinema De Paris, Edinburgh, Bilbao, Berlinale. Wishing you all the best, Stathis.

I continued reading the mind-blowing email about *The Neighbour's* positive reception across Europe. A dizzying sense of pride washed over me, and I had to read Stathis's email multiple times to fully grasp the magnitude of the achievement, but no matter how many times I read it, it just couldn't quite sink in. It was difficult to describe the jubilation I felt. A lad from the industrial city of Bradford was making international waves in the film industry.

My joy reached even newer dizzy heights when I learned I had won my first award for Best Actor at the Barcelona Film Festival. It was a monumental triumph that bolstered my confidence in chasing my dreams.

Instead of reaching for a whisky, I celebrated in style as I rocked away with pride, playing Aerosmith's *Crazy* on air guitar whilst standing on Wendy's kitchen table.

Later, I discovered that *The Neighbour* had also claimed third place at the Berlinale International Film Festival.

With accolades under its belt, the film was screened at the prestigious NYFA. Wendy was away and wasn't able to attend the prestigious evening with me, but I felt confident enough to invite Charlotte to the London screening. I had something that I could well and truly be proud of, and I wanted to shout it from the rooftops and share it with someone who had known my acting journey to get there. Gone were the days when my screen time consisted of a brief 10-second glimpse of my left shoulder. I was now not only an actor but an award-winning actor, and I wanted to share my screen debut.

On the premiere night, as I took my seat in the packed auditorium, nervousness coursed through every fibre of my being. I knew that all eyes in the room would soon be fixed on me, scrutinising my performance on the grand screen. Childhood memories came flooding back from watching my favourite big silent screen actors like Charlie Chaplin, Harold Lloyd and Laurel & Hardy on the small TVs at Sewell Road and Rosedale Avenue. It was now me who would captivate the auditorium full of cinema-goers.

The atmosphere in the cinema was electric and exciting. Most actors I knew or had read about found watching themselves on the big screen challenging, but I couldn't have been prouder on that occasion. I knew I had delivered a mustard performance, and I wanted to savour every moment: the ambience, the people, and the praise. It was a doozy moment, and my soul felt like warm apple pie.

By the way, Charlotte ignored my invitation and did not attend.

MY EGO SCREWED MY ACTING CAREER

NYFA, The Neighbour, Director Stathis Athanasiou.

44 MÉNAGE À TROIS

What about Greek? Xxx—A text had just flashed on my Blackberry.

It was from Charlotte and was another one of several that had been bouncing between us all morning.

Perfect, I'll bring the Greek. Anything else you want me to bring? I texted back.

In the space of a few weeks following the screening of *The Neighbour,* one apology text sparked a few more occasional ping-pong texts, which then escalated to more frequent daily and nightly texts and ultimately led to a rendezvous and a Greek takeaway at Hyde Vale, the place of her home and my former home in Greenwich. It was the first time after I'd left that we would be face-to-face with each other. Our texts had nicely heated the water and now we appeared to be both ready to dip our toes in for round two.

Prior to our date, I had an evening drama rehearsal for a play—*No Sex Please, We're British!*' I was in Euston, North London, 30 minutes away from North Greenwich station. If everything went according to plan, I was sure that I would make it to Charlotte on time. What I wasn't sure of was where this date would lead and whether it would mean getting back together again.

After rehearsals, my fellow acting friends and I went to have a few drinks in a local pub called The Jolly Roger. Somehow, the prospect of stepping into the known-unknown again with Charlotte was making me nervous, so a shot of some Dutch courage was much needed. But one shot led to another, which led to another and another, and it wasn't until several shots later that the group and I said our goodbyes.

I checked my phone and saw more than a few missed calls and a large number of texts from Charlotte. I left them unread as I hurriedly popped into Bharat's Off Licence and bought a bottle of French red wine, which always got the both of us in the mood. The Greek restaurant where I intended to pick up the dinner I had promised Charlotte had now closed. Almighty Aphrodite Kebabs, a shop en route to the station, was my only Greek option left. So I picked up two *chicken doner kebabs* with no garlic mayo and extra *tzatziki* sauce before I set off from Euston Station to Charlotte's. By this time, however, I was very drunk and very, very late.

While waiting for the bus at North Greenwich station, I looked over at two ladies who were looking over at me looking at them. They also were waiting for a bus ride. I walked over to check the timetable when one of the ladies enquired.

'Do you have a match?'

The woman's question was the instant spark for the conversation between Silje and Trudy (the two women) and me. Though I didn't have a match per se, their playful banter certainly was a match for mine. The tag-team-double were two Norwegian women living and working hard in London and, by the sounds of it, partying even harder. As the conversation heated up, Trudy flirted.

'How about you?'

'What do you want to know about me?'

'What are you going to tell me?'

'Of course, I'm going to tell you what I want you to know!'

Silje and Trudy giggled at my response.

'Okay, let me indulge you. A lot of people don't know this, but I'm quite famous.'

I flicked this over to Silje, a beautifully rounded being with a mischievous energy. She appeared to be just as curious about me as I was with her and her tag team partner.

'Famous?' Silje said wide-eyed.

'Yeah, I recently had a screening in a cinema, and I will be performing in a play, *No Sex Please, We're British!*'

'You don't have sex because you're British?' Trudy, the tad prettier one of the two, innocently asked, throwing me a crumb.

At that time, the empty 486 bus had arrived, and we all got on and sat together.

'What about sharing with us?' Trudy flirted, pointing to my bottle as they both giggled again.

'What, the wine?' I reacted to her innuendo, 99% sure I knew what she meant.

'Yes, why not? We like to share,' Trudy's giggles had subsided and were replaced with a smile and a look in her eyes to suggest she wasn't joking as the bus began nearing Charlotte's road. I could resist many things, but not temptation.

'Why not?' I responded, thinking it would be rather rude not to take up their invitation to share the bottle of *Côtes du Rhône* back at theirs.

As I entered Silje and Trudy's musty tiny bedsit, they invited me to cushion myself between them on the edge of their tiny bed. The three of us guzzled French wine directly from the bottle. It was the wine that I had bought to drink with Charlotte. Next to me, Trudy reacted to the tickling vibration on her leg.

'Jason...I think your jeans are buzzing!' Trudy smiled playfully, patting her hand around the epicentre of the vibrations.

It was getting late, and I knew EXACTLY who was trying to call me and what would happen if I went back to Charlotte's. She would either shoot me or wouldn't let me in the door.

I remembered how Charlotte once locked me out for coming home too late after a night out with my friends, and I ended up sleeping in the garden.

As I sat with Silje and Trudy, flirting wildly and downing the drinks, I did the most sensible thing I could think of at the time. I stood up, took my mobile phone out of my pocket, and I turned it off.

Trudy swelled up Christina Aguilera's *Dirty* and opened a bottle of gin then one gin led to another gin and then another until we'd nearly finished half the bottle.

I started to bust some moves on the only piece of floor available.

'Wooohooo...you are the partyyyyyyy,' Silje said as she joined me.

She proceeded to eat me up with increasingly suggestive dance moves as she ground herself onto me. Front to front first, and then, with her meaty bottom cheeks nearly swallowing my crotch, she lifted her hair from her neck and invited me to kiss it.

The drink had gotten to all of our heads by the time Christina Aguilera's Album had done its second rendition, and by that time, we were ready to hit the sack. There was a chill that the early morning hours had brought in, and with the heating appearing to be on the blink, the tag team sandwiched me between them to keep the heat in the tiny bed.

'*Godnatt*,' they said harmoniously. I'd be lying if I said I wasn't disappointed when the lights went out, and they went to sleep.

I tossed and turned between the two women until I got

reasonably comfy. We all had no option but to lay on our sides as the bed was so narrow. I spooned Trudy first, and her slight snores told me I would be wasting my time trying to entertain her. I turned to lie on my other side, and Silje responded to my movement by turning around to face me; she gave me the type of look that I could feel in my boxer shorts then one thing turned to another, and before we knew it, she had turned to face the wall and had pulled off her panties. The excitement of it all led to me entering her from behind as she took my hand round to her front to play with her where it counted for her. I did my best to multitask as she did her best to contain her moans of pleasure. I then followed her lead, which meant I had to carefully manoeuvre down the tiny bed. Now, she was flat on her back, and a warm welcome was awaiting me. When the housewarming party hit its peak, she nearly screamed the roof off, but by the sounds of it, we hadn't disturbed Trudy, who was still snoring like a broken tumble dryer. Silje returned the pleasure by giving me a sensational fellatio before we both fell asleep. I woke up a while later to Trudy's hand over my boxer shorts. Both still blurry-eyed but willing, I played, and she played, then I played again until she climaxed and released her moans of pleasure into her pillow so she wouldn't wake Silje, then she, unlike Silje, who swallowed, passed me a toilet roll so I wouldn't stain the sheets.

I had to go to work the following morning, but the late-night shenanigans had caught up with me. Silje and Trudy were still sound asleep. There was no alarm clock in the place, and I didn't want to turn on my phone to check the time because I was afraid of what messages I may have received from Charlotte. The sock monster had struck again as I couldn't find my socks or my boxer shorts, for that matter. Plus, the fog billowing from my breath indicated how stark-bollocking-cold it was inside and outside. I had no option but to leave for work like a snowman, freezing, pantless and sockless.

Luckily, as I was running late, the rat race rush had subsided, so I didn't have to be squashed like a tinned-sardine against a pretentious city worker. The stench of sex and stale booze on my unshowered body was pungent as I sat on the tube travelling to the office. However, this smell was overshadowed by an office worker sitting opposite me painting her nails; her antisocial varnish was so strong it probably could have been smelt 100 miles away in Birmingham. But my odour and the varnish weren't the only smells fermenting our carriage; as I peered into my bag in the front compartment, I saw the two *kebabs* I bought last night, which I'd totally forgotten about.

The office receptionist glared at me oddly when I arrived,

smelling of sex, booze, and *kebab* and looking dishevelled with drips of *tzatziki* sauce that had run down my jacket. I'd been promoted to charity team leader and was in charge of managing the fundraising team called The Pink Team. I picked up the paperwork I needed and, hungover, headed off to Charing Cross Road, Central London, which was only a 10-minute walk from the office. On the way to meet the team, my feet and bollocks were so cold that they felt like they might drop off. As I passed Foyles bookshop, I wondered what would be in store for my next chapter with Charlotte or had last night's shenanigans torn out the pages.

I set up my team, gave my assistant instructions and the necessary paperwork and walked away to bravely switch on my phone. As I walked past The British Museum, I hoped that the aftermath of what was to come wouldn't resemble its ancient ruins within.

I finally mustered enough courage to switch my phone on to see a barrage of texts. The texts which enquired about my whereabouts started off normally, but as I read through each of them, their tone became angrier and angrier with the addition of unrepeatable expletives that were harsh enough to make toenails curl. Charlotte had presumably received the delivery reports because as I read her last, very furious text, I received another from Charlotte, and this one had only just been sent. *MEET ME OUTSIDE THE DRURY THEATRE AT 12:30!!!*

The surprise that she wanted to meet up hit me as hard as the wrecking ball crane of a headache that throbbed inside my head, waiting for its next swing. I had no lust for any more swinging.

"Don't be a sinner, be a winner, don't be a sinner, be a winner, Don't be a sinner, be a winner."

The sounds firing out of the heavens reverberated in my hungover head. However, the echoes weren't God speaking to me, but a Liverpudlian preacher called Phil, with a megaphone, doing his rounds on the streets of London.

As the time drew nearer, I walked towards our meeting place, sat on a small wall outside the Drury Theatre, and observed the hustle and bustle in the sea of suits whizzing around the London streets as the big red buses passed and nearly choked my lungs with fumes. I began planning out my web of lies and contemplating different scenarios and plausible reasons why I stood her up and didn't text her. The reality was that I knew that I was like the Titanic heading for a humongous iceberg.

Dressed in a smart black pinstripe suit and a lace-collared white blouse, Charlotte stomped towards me in her black Italian leather boots. Before she said a word, I could see through her body language and facial expressions that she was livid and in no mood for pleasantries. I reached out to hug her, but instead, she pushed away my arms and demanded to know why I stood her up. I tried to blag it and pathetically pleaded with her, saying.

'Um I'm sorry...um...I love you...um I was just out drinking with my drama friends...and ummm....ummm...my battery died.'

Charlotte was not having any of it. She was a smart cookie, and her X-ray perception could see right through my brittle skeleton of lies. Instead of storming off, she kept her rage and irrationality cooly contained behind a reasonable and rational question she threw my way.

'...So you couldn't take the time to call me?'

This rationality caught me off guard. Then, there was a moment of pause, during which I could see the fire and pain in her eyes as she tried to pull back the tears that were beginning to well up. I read this to be a moment to hug her, and this time, surprisingly, she accepted, luring me into her web like a praying mantis.

She moved closer to me to kiss my lips, which she did, but her pulling away felt like yanking an Elastoplast from a very sore wound. In those stretched-out seconds, she raised her fingers to her mouth, cupped her fingers around her lips, and smelt her breath. The scorned Charlotte must have caught the aroma and taste of sex oozing from my breath; my *kebab* nibble had done little to mask the aroma, obviously! Without having to say the bleeding obvious, I knew that she knew, and she knew that I knew. All the bullshit I had served up was leading us into a perfect storm. I tried one last-ditch attempt to hold back the tide.

'...Charlotte...you've got to give me a chance to...'

'...You've had your chance, Jason. I'm done...You didn't even take the time to clean your mouth,' she said, her voice lowered but refused to tremble. As guilt wrenched the inside of my stomach and we stood silently, I was hoping that some sort of sense would come out of my mouth to try and salvage whatever was left of what we had. I looked up, and our eyes met. Charlotte wasn't backwards in coming forward to show me the meaning of *Hell having no fury like a woman scorned*. She proceeded to slap me hard enough to make it feel like that one painful strike was for every time I'd wronged her. As I held the left side of my face and checked if I could still move my jaw, she stormed away into the busy crowds of central London, and I went to the pub. Charlotte, if you read this, I apologise.

45 LOVE IS IN THE AIR

'Would it be okay if we skipped drinks? I don't feel like drinking anymore. I'm not sure if you noticed, but there's a hotel across the street?' Suggested a Cameron Diaz look-alike.

Her flushed face and stray strands of hair that hung from her loose golden French plait reflected how hard she'd been moving on the dance floor. The blonde took a sip of her strawberry Mimosa, the colour of which matched my shirt, and she waited for my response. I was standing at the bar of Expo nightclub, Soho. I was blown away.

The Swiss Eva Baumgartner was the latest in the long string of sweet delights I had met at Expo, who I'd mingled with, mixed with, made out with and more. She was a part-time waitress at the club who happened to be an aspiring actress reaching for the same set of stars that I was. Her pale complexion made her look unconventionally beautiful. Her red heels made her nearly as tall as I was. Her verve was just as intense as mine, and just like me, her seeming lust for fun and most things wild oozed from every pore. The vibe between us was strong and instant and was a vibe that led us both back to Herne Hill for a night of unadulterated passion.

The morning after the night before, Eva had been as quiet as a mouse as she left early to get changed for an acting audition, and as I was about to get some orange juice from the fridge before I left for work, I was stopped in my tracks.

'Jason, you're treating my home like a hotel!'

The normally kind Wendy, who was sitting at the kitchen table in wait, had obviously come to the end of her tether and wasn't holding anything back with her words.

'You're swanning in at God knows what time, God knows with

which…floozy!' she said in a volume that made it obvious enough that she was angry.

I didn't know what to say or how to pull out the arrow that Wendy had just shot, the arrow I hadn't seen but should've seen coming. The tired-looking Wendy unleashed her pent-up frustration, which I suspected had been on her chest for a while, when she delivered one last blow.

'I'm really not happy, you know. I'm not sure how much more of this I can endure!'

My life in Herne Hill contrasted greatly with that of my life in Greenwich. The affordable £50 per week rent included water rates, council tax and the opportunity to realise a new frame of mind. But though I saved on utilities, my new mindset needed saving from itself. Newly single and more than ready to mingle in London, I had entered a new and dangerous world of debauchery in which I became a more than curious tourist of firey spirits, recreational drugs and wild sex parties. My wild behaviour had snowballed. The only time I returned to my room in Herne Hill was for some clean clothes or occasional one-night stands.

I hadn't clicked then how much my wantonness had worn on Wendy, and a few days after meeting Eva, I brought home another woman I'd met at a local BDSM fetish Club called TG.

The morning after the one-night stand, I crept downstairs with the generously shaped, PVC catsuit-wearing, ruffled-looking redhead, of whom I'd forgotten her name; we were trying not to wake Wendy. However, Wendy had beat me to the morning. She'd left a note saying that she was feeling at her wits' end about our living situation, and she thought it might be a good time for us to talk. It was apparent what the talk would ultimately lead to.

Not long after we met, Eva, who became more than a casual fling, had come to hear about my Herne Hill woes, and though it seemed pretty rushed, she asked me if I'd like to move in with her. I knew I'd muckied my ticket with Wendy, and I didn't want to impose any more on her kindness, so I packed my big yellow rucksack, left my room and friendship with Wendy behind, and took Eva up on her offer.

Eva's apartment was above a women's boutique clothing shop located in Belgravia, which she shared with three other actors, Jody, Paige and Ryan, who happened to be the barman at Expo.

Belgravia was one of the poshest parts of the capital, with its ostentatious people, boutique shops, trendy cafés, bars and restaurants. It was certainly a change from anywhere I'd lived before.

The apartment and my flatmates were a contrast to the area

outside. The actors were undoubtedly not too house proud, and none of them seemed to be bothered about the 70s-style wood chip wallpaper, the thick lime green carpet, and the avocado bathroom suite. Eva's and my room had a view of the back garden and one single bed. Often, the sounds of chatter and creaky bed springs that bounced from the other actors' rooms would permeate through the paper-thin walls. In reality, living with four actors wasn't as heavenly as it first appeared it would be. When all of us were at home, we were literally crammed together with hardly enough room even to swing a skinny cat, but the rent was cheap at £75 a week, so I couldn't complain.

While flicking through Eva's impressive small collection of books by great authors like Victor Hugo, Franz Kafka and Virginia Woolf, one book jumped out at me; it wasn't George Orwell's *1984*, nor was it Dario Fo's *Accidental Death of an Anarchist*, or Irvine Welsh's *Trainspotting* but it was the *Kama Sutra*.

Apart from being cultivated and well-read, Eva, like me, had an immense appetite for sex, but for me, it was more than sex. It was a mindblowing encounter of two people becoming one. I hadn't explored the positions of the *Kama Sutra* until I met Eva. *The Lotus Blossom* position was new to me, but Eva had convinced me to try it when she finished showering one evening and sat on my lap, naked. The small window of our room was open. Our flatmates were all out. Only the fellow wild foxes would've been able to hear the howls of Eva the vixen. As I sat in position, Eva wrapped her long legs around my back, and it didn't take long before I knew that I'd hit Eva's G-spot.

While Eva went to make a green tea, I dog-eared the corner of page 52 of the *Kama Sutra* in the hope we'd try that new position: *The Snake Trap*, later on. Eva gifted me with what I'd wanted after she saw the page of her book I'd left open. The breeze of the evening cooled my upper body. The intensity was like something I hadn't experienced before. We both felt connected physically and emotionally as we climaxed.

'Ever thought how it would feel to be a woman, Jay?'

'I used to dress up in my mum's clothes when I was about eight years old.'

'Really, how did it make you feel?'

'You're the first person that I told that to. I quite enjoyed it; it was liberating, but walking in heels was near impossible.'

46 MILE HIGH CLUB

'Jay, Jay, Jay, are you awake? You won't believe it, I've got an audition FOR Zena De Wolf.'

'Huh...what time is it?... That's mustard... how did you get that?'

'Mandy, my agent, emailed, explaining that Zena had watched my showreel and loved it; that's all I know.'

'Back of the net...What time is it?'

I had been in the middle of a rare deep sleep and had been woken up at 8:00am with my ear being chewed off by Eva, who was as giddy as a schoolgirl, having just had word from her agent that she'd landed a big audition for Zena De Wolf, one of the world's leading casting directors. The audition was for a lead role in a feature film, *Echoes of the Spotlight*.

Eva spent the many days leading up to the audition with her head buried in the script. Her job serving tables took a back seat to prepare her for this opportunity, which could potentially serve her a different slice of life she had been longing to taste, just like me. The days and nights of rehearsals alone and together whizzed by like a speeding express train, and before we knew it, the big morning arrived. I Googled the symptoms of Gastroenteritis and laid on thick, an act of my own to my manager, who I could tell by her sarky tone didn't believe a word I was saying. But I wanted, or rather I needed to be there for Eva for moral support as we were both living the same clamber for recognition. I knew what it felt like to be in Eva's shoes and to want something so badly that it almost hurt.

'Break a leg...I mean, I hope you nail it...I mean, you will...they need someone...show them that, that someone is you, Eva...show them that you're the solution to their problem!'

Eva hid her body of nerves behind an uncertain smile that didn't know whether it wanted to go north, south, east or west.

'How did it go?' I asked as Eva came out of the building after finishing the audition, which seemed rather quick as far as auditions went.

'Let me get out of this bloody trouser suit...that was a disaster,' Eva snapped; her frustration was apparent and all too familiar.

'You never know what they are looking for...you never know.'

'Not what I gave them...they weren't looking for that! I want to go home!'

On arrival at Belgravia, we decided to join the masses in the café culture trend and grab an overpriced coffee and a piece of carrot cake at a local café. The Aristocafé. Eva had changed out of her audition attire into casual frayed jeans and a vest top, and I was sporting scruffy jeans and an Atari T-shirt. The café, with its leather upholstery and conservative decor, was pretty packed, and the only seats available were next to a highbrow middle-aged couple who were probably waiting for their clothes to come back into fashion. Their cups of tea were placed on floral patterned saucers, and their selection of fancy cupcakes and cucumber sandwiches looked too good to eat as they sat on a silver tray. As the man raised his pinky while drinking his tea, the woman smiled very superciliously while stirring hers. They appeared to be eavesdropping on our every word whilst looking us up and down. A what-are-you-doing-in-this area-type of look. The atmosphere in that corner of the café was off, and feeling uncomfortable, I wondered what ever possessed us to choose this café in the first place.

'Jay, envision a world where wealth and status don't divide. People care for each other and aren't stuck inside their bubbles or in their ivory towers. Picture a place where everyone is equally valued,' Eva's voice rose above the background music of Beethoven's *Moonlight Sonata*, her voice now catching the attention of the nearby earwigging couple.

Eva's intentional but eloquent to-the-manner-born dig appeared to have flown over to the next table and landed in the posh couple's platter of sandwiches like an unrequited spitball. This was met by the disdainful looks from the posh couple, to which I, of course, responded. Displaying manners which looked like I attended a finishing school for chimpanzees, I devoured my turkey salad sandwich like a starved primate who hadn't eaten in days, and then Eva and I both laughed, my mouth full of chewed white bread and turkey and Eva's with mushed falafel ready to swallow.

The prudish couple, less than amused, to put it lightly, moved their chairs back and appeared to be upset at our table manners and Eva's dig. Then, they got up to leave, no longer wanting to share their air space with the uncouth hoi polloi like Eva and I.

'How terribly rude,' said the woman, her voice trailing behind her and her angry-looking husband as they left the café.

'How terribly common we are, darling,' Eva quipped.

The couple were still in earshot as she gave me a high five. Her mind, at least for the time being, seemed to be off her audition woes.

Eva tried to bury the memories of the audition in a place that couldn't hurt her, and life, just like it always had to no matter what, just went on.

In the middle of making a bolognese, Eva answered a call that confirmed what her gut had told her. She hadn't landed the role, and her hopes plopped into the saucepan of boiling salty spaghetti water and fizzled away. I could see the pain in her limpid eyes. The pain in her soul was silent but intense. I felt it for her. I knew how rejection as an actor hurt—BIG TIME.

'I'm so gutted! I honestly feel that I'm not good enough.'

'Eva, I'm feeling you. You are good enough. The fact that you got seen by Zena De Wolf is a huge thing! I can't even get seen for a short film these days, never mind a feature film. All my applications are being rejected.'

'I just want to quit! I want to give in.'

'Come on Eva, if you believe you will achieve...acting, well, acting is the hardest profession in the world, you know, BUT it can be fantastic. You simply cannot give in. I know my words won't compensate for your disappointment, but you've gotta keep going...come on...think about what you'd say to me if I were in the same situation.'

With her tear gates opened, Eva's salty tears that she had held back for the past fortnight monsooned down her cheeks like hard, warm rain falling on a day when you've just hung out the washing, hopelessly hoping for a glimpse of the elusive sun.

'My feet are killing me; let's get a drink,' Eva shouted over Tiësto's *Love Comes Again*, which was blasting out over Expo's speakers.

'Leave the drinks to me, lovers!' Ryan shouted.

During a pause from getting hot and heavy sandwiched between Eva and our flatmate Ryan on the dance floor of Expo one night, Eva, with sweat dripping from her brow after dancing the night away, casually asked if I would accompany her on a trip to see her mum. It'd been three months since I'd met Eva, but she had a way of convincing me to do things. So I agreed. The plan was to go to have fun in Thun.

We were met at Zurich Airport by a glamorous divorcee whose English was just as flawless as her naturally beautiful face, which looked like it belonged on the cover of a celebrity magazine. She was Lydia Baumgartner, Eva's mother, who greeted us with a hug at the arrival gates of Zurich Airport Switzerland and then led us toward the car park outside in the rain.

'*Fröit mi*, nice to meet you, Jason; Eva's told me all about you.'

'*Fröit mi*, I hope it was just the good bits,' I joked.

'Eva, have you been drinking again? Take off those sunglasses...dark circles...Hmm. I knew it! How many times have I told you that drinking is bad for your skin? She never listens to me, Jason...does she ever listen to you?'

As I loaded mine and Eva's luggage into Lydia's Range Rover boot, I made sure I kept my sunglasses on because, to be honest, my circles were much darker than Eva's.

We took the ninety-minute journey and arrived at Lydia's home, in Eva's birth town of Lerchenfeld. Its quaint, pretty, fairytale-like thatched-roof houses looked like they belonged in a Terrence Malick movie. The town was carpeted in grass and flowers, and having come from the relative hustle and bustle of Zurich airport; we felt the difference in the atmosphere as soon as we got out of the car. We could've literally held the peace and quiet in our hands. If I could've bottled it, I could've made millions. I could've sworn that I heard a butterfly take off.

'Eva, show Jason to your room so you can put your bags down and I'll make us something to eat. I guess it's been a while since you've eaten some proper food. You're looking so thin, Eva.'

After settling in, we joined Lydia in the living room, which had more books on the bookshelf than in a library. Eva and I sat on the floral upholstered sofa, which matched Lydia's classy style. Lydia came from the kitchen and put down some plates of delicious-looking *fondue* and pieces of crusty *baguette* on the coffee table.

While taking polite bites of the crusty, crispy bread, catching the crumbs in my hands, Lydia sat beside me and invited me to enter her world of past memories that she kept in a maroon leather photo album. I continued to tuck into the warm *fondue* as Lydia flicked through the Baumgartner family memories of weddings, days out and birthdays and described some of their cherished memories. I nearly choked on my *baguette* in shock when she turned a page, and I saw photos of Lydia topless, sporting a shoestring thong on a beach! I quickly took a serviette, placed it on my lap and tried to think about baked beans to avoid becoming aroused looking at pictures of the beautiful, shapely, glamorous mother of the woman I was sleeping with. As I brushed away the crumbs that had fallen from the *baguette,* Lydia and Eva casually brushed the photos off, just like it was a simple photo in a museum or something. It was bizarre.

Eva had become unusually quiet during the last few days of our trip, and I wasn't sure why. Our flight back from Zurich to London was a different story altogether. It was a midweek early morning flight. Neither Eva nor I were morning people, and that particular morning, we had to get up at around 4:00am to get to the airport and catch our Gatwick flight on time. I needed coffee to wake me up; however, Eva had other plans for how to do this, and it wasn't coffee.

The overhead signs indicated we could remove our seatbelts. Eva removed hers, reached across my body to remove mine, and firmly dragged her hand across my thigh before cupping my groin with her slender hand.

'Meet me in the toilet in two minutes,' she whispered before she got up, squeezed past me and made her way to the aeroplane loo.

It was an early morning midweek flight, so the plane was barely half full. I waited until the hostess passed with her refreshment trolley. When the coast was clear, I walked to the loo, both nervous and excited.

I knocked on the door and quietly called out Eva's name. After a few seconds, the lock turned and opened slightly to reveal Eva in her sheer crotchless panties; her skirt was hitched up to her waist and she was smiling seductively. I turned and looked down the aisle, and a smartly dressed middle-aged guy was walking towards my direction. I knew this had to be quick.

I stepped into the toilet and locked the door behind me. Eva wasn't phased when I told her about the guy walking our way, as she unbuckled my jeans, unzipped me and continued kissing me. I sat on the toilet seat while she boarded speedily, but we had to be quiet. And after fumbling for a minute, we were riding high. Relishing the risk and pleasure. We both climaxed after a few minutes. I buckled up, as she pulled her skirt back down.

When the flight landed, Eva squeezed my hand tightly and looked at me nervously.

'You know, Jason, I think we have a few things to talk about when we get back home...'

47 BRIDGE OVER TROUBLED WATERS

'Jay, I've got something important to tell you,' Eva said hesitantly.

The 170 bus back to Belgravia was driving over the Prince Albert Bridge and crossing over the River Thames. I'd managed to snag the seat that'd just become free next to Eva and was now feeling slightly uneasy about the unusual seriousness in Eva's voice. My mind was racing a million miles a minute. Eva put her hands on mine, starting to stroke them as if this would offer me some kind of comfort. I pulled my hand away and pretended to scratch my chin without making my agitation appear obvious. I was a spontaneous and off-the-cuff kind of person, but weirdly, I didn't like surprises being sprung on me.

I got into the acting mode.

'What's up? Is everything okay?'

My mouth managed to deliver snappy words that came out in a calm contrast to Eva's.

'It's just that, um, and um,' Eva's words stumbled, her voice shook.

'Say it will you! Just say it! Let's cut to the chase and get real, shall we? We need a dose of straight talk here!' I snapped, now in an irritated tone that Eva hadn't known me long enough to feel the brunt of yet. I was aggravated at Eva, who appeared to be stretching out the jist of this news she had for me.

Though my tone surprised her, it seemed to force the words that she'd been holding back out of her mouth.

'I've been offered a part in a TV show in Canada, *Arctic Whispers*. My agent, Mandy, called me out of the blue whilst we were in Thun...I didn't want to spoil our trip...so I didn't mention it...I had worked with the director Olivia Chang before... It's a big opportunity...and I want to take it...I mean, what do you think? It's a big deal...but...'

'...You should've told me, you know...but yeah...that's great Eva... that's great...so you're going to take it then...Canada?...Wow...that is big news...big move...big change...yeah...a year did you say...?'

My stumped words were flying out of my mouth, but they were lost.

Eva nodded. Her words didn't have to say how much she didn't want to hurt me; her ocean-blue eyes said it all.

'But, um...you can come...but um...I know that you need to stay here...I mean, you have the Brook Uni Drama course you applied for starting soon...that would be good for you...and...um...you have that new NYFA film... what's it called *Broken*, um..' Eva, too, was finding it tough to articulate.

She was looking down now and scratching away the dry white stain on her skirt. It was obvious she wanted me to pass her some sort of lifeline.

Eva's news was both as much relief as it was a shock, considering the vignettes of different possibilities that'd just been running through my mind. Although for a split second, I contemplated joining her in Canada, I knew jumping into deep water with another woman after Charlotte was not going to be a good idea and to be honest, I wasn't entirely over, licking my wounds over that drama.

'Jay?' Whispered Eva softly as she netted my wandering thoughts and reeled them back to where we sat. She tried to find comfort in my arm as she moved closer to me to nestle herself in a hug I hadn't invited her to.

I sighed, a sigh that I wished I could've breathed back in as I didn't want to give away my disappointment. I ran my hand through my hair and placed my elbow on the backrest of the seat. I wasn't yet willing to let her have my arm and my hug to provide her with the reassurance that she wanted.

48 BROKEN

"Shhhhhh...any sound and I will cut you...Do you understand?"

She nodded her head. I removed my hand slowly from her mouth.

"Who else is in the house?"

"No one!"

Suddenly, someone rang the doorbell.

"Who's that?"

"I don't know!"

"I don't want you to invite anyone in...Do you understand?... Is that clear? IS THAT FUCKING CLEAR?"

Anubhav Bhasin, the director, called. 'CUT...I Love! Love! Loved it! You absolutely smashed that scene, Jason! Well done. Just want to check...You're free to do your remaining 'Harry' scenes tomorrow, right?'

I was on the film set of my fourth NYFA short film, *Broken*. I had just been filming some scenes playing a twisted, unhinged and vulnerable character, Harry.

I had thrown myself into acting with gusto and brushed the chipped shards of my Ego and smaller shards of my heart underneath the rug of my life. They were tucked and hidden away with the rest of the broken memories that I just wanted to forget about.

My heart yearned but was only slightly broken, partly because it was the end of a chapter in my and Eva's relationship, but more so because she was entering a chapter of her big-screen acting career, a place where I longed to be myself.

Eva's departure had coincided with the landlord's decision not to renew the tenancy. There was a lot of money to be made from selling properties in Belgravia at that time. He had an unexpected opportunity that had arisen, to move to Japan, so he decided to give our flatmates Jody, Paige, and Ryan only four weeks' notice. As I sat at the kitchen table circling potential properties which, in my budget, were as appealing as my cold bowl of porridge. My half-dressed housemate Ryan came into the kitchen.

'Fancy a clubber's breakfast, Jay?'

'Huh, what's that?'

'Well, basically, it's whisky, a cup of coffee and a cigarette.'

'I'll pass.'

'On second thoughts, me too!' he replied as he opened the fridge to look at what he could use for an edible fry-up instead.

'What are you looking at anyway, Baby?... Nah, nah...put that away.'

Ryan was referring to a property mag I'd been fingering through.

'You're coming to live with me, Baby! Sausage?'

Well, of course, it was rude to say no to the striking bartender who oozed such a sense of cool that he could have peed ice cubes. His tattoo on his torso looked like a Botticelli canvas, and the tattoo on his upper thigh stamped his whole ethos: Let the good times roll.

About a month after having the wind kicked out of my sails, and about a month of letting the new good times roll with Ryan, I took Ryan up on his offer when the tenancy to the Belgravia apartment ended. He had managed to bag a self-contained flat above Expo nightclub in Soho; the rent, at £100 a week, was certainly a bargain for central London. I packed my big yellow rucksack and was on the move again to join him and live it up on Greek Street in the heart of Soho. The two-bedroom, first-floor flat came with a shower that had a wild mind of its own and was so powerful it nearly took off our epidermis, dermis and hypodermis each time Ryan and I used it.

My new flatmate and partner in crime and self-confessed wild boy, Ryan Caradog Santiago, was as charming as he was striking. He was full of zing; he was the type of person who shared his smile with the world with his piercing eyes. Ryan, too, was a jobbing actor who had natural movie star looks, which led him easily to the point he was at in his 25-year-old life. His commitment to a career in acting was juggled with his other part-time pursuits: modelling underwear, whipping up snazzy cocktails as Expo's flair bartender and being the wildest party animal I'd ever known.

The trendy Expo, where Ryan worked, had an air of pretentiousness about it. Its high-earning clientele, who leant up against the exposed red brickwork and hobnobbed in their elite groups of friends in the leather cubicles, sometimes made me feel out of place. Still, the free drinks on tap from Ryan were the highlight of why I continued to venture downstairs from our flat on most nights. The VIP lounge was often filled with posh, totty and suited businessmen donning their expensive designer gear and sipping on their pricey cocktails and chilled champagne.

Ryan and I would often try out our cheesy and smooth chat-up lines in the bar and often made the most of having the luxury of an after-party pad being just a staircase away. Chat-up lines were not the only lines we'd do. We'd be lifted right out of this world with the help of our friend Charlie, which we'd take in various ways and forms until we hit Earth with a bump in the reality of the mornings.

The countless amounts of gatherings we had while Expo and most of London slept would more often than not evolve into wilder parties, which usually meant more drinking and more debauchery.

Ryan was holding a birthday bash at Expo. It was a film character costume party. So naturally, I decided to channel my inner gangster and rock up as Tony Montano from *Scarface*.

I hit the dance floor, dressed in a slick pinstripe suit, complete with makeup and a gnarly scar on my cheek, and a little secret stashed away in my pocket: a big bag of flour. I was just waiting to cause some mischief with my little friend.

As the night unfolded like a scene from a blockbuster, the dance floor was alive with characters straight out of Hollywood. Ryan was *Superman*, tearing up the dance floor to Kylie Minogue's *Can't Get You Out of My Head*. His date, Cathy, was rocking the *Wonder Woman* vibe like nobody's business.

But amidst all the glitz and glamour, I found myself striking up a conversation with a flaming redhead, Nuala, who was killing it as Vivian Ward from *Pretty Woman*. Sparks were flying, laughter was contagious, and before I knew it, we were all cosied up at a table in the corner of Expo.

After having a skinful, I whipped out the *pièce de résistance*, the bag of flour. I went to town, creating a mountainous line on the table.

'Jay, have you lost your mind?' Ryan said in disbelief, thinking I'd gone off the deep end.

Undeterred, I rolled up a £20 note, leaned in, and went for it—snorting flour like it was going out of style. The table erupted in laughter as I battled a fierce sneezing fit, flour coating everything in sight.

In the early hours, we went back to our flat accompanied by Cathy and Nuala, and about a couple of hours or so into us drinking and drinking some more champagne on Ryan's double bed, the two women were getting affectionately acquainted.

'Want some, honey?' Asked Nuala, passing me a small packet of white powder. I joined her and Cathy, who'd invited me to snort Charlie off their voluptuous breasts and devour the champagne out of their velvet undergrounds.

'Eat me like you stole me!' Nuala demanded as Ryan joined us.

The exotic and unfamiliar sights of London made my life immensely thrilling. I experienced, met and did things I'd never done before and rode the rollercoaster of excess and sexcapades. I didn't want the ride to end. I was excessively drinking, excessively taking drugs, and excessively fucking my way through London.

49 FRENCH CONNECTION

'You simply must recognise this.'

'Recognise what *Monsieur?*' The sultry *mademoiselle* replied with a noticeable French accent.

'The chemical reaction we have between us.'

I bubbled, excited at her fire.

'But I don't even know you, *Monsieur.*'

'But...'

'...Sorry, *Monsieur,* I'm not interested. I'm married.'

As I stood amongst the crowd at Brook Uni's busy Student Union Bar, my attention was drawn to a diamond standing out amongst the rough.

Although things were not going as planned, I didn't give up. I delivered my *pièce de résistance* over the Pussycat Dolls tune *Don't Cha*, which was pumping out of the speakers.

'This is cosmic. This is an enchantment. This is serendipity.'

Seeming not to be at all impressed with my words, her glare as she looked me up and down made me feel two feet tall.

'Maybe take your hocus pocus and make yourself disappear!' She snapped as she turned her head away, and the waft of her strong perfume slapped me hard in the face. I attempted some reverse psychology.

'I may not always be single.'

'Tragedy!... As anyone ever told you, that you belong on a lead.'

Ouch! I was gutted that I was about to end the night, not even knowing the French siren's name. It took all of two minutes from when I walked away, trying to salvage the smithereens of my Ego that the sharp-tongued woman had kindly smashed, when I felt a tap on my shoulder. I turned around, and the wicked-witted beauty smiled and held her bare hand in the air while wiggling her ringless wedding ring finger. She introduced herself as Nathalie Dubois.

'I'll have a red wine, and once you've got that, *Monsieur,* come and join me over there.'

I delivered what she had ordered, and this, unknown to me at the time, was to be the theme of our flaming love affair.

Nathalie Dubois, the supercilious French femme fatale firecracker, was an administrative assistant in the acting department at Brook University, London—the very same university where I was taking a one-year drama course, for which I had successfully auditioned and been accepted.

I had been juggling studying, trying to save the world through fundraising, and trying to carve a path for my acting career. My tireless efforts applying for different acting gigs did result in some, albeit a few, auditions, including one for a leading role in an Edinburgh-based feature film, *Castle Kings*, an audition in which I truly believed I'd done my best to blow the producers away.

Come to my place tonight! Don't forget the red wine.
Nathalie xxx.

This was the sixth text of the morning from the French firecracker, but its contents intrigued me. So, after finishing work, I did as she asked.

In the hip Shoreditch area of London, Nathalie buzzed me into the *chichi* apartment she owned, an apartment that'd been gifted to her by one of her former rich and older lovers.

'Take off your shoes, Jason, and come here...I have a gift for you.'

Nathalie was sitting on her *chaise lounge,* dressed in black slinky lingerie; I thought I knew what she was suggesting. She looked at the bottle I had in my hand.

'*Côtes du Rhône?* Hmm, not bad. I guess it will have to do for now!'

My budget did not extend to the pricier wines of *Cabernet Sauvignon* that she may have been expecting, so I let her comment slide over my head as it was superseded by another:

'Come, come, Monsieur Jason, bring the wine.'

Beckoning me with her index finger to join her in the bedroom, where she had now walked to. I, of course, followed her lead. On her bedside table was a red gift-wrapped envelope with my name on it. She tapped the space next to her for me to join her. I could resist anything but temptation, so I dutifully obeyed.

'Come here, come closer, *Monsieur* Jason,' she whispered as she grabbed the back of my neck and started wildly kissing me. Her *Îles flottantes* peeped out excitedly through her see-through bra and vied for me to taste them. Nathalie took total control, and we ended up on the floor on her Persian rug. As I lay with my back on the floor, excited by the animalistic passion of the French beauty working her way down my body, she ordered me to remove my boxer shorts, but as I did she must've got a whiff of *le pipi!*

'*Excusez-moi*, can you go and wash first. Then come back. Oh, and don't use the towels on display, Jason!'

Nathalie's bathroom had more towels dotted around it than Copacabana Beach. She seemed to have towels for every possible use: hands, feet, face, and hair. I dried myself on the robe hanging on the back of the door and returned to the siren.

Washed and ready to go, I manoeuvred my way on top of her and slid inside her as she demanded.

'Yes *Monsieur* Jason,...grab me... Beast...ah, *oui, oui, oui*...right there...*oui...Baise-moi, Baise-moi plus fort,* harder, scratch me Beast...' Nathalie screamed loudly. As we approached the finish line of our athletics, Nathalie said.

'Don't stain my Persian, Jason!'

When the siren went to the bathroom to freshen up, I reached over to the envelope on the table. Even though I wasn't entirely sure what I was expecting, it appeared that I completely got the wrong end of the stick. When I opened the envelope, I couldn't believe my eyes. It was a printout of an email thread between my drama course tutors, Miss Baxter and Mrs Douglas, and James McLeod, the producer of *Castle Kings*. James was enquiring about my experience and ability, and even though the message had notes of politeness, the undertones suggested that the reference about me given by my tutors to the producer wasn't as glowing as I would have liked. Nathalie came back to the room and saw me reading the printout.

'Oh, you've seen it. I never told you that you could open it, *Monsieur* Jason, you bad boy.'

I was livid at what I had read and, of course, appreciated that Nathalie stuck her neck out for me. I knew that I couldn't challenge my tutors, but I was really pissed off that they had potentially dampened my chances for a lead role in the feature film. Needless to say, that also completely put a damp squib on any more passion that evening, which Nathalie, of course, wasn't happy about.

50 GANGSTER RAP

Whoa, we're halfway there, living on a prayer, as Bon Jovi would say. Cheers for sticking with me up to this point, reader. Now that I have discovered acting, you might think that the following chapters would see me climb smoothly to the top, but as my life goes, this wasn't really the case!

There are more muck ups and fuck ups, and ironically, I'm back to being told what to do by who I despised most in childhood: teachers! I hope you can follow my rocky road to the end (not the end, end, but you know what I mean!).

'Less is more, Jason; remember, acting is also reacting,' explained Mrs Douglas.

The old earthy-smelling George Peele Theatre, Oval South London, set the scene for our weekly evening rehearsals. Miss Baxter, a very well-spoken woman in her late 30s, and Mrs Douglas, who was approaching the autumn of her years, were the main protagonists, otherwise known as my tutors. In the whole scale of things, I appeared to adopt the role that I'd often been typecast as in my life, the villain or the difficult one, with both of my tutors not backwards in being forwards about their dislike of MY preferred style of raw, gritty, improvisation and "Method Acting" on stage, which they felt was suited more in film than the evening rehearsals at the George Peele Theatre, but as always the game was on, by me learning and pretending to abide by their rules but really bending and breaking them without them realising.

We were in our sixth week and put into small groups. Each group had to create a 15-minute improvised scenario of our choice. In front of the long, red, worn cotton curtains, each group performed on the large wooden stage whilst the rest of the class watched on as they sat in the rows of old chairs until it was their turn. Our cadre, Timothy, Lance, Marie and I, created a gangster scenario, and of course, I put myself forward for one of the two villains. The first two groups performed their pieces, and Miss Baxter and Mrs Douglas fed back.

Now, it was my group's turn. The stage was bare, apart from two wooden chairs. We didn't have any props, so it was all about imagination. Timothy was playing a shop owner, and Marie was his assistant and wife. Lance Paterson and I were the villains due to rob the make-believe shop. Five minutes into the improvisation, Lance and I entered the stage, and Lance formed a gun shape with his fingers and demanded that the shocked shop owners empty their tills. I remained silent. I just cased the shop and looked out the window to see if any police were coming. The flat and trite scene seemed to last an eternity and needed some gusto. So, after Timothy refused to pay Lance as he was being held up at finger-point, I gave the scene the gusto it needed.

I walked menacingly across the stage. I tied Timothy and Marie to their chairs with curtain rope, then started lightly pushing Timothy on his shoulder.

'I'm not going to pay you anything.'

Timothy did not back down nor offer to pay up.

Then I (or rather I should say my character) lost it!

'Give us the bloody money, NOOOOOOWWWWWW!!!'

My dander had built up and my eyes rolled with anger. The thought of my tutors putting the *kibosh* on the *Castle Kings* leading role motivated me to prove to those very same tutors what I was made of!

I grabbed the back of Marie's chair and brought it from four legs to two. I then left Marie, Timothy, Lance and the whole class gobsmacked when I delivered my improvised line with a mephistophelean smile.

'Pay us NOW, you sonofabitch. You have one minute to cough up the cash before we fuck your scrubber wife.'

Timothy and Marie looked befuddled, Lance was speechless and the atmosphere had changed somewhat in the theatre as soon as those words jumped out of my mouth and exposed themselves on the stage. It was as if a bull with a Mohican had rampaged through the old theatre, leaving its onlookers dumbstruck. I loved the fact that I'd put the cat amongst the pigeons, and now all the attention was on me, but I hadn't finished yet. Still staying in character and still in a furious rage, I marched over to Timothy and started strangling him, so much so that he fell off his chair onto the floor and hung on for dear life to the curtain, which broke his fall on the way down. I then climbed on top of him, and like a raged mafia mobster, I made my demand. 'Hand over the fucking money, or we will kill you both.'

I, myself, was rather proud of my convincing performance. Judging by the fear in Timothy's eyes and the whiteness of his face whilst my hands were around his neck, I was doing a good job of being believable, so I continued. However, Miss Baxter and Mrs Douglas seemed to take umbrage, and they lampooned me, ordering me to STOP! So, I stopped acting. I said nothing.

I had to wait until the next group had finished performing their improvised scene depicting the serenity of a family picnic, while the dam in my mind felt ready to crash and flood with rage, and until the curmudgeon (Mrs Douglas) was ready to give me a piece of her mind.

'We thought you were going to kill poor Timothy!' And we didn't appreciate your foul language either!'

I called Timothy that same evening to see how he was, but he ignored my call.

51 NO CIGAR

'Try to imagine walking across that street and being hit by a car. Every time after that, when you cross that street, you're bound to be careful. It's not just the physical scar you'd be carrying from that incident; it's the mental one too. You're scarred for life. Now imagine waking up to the thought of seeing your friends dead at your side.'

I'd been preparing for our final showcase performance of a WWII play, Arthur Miller's *All My Sons,* when on the streets of Shoreditch, my path crossed with the path of a WWII veteran, Tommy Fetterman.

'I was a sniper and had killed many of my enemies. I felt no hate for them, you know, but at the time, during battle, it was either them or me. There were no winners in war...'

Tommy, who was a wheelchair user, had been fundraising for war veterans when I met him. He had been very open to talking to me when I introduced myself as an actor. He allowed me to step into the open door of his former world when I told him about wanting to gain insight into his experience as a soldier.

'In many soldiers' minds, the war is still happening. Those scars stay with us forever. Like wounds that just refuse to heal completely.'

I was due to perform *All My Sons* in a small, off-the-West End theatre, The Actor's Place, which held fringe plays throughout the year. I immersed myself in the character, studying his traits, dressing, and living as much as I could as if I were him.

My character was the lead role, Joe Keller, a crooked company boss. There was a 30-year difference between Keller's character and myself, so I added these years to my physical appearance by growing a thick trim beard and purchased a few items of clothing from yesteryear: a 50p trilby hat from a charity shop and a £5 white linen suit that I had found at a car boot sale. Keller was also a cigar smoker, so to enable me to feel more like my cigar-smoking character, I went to purchase a cigar at a small tobacco store near Waterloo Station. I wasn't a smoker myself, after being turned off of tobacco for life when, at the age of eight, I tried my Nana's filterless Woodbine cigarettes and almost choked to death. What I hadn't realised before buying the cigar was their hefty price tags—£50 or more for one decent cigar; holy smokes! I rehearsed and rehearsed with my pricey unlit cigar at home, in class and at work and made sure I didn't lose it as I didn't want to have to fork out £50 for another one.

The opening night at The Actor's Place was in front of an audience of around 200 people. Fellow actors had invited mainly family and friends, and the performance was also open to the general public. I didn't invite anyone.

The stage felt like one of the main West End theatres to me, with its heavy red velvet curtains draping down and framing the set, which had been designed skillfully with old furniture and an old record player on a carved oak sideboard. The set captured the zeitgeist of the 1940s. I felt nervous, but these nerves soon turned into adrenaline as the curtains went back and the theatre lights beamed down on me.

The play was going smoothly, and the actors were excelling. The audience's reaction concreted this. I had embraced Tommy Fetterman's powerful and painful words and tried to convey this emotion in my performance of Keller. Then, it was time for the scene where I had planned to use my cigar. I took out the cigar from the top pocket of my linen suit. Cool and calm, I placed it in my mouth and thought my next unexpected move would add even more authenticity to my character. I took out a box of matches from my top pocket, and while doing this, I felt the intensity of the moment in the silence of the audience. This was my moment to shine. I thought that I was going to blow my tutors away with this added touch because they weren't expecting me to do it. This was my *pièce de résistance*. Lance was playing the role of George Keever, Joe Keller's old neighbour.

"No, he's not well, Joe," explained George.

This was my cigar cue.

"It's not his heart again, is it?" (As Joe) I asked with the cigar clenched between my teeth.

"It's everything, Joe. It's his soul," George responded.

As I lit the cigar. My focus was on how to hold the cigar correctly between my fingers. What I didn't think about was the fact that I didn't have a clue about how to smoke a cigar. I never knew you shouldn't inhale cigar smoke. I remember trying to deliver my next line.

'....Ahem...Ahem...Ahhhheeeemmmmm.'

These weren't my actual intended lines; they were the lines that came out in response to the start of a dizzy rush and feeling like I was going to faint. Then, I fell to the stage floor, but again, this wasn't in the stage directions. It was because I INHALED and started to CHOKE. I rolled around, coughing on the stage floor in a heap. The audience wasn't aware that this wasn't part of the performance. As an actor on stage, no matter what happens, you have to carry on regardless and continue seamlessly. If any hiccups occur, you have to pretend it's part of the performance. So that's what I did. After a minute or so, I got up off the stage floor and ran my finger on the underside of my trilby brim, and I continued to perform to try to make it look seamless. However, out of the corner of my eye, I could see that my cigar wasn't the only thing fuming that night. Miss Baxter and Mrs Douglas were, too. *Oh fuck*, I was going to catch hell for this.

'Have you taken leave of your senses? You could've set off the fire alarms and wrecked the whole night for everyone else. Did you not think about that?'

I said nothing.

Me as Joe Keller minus the cigar.

52 HOLY GRAIL

'You know who you remind me of? James Dean, you have that, you know...living-on-the-edge...type of guy thing going on. Although he looked cooler than you when he was smoking,' Lance quipped one evening over beers at his mancave in Brixton.

He was referring to my cigar stage disaster and rebellious attitude that he had grown to know.

'You know Jay, like you, he gave some of his drama teachers hell! It's in his biography...Rumours had it he was bisexual. You and James Dean had a lot in common, don't you think?'

'There's only one way of finding that out!'

'What? How?'

'By turning the lights off and coming right here, my lovely.'

'Leave off!'

'Bloody hell, you have more Cow Pies than *Desperate Dan*!' I commented whilst pulling out two more cold Heineken's from the stack of reduced pies from Lance's fridge.

Lance Paterson was like me in many ways; we had become close friends following the drama course we embarked on together; often, our times and scrapes we got in were dramas in their own right. He had a similar insatiable desire to follow his dream to tread the boards. This love for the bright lights set him apart from people in his small hometown of Warminster in rural Wiltshire.

Lance's dad, Cedrick Paterson, was a vicar who disliked the frivolity of acting. He had wanted Lance to follow his religious steps, but Lance dropped out of theology lessons and turned his back on his religious studies to pursue his dream of becoming an actor in London.

'Lance, have you not heard of recycling? I thought my place was messy, but it looks like your place hasn't been cleaned this decade... it's like a scene from *Withnail and I*.'

Lance's place had the style of a movie cinema that had been deserted during some sort of mass emergency. It had an 80s home cinema projector, a big screen and multiple Tarantino movie posters keeping the living room wall up. The floor seemed to double as a landfill for half-eaten pizza, sweet wrappers, empty popcorn and McDonald's packaging, which were all strewn across the floor.

'Oh yeah, what happened on that date with Marie?'

'... She's not called me back since then...that was Valentine's night...yeah, she's not called or texted in about a fortnight...I really don't understand women...oh, but I did find out one thing, though.'

'What's that Lance?'

'She's still pissed at you for the crazy improv we did with Timothy, you know.'

'I thought that was water under the bridge?'

'Maybe your bridge, Jay, but not hers.'

'Anyway...Valentine's night...I didn't know you were a romantic, Lance...where did you end up taking her?'

'Burger King...'

'Burger King?'

'Yeah, for a hamburger...'

'...And you can't understand women...'

Lance walked towards his chest of drawers and handed me an A4 notepad and a Bic.

'Do you want me to write out your week's shopping list, Lance?'

Ignoring me, he opened his fifth can of Heineken and said.

'Jay, how about me and you write a script together?...imagine what we could come up with, with our talent?'

'A script? What kind of script?'

'You know, a film script.'

'I know what a script is, dingbat! I mean, what kind of genre? Looking to the ceiling won't give you inspiration!'

'Hmmmm...no idea yet.'

'Lance, I'm not Syd Field; you know, it takes weeks, months or even years to write something half-decent and not crap like you sometimes see nowadays...Hey...I've got a good title, though!'

'What's that?'

'*Talented But Crap!*'

Lance's thoughts were still away with the ceiling fairies until a text interrupted them. His expression looked as if he'd just received a meat pie in the face from a gnome with the hump.

'Get my broom quick...it's my dad, it's my dad...he's going to be here in thirty minutes!'

'What about the script?' I joked, knocking over the table as I got up.

Lance continued to get his knickers in even more of a twist rushing about like a blue-arse fly with the runs.

'And where's your broom, Lance?'

'Ermmmm...that's a point...where's my broom?...do I have one?...shit...no...I don't even have one...Dad was supposed to be here tomorrow...I was helping him organise a charity event...but he's coming like, NOW!'

'Lance, is your dad okay with semi-nudes?'

'What? What are you talking about?'

Unintentionally, I'd added to Lance's panic by pointing to a *From Dusk Till Dawn* movie poster featuring a scantily dressed Salma Hayek. Blinded by his infatuation with the Mexican movie Goddess, Lance blurted out. 'Dad may be a vicar, but he's not a fuddy-duddy.'

After a cleaning blitz of his flat, Lance, who was standing on a stool removing his Salma Hayek movie poster, raised his index finger towards me.

'Of course! YOU, you can do it, Jay!'

'Do what?'

'YOU have a talent; YOU'RE comfortable in front of people. You have that devil-may-care attitude! Blimey, why didn't I think about you all along...YOU'RE a funny guy, Jay.'

Lance literally sang his words with great enthusiasm, but I still didn't appear to be on the same song sheet as him.

'Lance, mate, you're talking like a riddle...I didn't think you drank that much! Are you pissed? What are you going on about, huh?'

'Well, uh, Dad needs a stand-up comedian, er, the one that was booked for the charity event. I sent you an invite, remember? Anyway, the comedian dropped out at the last minute; his wife texted to say he had the man flu.'

Lance handed me the unexpected plea along with a Brillo Pad he'd picked up from the sink.

'Jay, do you mind wiping that stain you made on the coffee table?' Before he went on any further, I replied, inspecting the mark in question.

'My stain? That's not mine Lance. You're having a laugh. That looks like it was made when dinosaurs were having a picnic on it...anyway, about the event... I'd love to help, but I'm an actor...not a stand-up comedian.'

53 CHEESED OFF

I didn't have a repertoire of jokes. I didn't have any comedy material, and I truly didn't have a *Scooby Doo*. What I knew about stand-up comedy you could fit in a pistachio shell. But obviously, I knew I could improvise. So, with a *dilettante* approach, I agreed to do the event.

The Cheesed Off event was a vegan night, and the funds raised that evening would go towards helping children living on the streets of India. The venue was a small, humble pub in Brixton, The Imperial Inn. Often used as a venue to host karaoke events or occasional open-mic nights, the tiny stage was more like a large box. It would be easy for anyone to take a few steps in one direction and fall flat on their face.

As it was last minute, I arrived at the venue without props. I was met by the hosts, Lance and his vicar dad, Cedrick Paterson. I asked the eternally grateful Lance if he could go to the supermarket to buy me some props.

'Some Rustlers cheeseburgers, plenty of tomatoes, and paper plates.'

'Some Rustlers cheeseburgers? But it's a vegan night! Vegans don't eat cheeseburgers, Jay.'

'I was testing my comedy! Don't you see? My comedy is lost on you, Lance! Anyway, forget about the cheeseburgers, but can you get me the other things?'

While Lance headed to the supermarket, I stood next to Cedrick Paterson, who had his jumper tied around his shoulders 80s style, just like you see older men doing while on holiday in the Mediterranean. He was a man of few words, but when he did speak, they were all long academic ones, the ones that you'd need a thesaurus to find the meaning of.

'Jason, it was frightfully good of you to do the comedy event. It will be awfully challenging to perform over the yakety-yak. Notwithstanding your convivial wit, you will prevail. I want to express my anticipation for an evening of unparalleled lexical finesse and intellectual merriment. Try not to get too pickled.'

After two minutes of nodding my head and downing my second whisky, I made my escape to the toilet, genuinely busting for a pee. I looked at the floor under the urinal, SHIT! My long wet shoelace was dangling in a puddle of stagnant piss. I had to remove the soggy and wet, piss-smelling lace from my Puma trainers.

As I prepared on stage, I tried to plan ahead to ensure that I would not trip up and tried to dig into the depths of past memories for some old jokes and jibes that I knew had had people I knew in hysterics. People were arriving at the venue, and before I knew it, the pub was packed. The audience was made up of around fifty new-aged bohemian-looking 20-somethings. I was now settled, as were my nerves, thanks to the further three shots of whisky I had just downed. Lance returned from the supermarket just in time to introduce me.

'Good Evening, Ladies and Gentlemen. We appreciate you coming, and I'm certain you will be entertained by the super-talented comedian Jason Croot.'

The chattering crowd didn't applaud.

Not only did Lance build me up, but he told them I was a comedian, great! Now I was cacking my pants. I instructed Lance to hand out the plates with the rusticly carved tomatoes and cheddar cheese that looked just as random as I felt standing there, and then I explained why.

'Hello, guys; in case you're wondering why you've been given cheese and tomatoes, well, for two reasons. The reason for the cheddar is that I know you won't eat the cheese because you're vegans, so I can probably eat it all myself later...and you've got the tomatoes because knowing my fucking comedy is going to be so bad, you can chuck them at me. But can I ask you to miss my head, please, but my chest is fair game...You're saving your applause for later, I see.'

As the evening went on, my improvised jokes dried up like a puddle in July, and they continued to be met with the brick wall of unamused guests.

'Why did the tomato turn red?...because it saw the salad dressing!.. What did the vegan say when they broke up with their plant-based partner?...lettuce, beet friends...'

Ba-dum ching! NOT!

They say that comedy is pain, and it seemed I was proving that theory right for both the audience and me. I was well aware that I was no Steve Coogan, no Richard Pryor or no Robin Williams, and let me tell you, this was a bloody tough crowd.

Only one lone lady in the audience found my jokes amusing, but I think she'd drunk more than I had that night. No smiles. No laughter. No round of applause. *Coup de grâce.* I died out there.

54 MEASURE FOR MEASURE

'Your jokes seemed as popular around here as an infected wisdom tooth!'

This comment from a pint-sized lady standing at the bar was served to me with a smile, so I tried my luck.

'Why, thank you. Are you a calendar?'

'A calendar...? Wait...what?'

The pint-sized lady asked, trying to figure out what I meant.

'Because you've got a date with me written all over you.'

'Sorry...tomorrow I'm washing my hair...next week I'm washing my hair and wait...the week after that I may be free...hold on...no, I'm not...I'm actually...knitting some leg warmers for a giraffe!!!'

The pint-sized lady was Miranda, the one and only person in the Cheesed Off audience who actually laughed at my jokes.

After the comedy gig, Miranda, a comedian herself, and I got talking at the bar. I had initially tried to chat her up, but this resulted in me falling as flat on my face as I did in my comedy act.

Miranda Kim-Mendoza was a London-born bohemian; she wore tousled-looking curly locks and was admirably imperfect. Though she wasn't necessarily traditionally beautiful, there was something deeper and more beautiful about her being. She went on to tell me that she was married to a prominent casting director, Lucy Kim, and they lived with Miranda's son, Brandon, whom she had when she was just 18.

'So, Jay, what's your day job? How do you make a living and all that?'

'Oh, I don't work for a living; I'm not actually a comedian, I'm an actor, allegedly.'

'An actor? You fooled me anyway! You seemed like you'd been

doing stand-up for years!'

An instant connection sparked between us, and before I left, we exchanged numbers.

Miranda had told her wife, Lucy Kim, about me as she had multiple industry connections, and a few pulled strings later courtesy of Lucy Kim I received an invite to audition for a potential place for me at the renowned Olympia Drama School. My hopes of getting into the Royal Academy of Dramatic Art had recently been rejected, so this Olympia opportunity allowed me to leave my beef about RADA on the table and go for this mustard opportunity with all the gusto I could.

My make or break rested on me smashing two audition pieces, contemporary and classical. I planned to perform as the character of Edmund Tyrone from *Long Day's Journey into Night* for my contemporary piece. It was one that I was quite confident in playing.

My classical piece, however, wasn't an easy choice. I'd opted for a character named Duke Vincentio from Shakespeare's *Measure for Measure*. Shakespeare's plays, up to now, had been the Achilles heel in my acting career. Acting as Duke Vincentio was proving to be more complex, more complicated, and more frustrating the more I continued to rehearse. As I just wasn't quite measuring up, I knew I needed help.

'Look at this photo of me at Edinburgh Fringe.'

'What were you trying to do, Miranda, stun them with your good taste? You look like you were going to the mad hatter's tea party!'

Miranda showed me a Facebook photo where she'd decorated her head with a brimmed rainbow and wore a matching dress. My witty response caused Miranda to spurt out her Moccona soy, which she had been trying to drink ever so carefully without spilling it on her white fox-patterned blouse.

We were at Riverside Blend Café London Bridge. As we got toasty by the coal-effect fire, I took a swig of my Americano, which was so strong it nearly singed my eyebrows off.

'God Jay, no way, you were on *Cook Me Up Some Love!* I used to watch that every Saturday; which episode? I need to watch it!'

'I also auditioned at Wembley Arena to be on *Big Brother*.'

'Jay, you'll go to any lengths to be famous, won't you? How was it?'

'First off, it was freezing cold because it was February after all. I was wearing my duffle coat, hat, scarf and gloves, but when I got there, there were women and men practically wearing nothing. So I stood out like a sore thumb!'

'That sounds about right, go on.'

'I remember now, this woman, probably in her early 50s, was standing next to me dressed like a Spice Girl. You know, Union Jack dress, red boots, the works....?'

'Yeah, I know. I've got the outfit.'

'Really? Can you wear it next time we meet?'

'No, don't be silly. Just kidding....go on...'

'So this Spice Girl look-alike asked me, "Did you come last year?" I told her, 'Nah, first time for me.' The wannabee said she'd auditioned three times before and had the cheek to call me a virgin.'

'Ah ah, wannabee, your comedy's improving! *Avante...*'

'Well, I stood in the big crowd freezing my knackers off; there were some real screwballs, werewolves, pixies, superheroes, you name it.'

'And you're in a duffle coat! Ah ah.'

'No one told me the dress code. Anyway, when the doors of Wembley Arena finally swung open, there was this huge roar, and everyone rushed in.... Shall we get two more coffees?'

'Finish the story first.'

'Where was I? Oh yeah, so it was jam-packed, just like a cattle market; you could feel the buzz. I guess for me, *Cook Me Up Some Love* had given me a taste of TV fame, and I wanted another slice. You know?'

'Nice pun.'

'I queued for an eternity until I was called in. I had to stand in front of five...I think...producers. They even had the *Big Brother* voice robot, you know, the one you see on TV. It was asking questions; I tried to be quirky. I threw everything, barring the kitchen sink at them; I was sure, no, I was CERTAIN, I'd nailed it.'

'Yeah, and?'

'I was....eliminated in round one!!!!'

After grabbing two more coffees, I mentioned my Shakespeare woes to Miranda. She rang her wife, Lucy Kim, and handed me the phone, offering her words of wisdom.

'...Jason, you should see a drama coach I know called Perry Rivera; he's great. A rehearsal or two with him before your actual audition may help. You'd benefit from his expert feedback. Perry would definitely have your back.'

That evening, I contacted Perry Rivera, and we arranged a date for a rehearsal at his place in Zone 6 in Epping, a quiet market town in Essex. Door to door, it was a ninety-minute journey from my pad in Soho.

The following week, I arrived in freezing cold Epping, where it was sleeting. I was welcomed with open arms at the station by a tall, camp Perry Rivera, a real natty dresser in his mid-50s. After we exchanged cheek-to-cheek air kisses, Perry shared his large Breton-striped umbrella with me, and he lightly rested his arm around my back, which I thought was a bit odd since we'd just met.

We walked down a country lane, and Perry must've noticed me shivering in the sleet as I had forgotten to bring my coat. He rubbed my arm as if to warm me up. We walked for about 25 minutes until we reached Perry's home, a beautiful Tudor-style house with a pebbled drive and two lavish Mercedes cars parked outside. To this day, I'm not sure why he hadn't picked me up in one of his cars.

I entered the spotless living room with high ceilings displaying old wooden beams. It was just like one of the lavish homes you see in glossy magazines, a home many would only dream about. The log fire and sheepskin rug made the ambience even warmer and cosier. As Perry wiped the sleet off his designer burgundy-framed glasses, I placed my big yellow rucksack on the leather burgundy Chesterfield sofa, removed my soaking wet boots, and began searching for my script.

'You have a really nice pad here, Perry.'

'Thanks, Jason, the only way to live enjoyably is beyond one's means. Earl grey?'

Perry swallowed the compliment in one as he poured the steaming Earl Grey tea into our cups, and I rested the script on my lap and warmed myself up in front of the fire. All warmed up and able to feel my toes again, I listened to Perry talk enthusiastically about Shakespeare, and then we began to rehearse *Measure for Measure*. Act III, Scene 1. A room in the prison. I envisaged I was a Duke as I stood tall on Perry's thick white carpet, trying to hide the hole in my sock. Perry must've noticed my shifty feet.

'Have you thought about your shoes, Jason?'

Unsure about what Perry was leading to, I asked.

'My shoes?'

'Yes, darling. The shoes that an actor wears are more than just footwear. You see...they're pivotal in shaping one's character, persona, and the very essence of movement.'

Perry's insight was not something I'd heard before, and he continued.

'Your shoes, darling, are like the silent partners on stage...they will aid you in crafting the very soul of your character...they speak volumes without uttering a word.'

With no alternative footwear other than my wet Karrimor

mountain boots, I remained in my holey socks. I was ready to deliver my lines as Duke Vincentio:

*"Son, I have overheard what hath passed between you
and your sister. Angelo had never the purpose to
corrupt her..."*

'RP, Jason, you are a Duke; a Duke needs to have Received Pronunciation!'

As I took a pause in the dialogue to think about the preceding lines, Perry faced me once again.

'Darling, you need to lose that; no Duke would be seen dead in that; wristwatches were not around in the 17th century, and certainly not plastic ones.' Perry said, pointing at my blue Swatch watch.

Perry used the pause as an opportunity to advise me on my posture as he put his hands on my shoulders and gently tugged at them, directing me to throw my shoulders back. To help me, he invited me to imagine that I was a member of the royal establishment.

On his advice, I continued:

*"I am confessor to Angelo, and I
know this to be true; therefore, prepare yourself to
death: do not satisfy your resolution with hopes
that are fallible: tomorrow you must die; go to
your knees and make ready."*

I looked at Perry and wanted some sort of feedback. Perry was observing me while massaging his jaw.

'You've got to loosen up, Jason. You seem so tense. Don't hunch your shoulders! You're Vincentio! You're a Duke! You're a member of the establishment!'

Perry came closer and again stood behind me. Pulled my shoulders back even more with his hands to correct my posture. While he did this, he tapped on the small of my back.

'Now, show me you're a Duke!' He walked around me to face me, lowered his glasses to the end of his nose and stood so close that I could decipher the brand of antiseptic mouthwash he used.

We rehearsed for a couple more hours; by this time, it was around 10:00pm. Perry sat down next to where I was while I was fumbling through my script pages to ensure that all were in order. It was at this time he squeezed up next to me on the large Chesterfield sofa and said.

'I'd like to make you feel a bit more relaxed, darling, because you seem quite tense at the moment.'

Without thinking anything more about it, I replied.

'Actually, I am feeling a bit tense, Perry.'

'We'll soon remedy that, Jason.'

'Come, lay on the rug. Close your eyes and relax.'

As instructed, I lay on the sheepskin rug with my eyes closed in front of the burning log fire, trying to remember what time the last train from Epping would be leaving. I hadn't noticed Perry had disappeared into another room until I opened my eyes when I heard a click. And I noticed the lights had been dimmed. Perry had also put on some sensual music, which just so happened to be by one of my favourite pop singers, Sade. Suddenly, I began to feel a touch uneasy, not knowing what to expect.

I was startled to see Perry walk into the room draped in only an unfastened dressing gown and very little else. When he asked me to take off my shirt and trousers so he could perform a deep tissue massage on me, I wasn't sure what to do. Reminding myself that Perry was only trying to help me out and that I should pull myself together, I did as he instructed, and he massaged me as I lay only with my boxer shorts on. The *Smooth Operator* song playing in the background was having the opposite effect, and instead of being relaxing music to my ears, it was adding to my unease. I hadn't signed up for this. It was selcouth, or in other words, bloody peculiar. To be honest, the massage felt good, and if I had been more relaxed, it may have even felt wonderful. It was only when the grandfather clock in Perry's hallway struck the 11th hour I realised the time. I remembered that the last train left Epping at 11:30pm, and it was now 11:00pm. Perry invited me to stay the evening because it was so late, but I politely declined the offer and got dressed quickly. He insisted on accompanying me to the station, and when we opened the front door, the weather had worsened without me realising it. Perry told me he'd be back in a second as he quickly ran upstairs. He returned with a full-length silk-lined leather coat and draped it over me.

As we walked to the station, the wind was unrelenting. It was starting to snow heavily. Now I was worried that the trains would be cancelled, meaning I would have to stay at Perry's house.

'Would you like to walk through the forest?' Perry threw out a suggestion that I didn't retrieve as I pretended not to hear. Whilst Perry's thoughts appeared to be on fumbling in the forest, I fumbled through my pockets to ensure I hadn't lost my return train ticket.

I was late. My steamed-up Swatch read 11:35pm when we arrived at Epping station; a good excuse for a quick but awkward thank you as I gave Perry back his coat and the £55 I owed him before running towards the platform.

55 LUCKY SOHO

'I'm fucking speechless that he actually did you like that? Half-naked? On his sheepskin rug?' Ryan commented whilst munching his snack.

'What did you say his number was again?'

He was half shocked and half listening as he added more *Dijon* mustard to his melted cheese, pickle and anchovy toastie as I explained my previous night's random massage session.

'Can you pass the Lea and Perrins there, next to you, Jay?'

'How can you eat that Ryan, mate?'

'Have you tried it?' Ryan asked in a tone that suggested he didn't quite understand that I wasn't as *risqué* as him when it came to toastie toppings.

'Nah, have I heck!'

'Well, you can't knock it if you haven't tried it, Jay...want a bite?... Go on live dangerously,' joked Ryan, who was egged on by the grimace he saw on my face.

I was living the wild life alongside my eccentric, living-on-the-edge, brother-from-another-mother flatmate, Ryan. I was enjoying the perks of living in Central London where opportunities to party, gamble and (whatever else) were right on the doorstep.

'I'm a member. I can sign friends in, so are you up for it, huh?' Ryan's invite was, of course, tempting and, of course, a no-brainer! So, after a few beers at home, Ryan and I made the most of his night off.

After the doormen of the Lucky Strike Casino in Soho patted us both down, checking if we were harbouring anything inconspicuous. RYAN CARADOG SANTIAGO autographed the members' book.

'Caradog?'

'Yeah, well basically, it's my middle name. It means love in Welsh. Only the folks back home in Llanfairfechan call me it. I hated it when I was a child. Before you start, keep any jibes to yourself.'

'Okay, Caradog, don't bite my head off...You're barking up the wrong tree, mate...I wasn't going to start, so stop your bitching!'

We stepped into the heaving casino, where we were hit with the cacophony of casino sounds, the chatter, the jingles of the slot machines and the oooohhs, and the aaaahhs of the winners and losers.

With our game faces on, it was each man for himself on a mission to win! Ryan had cast his eye on the Poker table, and I, on the other hand, headed straight for Blackjack.

I settled in at the Blackjack table and sandwiched myself in the gap between two suited Asian guys speaking loudly and expressively in what I assumed to be Mandarin. By the number of chips they were playing with, I could tell that these guys were big, high-stakes, win-big, lose-hard gamblers. My bet was £5 on the first game, whilst the other guys' chips were well-stacked and looked like they had a few hundred pounds riding on the game. I took a card from the dealer and lost, as did the other two guys. In the next game, I upped my stakes and bet £10, but I was dealt a poor hand and asked for another card. However, this action seemed to cause unrest with the guy sitting on my left, who appeared somewhat cheesed off, to say the least. As I turned to look at him, he stared at me with an annoyance in his eyes that seemed to burn a hole right through me and left me stumped as to why. The guy on my right was massaging his temple whilst staring at his dwindling pile of chips as I continued my gung-ho approach.

'Card, please,' I asked the curly-haired dealer, who looked like he wanted to go home.

Again, we lost the game. Again, the guy on my right banged the table. Again, the tension in the atmosphere hung over us like a guillotine blade. The losing streak was like the awful casino wallpaper pattern that repeated itself over and over for what seemed like an eternity. About 20 minutes into the game, I was over £100 down and not feeling so good. The two other guys seemed even worse for wear, as they'd lost thousands in that short time.

Chop Suey! We were all losing. By their expressions and banging their hands on the table every time I took an extra card, it was becoming increasingly obvious that these guys were getting pretty pissed off with me, but I still had no idea why. Maybe it was the strategy that I had been using in my card game, which was the strategy I used when playing Blackjack for fun as a boy with Dad and Martin. It was a strategy that won me many-a-game. But here, amongst the big boy high-stake gamblers, my normally good strategy screamed otherwise; I was not cutting it. The atmosphere at the blackjack table was like a house of cards.

That is until I turned to the guy on my left and asked him whether I was doing something wrong. Irritated, he cleared his throat and set me straight.

'Yeah, you need to do *Golden Rule!*'

I looked blankly at him, thinking, what the fuck is the *Golden Rule?* *"To know what you know and what you do not know is true knowledge" by Confucius* was the phrase that immediately came to mind. Before I could ask, the Asian stranger set me straight with the words that had obviously been erupting inside of him.

'The *Golden Rule*, very simple! You see, if dealer have 12, 13, 14, or 15 for first two cards, and you have same, you no ask for third card, OK? No more card! OK? Too risky!'

Could this secret fortune cookie *Golden Rule* be my way to becoming wealthy? I had now been warned. I now knew that my wrong moves were bringing the game crashing down, so I committed to the *Golden Rule*.

Slowly, my initial losses became wins. Game after game, by playing my cards right this time, my stack of chips grew. *KER-CHING!!! KER-CHING!!! KER-CHING!!!* The nodding acquaintances' tunes had now changed as their fortunes were up, too, which is more than I could say for Ryan, who had trudged over to the Blackjack table.

'Shall we get out of here and chow Jay?'

I was so caught up in my winning streak and drawn into the excitement and anticipation of winning more and more that I really didn't want to leave yet. I scooped up my winnings but wanted one more game.

I walked away from Lady Luck momentarily and took my phone out of my trouser pocket to check the time. I saw ten missed calls from Nathalie and several annoyed texts asking where I was. She had been hounding me about wanting a night out and had initially invited herself to come with me and Ryan. Instead, I suggested meeting her at Expo later on as the casino was strictly members only. I had been so caught up in the game I was now two hours late, so I decided to cash up my tidy profit before the chip on Nathalie's shoulder got any bigger.

'Drinks and dinner on you then?' Ryan suggested half-jokingly as I slid my chips to the cashier.

'Sure, why not? I think McDonalds is still open?' I said, laughing, before a polite and well-rehearsed cashier said in an Asian-American twang.

'Sir, I can cash these for you, but for these single £1 chips, Sir, you will need to get a £10 chip from one of the roulette tables, because I'm afraid Sir, that I cannot cash these here.'

'Red Number 21, red number 21,' announced the roulette robotic voiceover.

'Can I have a £10 chip for these?' I temporarily distracted a female croupier at a nearby roulette table with my question as she took the chips. By that time, the wheel had stopped spinning. I was competing with Chesney Hawkes's *The One and Only* song being strategically played on the casino speakers on full blast.

I turned around to see Ryan near the slot machines, tucking into the free sandwiches, so I walked over.

'I thought dinner was on me?'

I grabbed a mini cheese sandwich and a big smile from the heavily made-up and barely dressed waitress who stood waiting for a tip. I reached into my pocket and found a pound between an old tissue and my phone, which was vibrating again. Though it was hard to decipher, I'm sure I heard the waitress mutter under her breath.

'Last of the big spenders!'

She turned away and tried her luck with a dicey-looking customer in a pinstripe suit.

MY EGO SCREWED MY ACTING CAREER

The casino music played loudly as I returned to the roulette table. The wheel was again in full spin, the ball about to decide someone's gambling fate.

'Black number 10, black number 10,' the voiceover announced as the roulette wheel stopped spinning. I saw this as an in to get my £10 chip I had asked the female croupier for. The croupier put on a smile similar to the waitress's packaged one. 'Well done, sir!'

I had no idea what she meant until I saw £360 in a stack of chips. She'd misheard me and placed my ten chips on number 10. What a turn-up for the books. Okay, I wasn't *The Man Who Broke the Bank at Monte Carlo* (who also was a Bradfordian) but still, it was turning out to be a very, very good evening.

One of the Asian strangers from the Blackjack table was now sitting at the roulette table, waiting to try his luck on the next spin.

'*Zuò dé hǎo,*' the stranger said, holding up his whisky as if to toast me.

Ryan was walking towards me, now eyeing up the tray of free mini burgers approaching him. I tipped the croupier £10.

Whilst the cashier counted out the last in the modest bundle of crisp £10 notes, I then turned to Ryan and surprised him by giving him half my winnings.

' Here you go Caradog! Don't spend it all at once!'

'Woooah...are you sure?.... Thanks, Baby...how did you do that? Can you clue me in?'

'Lady Luck, Ryan buddy, pure Lady Luck...'

'Isn't life honey!' Ryan said with a mephistophelean smile.

'Talking of honey, weren't you supposed to meet Nathalie two hours ago?'

However, rather than heading to meet Nathalie straightaway at Expo, stir-happy Ryan and I hit the heart of Chinatown and were instantly met with food aromas that were strong but not intrusive. We both were tantalised by the smell of garlic, stir-fried with the smells of sizzling Asian foods of the surrounding restaurants, which happened to be winning the battle with the bus fumes that also hung in the air. As soon as we walked through its iconic red and golden gates we were spoilt for choice from some of London's finest restaurants; seated and settled we filled ourselves up on plates of *egg-fried rice, sweet and sour chicken* and *beef noodles* loaded with copious amounts of bean sprouts, oil and fried onions. Once we were stuffed to the brim to the point where we could hardly breathe, we rolled out of Mr Li's eat-all-you-like £5 buffet and headed to Expo.

When Ryan and I arrived, Nathalie was getting her groove on

the dance floor with a Hispanic-looking guy. Ryan and I settled in and began knocking back the free bottle of red wine that Ryan had brought over when a couple of Asian women in belt-like skirts, wearing enough material to make a pair of socks, made themselves comfy beside us on a burgundy leather L-shaped sofa as if they were familiar with us. Ryan smiled, and the ladies smiled back.

'If I told you that you had a nice body, would you hold it against me?' I tried my cheesy chat-up line with the ladies.

'I couldn't have said it better myself, even if I'd read the pickup line book he got it from!' Ryan quipped.

Nathalie spotted Ryan and I when she decided to take a breather from dancing. Her forehead and chest sparkled in sweat. Her aggravation with me seemingly ignoring her calls had subsided.

'Have fun, did you?' I asked as she squeezed herself between Ryan and me.

'You're the one I bed with! *Laisse tomber!*' Nathalie asserted defensively.

Her eyes threw daggers at the strangers sitting at the table. Her daggers were returned by them, with swords! Nathalie took a swig of my red wine.

'Wanna dance?' Nathalie asked with a tone as prickly as a cactus.

'I'd prefer to dance on shattered glass,' I replied sharply.

As the loud music banged on, Nathalie was working up another sweat on the dance floor with a more sluggish Ryan. The stringent sweet and sour sauce felt like it was repeating on me as I bathed in the attention of the two women who saw Nathalie's retreat as an opportunity to start inadvertently flirting with me, which, in turn, was starting to eat me up with curiosity. One of them sucked her straw suggestively and whispered something to her friend before they both headed for the ladies' toilets and a few minutes later, they came out smiling at me as they left the club.

As the women left, I spotted Nathalie bumping and grinding on the dance floor; she had gone back for seconds with the Hispanic guy once again, who was owning the dance floor with his every move and appeared to match Nathalie's zest. As she continued to make a show of herself, I decided not to stick around for the second act. I gestured to Ryan, who'd been dancing to Falco's tune of *Rock Me Amadeus* with a redhead whose silver shirt sparkled like the club lights.

'What's up, Baby?' A glitter-covered Ryan asked trying to throw his voice over the loud music and chattering.

'Have you got the keys? I need to look for something from upstairs! Let *Mademoiselle* know, will you? If she asks!'

56 BOMBSHELL

'Are you sure you don't want to share the sweet and sour?' Asked Ryan just before my phone pinged, revealing an intriguing message which read:
Are you busy tonight, honey? Love Simone and Lula xxx

'Who's that?' Ryan inquired as I swiped the phone away from his view.

'My agent.'

'You don't have an agent, baby,' Ryan replied sarcastically as he ripped open a packet of chopsticks.

'I need a fork...Can you get me one?'

'I'll think about it; my agent doesn't like me doing things for free!'

I opened the container of crispy seaweed and scooped up a pinch before Ryan returned with a fork and two beers.

'Are you sure you don't want any of this *sweet and sour* or *beef chow mein?* It's on point today.'

'Ryan, sweet and sour chicken is your fetish!'

'Huh?'

'It's the third time you've eaten sweet and sour chicken in the last 24 hours!'

'Uh, so?'

'If you start clucking and laying eggs, I won't tidy up the crap.'

For the life of me, I didn't know what made me think that over a Chinese takeaway whilst watching *Match of the Day* was the right time to confess to Ryan about Simone and Lula, the two Asian strangers at our table during our night out at Expo.

'You mean the two beautiful Thais? They were regulars before you started coming to Expo, you know...'

Ryan shovelled some egg-fried rice into his mouth and had taken a bite of a spring roll when he dropped some bombshells, which landed head-first into the pot of sweet chilli sauce.

'Baby, you know they were once male, don't you? I could've sworn we ordered some prawn balls. Have you seen them? Oh, by the way, Expo is closing. It means giving the flat up. We've got three weeks to get out of here...'

'We'll go Dutch, *Monsieur*.'

That evening, I met Nathalie; she had reserved a table at Oceana, a new boat restaurant floating on the Thames. It was one of those places where they hired handsome waiters and good-looking waitresses to keep you from noticing the eye-watering prices on the menus. A glass of water costs about ten pounds for the waiter to pour.

I reluctantly agreed. It was pricey and pretentious, and to be honest, the oysters looked as appealing to eat as the muddy River Thames looked to swim in. To appease Nathalie, we dined *alfresco*, and I sat freezing my bollocks off on the decking of the Oceana. But I felt a little sick, not at the sight of the slightly swaying waves, not at the platter of slug-like oysters, but at the £80 price tag on the menu just for a platter of six oysters with *tabasco* sauce. The table had so many waiters coming and going that you could hardly see the other minuscule feasts that were fit for jesters. I kept quiet, holding back my distaste for the stingy portions received and the extortionate menu prices. As we sat on the deck of the Oceana, Nathalie faced me, holding an oyster shell towards me, daring me to take it.

'They're an aphrodisiac, you know?'

I really didn't care if the oysters were the secret to eternal youth, so I refused.

'I'll stick to this, thanks!'

I took a swig of red wine and reached over to the basket of crusty bread rolls.

I could feel Nathalie's leg stretch over to mine playfully under the restaurant table. Her foot touched my crotch as she flirted.

'I had an erotic dream about you last night. It was vivid...do you ever dream about me, *Monsieur* Jason, huh?'

I dared not respond to her comment as I, too, had had a steamy dream, but not about her.

She was wiggling her foot, sipping wine, when she whispered in a sultry, playful tone.

'Beast, come here, Beast. *Voulez-vous coucher avec moi ce soir?*'

Nathalie, who already had one too many glasses of the pricey red wine, sometimes used the word Beast as my *sobriquet*.

'I want to get busy with you, Beast. *Je t'aime.*'

'...Yeah, so basically, we've got three weeks to move...bloody hell...I think we need to slow it down on the alcohol, Nathalie. Have you seen the prices?'

It was difficult to wrestle with the giant prices as I wide-eyed scanned the inflated menu again.

'More wine, sir?'

'We'll just have a jug of TAP WATER for now, please, TAP WATER!'

I reiterated to the waiter, who I could've sworn saw Nathalie's foot on my balls.

Nathalie's words were playful but slightly slurred when she asked.

'Do you think I'm...beautiful, *Monsieur* Jason...?'

'...hmmmmm...yeah beautiful yeah, yeah...seventeen pounds for a basket of *langoustines* with *pomme frites!!!*'

I was only partly listening to Nathalie as I was still scanning the inflated menu, still bemused by the prices, and trying to calculate half of the bill for what we had ordered so far.

'When I'm drunk, am I beautiful?'... Am I desirable to you when I'm drunk, huh?... I mean, you do still find me desirable, don't you, *Monsieur?*... I mean desirable for the long term...? You can come to stay with me.'

The tipsy but not so tipsy Nathalie subtly but unsubtly dropped in her suggestion, inviting me to live with her in her plush Shoreditch chateaux, and I responded with.

'Maybe!'

Though it was evident that her own sense of commitment was as stable as the tide of the Thames, the unusually perceptive Nathalie's tone changed as her hopes of me committing to her further had been crushed like a lobster claw with my one-word response: Maybe. Nathalie was no longer playing, and now there was fire in her tone.

'*C'est quoi ton problème?*' In seconds, her temper had risen from zero to a hundred. She yanked her foot away from my privates and caught my knackers with the heel of her Jimmy Choo's in the process. I held back my expletives as I leaned forward in pain as Nathalie exploded.

'MAYBE....? MAYBE...?...Well, MAYBE don't call me! Bastard! Wanker!'

Whilst the end of Michael Bublé's - *Everything* track played softly in the background, you could've sliced bread with the atmosphere at our table. The couple at the table beside us looked on in abject horror. The French firecracker then threw her half glass of red wine over my linen shirt as she repeated.

'Maybe...? Maybe...? Maybe? *Égoïste. Je me casse.* You can go to hell.'

'Okay, but can I finish my wine first?'

My sarcastic comment got a slight chuckle from the middle-aged man seated with his wife, who shot him daggers as he, obviously going through *le démon de midi*, watched Nathalie and her pert bum step over his tongue as she stormed away from the table.

I was left miffed, not by Nathalie leaving, not by my linen shirt now stained with red wine, but by the hefty £185 bill I had been left lumbered with, especially as she said we'd go Dutch. My head dropped dizzy. I had only eaten a few bread rolls and drank two glasses of red wine! *Putain.*

57 BIG TROUBLE LITTLE CHINA

The writing on the wall indicated the end of my relationship with Nathalie, as she still remained highly angered by my 'maybe' response to her proposal of us living together.

The writing on the wall signalled the need for change because despite my charity job covering my rent, I was feeling frustrated and stalled because each and every way I turned, nothing seemed to be surfacing in my quest to become a full-time actor.

The writing on the wall was also a mixture of vibrant graffiti art and gang markings. And was part of the new view through my window frame that I was now waking up to in my new room of the new Brockley apartment that I now shared with Ryan.

Our cheap rented apartment was on the wrong side of the tracks. At the time, it was notorious for being a crime-ridden area. However, be that as it may, once I got into the frame of Brockley, I found it to be an area that buzzed with creatives, it was an area that was filled with interesting and eclectic people, and it was an area that attracted beings that were wonderfully weird and sometimes just weird, as I found out.

'This is your Southern Train to West Croydon. Your next station is Brockley. Brockley is your next station.'

I was heading home after acting in a Tom Tranter film *Stray Balloon*, and it was quite late when I arrived by train at Brockley station. Feeling quite jaded and hungry, I needed something to nosh. My local Chinese takeaway, Little China, was en route, so I thought, why not?

The door sign said OPEN, but the door was locked. I could see a customer inside, but it seemed I'd arrived too late. I knocked and waited for a while and became hungrier than ever from the food smells coming within. My thoughts of food were interrupted when a stressed-looking Albert, the takeaway owner, stormed out from the kitchen, let me in, but locked the door behind me.

I checked out the tasty-looking pictures on the menu board nailed to the wall listing the dishes; alongside this was a statue of a smiling red and golden *Maneki Neko* cat waving its paw. The smell of frying garlic and the tempting aroma of *sweet and sour chicken* stir-fried my thoughts about what to choose and whether one dish was enough to satisfy my hunger. After placing my order at the counter, Albert stormed back into the kitchen without a word.

Having made my decision about what to buy, I didn't want to get tempted to order an extra portion of prawn balls by eyeing up the menu again, so while I waited, I eyed up a mature woman whose shapely hips waved a sweet hello as she paced up and down waiting for her food. Her eyes had a captivating intensity, as if there was an intriguing storm within them waiting to happen. Her suited and booted, no-nonsense city worker look suggested that this was a woman who would do anything to get what she wanted. Her look was whetting my other appetite and was now more appealing than the prospect of prawn balls.

From the kitchen, I could hear Albert rambling on, and by the look on the woman's face, something wasn't quite right. I clocked her, clocking me looking at her high stiletto heels that stood next to a broken plant pot. Latching onto this attention, the woman began to share her takeaway tale of woe with me.

'It was an accident...the pot just slipped and smashed...but then, believe it or not...that crazy man demanded £20 for the pot! Can you imagine? I refused outright...I mean, it's the principle of the matter, you see?... All I came in for was a *beef Chop Suey!*'

Her tone was convincing enough to nearly sway me, but while the woman was telling me her takeaway trauma, Albert must have overheard the woman's version of the story and stormed out of the kitchen, holding a spatula.

'Pfft, *beef Chop Suey*, you not having *beef Chop Suey*, you pay £20 first for the plant pot you broken, you *Jinǚ*.'

He yelled furiously, looking like he may herniate, turning to me.

'She crazy! She crazy! Not me!... She criminal, look she has tattoo!'

The wound-up Albert pointed to the Medusa tattoo on the woman's left hand whilst accusing her of throwing the plant pot on the floor. This was followed by a flurry of what I could only assume were Mandarin insults as he pointed his finger aggressively towards her and the broken pot. The woman stood in her spot defiantly and said.

'You'll see...I'll tell everyone about you...I'll leave you a CRAP review.'

'Crap! Crap! You crap! You leave, leave review, do it, do it, my food the best, I have good customers...him, him, him...he good customer...he not break plant pot like you...you *Jinǔ!*' Albert said, delivering his *kung pao* kick.

I wasn't banking on being a referee in a WWF match, but there I was, utterly flummoxed and stuck in the middle of a heated argy-bargy. I would have preferred to have slipped out of the takeaway if my *kung pao* chicken and egg fried rice had been ready and the door hadn't been locked. The way things were looking, it seemed that I'd never get home that night. As Albert and the alluring bombshell continued to squabble in front of the counter, the chef from the kitchen came in with my order in aluminium containers. Albert went behind the counter, and I paid him for my meal. I took out another £20 from my wallet and handed it to Albert as a gesture for the plant. This seemed to do the trick; his demeanour calmed, and he said to me.

'Enjoy your meal.'

As he unlocked the door. On the way out, the bombshell turned to me and said.

'That was very kind of you; I have a bottle of plonk at mine that would go very nicely with that takeaway if you like?'

My mysterious dining companion, Madison, told me that she was an estate agent working in the local area, and I revealed that I was an actor. We headed towards her apartment into a night that now belonged to just two people. The smell of her strong perfume, which was the type you could tell was expensive, wafted sensuously under my nose in the night wind. Her apartment was very close to my pad; a very small and instinctive voice inside of me was calling to my common sense to join alliances and go home alone; as it went, I ignored both and headed in the opposite direction from my instincts. There was something about Madison that tempted me.

The lights were on, but no one was home when we arrived at Madison's snazzily decorated apartment, which was kitted out like a showhome, and nothing on the surface appeared out of place. After sharing the takeaway and flirtatious suggestions, the bombshell Madison kept to her words and opened the bottle of wine she had promised, which we also shared.

'Let me show you the master bedroom,' she invited as she led me to the shocking pink-walled room, where she slowly undressed,

'Fuck, it gets me in the mood.'

She sprinkled what I assumed to be Charlie on the table, rolled up a £20 and snorted a line.

I decorated my gums with some, and then, one thing led to another.

'Watch me,' she tempted as she unzipped her cotton black skirt, unbuttoned her peach silk blouse and unclipped her hot *Fuscia* pink bra. I did as she asked and observed her sitting and undressing on the edge of her king-size bed.

'Do you like?' She asked as she showed me her sheer black silk stockings, her matching suspenders, and her patent red high heeled *fuck me shoes,* which for me, were a big turn-on.

'Hold on...I nearly forgot!' she said in an intriguing tone as she opened the top drawer of a wooden bedside table, took out a black and gold sequin eye mask, and put it on; it was at that point she had me eating out of her hands.

After a few rounds of steamy foreplay with the knockout, masked temptress, we engaged in intercourse, but it was during our athletics that she began talking—not just dirty talk.

'Would you like to come back over next week, huh? I'll cook for you.'

Madison was running before she could walk with her thoughts of where this was leading. The masked madame was nuzzling my groin; at that moment, I let her comment slide between the passionate kisses she was laying on me, and she continued.

'I'll dress in my French maid costume...if you like my mask, you'll like that too!'

The thought of Madison's offer was captivating as the masked temptress had now worked her way further up my body, her lips now kissing my bare chest as she rocked back and forth. She began whipping me with the ends of her long blonde ponytail she had bunched up in her hand. Then Madison followed this with words that began to burn a hole in my ear.

'Yes...yes...ahhhh...yes...I'll put on my...ah...8" strap-on dildo...ah oh fuck...yeah I'll be the man, and, fuck you up the arse...will you come?... Oh my gosh, yes...please come!!!'

Madison's eyes through the black and gold sequin mask shone wickedly with a kinky devilment as she bounced her invite on me between her heavy but sweet panting.

I was feeling hornier rather than perturbed by Madison's

outlandish offer of round two until mid-copulation, the bombshell dropped a bombshell of her own.

'Yes...yes...mmm...that feels so good...ahhhh...if my boyfriend found out...ahhh...what we were doing right...ahhh...NOWWWW, he'd...mmmm, he'd be so...ahhhh fucking...yessss...fucking yeah, fucking angry at you and...ah...ah....ah...don't stop... he'd put your head through the...fuck...yeeeessssss...right, right, RIGHT THROUGH the fucking windowwwww...he's a boxer, you know... mmmmmmm.'

Ding! Ding! Ding! That was my signal to get out of there.

The red-hot woman whose thrusting hips I held in my hands had set my alarm bells off because, now, I had a red-hot problem. I needed to get out of there before my chin got carpet burns from meeting Madison's bedroom floor courtesy of her apparent boxer lover. I had appeared to make all the right moves, but as was becoming increasingly obvious, it had been at the wrong time, in the wrong place, and with completely the wrong woman. Madison had *Shanghaied* me.

58 AMOUR FOU

I can't take my mind off of you. Call me. Madison xxx
I had lost count of Madison's barrage of daily messages and calls over the weeks following our initial meeting at Little China.

Ryan told me he'd seen a shifty-looking blonde woman loitering around outside our apartment. I was becoming slightly unnerved, and this feeling worsened as the calls from Madison continued to come in. Turning off my phone wasn't an option, as that would mean missing out on potential castings and the all-important call from Olympia Drama School. So, the drama of my own continued.

Three months went by
'What's the point of those? I can't see the point of those,' Ryan said. He had observed me wrestling with one of the fortune cookies I'd just taken from a bag of Chinese takeaway that we were about to devour while watching Luc Besson's *The Fifth Element* on TV.

'I'd love to be in a Luc Besson movie.'
'Wouldn't we all, Baby. Are you on IMDb?'
'IMDb, what's that?'
'Pass me those spring rolls; you've never heard of IMDb? Where have you been, Mars? IMDb stands for International Movie Database, basically, it's a website for everyone who is anyone in the film industry. The gospel for actors, if you like. Every top actor and film director is on there. It's the be-all and end-all. You gotta be on there!'
'How do I get on it? Do you have to pay or what?'
'Pass me my laptop and those napkins, and I'll show you, Baby; it's free. You need a profile; all those NYFA short films you did should be on there,' Ryan explained as I flung the fortune cookie onto the

table and reached for the *kung pao* chicken.

I was just about to speak when there was a knock at the front door, and Ryan went to answer it.

'...to tell you the truth, I don't know. The last I heard, Jason was in America, shooting a movie. He'll be away for a few months, I reckon.'

'Can I come in?' I heard the female enquire.

'And you are?'

'Madison.'

'Sorry, MADISON. Like I said, Jason's out of the country. I'd forget him if I were you...but that's your prerogative.'

Ryan had given an Oscar-winning performance to Madison, who, out of the blue, had appeared on our doorstep.

'Yes, it's my prerogative, so don't tread on it. Tell Jason that I've been,' voiced Madison coldly before she departed back into the night.

'Hear that crunching? Those are the eggshells you're walking on with her... you've got a lot on your plate there, Baby,' said Ryan, stating the bleeding obvious.

'Try celibacy like me. It's the way forward...Sike!!! I'm going to the new Bubblegum Club in Deptford later. You coming, Baby?'

'I'll give it a miss. I'm doing that NYFA short film tomorrow, remember?'

The morning after the relatively quiet night before, en route to the shower before heading for filming, strange murmurings were coming from the vicinity of Ryan's room.

'Um...I'm not well...um...Hi, I can't come in today. I feel terrible...um, hello....I've been up all night and....'

'Ryan? You okay in there, buddy?' I asked through a gap between Ryan's open bedroom door, genuinely concerned.

'Yeah, I'm fine, Baby; why?'

As I opened the door ever more slightly, Ryan was lying flat on his back in bed, wearing only a mud facemask and two slices of cucumber on his eyes.

'I'm just practising before I pull a sickie, Baby. I've got a shoot today.'

Next to Ryan, facing away from the bedroom door, was a naked blonde asleep on his bed and on the floor, there was a pair of very familiar *fuck me shoes*.

A few weeks later, I went to watch Miranda perform *The Vagina Monologues* at the Jolly Roger pub. After the performance, Miranda and I headed to the nearby Chalk Farm to Marathon kebab shop. Whilst we chowed down on our food, Miranda updated her Facebook page by posting some photos of the both of us eating and of some snaps of her earlier *Vagina Monologue* performance. This was accompanied by a tongue-in-cheek caption: *It's hard to be funny and sexy at the same time.*

From an unknown location in the world of social media, Nathalie responded to the post.

Miranda, I don't think sexy is your thing! Stick to being funny!

'I'm not sure Nathalie enjoys you going out with another woman,' Miranda said, laughing off Nathalie's bullet.

Miranda's words were just barely audible amongst the singing revellers at Marathon kebab shop that night, who appeared to have that Friday feeling as they boogied on down. Marathon kebab shop was one of a kind. It was fully licensed, and it always had the atmosphere of a bustling nightclub. Its customers, more often than not, came for more than just its legendary chargrilled chicken *shish kebabs*. A few more drinks later, it was 1:30am. I saw to it that Miranda had gotten a cab safely back to her home in Wimbledon, but I had missed the last tube.

I eventually arrived back in Brockley, and by this time, it was almost 2:30am. I was tempted to grab a few beers from an illegal late-night alcohol shop near Brockley Cross, but took seconds after I saw a group of lads fighting in lumps. I hopped off the N343 bus and headed to my apartment. However, as I neared home, a blonde woman caught my attention as she stood directly outside my building, suspiciously looking up towards my apartment window. As I edged closer, I realised it was Madison! She was accompanied by a man built like a brick shit house.

My heart was pounding, and I wasn't sure what to do. Fortunately, a bus stop was in sight, and fortunately, within seconds, I was able to jump on the first bus that stopped. I had no thought about where exactly I was going, but I had the sheer relief that at least it was away from Madison and the brick shit house of a man. Ryan wasn't answering his phone; I didn't want to disturb Miranda and Lucy Kim; Lance was away filming in Wales. It was too late to call any drama pals or charity colleagues, so as a last resort, I called Nathalie and asked her if she was busy.

'*Excusez-moi* Jason, you've got some gall calling me...You can come, but don't expect a blowjob or anything; your scorpion hands are going nowhere near me, and don't think you're getting in my bed; I'll leave the door unlocked, don't wake me!'

When I arrived at her pad in Shoreditch, Nathalie was waiting up. Dressed in silky white lingerie, she looked like she was waiting for me to say sorry. I shared as much as was necessary with her about the Madison saga. She appeared not to want to hear anymore when she cut me off mid-sentence and left me to sleep on the *Chaise lounge* with no blanket or pillow.

It had taken me an eternity to actually fall asleep, but I was woken from my fitful sleep by Nathalie tugging at my shoulders. The light pollution coming from the streetlamp outside her living room window suggested it was still really early. Without a word murmured, we did what we both knew was on the cards.

'You're a mind-blowing curiosity, Beast...Why did you turn me down?... I don't get it. Why did you not come and live with me, huh?'

Nathalie lay her head on my chest and waited for my response. Of course, I snored convincingly, pretending that I'd left for the land of nod.

Around late morning, the smell of sausages, hash browns and muffins accompanied Nathalie as she woke me with a cooked breakfast, which she brought me dressed in the *Cook Me Up Some Love* apron I had once gifted her. Nathalie sashayed to get the freshly squeezed orange juice she'd forgotten in the kitchen, revealing her bare back and pert, shapely bottom. She came back in all her golden glory and moved towards the bed like a feline in search of cream. The feline then sprawled herself on the bed as I finished off one half of a buttered muffin.

'If you're still hungry, you could eat these hash browns,' she tried wheedling her way into my appetite by dangling the hash browns in front of me. I reached out to take them...

'You know what'd be nice, Beast?'

After we had both shared the delight of me devouring the hash browns, Nathalie explained she had a gift for me and handed me a wrapped parcel. I opened it.

'You know, next time, you may find I'm not so forgiving...'

'...Pink, my favourite colour,' I swerved, holding up Nathalie's gift: a T-shirt with 69 printed on it.

'You can wear it when we go and watch a film together?'

'I was planning to have drinks with Ryan tonight.'

If looks could have killed me, I would have been dead on the spot!

'Which one?' I asked as I picked up the remote and started flicking through to find the film channels before she erupted.

'No, not on there!'

'What...you mean?'

'*Oui*, get ready!'

It was tough to argue with Nathalie; she was just too persuasive, but I was quite partial to a little friendly persuasion.

Nathalie had put on nude stiletto heels, and her shapely hips beckoned me with a tantalising sway as she moved towards me in her new short blue mini dress, which was so tight it was like her second skin.

'Tu es très beau Beast....' Nathalie said with a look in her eyes that turned me on.

'Does my hair look alright?' Nathalie asked me as she finished spraying perfume in between her shapely thighs.

After a quickie, we headed down to the local independent cinema, which mainly showed foreign films. We were in time to catch the start of the French Love story *Last Tango In Paris*, starring the great Marlon Brando. A group of young men were standing smoking near the cinema's entrance. As we entered, Nathalie stepped over their tongues.

We headed to theatre number 1 with our butter-sweet and salty popcorn.

We settled into the back row of the virtually empty theatre. Nathalie lifted up the armrest that divided us, took my arm, put it around her, and squeezed up closer to me. We attempted to put French back into kissing. It wasn't only the lights that went down. I was trying to act natural as Nathalie took me through the commercials. I felt sleepy but knew I had to return her mind-blowing act.

I looked around to see only a few people spaced out in front of us, so I slid onto the floor. That night, we gave butter-sweet and salty popcorn another meaning. My neck, however, was killing me.

59 IN NO MOOD FOR PLEASANTRIES

'What makes you think that you're entitled to turn your feelings on like a tap? I'm through with you! *Je m'en fous!'* yelled Nathalie as she buttoned up her blouse.

Our fiery afternoon of heated passion had evolved into a blazing argument, which, for us. Yet again, we were able to do the second thing we were best at together, which was to find an argument in even the most minuscule of subjects. Yet again, this all too common pattern was followed by one of us (Nathalie this time) to storm out of the apartment. Yet again, the door closed on that film-noir-esque drama. Plus, there was a new drama happening.

"*O Romeo, Romeo! Wherefore art thou Romeo?*
Deny thy father and refuse thy name;
Or, if thou wilt not, be but sworn my love,
And I'll no longer be a Capulet."

The setting was Olympia Drama School, the scene was a *Romeo and Juliet* rehearsal, and the character Juliet was fellow classmate Gina Ricci, who was looking out of the window on stage with her back to the class as she performed her lines. The villain was not Lord Capulet but Franco Carluccio, a salt-n-pepper-haired, erratic man with no qualms about pushing it. Franco Carluccio was our teacher who was never in the mood for pleasantries. He stood up and gave Gina what seemed like a slow, sarcastic applause followed by.

'...Hmmm, where do I start...Tedious! Tripe! Terrible! Gina, Gina, Gina...this is not acting, my dear! You gave a fantastic performance—with your back to the audience! If only you could act anywhere near as well when looking at them.'

Gina paused before bursting into tears. While she sobbed into her hands, the rest of the class remained silent and stunned. I, on the other hand, was thinking Fuck! It's my turn next for the chopping board.

I walked across the stage in character as Romeo towards the tear-stained Juliet, who was waiting for me to deliver my dialogue. As I looked up at Juliet, however, I drew a blank as I tried to remember my lines. My stomach was churning as stage fright kicked in. It was unlike me to be overcome by nerves, but the 30 seconds that passed by felt more like three hours. I had nothing. I said nothing. I paced up and down the stage to bide my time; my last liaison with Nathalie had left me walking like a cowboy, which didn't suit my character as the suave Romeo; all my efforts to practise Romeo's traits had gone out of the window. Finally, my words caught up with my brain, which is more than I can say for my confidence as I tried my best to get my words out:

"O, speak again, bright angel, for thou art
ahem
As glorious to this night, being o'er my head,
ahem
As is a wingèd messenger of heaven
Unto the white upturnèd wond'ring eyes
ahem
Of mortals that fall back to gaze on him."

The words of the great Shakespeare flew out of my mouth like a pile of clothes on a table in a church jumble sale. It was a lousy, lacklustre performance, but I had to go on. Franco Carluccio, who I had seen out of the corner of my eye vigorously massaging his jaw, could not take any more of my butchery.

'Stopppppppp! Stopppppppp! Pleeeeasssse stop! Jason, where is your pathos? Where is your character's minutiae? Where are your nuances?'

My head was now on Franco Carluccio's chopping block but Before Franco could give me his cutting comments, I interjected and started a cantankerous Carluccio-esque critique of myself in front of my stunned class.

'...Jason, that was terrible. You are such a shocking performer. Jason, that was tripe, so damn tedious.'

It was as if I'd lost my marbles. During my rant, the great quote by *Aristotle* sprang to mind.

"There is only one way to avoid criticism: Do nothing, say nothing, and be nothing".

However, I ignored the wisdom of the great Aristotle, and I

continued to critique myself anyway.

A graveyard silence fell over the class, and Franco looked stunned. Did he critique me after that? Well, no, he couldn't. I'd covered all bases. There was nowhere else for him to go with it.

'Gina and Jason, can you both stay behind?'

All the other students left the class and left me, Gina and the ticking time bomb Franco on the stage.

'Gina, you earned your spot in this drama school; every time you perform, you must be convincing...You know, Gina, when you acted alongside Jason, I saw a bigger improvement, but it seems that you're not taking it seriously until you're under fire; you've got to be ready for every crucible of acting... see you next class.'

Franco and I were then the only ones left on the stage. I wasn't sure what to expect. He looked me in the eye, placed one hand on my shoulder and said.

'There's one thing I will advise you on, Jason. That is, never, ever, ever criticise yourself. Especially in front of an audience, never say you've given a bad performance, even if you believe you did. Because there's going to be one person or two or maybe all of the audience feeling you'd given a fantastic performance. So for you to critique yourself in that way was a huge error.'

Franco looked to the ceiling, leaving me hanging as he paused in thought. When what he appeared to be searching for, had found its way to his mind, he asked.

'By the way, Jason, you don't have an injury, do you? You seem to be walking quite oddly.'

60 THE OFFER

'Jason, everything about your performance HAS TO warrant an exclamation mark, NOT a question mark... GIVE ME a symphony. GIVE ME a more telling and more convincing performance! I can teach you acting, but I cannot teach your soul...Acting has many different levels, it has many different notes and it has many different tunes. Acting isn't a one-note performance like the one you just gave me!'

These were the drilling words of Franco Carluccio that bored a big hole into my naive Ego. Because, this time, I hadn't escaped his lambasting.

Harold Pinter's words were being butchered by me, and my rehearsal of the *Betrayal* play at Olympia Drama School wasn't going well. Franco, of course, wasn't backwards in coming forwards. Once again, I was on his chopping board, and once again, he hadn't minced his words.

'Rather than commanding this room, Jason, it's as if you're apologising for being in it!'

The frustration in his words and his face were evident, and this was concreted when, without another word, he turned around, and the eccentric and highly irate, ticking time bomb of a man, Franco Carluccio, went off and left the building and didn't return for the remainder of the class.

I never could retain much from rigid, structured lessons, but I retained thousands more things from unplanned lessons, and this particular occasion was a perfect example of that. I knew Franco Carluccio's credo was right. I needed to dig deep, focus, and learn my craft. I knew there was a key to everything and that if I was going to break into the film industry, I needed to latch on to it fast.

Greenwich (old haunt)

It was now almost five years after arriving in Greenwich, with a head full of dreams and a VHS copy of *Two Faced*. Ironically, I was invited back to Greenwich, but not by Charlotte this time. I was back at the first base where my journey had begun in London to attend an audition for a Trickshot Films production, a low-budget black comedy feature film, *Incidental Weekend*. I was fully focused and determined to land the lead role of Will, a middle-class narcoleptic author with a terminal brain tumour.

The audition was held in a rented office facing the Greenwich cinema, not far from my old house on Hyde Vale.

After having my chances scuppered as the lead role in *Castle Kings* feature film and after having lots of rejected applications, I desperately wanted to land this part. I was *All Fired Up* as I sat on the 177 bus with Pat Benatar, humming through my ears, when I felt a tap on my shoulder.

'Jason, long time no see.'

'Ahem, Monica.'

'Are you living back in Greenwich, Jason?'

I stayed quiet. What were the chances of me bumping into one of "The Troop"?

'What are you doing these days?'

'I'm an ACTOR.'

'Ah, I see, you're still trying that...but you know what I mean, where do you actually work, to pay the rent, I mean?'

I ignored Moo-moo-Moonica's cow-pat jibe and left the bus without as much as a goodbye. The focus now was on my big opportunity. I really wanted to silence and prove the doubters, the critics, and all the creative killjoys wrong, and stuff my smelly socks down all their throats when I hit the BIGTIME!

I sat nervously in my lucky pink Oxford shirt on a hard plastic seat in a cold corridor. I eyed up the other actors, weighing up my competition as they were called into the audition room individually. I heard each one read aloud through the paper-thin walls, and then it was my turn.

The directors at Trickshot Films, Nick Kirk and Rich Allison, introduced themselves to me as I took a seat. Nick Kirk was the first to break the ice.

'Jason...do you prefer to be called Jason or Jay?'

'Call me anything you want, Nick, as long as you give me the role... that's just my sense of humour, by the way,' I added, waiting to see the directors' reactions.

My light joke was returned with chuckles from Nick and Rich as I let out a sigh of relief, and then Nick Kirk (a standup comedian himself) kicked off the discussion.

'Jay, we had over 100 applicants for the role of Will, you know.'

Rich Allison added.

'You, Jay, you've got something special...and we can see it. Just relax and do your best.'

Nick Kirk's and Rich Allison's laid-back, warm natures made me feel more at ease just before I was asked to read my scenes.

I'd spent days learning my lines and trying to get to grips with the character Will. I had two scenes to read; one was a light scene, whilst the other was a more concentrated, heavy scene in which Will had to tell his friends in the film that he was going to die soon. For this scene, I tapped into my emotional memory of all my heart-wrenching losses of the people I'd loved.

I believed it went well, but I had been there before. There were no certainties when it came to auditions. I very rarely ever got a definite the-part-is-yours indication straight after an audition. So until the phone rang and I was told the part was mine, I refused to ever let my mind completely go there. Instead, I hung onto a prayer that I'd get the part.

'Happy Birthday Luv...I remember yer Dad coming into the delivery room and saying he's beautiful Alice; he looks like a movie star...So yer going out for yer Birthday meal then? Make sure ye ring me when ye get back home, won't ye? The restaurant's not far from ye, is it?'

'No, Mum, it's not far, don't worry and I'll ring you later.'

Sometime later in the evening, I was celebrating my birthday at Sal's, an Italian pizza restaurant in Covent Garden, with Lance, Ryan, Miranda and Nathalie (don't ask!) when I received a message on my phone from the *Incidental Weekend* directors.

Hi Guys and Gals, congrats on getting the parts.

Whaaaaaaat? I couldn't believe my eyes. FINALLY! After all this time, I had LANDED a part in a FEATURE FILM as the LEAD ROLE. I was on cloud nine and ecstatic. In the middle of the packed restaurant, with many people chowing, I jumped up and shouted at the top of my voice.

'Yeahhhhhhhhhhhhhhhhhhh, Baaaaaaaaabbbbbbby.'

My hard-to-contain elation had jumped in every diner's plate as all eyes were now on me.

'Who's that? Madison?' Nathalie asked, sounding agitated as she pulled me back down.

After composing myself, I read the rest of the message, which contained filming details. A read-through was planned in Greenwich, and the main shooting was to commence a week after that. The message ended with.

We're both thrilled, and we can't wait to get working with you all; this is going to be a fantastic project!!

Best regards, Nick and Rich.

I couldn't quite soak it all in. The added bonus was that the majority of it was to be filmed abroad on location in Bulgaria. Nick Kirk and Rich Allison had given me the break I longed for, and I wanted to repay their trust in me by giving the production my all.

Now, feeling like Al Pacino, I shared my good news as we all raised our glasses, and I was the toast of the town.

'It's about time, isn't it? We all knew you had it in you. You're gonna rock that lead role...can we go for Chinese next time?' Ryan said, his mouth half filled with the pepperoni pizza he had just bit into.

'Cheers, Caradog buddy, sure we can,' I replied, accepting the support, which didn't end there as it was followed by a grinning Lance who echoed the sentiment.

'One for the books, Jay, what next, a Tarantino movie? Starring alongside Salma Hayek, maybe?'

Nathalie rolled her eyes at Lance's comment.

'Cheers, Lance, I wouldn't say no.'

From seventh heaven, I returned Lance's comment and then received another from Miranda, who teased playfully.

'A feature film? Well, you'll have to start practising your speech for the Oscars!' Miranda leaned over the table and showed her genuine support by kissing me on the lips and whispering.

'Well done, you! So proud of you!'

'Cheers Miranda.'

Lastly, handing me a napkin, along with a swipe from her blade of envy, Nathalie morosely muttered.

'Here...wipe your mouth, Jason.'

61 INCIDENTAL WEEKEND

Me and Hayley J. Williams on location in Veliko Tarnovo.

I ignored Nathalie's jibe. After the table of supportive friends had arranged for a surprise New York cheesecake to arrive at the table with a candle, I made a wish as I flushed with triumph. From cloud nine, I ordered a bottle of *Moët & Chandon,* and with my frugality going out the window, I footed the £302 restaurant bill without flinching.

'Ahhhhhhhgggh fuuuucck!' I yelped after the area of my old rib injury had taken a hard sharp blow, which consequently took the wind out of my sails.

This was day one of the *Incidental Weekend* filming. The location was an apartment in Islington, North London, where a fellow actor and I went straight into character and straight into an improvised fight scene.

After taking five, Nick and Rich asked if I was okay with continuing. Although in pain, I was determined nothing was going to stop me from completing this feature film till the very end so we resumed filming.

It turned out that I had cracked my ribs, but my hunger was still very much intact, even more so in fact. So I carried on.

'...I fell down the stairs. I've busted my ribs.'

'Jason, as a charity team leader, you have to lead by example and show responsibility. You simply can't keep taking time off like this, you know. Can you come and see me when you are feeling better?!'

I had called in sick for what must have been the 85th thousandth time, and my boss was getting sick and tired of my neverending flimsy excuses. But I had really broken my ribs, though not from falling down my stairs like I had told my boss. Plus, I wasn't going to be resting up; I was heading to Sofia for filming.

'...This is a call for Speedy-boarding passengers for flight 1158 to Sofia...Please go to Boarding Gate 11...would all Speedy-boarding passengers for flight 1158 to Sofia...Please go to Boarding Gate 11...'

After completing the UK *Incidental Weekend* scenes, we travelled to Bulgaria for nine days of filming. I'd never been to Bulgaria before and had no idea what to expect.

Nine of us, the two directors, cast and crew, took the three-hour flight from Heathrow to Sofia, the Capital. A coach was waiting outside the airport and took us to the filming location, a picturesque town called Veliko Tarnovo (the old Capital).

During our journey down country lanes, as I stared out of the window at the countryside, I listened to *Café del Mar* on my iPod, and soaked in the Bulgarian surroundings. I was like a farmer in August who had gone five rounds with Tyson. I was trying not to get ploughed under with my doubts about whether I could get through filming with the injury that wouldn't stop reminding me it was there.

Ding! Ding! Ding! The coach braked briefly for a bicycle to pass before turning the corner to stop at the bottom of a steep cobbled hill. There, we were told that the coach couldn't be driven further, and we had to walk the rest of the way to our hotel. At the top of the hill!

Though my ribs were still causing me a lot of pain, I soldiered on, grateful to be where I was, getting ready to do what I loved. We eventually arrived at the hotel with its half-timbered façade that had a certain *je ne sais quoi*. Set above the winding river valley, the hotel overlooked the picturesque town, and it was surrounded by luscious greenery. I unpacked my big yellow rucksack, and after showering, I joined the cast and crew and went down to the town for our evening meal, which included plenty of drinks. Alcohol is thought to be a form of painkiller, but the proof was in the pudding. I planned to have a lot of pudding that night and prove the theory correct.

All nine of us sat in the restaurant ready to experience Bulgarian culinary delights. The menu showed plenty of options, and we were spoilt for choice. However, we had difficulty choosing what we wanted because the pictureless menus were written in Bulgarian. None of us had considered bringing a phrase book or a translation dictionary.

'*Dobŭr vecher,*' the waitress greeted, which we figured out meant good evening.

She had as much English in her linguistic repertoire as we had Bulgarian in ours, and it would've been helpful to know that head nodding in Bulgaria (or at least in this region) meant "No" and that moving our heads from left to right meant "Yes."

The food prices on the menu appeared dirt cheap but the only downside was that without photos of the dishes on the menus, choosing our food was hit and miss, so each of us chose a meal and hoped for the best.

When our food arrived, some of us who thought they ordered chicken were given fish, and those who thought they ordered beef got pork.

'What did you order, Jay?'

'*Shkembe chorba* Nick, I think it's chicken soup, but I'm not sure it's ever seen chicken!'

I later discovered that on that first night, what I actually ate was *goat intestines.* This explained why what I thought was a chicken dish tasted more game-like and smelt more like smelly feet than chicken, but I was so hungry that I could have eaten a horse, which might well have been on the menu, but we were none the wiser.

'What about you, Rich?'

Rob Allison asked his perplexed-looking brother.

'Well, I think I ordered *Kebapche,* I think it's meant to be meat on a stick, and the waitress brought this!'

All of us looked at Rich's meatless plate to see it filled with enough salad for a banquet fit for *Bugs Bunny*, and this was ever so elegantly garnished with an empty stick!

'This must have been a mistake,' Rich said, half-joking and half-bemused as the cast and crew burst out laughing; it was like unwrapping Christmas gifts because we had no idea what to expect.

'That's a wrap, guys!' Called Nick Kirk. We'd just finished a long day's filming and Nick's next words were music to all of our ears.

'Drinks on me, guys!'

We had been filming in the local pub, Pepy's Bar, and we'd stopped work for the day and walked a few footsteps to the bar to collect our well-earned, ice-cool *Kamenitza beers*.

A few pints later, Nick and Rich headed back to the hotel and I stayed on at the bar with some of the cast and crew for a few more rounds. When it came to my round, I chatted with the English-speaking barman Vlad whilst he pulled the pints and asked him if he could teach me a few Bulgarian words for me to do some pulling of my own. A crash course on the idiot's guide in Bulgarian was all it took for me to down the phrase: *Mnogo si krasiva* (which translated to, you are so beautiful). Armed with my new phrase, I left the bar and gravitated my way towards two local women sitting down at a nearby table. I sat down with my tray of drinks and tried it out.

'*Mnogo si krasiva.*'

My face was burning red and stinging. I was even starting to hear bells in my ears after being walloped in the face several times. However, this wasn't from being slapped by the perplexed Bulgarian strangers but by my co-star Hayley J. Williams.

In this particular scene at Pepy's Bar, Hayley's character Charlie was due to slap my character Will for lying to her. I remembered what Olga Antonov had taught me during my "Method Acting" classes, and I insisted to the directors that Hayley should slap me for real and that she should do it hard so it looked authentic.

'Not like a fake slap?' Nick Kirk questioned.

'Are you sure, Jay?' Rich Allison questioned.

'Yes, it needs to look realistic,' I replied.

Nick Kirk called. '*Action.*'

Hayley's character, Charlie, walked over to Will (me) and accused him of lying to her before she slapped him and stormed out of the bar. Though it was my idea for Hayley to really slap me, it actually really did hurt! We needed to film the same scene a few more times. By the eighth take of the same scene, I started to question why I ever said:

'Let's make the slap for real, not a fake slap.'

Fortunately, we got the scene in the tenth take.

Over nine intense days, we filmed in various locations from dusk to dawn. Curious onlooking locals observed us, probably intrigued at the sight of a film crew in their neck of the woods.

On the final day of filming, I had really gotten into the frame of Bulgaria and had fallen in love with the charm of the location of our final scene. The beautiful part of Veliko Tarnovo was a spectacular large square looking down on the blue Yantra River and the old town. The hilly terrain created a stunning backdrop making the scene look like we'd stepped into a postcard. Despite it looking amazing, Nick and Rich had their work cut out, having to deal with some sound issues, namely dogs barking and construction work.

Our characters Will and Charlie were ready for a long reminiscing scene. The camera operator, Rob Allison, had lined up the shot. Finally, everything was as calm and quiet as a sleeping dog in terms of sound. Literally, all we could hear was the burbling of the water running down the Yantra.

Rich Allison called. '*Action.*'

Rob Allison, with camera in hand, ambled towards us, Charlie (Hayley) and Will (me), as we acted out the scene. On a wooden bench, we delivered our dialogue.

Charlie: *"Come on. It's been years; you can't have already run out of things to talk about."*

Will: *"I know, but I have just been thinking about it recently. I don't think I've done much..."*

'...SHHHHHHHHHHHHHHHHIIIIIIIIIIIIIIITTTTTTTTTTTTT!!!'

The scene had been flowing like the Yantra when, with no warning, out of the blue, Rob (following a loud expletive that made us jump) dropped the camera. He'd been spooked by something over mine and Hayley's shoulders. Hayley and I turned to look behind us and saw a huge husky-type dog trying to jump over the wall. Rob had spotted this, which had consequently freaked him out whilst he was looking down the lens. Nick Kirk called. '*Cut.*'

We all broke out into hysterical laughter. Fortunately, the camera was still working, and the film-bombing Husky gave in, and decided he didn't want to be part of the limelight.

I, however, basked in the rays of limelight that shone on all of us. Filming my first feature was like 1000 summers crammed into nine glorious days—full of good times, full of laughs, and full of the unexpected. This superseded the physical pain of my cracked ribs by far.

Incidental Weekend was a doozy moment in my life where my soul felt like warm apple pie.

62 THRILLER

Elizabeth,
In answer to your question, so far, I've appeared in over 15 short films, including six NYFA films, and I've played the lead role in a feature film, Incidental Weekend. Also, I've quit my charity job to dedicate every fibre of my time to my acting, so I'm open to being put forward for anything and everything suitable. Bring it on!
Best regards,
Jay

I was ready to roll the dice and take the gamble to become a full-time actor. Being cast as the lead actor in *Incidental Weekend* gave me more leverage to hook in an agent. I needed someone who was singing from my corner, someone who had the drive, ambition and hunger that I had, and someone who had the potential to pull in the big guns.

Miranda Kim-Mendoza's casting director wife, Lucy Kim, knew someone who knew someone and that someone, was Kipper Talent's Agent, Elizabeth Grolle, who, after a rally of emails, left the ball in my court for me to impress her with my charm at a meeting with her at Riverside Blend Café.

Elizabeth Grolle was an ambitious businesswoman, a former model, and a part-time photographer. Over two strong coffees, an Apple Danish, and *scrambled Ackee & Tofu*, she snapped up a hungry actor, and I snapped up an ambitious agent. That very afternoon, she snapped up some fantastic headshots that would help kick-start my game with the big guns.

But it didn't take long for frustrations to kick in. After a few months of initially signing up with Kipper Talent, nothing appeared to be coming to fruition, despite Elizabeth trying every which way but loose to get me to where we both wanted me to be.

I was snapped out of my blues when Elizabeth emailed me one day to attend a last-minute audition. The only information I received was about the time, location, and instructions to take a pair of shorts. I knew nothing about what type of audition it was for, but of course, I jumped at the chance and was available to go.

I was butt naked in the shower when I received a call from a withheld number. Bummer, I slipped on the wet floor and missed the call. Still steaming and soapy from the shower, I listened to the voice message as I wiped the steam off my bathroom mirror.

Jason,

I hope you listen to this, erm how to put this...I hope you're thinking of me like I'm thinking of you. You know...I haven't been able to get you out of my mind...it's just that uh...I want you to know that erm...from the moment I first laid eyes on you, that very moment...I know you'll remember...I've been carrying this...this...longing...I can't shake it...God only knows I've tried...I think I'll carry this feeling, this longing, this need I have for you until the day I'm laid into the ground...You really need to call me. Madison.

I can only put the reason of curiosity down to what possessed me to continue listening, even though her words felt like she had clamped my testicles tightly together with a metal vice. Alarm bells should've reminded me that curiosity is what killed the cat! It had been almost two years since we first met and nearly two years since we shared a one-night-only fling.

At that moment, there was nothing I could do. I had an audition to attend, so I took caution when walking out of my building and to the bus stop.

I hopped on the packed 343 bus to Central London. A hairy man who took up three-quarters of the double seat added to my agitation as he played Snake on his Nokia, inadvertently nudging my ribs with his elbows at the same time. This lasted all of 45 minutes until I gladly got off at the stop for the Melon Studios.

    I walked through the double doors with the handwritten sign saying CASTING stuck to it, indicating I was in the right place. It was a spacious and well-lit room with tall mirrors that lined the walls, and some people who were already there were adjusting their hair and makeup. Others were moving up and down the polished wooden floors, already dressed in their sports gear, stretchy pants, jogging bottoms and all that jazz. Several people were talking to a lady with a clipboard. Behind her was a long table with three people sitting down sorting headshot photos of the auditionees. The lady with the clipboard beckoned me over. She asked my name and checked it off her list before instructing me to get ready. I put on my shorts, still not knowing what the audition was for. Then, a blond guy dressed in a tracksuit who introduced himself as Alex stood at the front of the room and began instructing the auditionees.

'Alright, everyone, gather around! Let's go over the moves.'

The eager auditionees formed a semi-circle around Alex, and we were all focused and ready to absorb his instructions.

'Let's do this. Are you good? Are you great?... We are going to start scuffing...left, right, left, then you hold...5,6,7,8...then you're going to pull across your body...'

Whilst everyone began dancing to his tune as instructions were being fired out faster than bullets on a firing range, my neurons were doing the *Macarena*. Bloody Nora! The people in the room were not actors. They were bloody dancers, and I'd been sent to a bloody dance audition. It was Danceville! Sure, I could bust some *Gangnam Star* moves after a few beers, but I was definitely not designed to move elegantly on the dance floor. I was definitely no hip-hop dancer, and I definitely knew I wouldn't be able to replicate what Alex had shown us without looking like a proper melon. There was NO way I could do this!

We were placed into four groups. Mine was to be last to perform. I observed each group. Each dancer moved with rhythm and flexibility to the upbeat track of Michael Jackson's *Thriller*, which was pumping up the studio floor. As I continued to watch in horror, my courage to "give it a go" went out of the studio window and made its way home.

As they got their groove on, every single dancer breezed through and looked so professional, busting their sick moves. There was no way I could ever reach that standard in such a short time, if at all! I felt sick, and my nerves were pulling me to pieces. I needed a quick excuse in order to leave because there was no way I wanted to dance in front of the professionals. I could improvise till the cows come home in acting. I could dance to make people laugh. But in front of me were a tonne of professional dancers, who I didn't believe would've appreciated an amateur like me in my blue floral Bermuda shorts butchering their art. I mean, I wasn't built in any way for agility or grace, and when it came to dancing, I was a *dilettante*.

Next up was the turn of group four, my group. I felt nauseated to the stomach. My heart was going mad and thump, thump, thumping away. I was sweating and wondered how I would get out of it. I said to myself: I didn't sign up for this.

During group three's performance, I pretended to look like a pro dancer by doing some warmups and stretching down to the floor before dramatically falling to the ground and yelping, acting like I'd pulled a muscle in my back. It was the only thing I could think of to get out of the performance. Ambling around the floor, holding my back and acting like I was in excruciating agony, I gravitated towards the casting director and told her that I couldn't perform due to a pulled muscle and explained that I didn't want to cause myself any further significant injury. Sympathetic to the situation, the casting director said. 'I understand completely; your well-being comes first. Thank you for coming, though. I hope you feel better soon.'

Like a flash, I left the audition. I called Elizabeth and explained that I was, in no way, shape or form, Rudolph Valentino or Travolta.

63 LITTLE FREAK

"You sick little freak, you told me you were dying for a sympathy shag; that's really twisted!"

These harsh lines from a scorned lover reacting to the most unforgivable lie were as sharp as an executioner's axe being held up in the air waiting to fall. The tension in the room of 300 or so people hung there with it. When this tension fell, and the lights revealed reality, a round of rapturous applause and cheers spread across the room like wildfire.

These cutting lines shot out from the mouth of Charlie, a character played by Hayley J. Williams, and were aimed at my character, Will. This was just one of many lines of a fantastic script. Hayley J. Williams and I were amongst the crowd of 300 at the Curzon Cinema Soho. This was the premiere of *Incidental Weekend*. This was my second experience of a cinema screening in which I had played the film's leading male. As I watched the film from my cinema seat and saw myself on the large cinema screen again, I was left gasping for breath, nearly choking on the ball of over-excitement. I had a mixture of nerves and self-criticism, and I vied for the golden liquid of audience approval to wash this down. The audience reactions, the applause, and the affirmations gave me what I needed.

After the film ended, we drank wine in the lobby with the red carpet touch, making the ending good enough for a shot in *EMPIRE Magazine*. I wanted Miranda to share the momentous moment with me, but she was away working at a comedy gig in Leicester. My next choice was Nathalie, but given that I had some kissing scenes with a co-star, Henrietta Meire, I took a raincheck on that idea.

On the bank of the River Thames, on the days that followed the premier, there was a downpour. Nathalie's demands and negativity were raining down heavily, and of course, I hadn't brought an umbrella.

'I told you, Nathalie, I wasn't allowed to bring guests!'

'But you could've snuck me in...I could've worn my new Gaultier dress!'

'I told you I couldn't.'

'Oh, you're so vanilla! Why don't you ever take a risk for once in your life?... I think you should come with me!'

'Where?' I wondered where the direction of this conversation was heading now.

'Paris, of course. It's only one hour from London!... There's nothing else for you here.'

Nathalie's words took the atmosphere from light rain to unexpected heavy hailstones that hit hard as her pitch grew in irritation. My silence in the minutes that followed Nathalie's proposal, I sensed, was now threatening to rip the several bandages from our on-again-off-again relationship as we sat on the bank of the River Thames.

'Hmm, I dunno...Paris...erm...Perhaps!' I murmured.

These were the only words I was willing enough to muster. With her tone now even more raised and even more demanding, she laid it straight to me right there on the river bank.

'Jason, do I really have to spell it out for you? If you don't come, we really, really, really are through. I mean it this time. You'll never see me again!'

I always hated feeling like I was being trapped and shoe-horned into anything by anyone. In the bid to battle my way out of Nathalie's Jimmy Choo's, I responded.

'We started off like a couple of animals...It was merely a dalliance...as I remember, you were happy with that...everything was cool with us...but now Nathalie, you want more...'

Nathalie remained silent, but I needed to reiterate where I stood as my voice softened.

'Nathalie, what you want...is more...more than I can commit to you...and more than I can offer you...'

Nathalie's harbouring thoughts of us living together had now been shipwrecked by my noncommittal words. She appeared to be staring at a tour boat approaching from a distance.

'...Nathalie...I had to be honest with you...we can't continue to be gluttons for punishment...particularly if you're shifting gears AGAIN to what you want from me...I'm not sure what else you want me to say?'

'Nothing! There is nothing you can say! I can't believe I fell for you once again. *Je m'en fous.* I wouldn't care if you fell off the face of the earth. *Égoïste!*' Crazy-mad Nathalie barked and again, in true Nathalie-style, stormed off, taking her *mauvaise* attitude with her.

While the distant sound of her designer heels crunched, crunched, crunched away on the dregs of the river bank, I felt neither sorry nor sad as I sat alone with the waves of my thoughts. Why did I always let my guard down? Why hadn't I pulled up my drawbridge sooner? Was this whole love thing just something found in feel-good movies? Was I destined to sail solo forever? Would I ever find someone who I didn't feel anchored me down? Did I even really give a shit? *Je ne regrette rien?*

The shrillness of a tour guide's voice on a passing tour boat reverberated on the surface of the water:

'...The Prospect of Whitby, one of London's oldest pubs on your left, was said to be often frequented by pirates...'

These words were ironic because I had just been literally made to walk the plank, and in my haste, my response of 'perhaps' to Nathalie's attempt to hold me to ransom meant my ship was now in troubled waters, *mal de mer.* There was no way back to rebuild the bridge that once satisfied us both. I got up from the bank and made my way to a nearby pub for a stiff shot of whisky.

'I can see the pub from here!... That Sheila wasn't good for you anyway, sport,' said Lance in a put-on Australian accent that was as genuine as a crocodile in Hyde Park sipping Earl Grey.

He had Skyped me from Sydney, Australia, where he had travelled to, straight after accompanying his dad to do some voluntary work with Indian street children. Now, Down Under, he was already three months into a year of a screen acting course.

He wasn't the only one to say goodbye to Old Blighty, as I saw when a Facebook video popped up on my feed a few weeks later showing Nathalie posing, her lips painted and pouted, dressed to the nines and behaving like she didn't have a care in the world. The caption under her photo read:

I'm ready for my new chapter in Paris.

Ryan, too, was soon to depart and was currently eyeball-deep in clothes and food packages from his mother as he was preparing to go and live with his friend Cecil Zimmerman in San Francisco.

We were spending our last night in Brockley together before he left for America. While I was cooking, Ryan was sorting out the belongings he was chucking and taking before we planned to settle in to watch Vincent Gallo's *Buffalo '66* together.

'Is the chicken ready, Jay?'

'Well, it is if you want it raw! Master chefs shouldn't be rushed, you know.'

'Come on, Jay, I'm starving, and don't make a mess.'

'Stop ya nagging; you've got the wrong look to be a mother!'

Our regular Chinese takeaway, Little China, had been temporarily closed due to hygiene issues. So, I took inspiration from a *Lemon Chicken* recipe that I gleaned from a Ken Hom cookbook, which I picked up at a charity shop, and tried my hand at whipping something good up in the kitchen for Ryan, who was to Chinese food what Rick Stein was to cooking.

'Mmm, pretty good, Baby.'

'You like it?'

'I hope I can actually get on the flight because I'm not sure now.'

'Why do you say that?'

'Well, with the amount of arsenic in this chicken, I'm not sure I'll get past the American border security.'

'You've eaten Chinese almost every night for the last two years; if you weren't going to America, you'd be able to teach me Mandarin!'

'There's one way to improve your cooking.'

'How's that?'

'Cut off the electricity!'

'Cheers, Caradog.'

'*Yaki dah,* Baby.'

'You know I'll miss you like a hole in the head.... But who knows? I might be going transatlantic too!'

'Yeah?'

'I dunno, maybe to The Actors Studio in New York.'

'I saw online that Eva auditioned to get in, but I don't think she did. Last I heard, she was touring a play in Canada...you know you can still take over the tenancy...will you be okay house-wise?'

'I'll be okay, Ryan buddy...I simply can't afford this place on my own...now that I've quit my charity job.'

'Where will you go?'

'Oh, I don't know... we'll see... I'll just have to try out different places for size.'

'Promise me one thing before I go, Jay...just one thing, will you?'

'What's that?'

'Don't accept sweets from strangers you meet in Chinese takeaways!' Ryan joked whilst shooting me that smile that always made me smile.

During the course of my and Ryan's colourful friendship, we were able to say, do, and share most things together. Our sadness was too awkward to express verbally, but without words, the bear hug between us said all that needed to be said. Well, I must admit, I was going to miss him.

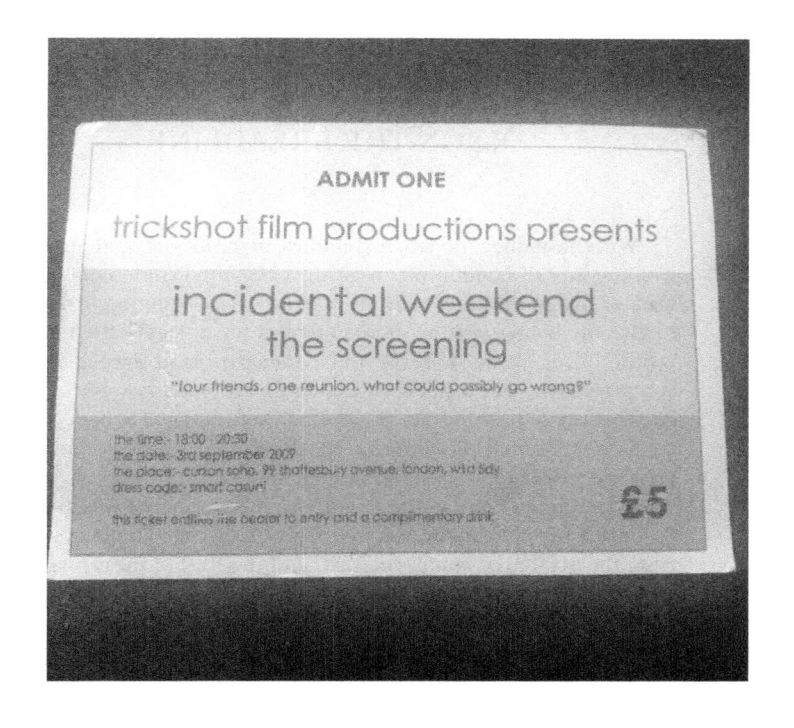

![ticket: ADMIT ONE — trickshot film productions presents incidental weekend the screening. "four friends. one reunion. what could possibly go wrong?" the time:- 18:00 - 20:30; the date:- 3rd september 2009; the place:- curzon soho, 99 shaftesbury avenue, london, w1d 5dy; dress code:- smart casual. this ticket entitles the bearer to entry and a complimentary drink. £5]

64 ON THE BREADLINE

With no money, no job, no buddies, no girlfriend, and nowhere to live, the lure of London was wearing a bit thin. I contemplated going back to live in Bradford, but my last shred of Northern grit drove me to give my London acting dream one last push. Maybe there was still a little bit of life in it. I was up for the crucible of the Big Smoke. I contacted everyone I knew in London who had a spare sofa; then I leapfrogged all over the city from sofa to sofa and bed to bed.

'Yes, Mum, everything's okay, Mum, and I haven't had supper yet...and yes, Mum, I'll ring you tomorrow.'

Mum didn't know at the time about the sacrifices I was making to become a full-time actor and that I was living like a nomad, moving from the north, the south, the east, and the west of the capital. I also had to resort to cadging a few pounds here and there when I really needed to. I found out that there were many good, supportive people I knew; I just had to shop around.

'Jay, we'll be away in Edinburgh for four weeks; you can stay here, rent-free. Help yourself to all the food, but (sorry about this) Lucy Kim told me to tell you that you should leave the house as you find it! And a mother-like comment from me. Make sure you recycle your packaging! Okay, Jay...Oh, keys, hmm, I will leave the keys under the *Skimmia japonica* in the wooden barrel flower pot near the front door...And no wild parties!'

Miranda called me to tell me that she had persuaded her wife, Lucy Kim, to allow me to stay at their house in Wimbledon while Miranda was doing four weeks of stand-up at the Edinburgh Festival. I had one task: to take care of Toby, another tri-coloured crazy cocker spaniel. He had the crazed spirit of my own childhood pet spaniel,

Beulah.

The cupboards looked like Miranda and Lucy Kim were ready to open up a health store, and the fridge was full of culinary delights: King prawns, *Kimchi,* and crab, plus lots of Miranda's vegan food I'd never heard of and much more. Toby and I lived like kings in Wimbledon during those few weeks. However, my feast was short-lived. After Lucy Kim, Miranda and their son Brandon returned, it was all downhill from there and back to famine.

I was broke, struggling to keep my head above water while the waves lapped at my jaw. Living out of tins and on mouldy bread had become the norm.

As the saying goes, man does not live by bread alone, AND living on bread alone, I wasn't.

'Are you sure it's no trouble?'

'No bother, brother, I've slept on many couches myself; you can doss down here,' Cosmo said, pointing to a two-piece dishevelled settee that had seen better days.

Cosmo Banduka was a 35-year-old free-spirited Greek-Serbian. Like me, he was a creative who had moved to London to follow his dream, which for him was sculpting in the art world. Like me, he was raised in a working-class family. Our instant connection had grown from when we had met at an art fair in Brockley.

He sported a rugged mutton chops beard and formidable wild walrus moustache that matched his gritty and eccentric character. He was truly the salt of the earth and truly *simpatico.*

Cosmo had offered me his sofa to crash on in his bedsit rent-free. The deal was that as soon as I got a job or acting gig, I'd chip in for the bills and food. I did consider signing on the dole, but the thought of it depressed me.

Cosmo and I lived cheek-by-jowl in his rented tiny, musty-smelling Deptford bedsit. It had only a few pieces of bric-a-brac furniture that looked like they'd been picked from a car boot sale. There was a recycled recycling bin that Cosmo had built. Between the fridge and cooker, humane mouse traps lay in wait and the clothes cupboard was so chaotic that even the moths must have considered hiring a personal trainer to tackle the clutter. It was certainly minimalistic.

Neither of us were exactly house-proud after growing up with mothers who were devout worshippers of keeping their homes spick and span. Cosmo and I had both denounced this belief. And washing up, as it may have appeared to some, wasn't part of our daily priorities. Our sink looked like a scene from the film *Withnail and I.*

We nearly had our very own leaning tower of Deptford with weeks' worth of dirty plates and bowls stacked to the ceiling, screaming, 'Wash me, wash me.' The heating system was nonexistent, so the room was more often than not, far from toastie. Cosmo and I breathed out more fog inside our flat on cold days than there actually was outside. On top of that, the electricity key was dicky, which meant the power kept on going on and off and on and off. Our electricity was dodgy, our heating was hinky, and our internet connection was unreliable mainly because we'd tapped into it from our neighbours Witney Thomas-White the Estate Agents next door. Despite all this, there was one thing that was strong and solid for sure, which was the synergy between us.

Cosmo's pad, as a temporary measure, suited me just fine. His company kept me sane, and we kept each other on track. He had been in London for ten years and strictly lived without set forward plans, living from day to day, using all his survival knowledge to survive in the smoke.

Both canny and frugal, Cosmo showed me how to save some money at the salad counter in our local hypermarket. The price of a container of salad would cost around £5 or more. He showed me how to fill the container with salad and weigh it cannily. Rather than put the container onto the weighing scales, we held it, touched the scales lightly and printed out the price on a barcode.

'Watch and learn, Jay, we'll get the salad for a fraction of the price.'

Cosmo was right. For the mountains of salad, which should've been £5 or more, we'd only pay 50 pence, a tenth of the actual price.

Cosmo wasn't the only one with tricks in his hat, as he discovered one freezing cold day on our way back from the hypermarket.

'Fancy a tea, Cosmo?'

'Have you seen the prices, mate? Over £5 for two cups.'

'It's on me,' I said as we entered the well-known branded café. Cosmo took a seat, and I headed to the counter; when I returned with the two takeaway cups, I sat down and popped off the lids.

Cosmo looked down, miffed at the steaming hot water in his cup.

'Now you watch and learn, Cosmo.'

I went into our bag-for-life shopping bags. Under the table, I took out two tea bags, popped them in our cups, and put the lids back on. I spied an almost untouched brie and cranberry sandwich left on our table.

'Want a bite?'

'I'm okay, thanks, Jay.'

After we warmed up our cockles, we left. Our internet was down yet again and there was more freezing going on than in Iceland. I needed to do my daily trawl into the virtual world to look for work, so I headed for Jambo's Java Tropical Internet café, and on the way there, Cosmo gave me another pound-saving nugget.

'After you use the computer they give you, go back to the counter after 15 minutes and then complain it's running like a tortoise. They'll give you a new computer and another 30 minutes. Works every time! See you later on, mate....'

'Take number 16... that's £1...30 minutes, right?' Voiced the mardy internet café worker, his eyes barely looking away from the India vs Pakistan cricket match on the 24-inch television behind the counter.

I used up my last £1 for 30 minutes, which was a bit of a rip-off given the sloth-like speed of their computers. Their computers were only a tad bit faster than ours, and they were so noisy that I thought they would take off any second and would be better suited at Heathrow Airport.

With only 30 minutes to check my emails and acting sites, I'd almost finished the daily chores of my trade when, to my astonishment, Elizabeth, my agent, had emailed me about a last-minute audition in Feltham in zone 6. Despite not having a pot to piss in to get to the other side of London, I emailed her to count me in for the audition. I simply had to get there, by hook or by crook. It was one of the many instances where I had no option but to use chicanery and subterfuge to get where I needed to be.

Back at the bedsit, one of my first ports of call was one of the dusty shelves where I picked up and pocketed Cosmo's self-made A-to-Z map of London train stations without ticket barriers. Cosmo was still out, and there wasn't a penny in the bedsit. All I had was a handful of crumbs, a dead woodlouse, some frayed thread that had got stuck to my blue swatch watch and a half-eaten Twix bar from the sofa where I'd just tried my luck in the hope of finding some spare change. In an old coat pocket I heard the promising sound of jingling, digging deeper, BINGO! NOT! I found 52 pence! But undeterred, I had an idea.

'How much will you give me for this?'

'Hmm, in the condition it's in...hmmm.'

The local Cash Converters pawn shop assistant was searching for something in his mind as he examined my blue plastic Swiss-made Swatch watch and its matching rubber strap, looking at it like I had handed him a wet kipper. Granted, I knew it wasn't a Rolex, but it had been a great timekeeper for me.

'Five pounds, I'll give you five pounds!'

'Any wiggle room on that, mate?' I asked, hoping the West Indian pawnbroker might budge slightly.

'No, sorry man, no wiggle.'

Reluctantly, I agreed on the measly £5, which was not enough for a zone 1-6 card, which cost £6.50. I was short on time and short of 98 pence. Bloody hell, I was in a bind. I knew for sure that I couldn't haggle for a cheaper ticket, but I remembered something else Cosmo had taught me.

Back then, the best (but not always honest) way to get around was by purchasing zone 2-3 travel cards, being canny by getting on and off the trains at the right places and getting into the more expensive zones 1 and 6 for half the price. So, I bought a zone 2-3 card and combined my creativity with information from Cosmo's homemade A-Z no-barrier train map. I needed to get to zone 6, where my audition was. As canny as a London underground rat, I jumped on the train, hoping not to get noticed. All was good as the train passed Zone 3, Zone 4 and then Zone 5. I thought I was home and dry and on schedule for my audition as the train almost neared Feltham. But then things happened.

A train inspector was walking towards me with his clipper.

'Tickets, tickets, tickets, please. Ahem...sir...ahem...ticket please, sir.'

I'd acted completely on impulse pretending to be in a deep snoring sleep.

65 FOR THE LOVE OF ART

'Excuse me, excuse me. Where are we, huh? Oh, God, noooooo!' I hollered, waking up from my pretend sleep.

The startled inspector responded.

'We're nearing Feltham station.'

'Noooooooo, nooooooooo is that near Putney?' I inquired whilst appearing to be frantic.

'Nope, we passed Putney 30 minutes ago.'

'No, no, you're joking. I've got a job interview in Putney. If I don't get to the job interview, I'll not get the job, and I won't be able to pay my rent.'

My panic, by now, had evolved into a pretty impressive hysteria. Fortunately, he was a kind inspector, which was reflected in his advice.

'Calm down, son. It's okay. All you need to do is get off at the next station, cross over the bridge and get on the next train. You'll be in Putney in 30 minutes.'

The inspector never bothered checking my invalid ticket as I stepped off the train. Ironically, the next station was Feltham, home to one of London's prisons and the venue of my next make-or-break audition.

Back in Deptford

'How much did you say he was offering, Cosmo?'

'£950!'

'What? And you turned him down?'

Cosmo had the soul of an artist, working night and day to perfect his craft, but for what he did, he earned a meagre living.

His designs included spectacular recycled perspex artwork with intricately carved macabre cardboard figures inside. His oeuvre of artwork was shown across Europe in many exhibitions. One art creation normally took Cosmo around six months from start to finish, which he would then sell for up to £1000 per piece, BUT he never compromised his incandescent love of art for ANYTHING. Art over everything else was Cosmo's dogma.

'That's right…I turned him down…do you want another beer?… You see, Jay, I value my art more than money…money…well, money just kills creativity..'

'But what if that means that you're skint most of the time?'

'…But I'd rather be skint and keep my art away from the wrong hands…you know?… It's about the love for my work, not just making money. Money is not the name of the game for me…money can fill your fridge, but money can't fill your soul; money can only buy you objects and luxuries; it can't buy you love, passion or creativity,' Cosmo explained as he took another swig of his can of Skol, the froth of which clung on to his walrus moustache, as he continued..

'You know, the biggest selling industry in the world?'

'Sex?'

'No, Jay, it's fear!'

'Fear?'

'Fear is related to almost everything we are sold, you know, from toothpaste and anti-ageing creams to locks on doors. We're conditioned, from the fear of getting old, and our teeth going yellow to having a thief break into our house. We're cajoled into buying whatever companies want us to buy, you know…it's all money spinning…And fear is always in the driving seat cruising down the motorway of vulnerabilities.

But all these fears cost money, you know. We've paid for them more often than not with money we didn't have, with money we had no intention of spending; before you know it, because of all of this fear that's been planted in our psyches, we've maxed out our credit cards and the vicious circle of fear goes round again like a roundabout that we just can't get off. Beer?'

Cosmo's words struck something inside, but I wasn't quite sure what. His philosophy was rubbing off on me. It was like we were cut from the same fabric. It was my turn to be profound.

'There's enough money spent on stupid wars and sending space rockets to the moon, which are unimportant; why not put a bit of money back into the arts…don't you think Cosmo?'

'Absolutely…war creates more money and destruction than the

arts would ever do.'

'John Lennon had it right, Cosmo, *Power To The People*.'

'People are strange creatures, Jay. They show you what they want you to see. Life is complicated, and everyone has problems you know, but they rarely display or talk about what they're genuinely feeling. They go into their autopilot of I'm great, everything is great, my job, life, and marriage are all great, BUT are they, really? Jay, there is so much falsehood, façade, and fake.'

'I don't want to be fake; I do not want to be someone I'm not; I just want to be me.'

As the night wore on, our conversation went back and forth like a superlong rally at a Wimbledon tennis match. We drank some more beer and then some more.

'All you need is a strategy...you know... philosopher Lao Tzu had it right when he wrote.

"The journey of a thousand miles begins with one step."'

Cosmo's and Lao Tzu words were paused in the airspace above my head because while waiting for him to get another four-pack of beers from the cold water sink, I opened an email only to find that after traversing through the monopoly board of London to get to my Feltham audition. I received a message to find that I hadn't landed the part. I was back to GO again.

I snapped open one of the cold beer cans Cosmo handed me, which fizzed over my shirt.

'Shit...I feel like getting out of England... I'm fed up with acting...sometimes I just feel like packing it all in... I'm losing my edge... I just can't seem to get my name out there... I'm just hitting a brick wall! I'm getting nowhere fast.'

'The sacrifices of life are the joys of art, you know. Pass me those chips, Jay...A couple of years ago...I felt the same. I was going to quit my art..., but like you, I love it too much...so I simply couldn't quit...just because you aren't yet a household name doesn't mean that you are less talented than those who are. You just have to persevere.'

After hearing Cosmo's advice, I drifted into my own world and thought to myself. Who was I kidding? I couldn't quit, and I shouldn't be complaining; after all, I chose to be an actor; nobody forced me to be one. I knew that I needed to roll the dice again and needed to PASS GO. My trance was broken by...

'...Got it, Jay!...'

'Huh, got what?'

'I think you should mushroom...'

'What?' I asked, perplexed, thinking he'd taken some magic ones.

'You know...you should mushroom yourself a bushy beard...the power of the BEARD,' Cosmo said, his words stumbled and infused with Skol.

I thought he was joking or just so pissed up that his wisdom had disappeared out of the window.

'Fuck! The lights? Do you have any change, Jay?'

'Well, I was doing our weekly budget.'

'Yeah?'

'And I've worked it out.'

'Yeah?'

'And we have...the square root of fuck all!' I said, trying to lighten the mood.

Our pre-paid electricity meter designed to help those in debt actually chewed electricity up like a school of ravenous piranhas. Our home was often freezing cold with no heating, instant hot water, very little food, and no money, and this was just a normal day in our paradise. It was a life to which we'd become accustomed. We were both living the same struggle to clamber for survival.

Cosmo and I would often drink, play cards or board games till 4.00am, having drunken talks about everything and nothing; we would often wake up at noon.

We both landed a side hustle working part-part-part-time at Ali's Kebab shop in Peckham. The pay was low, but at least we had some decent food to eat. I named it—*The Dinner of Champions* because it beat all the other crap we had in our almost empty fridge.

When I wasn't serving drunk customers at Ali's, most days were spent surfing the internet, looking for acting work. I was trying to be creative, trying to suss out different angles to get into productions, and trying to think outside the box. But all my attempts to find acting opportunities seemed to be falling on deaf ears. Finding an acting gig was like finding a puddle in July. I was hitting a creative wall. I called my agent.

'Elizabeth, I'm willing to take on ANY acting work...absolutely ANYTHING. I'll do film, TV, music videos, voice-over work or modelling...ANYTHING. I'll even be the face of Tampax.'

'Leave it with me, Jay.'

True to her word she bagged me an audition for a part in a Caspa Codina music video. I was again short on money to travel and again, I took a chance to get there with little money by taking a risky train journey. This time, I got on the train in Deptford with a ticket three days out of date.

After I got off the train at Tower Gateway, Central London, I thought I'd reached my destination unscathed. That is until I was stopped in my tracks because I spotted a person dressed in plain clothes with a clipper board. Bollocks! It was a train inspector, armed and ready with his clipper. He stood intimidatingly waiting to take my ticket. I flashed it quickly, hoping that would be sufficient.

'Hold on...the ticket is out of date,' the inspector retorted militantly, not falling for my ruse.

Fuck, my goose was cooked!

'Sorry, it's an oversight on my part,' I uttered.

The waspish, overzealous inspector proceeded to write me a penalty ticket, giving me every chapter and verse about tickets. I knew I had at least an hour to spare, and the audition was only five minutes away by foot.

'You can write a statement to contest the penalty,' the inspector voiced, disinterested, as he continued to write on his clipboard. He didn't even look up at me.

The inspector was probably too busy calculating his commission, but as he calculated his profits, I calculated my plan to get out of the situation and get to my audition. I agreed to write a statement. Being the fastidious person that I was, it was imperative that I wrote each word and each line of the statement very, very, very carefully! I was hoping my tactical gambit would pay off.

After about ten minutes, the inspector rubbed the bridge of his nose and couldn't contain his impatience when he harrumphed and then snipped.

'For heaven's sake, can you hurry up, huh? I'm busy!'

The cantankerous inspector had tried to step all over my prerogative. But to his annoyance, I matched his sour tone by flippantly saying.

'You being busy is beside the point! This is my statement, and nowhere on this form does it say that I must write it in a specific time frame!'

But I knew that was my long suit because another ten minutes passed and the next train entered the station. Now even more irate, the megalomaniac inspector was about to face another trainload of people, and I was interrupting his snare. His patience metre just broke as he put his face into mine so close that I could see his deep vertical furrows on his glabella, which looked just like the train tracks. His plans now derailed. He snatched the statement from my hand, tore it into pieces, and shouted, outraged.

'People like you should GO TO JAIL!'

His voice trailed behind me as I headed out of the station. He obviously took umbrage to my tactics.

As I took one final look over my shoulder, I saw two of his inspector colleagues alongside him, probably wondering what the ruckus was all about.

It was freezing cold as I faced the wall. I was dressed in a fur coat, bearded and plastered with women's makeup. A man tapped me on the shoulder, indicating he was looking for his lost love. This wasn't the bathroom of a men's prison, though. I had smashed the audition that day and landed the part in a Caspa Codina Music Video—*Used To Go Dancing*, playing a bushy-bearded transvestite hooker.

Poster of Caspa Codina's Music video with me as a bearded transvestite hooker.

66 GRANDMA

'Rio de Janeiro!!!... 29 thousand pounds!!!....'

These words sprayed out of my mouth along with the flaky crumbs of a dry-as-a-bone croissant I'd been eating. I had just received a callback audition for a VW commercial in Brazil, playing an Angel. Okay, it wasn't an offer, but a callback had dwindled down the potential competition from hundreds to just three or four actors, including me. Just as I was about to confirm that, hell yeah, I'd be there, I groaned.

'Cosmo, can you sort this pile of shit out? It's doing my head in!' I rattled, trying not to get frustrated at the appalling speed of the internet connection that had just crashed.

I was about to throw the laptop out of the window when I received a phone call from Mum. Her voice was shaky.

'Hello Luv, sorry to ring yer like this, but it's yer Grandma...'

I dropped everything and rushed back to Yorkshire.

Grandma Croot

Just before I left Bradford to pursue a life in London, Dad's mum, Grandma Croot, had come to live with Mum, Dad, Martin and me, which was when I learnt much more about life, love and lost connections.

Grandma Croot's deep wrinkles were just like an olive-coloured antique map which harboured a thousand stories and a thousand more secrets. She had not long undertaken a return journey back to the comfort of her Bradford nest after leaving to live in Toronto, Canada, for a few years with another of her grandchildren and my cousin Bernadette.

Whilst everybody else was busy getting on with everyday life, over a brew, Grandma Croot told me about someone I knew very little about. A strikingly handsome Dutch Jew, her first love, my Grandad, Stanley Croot.

Grandad Croot
'He was very handsome, just like you, he looked like Ray Milland, all the ladies would swoon over him...he was adventurous...you know...he had an inborn *wanderlust*, just like you.'

I held onto every word as if she was telling me a story from a book, fascinated by the larger-than-life character she was presenting to me.

This was my first time learning more about the man I had known as Grandad Croot, a man I'd never met. As she relayed her memories through her stories about Grandad Croot, I wanted her to spend longer on each page as my mind filled with questions. I had been drawn in by her intriguing recollection as she moved on to the next story about the real-life *Gulliver*. Her romanticised words painted a vivid picture of Grandad Croot's love for moving from town to town, city to city and country to country.

'He had a wild streak, you know?...oh yes...that he did...it was the merchant sailor in him that gave him the taste for travel.'

'Where did he go...?'

Grandma Croot dug deeper into her memories; she was just as encapsulated in telling me her stories as I was in listening to them.

'New York...was one of the places where he spent some time...he was insatiable was your Grandad Croot...never could stand still...he had a curiosity and wonder he needed to fill.'

He sounded different from most of the family, apart from just one exception: me! I didn't know why words had remained up to now, unspoken about him other than those from Grandma Croot, but I savoured those slices of enlightenment as she shared more about him, as they somehow became part of a food, which seemed to nourish me.

'...There came a time when he disappeared for a whole year, you know.' Her tone remained calm as if she were talking about a routine event rather than a revelation. It was also as if what she had just said was no different nor any more dramatic than the other stories she had just told me. To me, though, her words as she spoke about Grandad Croot continued to glitter with the mystery around this fantastical character.

'A year?' I inquired, wanting to clarify that I had heard right and I had.

'Yes, a whole year...He set out one morning, saying he was off to buy some groceries... I remember now that he told me he was going to buy a Hovis loaf. But he ended up in London, that's where he was born, you know... he stayed with his sister Jessie in Hampstead...he stayed for a year.'

I was astonished by Grandma Croot's poise. She continued to speak with unalloyed pleasure about him and did not make any resentment toward him apparent. Instead, she continued to tell the story as if that was the way it was meant to happen. She continued to tell the story with love.

'That's where the Croot family had their big houses...'

It was the first time I heard that I had any family ties in London...a family whose opulent lifestyle contrasted greatly with the family I knew and belonged to.

'...But how did you find out he was in London?...' I asked, genuinely curious how this could possibly be, pre-social media days when privacy actually was a thing.

'I didn't know...until he came home to where his heart belonged...back here, with me.'

This, however, wasn't the last of Grandad Stanley Croot's days leaving Bradford. It was back in London, in his late 40s, that he sadly died tragically as a result of an accident. He had fallen through a trap door behind the stage in a London theatre where he'd been working.

'That was such a tragedy.'

Grandma Croot appeared to hold back her tears as she took a swig of her tea, and I tried to steer the conversation.

'He worked in a theatre?'

It had piqued my interest that there actually was someone in the family involved in the world of arts other than me.

Great Aunty Ellen Croot

'Yes...like your Great Aunty Ellen...your Grandad Croot's sister...but she worked on stage...in front of the audience...she was an actress and performed in the West End, you know?'

No, I hadn't known; no one had ever spoken of this huge detail. I could've been blown down with a feather as Grandma Croot shared another revelation. I knew absolutely nothing, until then, about a family member who was a fellow actor and a person whose soul was lit up when performing. Until then, I never knew acting was literally in my blood.

'Did you ever watch her perform?'

My mind was caught up in yet another story that no one had ever let me in on. She paused, looked to the heavens like she was searching for an answer, smiled and said.

'Only once when she was touring. She was very beautiful; she reminded me of Joan Crawford. Aunty Ellen had a similar magnitude, which meant that you couldn't quite take your eyes off of her. She performed in Bradford at the Alhambra theatre, you know...her acting days stopped when she caught the eye of a wealthy South African diamond merchant and got married...what was his name again? I can't quite remember...Can you make me another brew, love?... Ruan, that's it. Ruan was his name; I think that's what he was called.'

Grandma Croot said as I passed her, her third cup of Yorkshire tea after her second had actually gone flat cold.

I had been drawn in and connected with two people in my family I'd never even met. I knew that there were always three sides to every story, but Grandma Croot's version was one that I wanted to hold on to. However, her stories raised more questions than they answered.

The Journey

'No worries, Jay. Is £50 enough?' Asked Cosmo.

It was enough for the fare of the first available coach I could book from London, Victoria, to Leeds. The traffic in Leeds reflected the urgency of people, all of whom had somewhere to go, all of whom were probably feeling the same frustration and exasperation of being stuck in the rush hour gridlock with no indication that any of us were going anywhere in a hurry. Mum's worrying was also evident when she rang me again.

'We got a call Jason, luv...where are ye now?'

'I'll be there soon, Mum... I'll be there soon.'

'Is it okay if I get off here, mate? My Grandma is very sick, and I need to get to her.'

'No can do, sorry. That's the rule. I'd get the sack, sorry.'

The coach driver turned back to look ahead at the river of choc-a-block traffic. But desperate times called for desperate measures, and I remembered a trick I'd learnt as a boy on how to open the bus doors without needing the driver to do so, so I did that. I grabbed my big yellow rucksack from the suitcase rack, hit the button above the passenger door and jumped off the now-moving coach. It was dangerous and irrational, but in my world at that time, it was necessary.

I flagged down a taxi and headed to my childhood area of Allerton, where my Aunty Lynn's home was and where Grandma Croot was staying.

I walked down the long path. The cloudy sky darkened with every step, the leaves swirled in the wind, and the wilting tree branches sagged as the heavy raindrops hit them.

Grandma Croot's wish was not to go to the hospital. She was a fighter, just like Dad, and she held on. She was still alive when I arrived, and we sat by her bedside for a few hours before she passed away.

67 MEMORIES

'Mum, where are they?'
'I put them in a safe place, I can't remember where...'
'Mum!... I need them!!!'
'I'd be willing to bet that you've been gambling again. Jason, eh?'
'No, I quit my job.'
'What???... That good charity job?...Why?...What are ye going to do? Eh? What are ye going to do now, Jason?'
'Mum! I'm an ACTOR!'
'Why don't you want a proper job?'
'ACTING is a proper job Mum!!! Stop pushing me, will you?'
'Pushing ye, Jason? I'm not pushing ye!... What about yer savings? Where ye going to live? What ye going to do? What ye going to live on? You know money is like water!'
'Mum!!! I really don't need to hear this, you know... You always say there are no pockets in shrouds!'

My holy reference seemed to temporarily silence Mum's *Miss Marple*-esque interrogation, and with no way to return from this, she had no further comment, apart from.

'They're in my top drawer, underneath my white thermal Damart vests at the front.'

After my little tiff with Mum, who always believed that I had a head full of dreams, I found my Star Soccer football cards.

'Have you seen my *James Bond* eject car?'
'Was it on the shelf in the cellar?'
'Yes, Mum, why?'
'I didn't have any room for it Jason; it was cluttering up my house; sorry, I didn't know ye wanted it!'

'Mum, it was a three-inch car!'

As a goodwill gesture, Mum often donated some of my memorabilia and old toys to the St. Peters's church jumble sale. This was all well and good, but more often than not, she did this without telling me until after the fact. So, finding any of my old treasures where I'd left them when I went back to Yorkshire was always a surprise.

An old box on the top shelf of my wardrobe that was out of Mum's 5'6 reach was a pleasant surprise to find. So when Mum was busy watching *Columbo* on her 42-inch TV, I tipped the box out in the middle of Mum's guest living room, which was only reserved for special guests, and began sorting the box out. During commercial breaks, Mum came to see what I was doing, and she seemed less than pleased.

'Jason!... for cryin' out loud... what ye done? What yer rooting for?...my house is like a tip now...Sister Pat is coming in the morning...what yer trying to do torture me, eh?... I just can't have the house like this...I just can't, Jason!'

'I'll sort it out, Mum.'

'Why are ye so come day go day, Jason?'

In the box, which reeked of mothballs and housed a now aggravated Daddy Long Legs, I discovered treasures that were once the simplistic key to some of the happier moments in my childhood. Items that, when adulthood came, were packed away and simply left to gather dust. As I went through some items and checked their prices online, I realised I may have had a small pot of dusty gold in front of me. I continued rummaging through my old belongings and unearthed my Atari, Zx Spectrum, and Nintendo handheld game and watch. As I was flat broke, I needed cash quickly. I knew that I'd have to sell them if I wanted to continue pursuing my dream of making it big in London. So I had to ignore the nostalgic tug inside me and place all my retro belongings for auction online, but I kept my rare set of Ace Star Soccer cards. These were more difficult to bear to part with.

'Just don't worry, Mum...'

'But what are ye going to do...'

'I can't really speak about that right now...'

'But what about yer food...'

'I'm on the coach, Mum... I'll call you when I get home.'

I was on the way back to London and had just hung up on a flustered Mum when I slid my phone into the same jacket pocket where I'd put my treasured football cards.

'...Giz me back my Kenny Daglish card! You wazzock!...'

The voices of childhood friends were as clear as if they were yesterday, and they ran carefreely through my thoughts as I reminisced about swapping football cards at school and using them as a lifeline in return for getting out of strife. And as Luther Vandross's *Dance with My Father* played on my iPod, I thought of Dad: his football Yorkshire County Cup victory, his patience, and his share of big dreams and hopes. I remembered what he'd said to me.

'It was all alright in the end though, Lad... like it always is... it's always alright in the end.'

'We're expected to arrive at our final destination, London Victoria, at 6.30,' announced the ambitious coach driver.

We had just passed Hampstead and were caught up in the rush hour traffic of Golders Green. The view from my window was the window of Carmelli *Kosher* Bakery, displaying its beautifully shaped, shiny loaves of bread.

'...He was going to buy a loaf. But he ended up in London...he stayed with his sister Jessie in Hampstead...he stayed for a year.'

My thoughts had driven me back in time to when Grandma Croot told me about Grandad Stanley Croot, the wanderer who'd disappeared.

Even though the people around him may not have understood his drive to just up and go to do whatever he needed to do, he did it anyway.

The sharp horn of the coach driver who'd swerved away from some intrepid school children on the road diverted my thoughts back to where I sat on the coach to Victoria. I glanced at my phone to check the time and found myself in two minds about whether I was brave enough to check my emails, which I'd blanked whilst in Yorkshire, knowing that I couldn't attend an audition even if I had one. I'd tried to forget about the callback for the VW commercial in Rio de Janeiro that I couldn't attend, due to my Grandma Croot falling ill.

Before going to Yorkshire, I'd applied for ten or more feature films but had been getting out of my mind frustrated, waiting for someone to respond. I dared to read my unread emails.

Woah, *Mama Mia!* An email from a director, Dave Antonelli, put the brakes on my wandering thoughts.

68 FROM COFFEE TO CAMEO

Jason,
After reviewing your resume and showreel, I would like to consider you further for the lead role of Martin in my film *Inbetween*. I have attached the script for your perusal and will fly to London from Canada in the next few weeks for auditions. If you have any questions before then, do not hesitate to ask.
Sincerely, Dave.

I excitedly opened up the attachment and started reading the script. *Inbetween* was a psychological thriller by Dave Antonelli, who'd adapted the novel into a screenplay about love and redemption in the face of violence and futility. The storyline was loosely based on a left-wing West German terrorist organisation in the 70s who were devoted to the fierce overthrow of capitalist society, the *Baader-Meinhof* Gang. Like this gang, the terrorist group in the film *Inbetween* tried to cause tension between the East and the West through a series of bombings.

When I returned to Deptford, I began preparing for the audition by ordering several DVDs to help me research the *Baader-Meinhof* Gang and study their every nuance.

Four weeks passed, and I was fired up and ready to audition for this role. I left my pad with my heart full of fire and rocket fuel in my step.

The audition was held in a lobby of Knightsbridge Hotel, where I met the writer of *Inbetween*, Dave Antonelli himself. I hoped the weeks spent preparing for the scenes and trying to get into character would pay off. The audition also gave me a chance to show off my skills to blow the director out of the water through a performance of a two-minute piece of my choice. I chose Eugene O'Neill's *Long Day's Journey into Night*.

'Very good, Jason... your acting has a powerful, Al Pacino or Sean Penn kind of aggressiveness with a touch of European refinement...and...and a noticeable sensitivity under the intensity,' Mr Antonelli complimented following the audition.

On the cosy leather sofas of the plush hotel lobby with only a dash of people around, over coffee, I got the opportunity to learn more about the profound film director. It was a pleasure to share common interests and a rare chance to chat straight after an audition with a director. Like me, Mr Antonelli, who carried a certain cachet, had a great love of films; we discussed the greats from Ingmar Bergman to Federico Fellini to Jim Jarmusch and other filmmakers. I bathed in Mr Antonelli's knowledge of film and left with a great feeling, hoping that I would land the lead role of Martin.

Two weeks later, whilst eating breakfast, I received an email from Mr Antonelli, who wrote that although he loved my intensity and rugged look, he had found someone else who matched more of his vision of the character Martin. I thought I'd done enough, but clearly, I'd jumped the gun! I pushed my concentrated orange juice and my plate of salt and pepper eggs away as I pushed myself to read on. He also added this had nothing to do with my obvious acting ability and that it was just a question of niche. Mr Antonelli hoped we could work something out, and he still wanted to offer me a role as Yorkie, a gang member for the terrorist organisation. That news was certainly a brain fry for that time of the morning. My thoughts were as scrambled as the half-eaten eggs staring at me from my plate; Being offered a much minor role had certainly beaten my Ego. I needed time to mull it over. I snapped my computer shut and couldn't bear to look at any more emails for the rest of the day.

The day got even worse when I went to the Happy Shopper and got more than the milk that I had gone out for. A gigantic billboard poster with the face of an actor as an angel soured my mood as he overlooked Rio de Janeiro. It was from the VW commercial that I had to pass over, on account of my unexpected trip up north. Nevertheless, as I stood on the pavement looking up at the actor who looked very similar to me, I felt light-headed and sick to my stomach. I knew that I was developing a really bad case of the fuck-if-onlys.

Mr Antonelli's email mentioned that he would return from his Canada trip to London again the week before filming commenced. So, after a bit of time licking my wounded Ego, I contacted him, and we arranged to meet and discuss his offer.

We chatted over a strong, bitter Americano at Riverside Blend Café, overlooking the River Thames. Mr Antonelli's kind, gentlemanly approach made me feel relaxed straight away, and not a fan of formalities; he told me to call him Dave.

The astute director somehow sensed the cloud of disappointment of not landing the lead role, which was lingering over me.

'...Often, the hopes that actors hold onto just these big roles can create a factory of illusion...If a casting director looks at your resume and it shows huge gaps, they won't be likely to cast you.'

I listened and tried to let Dave's honesty sink in.

'Jason, a short film is better than no film at all. A feature film is better than a short film. Many great actors have taken small roles as cameos, and many of these roles have ended up being classic performances.'

Dave's silver tongue convinced me to take the cameo role of Yorkie and taught me something new about how I had been approaching my acting journey thus far. I appreciated Dave's candour and was now more open to dancing to his tune.

'Quiet on set, please,' hollered the assistant director.

Tower Bridge was the location where filming commenced one week later. The London landmark symbolised history and elegance that spanned over the River Thames with its majestic towers and raised bascule section. I had accepted and embraced the part of Yorkie. I was ready to blow my perceptions that I needed a lead part to deliver a stellar performance...right out of the water.

The bridge had to be cordoned off by the London Metropolitan Police for filming, which temporarily held up the traffic. The scene was set to be action-packed and a pivotal part of the film when the gang had taken two hostages, Jan and Liisi, at gunpoint.

Jan was a terrorist and part of the gang until he got cold feet to go through with the organisation's plan to bomb a hotel. Instead, he ran away and was then captured.

The dark nature of the scene was enhanced by the gunmetal grey sky over Tower Bridge. It was radiantly gloomy, it was biting cold, and it was about to chuck it down buckets, but I had never felt the feeling on such a day as I did then.

Dave Antonelli called. *'Action.'*

"Maybe I die today, but you'll always be a worthless bastard" (Jan to Luinstra)

".... it's time........walk.....or she dies...." Luinstra replied.

Jan was directed by his former gang leader, Luinstra, to cross the bridge armed with a detonator. The intention was to cause mass casualties, which included the planned targets of the entourage of English politicians and a Russian delegate who were crossing the bridge when Jan was due to set the bomb off. With the despair of impending doom, Jan slowly walked across the busy tower bridge, leaving the rest of the characters on edge. Jan was set to press the button, but just before he did, a gunfight ensued—this was my action part. The rebelling Jan, refusing to follow Luinstra's instructions and see innocent people killed in cold blood, ran with the detonator in his hand and threw it in the River Thames.

"*Fuck you, you Bastards!*" Jan yelled.

Gunfire rang out as characters fired guns from different angles. While this was happening, I, as Yorkie, ran across the bridge with a submachine gun to kill Jan. My heart was beating as fast as the raindrops that were now pelting on my face. After catching up to Jan, he laid punches into me, and a struggle broke out before I fell to the floor. This is where Yorkie and I met our end. After being shot and killed by Jan, Dave Antonelli Called. '*Cut.*'

That was that! My cameo role in *Inbetween* was shorter than the drop from Tower Bridge to the River Thames.

Inbetween Tower Bridge scene.

69 SMOOTH CRIMINAL

'Jay, are you sure this is a good idea?'

'No, Lance, it's a genius one!'

Armed with balaclavas and baseball bats bought from a sports shop, we ventured around Brixton in Lance Paterson's weathered Fiat Uno car on an early morning drive. The dashboard clock read 2:00am, and the chilly breeze and eerie darkness amplified our excitement. We felt like kings navigating the run-down streets of Brixton, with only the small kebab shops and chicken joints still open. We had no concrete plan in mind, and we were on the road to nowhere.

'What music is this, Lance?'

'Lil' Kim - La Bella Mafia, I want to learn some gangster lingo. I thought it might inspire us, you know.'

'How will American gangster rap inspire us? Our roles are Italian gangsters!'

'Sorry Tony Soprano! What music do you want, huh? Ennio Morricone?'

Lance and I were cast in the same low-budget mafia film and set to play Italian gangsters Umberto (Lance) and Marco (myself). It was a film which would transport us from *Genoa to Roma*, despite filming all of our scenes in Burnt Oak, North London.

We decided to immerse ourselves in our characters by exploring the dark alleys of "Method Acting." Our objective was to grasp criminal emotions. The *Genoa to Roma* scenes we were rehearsing for involved our characters robbing stores and banks, a world so far removed from our own.

We ended up in Canary Wharf.

'Nice, aren't they?' Said Lance, admiring the plush modern penthouse riverside apartments that took up the landscape.

'Nice? Huh, nice? Chips are nice, Lance! Those lavish apartments are not for the likes of you and me; they're for the elite. We can afford our cheap rent in Brixton and Deptford right now, but that will change in ten years, you know. Once the fat cats invest in an area, the real people are pushed out, and some are even left homeless. Can't you see the moral decay that has come with all this prosperity? It's wrong, Lance—it's just wrong!'

'Bloody hell, Jay. I only said they were nice! I didn't expect a Noam Chomsky lecture!!!'

We circled the area before we dared to go into a 24-hour petrol station. It was now almost 3:00am, and it was our only option for action at that ungodly hour. We pulled into the forecourt.

'Pass my balaclava on the backseat, will you...oh, and the baseball bat while you're at it...come on Lance, quick, hurry up!'

'What? No! You're not ACTUALLY going to do it, are you, Jay?'

'I'm not sat in your freezing cold Fiat for the fucking fun of it!'

'But Jay...'

'...Keep your hair on dingbat. I was only pulling your pisser.'

'You're crazy, you know...you had me going there, you're just about the craziest man I've ever met.'

'What?'

'It's like stepping into a haunted house with you...I swear!'

'What is, Lance?'

'Being with you, Jay.'

'What do you mean?'

'I never know what's going to happen next with you... you're always making mysteries.'

'I'm starved, *Scooby!* Fancy a *Scooby* snack?'

'See if they have any cornish pasties, will you,' Lance asked as he handed me some loose change from his dashboard. I made my way into the shop.

'Cold out, isn't it?' Said the tired-looking, salt-and-pepper-haired cashier. He commented in a friendly tone that sent out the need for a glimmer of human conversation from the world outside of the petrol station. I was familiar with the sheer and utter boredom he was feeling, having worked in a similar position at 18 years old.

'It is! They're talking of snow next week, too!' I responded to him, temporarily satisfying just a fraction of the cashier's hunger before it was interrupted with a loud beep and...

'Bugger, drive off... not another one!' hollered the slightly panicked cashier.

'Mustafa... it's another one...check the cameras, please.'

'Okay, Boss!'

The cashier directed the request to his colleague, who was stacking Weetabix on the other side of the shop. He was looking on towards the forecourt as a blue BMW car with four men had just screeched off without paying.

After paying for Lance's petrol and food, I returned to the car, my hands filled with two coffees and two discounted meat and potato pies.

'Did you see that?'

'See what?

'The drive off!'

'No. There was a drive-off? You want ketchup?' Lance enquired, pulling a bottle from his glove compartment as he squeezed it all over the pie I had just handed him.

'Why don't you put some pie on your ketchup!...it was invented in China!'

'What was?'

'Ketchup?'

'Getaway! Are you sure about that?'

'Yeah, it was originally made from fish guts in ancient China,' I said as Lance took a bite of his lukewarm pie.

'Thanks, MATE...that put me right off this! The thought of it is as nearly as bad as the kangaroo and kidney pie I ate in Sydney...I vomited for nearly a week!...fish guts, that's disgusting! I think I'll eat that later.'

He placed the bitten pie on his dashboard and pushed an open packet of chewing gum and some wooden prayer beads out of the way towards the passenger side before opening the lid on his coffee.

'Ever regret not being a vicar like your old man, Lance?' I asked, genuinely curious whether his mind ever questioned his decision to follow a burning dream.

'Not a chance in hell, Jay! Forgive my French! You know I chucked it up. I belong there as much as you do...it didn't suit me. Acting suits me. Acting is where I belong! I hope I can make it to the top.'

'Lance, the cream always rises just like in a coffee cup...acting isn't for the weak-spirited.'

After taking our last gulps of coffee to mask the taste of the disappointing, highly processed meat and potato pie, we decided to call it a night and head back to Lance's flat.

'I'm still starving, though!' Lance said while routing around his dashboard.

'Lance, you eat like there's no tomorrow. Do you have worms?'

'Ah...bingo,' he said as he found a slice of leftover garlic bread behind the prayer beads on his dashboard.

'Are you sure you want to eat that?'

'Why not? There's nothing wrong with it!' he said, his mouth half-filled with the big bite he had just taken.

The whiff of the God-only-knows-how-old garlic bread on Lance's breath was too much of a temptation not to comment on.

'Bloody hell...pew...what is it...chemical warfare with garlic?'

He blew a mouthful of his garlic breath in my face in retaliation for my jibe before he said.

'Let's get out of here...SEATBELT!'

As Lance drove back to Brixton, he made a wrong turn.

'Lance, your Sat Nav is about as helpful as asking a pigeon for directions,' I complained before grabbing his A-Z from the glove compartment.

Several wrong turns later, my own smart navigation system, named Common Sense, had gotten us out of an unknown territory, or so we thought.

'I think I know where we are now...yeah, I think I do...*Charlie Chaplin* used to live over there...see right there?'

I pointed to a house on Brixton Road.

'I don't believe it, I'm going bald!' Lance said as he looked through the rearview mirror.

'You are Lance. Do you blow-dry your hair?'

'Yeah. why?'

'Lance, it's well-known that blow-drying your hair regularly makes you bald.

'Jay, how do you know this shit? COPPERS! Sweet doodle fuck! I wasn't speeding, was I?'

To read the map better, I had switched on the interior car light, only to have it overshadowed by another set of lights — flashing blue ones! Lance and I exchanged alarmed glances; this wasn't part of the script.

'Don't press the panic button yet, Lance.'

Lance pulled to the side of the road. I quickly switched off the interior light as the two officers approached our car. One officer went to the back while the other approached Lance's window and demanded.

'Wind down your window.'

To which Lance complied, his nerves palpable.

The officer, wearing a stern look, leaned in, noting.

'You know your rear light is broken, right? And the interior light being on while driving is illegal.'

Lance who was in a tiz-woz stammered.

'Yeah, yeah, I know...I know...officer. Um, sorry...sorry about that. I was...um...reading my map and um...intended to fix the backlight. I've...um...just been busy.'

The officer, unimpressed.

'Pfft, reading the map while driving, huh?'

His words made us feel like snowflakes just about to fall into a bubbling volcano. Meanwhile, the officer at the back of the car shone his torch onto the back seat, revealing the baseball bats and balaclavas. He shouted.

'What's all this then?'

70 CRADLE OF FILTH

'Watch out, De Niro and Pacino!' Joked one police officer to the other as they walked back to their patrol car. After realising we were actually actors, the police officers had let Lance and me off with a stern warning. Fortunately, we'd swiftly avoided the long arm of the law. However, one man who hadn't was the character for the next role I'd landed, *Giles De Rais*.

De Rais was suspected, accused and found guilty of heinous crimes such as cannibalism. He was a 15th-century French activist whose love interest was *Joan of Arc*. Many believed he was not guilty of the crimes he was accused of and that he was set up.

My agent, Elizabeth, had set me up with an audition, and consequently, I was cast as the lead actor to play *Gilles De Rais* in *The Death of Love*, a music video for the extreme heavy metal rock band Cradle of Filth.

Like always, I researched my character and storyline, which was an integral part of my preparation process for filming. The music video's premise focused on the fugitive *Giles De Rais* being targeted by the French Government, who wanted him sentenced to death. The love of his life, *Joan of Arc*, had been burnt at the stake, leaving *De Rais* flashing back to the memories of his relationship with Joan. The filming was to involve graphic vignettes centred around death and murder.

On arrival at Pinewood Film Studio, the Cradle of Filth band members were rehearsing on a purpose-built smoke-filled set that depicted the 15th century.

After spending over an hour being kitted out in costume fitting and having my beard primped and primed in hair and makeup, I emerged from the dressing room, ready to rock. Though moving in the heavy costume I had on wasn't easy, I remembered what Perry Rivera, the drama coach and masseur extraordinaire, had told me about an actor's shoes being their silent partners that helped craft the very soul of their characters. True to what Perry had said, I could sense the heaviness of my boots, weighing me down with each and every thud I made; they spoke volumes and, without uttering a word, reminded me to make my steps slow and ominous, reminding me of the sinister presence I needed to reflect and reminding me how to channel the dark and unhinged character of *Giles De Rais*. Donned in costume: a cumbersome military-style coat and heavy military boots

Will Wright, the director, called. *'Action.'*

As my character, *De Rais,* emerged sinisterly from the fog billowing into the air from the production's smoke machine, the smell tickled my throat big time! Fortunately, my character was silent. Dani Filth, the lead singer, sang the electrifying song *The Death of Love.* The band of three electric guitarists, a drummer, and a keyboard player blasted out tunes of heavy rock.

My character, *De Rais,* a tortured soul with a tragic past, wandered through the film set ruins weighed down by his heavy coat, his heavy boots and his heavy heart. As the song's haunting melody intensified, *De Rais* sought solace following the execution of his lost love, *Joan of Arc.*

In the far corner of the film set, I, as *De Rais,* sat on a wooden throne-like chair at a long table covered with a pure white cloth as the band continued to play. Silver trays contained chicken meat that symbolised human flesh, and the vintage pewter goblets were filled with red grape juice, symbolising the human blood of his victims. I gorged on the *Smörgåsbord* of food and drink that was spread in front of me as the raw music continued to rage on in the background; then, in a spurt of madness, I stood up and savagely ripped the cloth from the table and, in one swift motion sent the platters of carcass and the goblets of human blood to soar into the air in a chaotic display. My heart beating against my chest matched the frantic tempo of the track. It was imperative to nail this in one take and I did as the director, Will Wright, called. *'Cut.'*

In the end, *The Death of Love* music video left a lasting impression on me and the audience of over 30 million viewers worldwide. Working on this production stimulated the hungry beast inside of me.

MY EGO SCREWED MY ACTING CAREER

Me, Will Wright, and Dani Filth, on the set of The Death of Love.

71 SHOWREEL DRAMA

'You talking to me? Are you talking to me? That was a great De Niro impression!'

'Cheers, Lance.'

Lance was referring to my performance as a hinky, Californian motorcycle cop on Cage The Elephant's - *Ain't No Rest For The Wicked*.

'With over 50 million views, you've got to put that one on your showreel. It'll look cool alongside the Cradle of Filth clips... So about your reel, there's this guy, Nigel; he's cheap, and he'll do a good job. I'll get his number for you and text it to you. Are you coming over tomorrow to rehearse for *Genoa to Roma?*'

'Cheers Lance. Yeah, I'll be over after eight.'

Now that I was privy to the power of the BEARD and had landed many more roles, my first showreel needed replacing. But with the eye-watering cost of £500 to have one made, I insisted on shopping around. Lance knew of someone who knew someone, who knew someone—namely, Nigel, a student film editor at the Ember University of London.

My film clips were the only master copies I had, and at the time, I had no access to tools to burn copies. Back then, it wasn't uncommon for filmmakers to provide an actor with only one copy of their film, and most of these films I worked on were expenses only, with the DVD being the gold nugget. Needless to say, I was hesitant and uncomfortable about sending Nigel my only ones just in case they got lost. As I desperately needed a showreel, I contacted Nigel.

'Of course, man, I can do a reel for £200...just post all your

DVDs to my campus at Ember University. I'll have your showreel sorted for you in no time, man,' Nigel said confidently during our initial phone call.

Bubble-wrapped to the heavens, I sent my DVDs off.

The next day, I was relieved to receive an email notification from the DHL courier service informing me that my material had been delivered and signed for at Ember University. I hoped that Nigel could make my new reel in a couple of weeks so I could send it to potential film and casting directors.

I already put £100 in Nigel's bank account, half of the agreed payment, so I was expecting work on my showreel to commence soon, given that he promised to do it in no time.

Three weeks had passed since Nigel had received my parcel, and I hadn't heard a dickie bird from him, so of course, I pinged him an email. His reply was infuriatingly slow, and when he did respond, it went along the lines of...*sorry man, I've been down with the flu...I've been feeling like crap...I'll get on it today.*

Over the next fortnight, the following emails ping-ponged in the same pattern: me batting over questions about what the score was with updates, and Nigel only returned me a list of reasons why my reel wasn't ready. I didn't believe there was a kernel of truth in what Nigel was saying.

Eight weeks after sending my DVDs, Nigel's emails bounced back, showing a non-delivery report; phone calls to him went straight to his voicemail. It was as if he disappeared from the face of the earth. Why was he ghosting me? I had become extremely anxious about my material. This was my career on the line here. I'd be lost without the footage, which was several years' worth of acting work for me.

The following weekend, I headed out to Ember University in West London, where Nigel was studying and living on the campus. My blood was boiling like I'd eaten 85 scotch bonnet hot chillies. I needed to remain composed.

On arrival at Earls Court tube station, it was pissing down; even the rain couldn't wash away my bad mood.

I arrived at the security desk and gave Nigel's name to the security guard, who looked like he was tired of life. After checking his name list, he said.

'Just down there on the left, just after the bin, you'll see a white door.'

I came to the white wooden front door with twenty or so metal buzzers. I pressed several buzzers with various names on them. I made sure not to press Nigel's. I wanted to surprise him as he probably wouldn't open the door if he knew it was me.

Then Bingo! Someone answered.

'Pizza!' I chimed.

It was a trick I'd seen in a movie, and it worked a treat.

The door opened. I stormed upstairs and went to number 22, Nigel's room. I banged on Nigel's door. There was no answer, although I thought I heard a noise inside the room. I knocked again and again, but no joy.

Extremely agitated, I crossed the landing and sat on a hard, white plastic chair in the canteen, facing Nigel's room. A bohemian-looking student came in and popped something in the microwave. It smelt like chicken curry. The student waited bleary-eyed, watching the dish spin inside the microwave until the ping woke her from her daze. The bohemian removed the fragrant dish from the microwave and left the canteen with her poultry dish while I waited for the paltry excuse for a man: Nigel.

It wasn't until about 30 minutes later that Nigel's door opened, and a spikey-haired guy in his 20s walked out and passed the canteen's open door. I stood up and quickly followed him. Before he reached the staircase, I put my hand on his shoulder and said. 'AHEM, NIGEL?'

He turned, shot a look at me and realised who I was, replying sheepishly.

'Hey, what's up, man? I...uh...wasn't expecting you...I mean...why are you...'

'...Why?...Why? There are a hundred reasons why! Check your bank balance if you can't remember...MAN!... I've waited over two months, which is hardly, quote-unquote, "Done in no time," is it, huh?'

I was as calm as a raging bull when I directed him.

'You've got a minute to go into your room, get my showreel DVDs, put them in a bag and bring them out to me.'

'Okay, man...okay, I'm going, calm down, man!'

'This IS MY CALM NIGEL !'

'We'll cut here?' Suggested my new editor.

It took one cutting look from me to tell him that I disagreed.

However, he tried to make another suggestion.

'Are you sure you want to leave so many scenes in, huh?... It's eight minutes long, you know...I don't think...'

'...Yes!!!'

I fired across to him another glaring look to reiterate that I...MEANT...BUSINESS... Of course, I knew better. I was the ACTOR, after all.

'Okay, have it your way!' he replied, the inner corners of his eyebrows creased as they pointed south towards bloody hell.

I'd found a new editor to do my new showreel—one who was a better communicator. One that I could sit in with while he made it. I insisted that a clip from EVERY film I made had to be in that showreel, much to the editor's dismay!

A week later, it was ready. Thrilled and excited, I tried to upload it onto various acting websites but then found that my eight-minute reel could not be uploaded because, on average, two minutes was the maximum length allowed. I was gutted, to say the least, because I had to feed my overly indulgent Ego a humongous piece of humble pie and then edit the reel down all by myself.

72 THE HEIST

"Drop your weapons now, or I won't hesitate!"
"You really think you can take us both down, old man?"
"I won't go down without a fight!"
"You must be itching for early retirement, huh?... shall we give him a retirement party, Umberto?"
"You'll never make it out of here alive!"
"We'll see about that! Say hello to the fireworks, old-timer! It's time to light up this joint!"

'What do you think?... Good?'

'Lose the teeth-gritting Lance; no one grits their teeth when angry, and what's with the eye crinkling?'

'Clint Eastwood does it!'

'Lance, you have delusions of grandeur...you look more like Squint Eastwood than Clint Eastwood... What about me? Watch this, Lance!'

'Jay, we are not doing a Bollywood movie, are we?'

While Lance tried to get his facial expressions right, I focused on my movement. We were rehearsing our scene over coffee and burnt toast in Lance's Brixton flat. Lance and I hoped that our filming of *Genoa to Roma* would go a bit smoother than our rehearsal when we almost got arrested for carrying balaclavas and baseball bats in Lance's car.

'You were shitting yourself, weren't you, Jay? Your face changed colour!'

'No, Lancelot, your garlic breath did that!'

'Very funny...speaking of garlic, did you know Rudolph is planning to make a *Dracula* movie too?'

MY EGO SCREWED MY ACTING CAREER

Rudolph Assasini was born and raised in Naples and came to London after he left film school to pursue his dream of making films. His future plans included a black and white *Dracula* feature-length movie, but like us, the project he currently had his teeth sunk into was *Genoa to Roma*, the film he was directing. Because of the budget restraints, there were only a few scenes. Rudolph intended to film the majority of the production in Italy. In the edit suite, Rudolph planned to cut back and forth using stock clips, making it look like Lance and I were in Italy when, in fact, our scenes were all filmed at night in Burnt Oak, London. The film's premise centred around Lance's character, Umberto, and my character, Marco, both striving to make their ultimate dream of owning a Naples-based casino business happen. However, in the script for Umberto and Marco, the only way to make the dream come alive was to generate money through a string of robberies and bank heists at gunpoint.

A few weeks later

It was a dark winter's late afternoon, at about 5:00pm, when the two camera operators, Christen and Sam, the director Rudolph Assasini, Dapo, who was to play the security guard, Lance, and I were all preparing to film.

The location was a derelict building in North London. We had to get this scene perfect because the budget was tight, only stretching to allow us to film for one hour in the now-abandoned bank.

Rudolph Assasini opened the back door to the rented building. The stale, musty, damp smell hit as soon as we entered. There was no electricity, so we used torches to see our way around.

'Jay, I really appreciate you helping me get this. I really was desperate for a role.'

'You could have gone to the bakery, Lance,' I quipped as I brushed over his sentiment.

'FIRST POSITIONS!' yelled the nervous-looking director.

'This is it, Lance,' I ear-kissed.

'Call me Umberto; I like to be referred to as my character when on the film set.'

'Okay, *Batman!*'

While Lance and I were getting into character, Christen and Sam had set up the generator, the cameras, and the portable lights inside and outside the bank, and Rudolph Assasini called. *'Action.'*

Our characters, Umberto and Marco, broke into the bank through the back door using a crowbar and were careful not to set off the alarm. The bank was closed for business, and no staff were supposed to be working. It was pitch black inside the bank as we used our torches to case the joint, looking for the vault. My gun was in my inner jacket pocket, ready for the next part. I had watched many episodes of the hit 70s police series *Starsky and Hutch* to get the movements spot on, and I was smashing it.

The vault at the back had a robust metal door, but our characters were not deterred by this. The next part of the scene involved Lance and me using fake explosives to blow the door off its hinges. To our characters' surprise, Dapo, the African American security guard, was on duty, and we both found ourselves face-to-face with his loaded gun.

"*Drop your weapons now, or I won't hesitate to use my gun!*" Ordered Dapo.

"*You really think you can take us both down, old man?*" Marco replied. The script then planned for Lance and me to react in that split second by pulling out our guns and aiming them towards Dapo. I pulled out my gun, which got stuck momentarily in the hole in my jacket pocket. In my panic, I yanked it hard but then accidentally dropped the decommissioned gun, but this wasn't part of the script. I picked up the gun, and we continued the scene, which resulted in us escaping with the loot in hand and a dead security guard.

"*Did you have to kill him, Marco?*" Umberto yelled, trembling.

"*I had no choice, kid,*" Marco replied coolly.

Then Rudolph called '*Cut.*'

It was only after the filming had ended that I realised that in my panic of yanking the gun out of my holey pocket and inadvertently dropping it on the floor, I had dented it.

When filming ended, all the cast and crew headed to The Black Horse, a nearby pub. I sat next to my other two fellow Stooges, Lance and Dapo.

'This place is hinky, guys...Look at how watered down this beer is,' Dapo commented as he examined his nearly translucent pint.

'Watered down? This is not beer; it's brown water! That round cost me a ruddy £35. London's becoming too bloody expensive!'

'£35? That's Daylight robbery,' I quipped as I talked on.

'A cocktail at Expo was £35, you know.'

'No way? You used to pay £35 for one cocktail.'

'No, dingbat, how long have you known me? I'd never pay £35 for a cocktail.'

'Not even if you were buying one for Salma Hayek, Jay?'

'No, not even for Salma, Lance!'

'I'd be her bodyguard any day!' Dapo teased, prodding for a

reaction.

'Dapo, you couldn't even secure a bank! Never mind securing Salma Hayek!' I joked.

Lance's Heineken shot up his nose from guffawing, which he spurted all over the table.

'I'll put that line in my book!' Lance said with gusto.

'You're writing a book? You never said. Everybody's writing a book these days. What's it about?' I inquired curiously, wondering why he'd kept it under wraps.

'Didn't I say? Before doing my screen acting course in Sydney, I harboured many thoughts about life, acting, and choices. That's what it's about. When I was sailing around Oz...I had a lot of time to think, you know.'

'It's your round, *Sinbad.*'

Lance ignored me and talked on.

'I'm hoping people can relate to it... I'm hoping people will buy it... It's called *Acting Unmasked.*'

'I'll buy it!' Dapo chimed.

Lance put his arm around Dapo in a sign of appreciation.

'Be careful of Stockholm Syndrome, Dapo...Jokes aside, Lance, I support you and your dream. I hope it's a bestseller.'

'Me too! I'll even leave you a review,' Dapo said.

'Cheers, guys. As long as it's a five-star one!' Lance joked as he went into a gigantic monologue.

'People are funny, aren't they? Not many bother to leave reviews when everything's fine. But something goes wrong, and suddenly, everyone's eager to jump on the bandwagon of blame, clicking that one-star button and leaving a scathing comment. They're like vultures circling overhead, waiting for the slightest hint of weakness to swoop down and tear apart their prey... It's not just strangers either...Not everyone is like you guys...In terms of being supportive, I mean....Even the ones you thought were friends that you've helped out once upon a time... It's like lending someone an umbrella on a rainy day, and then they forget your name when the sun comes out. People do have short memories, don't they?'

Over copious pints of watered-down beer, we chatted more about the day's filming and Lance's novel whilst Rudolph, the director, returned the gun to the nearby arms rental shop in North London.

When Rudolph returned, he came straight over to me and handed me a supermarket carrier bag.

'It's just a small token of my appreciation, Jason. Don't open it here. Wait till you get home.'

73 JUMPING THE GUN

'*Ee-se malaka, malaka, malaka!* Are you out of your mind!? huh...? What the fuck is this doing here..huh? We can both get an eight-year prison sentence for this, don't you know that? Huh? What have you been doing?'

'Huh? What?' I groggily replied, wondering what I'd done to aggravate this rather irate grizzly bear who sounded just like Cosmo.

After having one too many watered-down beers, my head was about to explode. I didn't have the foggiest idea what all the brouhaha was about, but I tried to convince my eyes to stay open so I could find out.

The morning after the night before, at home in Deptford, South East London, which at the time was one of the most notorious areas in the capital for gun crime. The ordinarily laid-back, stoic, wouldn't-hurt-a-fly Cosmo appeared discombobulated and now angry. He'd awakened me from my slumber on the sofa, shaking me frantically, pointing with his yellow marigolds at the supermarket bag Rudolph Assasini had given me. I could now understand why Cosmo was getting his knickers in a twist. Rather than the gift from Rudolph being a box of chocolates or something similar, I was shocked to find that Rudolph had gifted me the Beretta 92FS decommissioned and now recently dented gun from the film. I felt honoured to have received such a kind gift and souvenir from my fantastic filming experience, but in my inebriated state, I hadn't realised that I had travelled across London on the bus and tube with a gun. And when I got to Deptford, I just passed out on the sofa, without checking the bag's contents. The reality of having a gun began to dawn on me as I tried to get my bearings. *Fuck!*

'What's going on? I thought you brought home some food or something. I opened the bag to put whatever was in it in the fridge and saw THAT thing!...what have you done, man? I thought I knew you...but clearly... I don't know... Communication, Jay, speak to me; you NEED TO COMM-UNI-CATE.' The ordinarily stoic Cosmo paced up and down, beating his chest and then rubbing his face like a crazed man as his blazing brown eyes shot a look at me.

With as much rationality as I could muster, I filled in the blanks to Cosmo as to how the decommissioned gun had come into my possession. Though this gave him a slight (albeit temporary) relief that I hadn't committed a heinous crime, possessing a firearm was a crime all the same. What on earth was I going to do with a gun? I couldn't sell, give, or throw it away. Surely, because it was just a gift, and I didn't intend to do anything with it, the eight-year prison sentence for possessing an unlicensed firearm wouldn't apply to me, would it?

A few days later, at home at around 3:00pm, while I was doing my daily trawl for acting roles online, a bang similar to fireworks made me jump. I stuck my head out of my window to see what it was but didn't notice anything apart from the smell of burning. I put it down to the bored local teens trying to mess around with fireworks, so I didn't think anything more of it.

It was just after nine at night, and Cosmo was at an Art festival in

Shoreditch. He still hadn't quite forgiven me for the gun palaver and was even more pissed that I hadn't yet got shut of it. I hadn't eaten, so I ordered a Mediterranean pizza from Pizza Italia. It had been over an hour since I placed my order. Starving and bored, I started playing with the gun, imagining myself as Detective Dave Starsky. I bounced around my pad, holding the gun as if I were in one of the *Starsky and Hutch* episodes. Then the door went. I put my gun down the back of my trousers with only the loose elastic to hold it up.

I answered the door; however, it wasn't my Mediterranean pizza at all but a uniformed police officer! *Fuck!* Before he had a chance to speak, my life literally flashed before my eyes, along with the irrational thoughts that he had found out about the gun. I stood at the door with my gun lodged near my butt. The potential eight-year prison sentence shone in luminous lights right before my eyes and right up my arse. What on earth would I say to my mum? I felt drop dizzy. Come on, Jay, pull yourself together; you're an actor. You can get out of this! I thought before the police officer said.

'Good evening, sir; we are making routine enquiries about an incident involving a firearm.'

74 NEW BEGINNINGS

As I closed my front door, I clasped my hands together and looked heavenward. I praised God; in fact, I praised every God I could think of.

It turned out that the police officer was inquiring whether I had heard or seen anything about an incident that happened around 3:00pm that day. The incident that I put down to rogue teens setting off fireworks on the pavement was not this at all. It was related to suspected gang warfare that had been rife in the surrounding area. The crime committed: A near-fatal drive-by shooting, which nearly injured two men as they sat eating pizza in the front seat of their car. The bullet had bypassed them and their pepperoni pizzas and shattered their car window instead.

'£11, please, mate.'

'Keep the change, buddy,' I said, handing the pizza delivery guy a screwed-up £20 note.

Following the police visit that had scared the bejesus out of me, I had to destroy the gun. I had no option.

It took me about a week or so to break the gun into pieces, then I discarded it, bit by bit by bit, making sure that there was no way, no shape or no form, that the pieces would be a potential danger to anybody who found them. I was a massive hoarder and hated throwing things away, particularly items that had significance in my life, so before breaking the gun into smithereens, I seriously contemplated storing it in Mum's basement cellar on my next trip to Yorkshire, but if Mum had found it while doing her *Miss Marple* routine, no doubt she would've gone absolutely ballistic.

I had debt coming out of my wazoo, and I had run out of money. Desperate times called for desperate measures; sadly, I decided to put my Star Soccer cards up for sale on eBay. I was compensated for this, though, as they sold for £2155. However, as the cards were attached to so many memories of the good old days and good old friends, they were not easy to part with.

Those were not the only things I had to part with, though, as Cosmo had suggested, a new environment, i.e. a new place to live, could lift my spirits. I completely understood the message loud and clear.

'No hard feelings, Jay, huh?'

And now, with just enough money to rent my own place and pay back what I had cadged from Cosmo, I found a new place where at least I could sleep in my own bed. I'd seen a small ad placed in Ha-Noi oriental supermarket shop window in Deptford advertising a luxury flat for rent at £80 per week, with rent prices increasing every millisecond. I called the landlord, Sammy, and after a brief chat with him, I decided to take the place without viewing it. Sammy gave me his office address in Deptford, where a week later, I signed a rental agreement, paid the rental deposit and picked up the keys. With my big yellow rucksack, I left the office and took the 172 bus to make the short journey to my new pad.

I usually play poker blind, which is a big gamble, and signing a lease on an apartment without seeing it was an even bigger gamble, as I soon discovered. When I arrived at the apartment to move in, I wasn't expecting Buckingham Palace, but it was immediately evident why the rent was so cheap, and I certainly hadn't hit the jackpot. The advertised luxury flat was a bedsit hovel in the notorious Peckham, South East London. It was one of many bedsits in a large building near my old workplace, Ali's Kebab shop. The dimly lit room was like a museum of horrors with a long, full-length, cracked mirror and furniture that'd seen better days. In the corner of the room was a chair that probably hadn't been cleaned since the day it was made, which was most likely to be before I was born. There was something resembling a desk in the corner. And against the wall was a gas heater that looked like it was made in a different decade. Every window was stuck down with paint. Plus the toilet was so close to the kitchen I could've fried bacon and taken a crap simultaneously. By no means was it *bijou*, but for now, this had to be the paradise I would call home!!!

I spent many hours in my new Peckham paradise, immersed in Pacino classics like *Dog Day Afternoon, Serpico,* and *Carlitos Way,* and in awe of gems like De Niro's *Taxi Driver, The Deer Hunter,* and *Once Upon A Time in America.*

'Wayk uhp and smel thuh kaw-fee...noo yawk, noo yawk...liddl baddl dwader...'

My newly purchased American accent book was proving to be much more difficult to get to grips with than I had initially envisaged, but I needed to get the accent as down as I could get it, as it could only help me get nearer to taking a bite of the BIGTIME I hungered for.

There were a few companies at the time that were charging $7,500 or more for three weeks to guide aspiring actors around American studios during the Pilot Season. During this busy time each year, new TV productions were trialled, and their mainstream potential was weighed up. In hopeful actors' eyes, this had the chance of bringing up plenty of opportunities for them to appear on new shows. The companies also promised possible introductions to film industry contacts. After researching, I realised that, realistically, the three weeks weren't long enough to make an impact, and it wasn't as fruitful as the promises being sold. I wanted to cross the Atlantic to make a long-lived impact and prove myself. I planned to find an acting manager in the United States and set my sights on New York. Top actors like Pacino and De Niro had managers, so why couldn't I?

After sending tons of emails to American managers, I heard nothing. This was proving not to be a cinch. I was getting frustrated, waiting, waiting and waiting some more. THEN, in a stroke of good fortune, I found a message in my spam folder that had lost its way. It was from VSZ Management. I did my checks on Google to see that it was a proper company and not one trying to sell me Viagra or steal my bank details.

The *kosher* email was from Verona Sanchez, a Manhattan-based manager at VSZ Management.

Hello Jason,

Thank you for your interest. I would love to meet with you. When will you be in New York? Once I hear back from you regarding your plans, we can arrange a meeting.

Thank you

Verona Sanchez

Although I know I should've taken my time to think about it and reply, I waited for a total of two whole minutes before I impulsively typed up my email response.

Dear Verona,

I'll be in New York next week. Let's meet up. I look forward to

hearing from you.
Best regards
Jason

My Ego and heart swelled with excitement as I danced to James Brown's *Living in America.* Mid-dance, it dawned on me that crossing the Atlantic would cost money. My kebab dinner reflected how healthy my bank account was or rather wasn't.

As usual, my sense of rationality was overtaken by what I wanted there and then.

'Let's see. Heathrow to JFK return flight would be, hmm, £750, not including baggage. How does that sound?' Enquired one of the Flight Centre's friendly travel agents.

75 ENGLISHMAN IN NEW YORK

It was about 9:00pm on a pitch-black, freezing evening. I'd soon forgotten the February cold when I reminded myself where I was and that this was it. I was finally living the dream.

I had arrived at JFK Airport in The City That Never Sleeps, New York. I was on a limited budget, so I skipped taking a cab and headed to Brooklyn via the longer, cheaper option of the Q7 bus, which was more within my budget. I sat on the first empty seat I saw. On the seat across from me was an old guy snoozing, and in front of him sat a trendily dressed woman. After 30 minutes or so, the old guy woke up, started coughing and then sneezed but failed to cover his mouth. To my disgust, a globule of bright, green phlegm tinged with blood flew out and landed on the lady's jacket before him. Needless to say, the ghastly sight put me off the salmon and avocado bagel I'd bagged from the plane and intended to eat later.

Finally, I arrived at my destination, and I'd be lying to say that the apprehension didn't hit me as soon as I stepped off the bus. As I'd expected, the area was slightly sketchy, so I quickened my pace to the subway, where I had to take a quick ride to my hotel stop, Metro Myrtle-Wyckoff Avenues. The area had an eclectic mix of stores and restaurants, and the graffiti-sprayed shutters and walls boasted some art that Banksy would have been envious of. I spotted a Chinese takeaway. The smell was tempting me, but my track record wasn't so good at those joints, so I passed. I was disorientated but didn't want to pull out my map. My big yellow rucksack already made me stick out as a tourist. Having seen many films based in New York, I had come armed with the knowledge that the city had a reputation for crime. I knew that I needed to get to my hotel quickly. Fortunately, I made it to my accommodation without being held up at gunpoint, and I checked in.

The Red Carpet Inn was hardly the most beautiful place I'd seen, but I chose it because of the name and cheap price, not the aesthetics.

My room was on the 2nd floor, and the elevator was out of order, so I had to take the stairs. I opened the door to find a room that contrasted hugely with the plush New York hotel rooms I'd seen in the movies. Nothing fancy; It was a tiny, no-frills room with a toilet but no shower. It had a double bed rather than a four-poster bed. Stuck next to it was a crinkled travel-themed picture off-kilter on the stained wall. It was clear that I wasn't living the high life yet!

I was due to meet Verona Sanchez at 11:00am in her office the following day. My restlessness itched at me like an overactive flea with the fleas. Before I knew it, it was almost 4:00am. The local bin trucks were causing a racket, which woke me from my fitful night's sleep. Restless, I flicked through the TV channels to find something dull to watch. Ironically, I stopped on the scene of a famous 70s movie where the lead actor was told:

"Mr Grillo, you've got the job. Welcome onboard."

Grillo then went out where an office party was in full swing and yelled.

"I love New York!" In his ecstasy, he kissed a startled stranger.

'Colour me surprised. I wasn't expecting to see you there, boy,' voiced a large, hairy, middle-aged man with a thick Texan accent.

He was occupying the only shower cubicle on the whole floor, and I'd obviously startled him as he came out of the shower with a towel so small that one side of his hairy butt cheek peeked out from under his towel. Maybe he was playing a game of Texan hold 'em in there.

When he left the shower, I jumped in. The smell of the hairy man's lavender-scented shower gel overpowered the shower cubicle, and stray pubic hairs, which were not mine, floated around my feet on the yellow-stained floor, but my mind was on other things.

Suited and booted, I left the hotel lobby and popped into Martinez Grocery Store and bought a Sky Bar; after my chocolate fix, the sky was the limit. I'd initially wanted to find Katy's Candy Store in the hope of bumping into its owner, Katy Keyzer, who was famous on social media for the great quote.

"I speak three languages. English, Spanish, and Mother Fucker."
I loved that!

I opted to treat myself to a cab and tried to flag down a yellow cab like they did in the movies. I mustn't have been doing it right as one cab after the other passed me by. A scruffy-looking guy smelling of alcohol walked past me and said in a strong New York nasal accent.

'No cabs, stop in this hinky area, buddy.'

'Cheers, buddy,' I replied, testing out my American accent (which obviously didn't work).

'You're from whatchamacallit? Hmm.. England, yeah, England.'

The whiff of sizzling street hotdogs from a food truck intertwined with exhaust fumes and coffee from nearby cafés wafted up my nose. Minus the fumes, the aromas of the Big Apple were as refreshing to me as my favourite childhood smells of happiness, fresh Yorkshire country air and Nana's newly baked apple pie. I was in my element and wanted to breathe in the oxygen of the movie legends De Niro and Pacino, natives of this great city.

After a few attempts of being ignored by the yellow cabs, I realised there was a New York way of doing it: by slightly stepping off the pavement into the oncoming New York traffic. I eventually stopped one and gave the driver the address: Duane Street, Tribeca, Manhattan. The cab journey took me over the Manhattan Bridge, one of the iconic filming locations of *The Godfather, Once Upon a Time in America* and Woody Allen's classic *Manhattan*. My mind worked overtime as we drove down Broadway; dreams of the BIGTIME were now becoming reality. I was enamoured by the vibrant atmosphere of New York City, and it was certainly a contrast to the one-eyed places I'd lived in in the past.

The cabby was a middle-aged guy. His dashboard ID highlighted his name, Lorenzo. The friendly driver commented on my British accent as we got into a conversation about me being an actor.

'You're right in the thick of it, kid. It's the city that never sleeps, the city of broken dreams... I've had my time treading the boards, too, you know!' Lorenzo revealed as he took a bite of his sweet-smelling cinnamon doughnut while stuck at the traffic lights. Lorenzo's words hit the brakes abruptly on my vision of making it big in the USA. I sat through the rest of the journey, thinking about making the huge move to the States, only to find myself in Lorenzo's position. I didn't want to be driving a cab. Not that there was anything wrong with that job; it was just that I wanted to be a STAR...But was this even possible?...or did I need to wayk uhp and smel thuh kaw-fee? I knew I had to take every risky opportunity to get to where I wanted to be, regardless of the odds stacked against me.

We arrived outside Verona Sanchez's office before any further fears became gridlocked in my mind. I paid Lorenzo, tipped him five dollars, and he said.

'Break a leg, kid.'

I felt like I'd left my stomach in the reception area that I'd just come from, and I was hoping that my nerves working overtime wouldn't lead to me needing the restroom. I arrived on the 17th floor and entered the bright, beautifully furnished office where after a quick greeting, Verona's assistant went off to tell Verona that I'd arrived.

Boom, boom, boom, shake the room! What a stunning lady, very Junoesque. I hadn't actually envisaged what Verona Sanchez would look like. As we walked into Verona's swanky office, I was glad she hadn't noticed my hands trembling. Her initial words were a blur, which became more comprehensible with the quick caffeine fix her assistant had brought me. It was not long before the straight-to-business Verona Sanchez shared her perspective on the many actors she'd encountered in their early days.

'...Fiery, passionate actors can be truly great when they start out, you know? They've got the hunger and eagerness...over time, some tend to coast on their initial successes. They rest on their laurels. You know? They think that they've made it. And they no longer think they have to try. They lose their drive...'

Verona was talking at a speed like a train travelling a million miles a minute. At this point, I was trying to figure out where this was going. I hoped my transatlantic journey would not be a waste and that Verona's response would not derail my dreams in the following seconds.

Verona looked me straight in the eyes and said nothing. She held this look for a few seconds, which felt like an eternity. Maybe she was looking for my hunger, my desire and my want. She then smiled.

'I have a nose for talent. I'm happy to tell you that I want you on my books. Oh, by the way, you will be the first European actor to join.'

I began to sign the first page of the five-page contract, but I hardly even read it. I could've been signing my life away. I could've been agreeing to work for free. I noticed the clause about her 15% commission, but to be honest, at that point, I would have agreed to give her 85% as I signed the deal.

The New York breeze was like champagne, and my energy was like a supernova as I left the office light-headed and euphoric. A swell of different emotions came over me. Although my stomach had found its way home, my sense of inhibition flew as tall as the high-rise buildings surrounding me. I walked through the dash of people towards a middle-aged woman walking her Chihuahua dog, gave her a big kiss on the cheek, and said.

'I love New York.'

'I do too, sugar,' she replied, smiling.

I left her looking stunned but still smiling, and fortunately, I managed to get away from the aggravated and yapping Chihuahua before it nipped my ankle.

I had a few dollars left and two days left to explore the city that never sleeps. It was the city of wonderful dreams, the very same city that filmed the TV programme *Fame,* that had inspired me to dance on Rosedale Avenue as a boy. I wanted to make the most of my trip and have a long-awaited slice of this place they called the Big Apple.

The New York Water Taxi sailed down the Hudson River as I looked towards the magnificent skyline of New York. My thoughts were of my intrepid Grandad Croot, who was here 50 years or so ago. The boat arrived at the torch of enlightenment, which was held high and proud by the Statue of Liberty. My eyes misted up due to the New York smog, of course. Quickly, I wiped away the tears that dared to fall.

76 MAN AFTER MIDNIGHT

Jason,

You will need to join SAG. This is not hard if you work on a commercial in America, for example. You need to be looking at moving out here as soon as possible. I will be away in LA next week but will be in contact soon. Regards Verona

This email made everything that had just happened all the more real, having just landed a New York manager. I was on fire.

However, a few weeks went by when the highs of the events in New York were fading thick and fast, and I started to feel melancholy. My mind was cluttered with the should haves, could haves, and would haves. I should've booked a more extended trip. I could've looked for film roles in New York, and I would've at least been starting to make leeway by carving a name for myself across the Atlantic. And why didn't I try an American-style Knickerbocker Glory, just like I'd seen in the *Laurel & Hardy* flicks?

I soon perked up after reading Verona's email and a text from my old flame, Nathalie.

Let's meet in London next week! I'm staying at Hotel Leonardo. N Xxx

It'd been over a year since we stopped seeing each other, but we had an alchemy, which meant there had never been a full stop at the end of our sentence. Nathalie was due to travel from Paris to visit some friends in London, so we arranged a *rendezvous*.

After taking down a lacy bra from the hotel chandelier, I also had to lug a new colossal plasma 30-kilo TV up to the room to replace the hotel's one I had completely smashed.

'Let's do that again, Jason!'

My insides huffed, but my face remained composed. This was the 20th time I had done it! I had to be careful not to drop the enormous TV. My arms felt as though they were going to fall off at any second, and my head was pounding—reeling from a rock star's hangover. The smirking and laughing, however, made me slightly paranoid.

The scenario was far from a kinky night in a hotel with Nathalie. It was actually an online commercial I had just been filming. It wasn't until late afternoon that we finished, and I sat down next to Martina Bruno, the producer of the online commercial.

The premise was that a rock star had trashed a hotel room by smashing up the hotel furniture and TV, but instead of walking out like a rebel, my character was directed to tidy up what I'd just trashed when the hotel manager came to inspect.

'Do you know that scene you did with the plasma TV, Jason?' Martina asked.

'Yeah?' I said as I gulped a mouthful of much-deserved coffee.

'You know, we actually got it in the second take, but we thought it was so funny every time you walked into the room with that massive TV, so we kept rolling the camera and doing more takes,' Martina said as she burst out laughing.

I had wondered what was happening and whether it was a technical problem or, worse, my acting. The words that floated out of Martina's mouth to me sounded like a choir of angels singing in my ears.

'It would be amazing if we could work together again, Jason.'

Her tongue nearly touched my tonsils as her affection towards me in front of a busy crowd was more French than Coco Chanel. After a great day's filming, I wrestled through the crowds of antisocial umbrellas held by city workers at London Bridge to meet Nathalie, who had arrived fashionably late.

It felt like it had been hours rather than a year since we last saw each other. Nathalie's fleeting interest in how I'd been doing made it apparent that not much had changed between Nathalie and me. After a few minutes of talking about my day filming and my New York adventure, I was interrupted with...

'...I'm sure it's over here. You remember, don't you? Did we have to cross over here, or was it down there?'

Nathalie insisted that we revisit Oceana, which overlooked the River Thames, the very same place where we had the big 'Maybe' row. It was bouncing down, and the wind was blowing raspberries. As Nathalie had just had her hair done, she decided we wouldn't eat *alfresco* in the extremely expensive joint that wouldn't have been my choice at all.

'Spare some change, brother?'

'Don't, don't, don't, Jason, he might rob us.'

'There you go, buddy.'

'Thank you, brother, God bless you, be lucky.'

'Why didn't you listen to me, Jason, huh?'

I said nothing but felt an overwhelming sense of guilt when we then entered the suave restaurant whilst the homeless guy had to endure sitting out in the freezing rain.

Nathalie chose a table by the window and shed her long winter coat, revealing a tight haute couture dress almost ready to peel off. The dress was so flimsy that if she sneezed, she'd be completely nude.

'Do you have anything under that dress?'

'Just my *Terre D'Hermès, Monsieur!*'

Hot and bothered, I got up to use the toilet. On my return, I found that Nathalie had ordered me an *amuse-bouche* of Alaskan king crab, a plate of oysters and a fillet steak. My taste buds actually had been gearing towards the sea bream, so I was miffed she had gone ahead and ordered for me without asking. Since she said it was her treat, I took it on the chin. I broke the awkward silence as we waited for the food to arrive. I could see from her eyes that she had something she wanted to say, but I wasn't entirely sure yet what it was.

'Something on your mind?'

'You're on my mind, *Monsieur* Jason!... You've grown your hair and beard, and you look so sexy. You know...you remind me of the caveman, you know, Sébastien Chabal...the French Rugby player...*Merci Beaucoup*,' Nathalie said to the waiter who delivered the plate of oysters.

Just before she swallowed another oyster, it appeared she was suggesting that she was wetter than the weather.

'They make me horny, remember?'

Next arrived the *Burgundy* red wine Nathalie had ordered, which she knew always got me in the mood. We both knew exactly where this night was heading: back to Hotel Leonardo, where Nathalie was staying.

It was almost midnight. After settling in, Nathalie went to the bathroom and returned dressed in a red see-through *frou-frou* babydoll nightie. *VAVAVOOM!*

My little head told my big head what to say mid-copulation as I grunted.

'I love you!'

'What's there not to love, *Monsieur* Jason?'

As Nathalie lay beside me on the bed, she handed me a gift-wrapped box.

'Open it. I hope you like it, Jason.'

I opened the gift to find Kouros, a strong French cologne. Since I had no gift for Nathalie, I paid her back in kind.

'How did you do that again, Beast? You blew my mind...I thought about you when I was in Paris, you know?...A thousand times I've reached for my phone to call you, but...'

Before she finished her sentence, she cut straight to the point she was leading to.

'I'm glad that you still have love for me, *Monsieur*, Jason...I'm so glad...*je t'aime*... Come live with me in Paris. It will be so wonderful...It's lovely for newlyweds.'

Zut alors! Stumped again by Nathalie's second attempt to have more out of me than I could give, I knew I was partly to blame for telling her I loved her less than twenty minutes ago. But *Sacré bleu!* I needed to set her straight.

'Nathalie, don't you understand that acting is my everything? Now isn't the right time for me. It's not that I don't CARE about you, but everything that I've been striving towards is starting to come into shape. Like I said earlier, I might move to New York...You understand, don't you?'

This time, it was the truth and the best thing I could think of without directly answering her question.

'Acting, you spend too much time on your acting. Nothing's changed with you, has it? Isn't it time for you to focus on the better things in life? like me!' Nathalie snapped before she turned her back on me and turned the lights off.

I can't be with this woman anymore. She's too bloody demanding! I love her, but I can't. I just can't. I should put my foot down! I will put my foot down! Oh, Lord! What shall I do?

The following morning, I was woken by my phone vibrating. It was a text from my good friend Miranda, distraught about the crumbling state of her marriage with Lucy Kim, which had hit rock bottom.

'Who's that? Let me see?' Nathalie asked, reaching for the phone in my hand.

'It's my agent.'

I pulled the phone away from her sight. I knew that if she'd seen the text from Miranda, she would blow her French horn and hit the roof, and I would have to face a French inquisition.

When I stood up to find my jeans, Nathalie responded as sharp as the belt buckle I'd tread on.

'Agent? Hmm...I see...oh because you're a professional actor? ...Professional liar, more like! *ÉGOÏSTE!*'

'As I said, I need to sort out something with my agent,' I murmured hastily, ignoring her jibe.

'*C'est n'importe quoi?*... Absurd...bullshit...So you have another woman, is that it? Is that who was texting you? Is that who you are going to meet now, huh? Perhaps you're sorry you slept with me instead of Miranda!'

'There's no perhaps about it, and who said I haven't. Jealousy doesn't go well with your new designer shoes, Nathalie!!!' I barked after nearly tripping over her Jimmy Choo heels. I talked on.

'I can see your agenda for the rest of the afternoon: My relationship with Miranda...so on that note Nathalie... I'm off.'

Nathalie was making much ado about nothing; she was really busting my balls and twisting the hell out of me. So, without bidding her *adieu,* and with a *laissez-faire* attitude, I left.

After having started the day off on the wrong foot, I texted and arranged to meet Miranda for an uncomplicated coffee at the Riverside Blend Café. As the place was heaving and it was nearly impossible to find an empty seat, I suggested we grab the coffee to go.

'Have you noticed there aren't enough female superheroes?'

'Pretty random comment, Jay, but I guess so.'

'It's your dress.'

'My dress?'

'Yeah, that dress on the sofa, the one that you were wearing earlier. You had that superhero thing going on, you know, with the blue and red scoop neck. I assume that was the look you were going for?'

'Um, I'll take it as a compliment...I think!...but it wasn't a look I was really going for. I just grabbed the first clean dress I could find.'

'You have a real style about you, Miranda. You can't find that style in a catalogue, you know.'

Miranda's mood seemed to momentarily lift as she couldn't hold back a giggle at my nonsense, but understandably, her mood continued to bounce all over the place like a ball in a squash court.

'What am I going to do, Jay? I don't know how much more I can take from arguing with Lucy Kim. It's affecting Brandon...her idea of fidelity is not having more than one woman in the bed at the same time...I seriously think I'm going to file for a divorce.'

'I'm hardly the best person to advise you on

relationships...working women out is tougher than crocodile skin. Look at who I've been dating. Mine and Nathalie's, whatever you want to call it, is hardly *Hello* or *Vogue* magazine happy relationship material. I reckon Nathalie couldn't make me completely happy; now that I think about it, I don't think she ever did make me happy.'

'Jay, if I had a pound for every time you said that the egomaniac Nathalie made you happy?

'Yeah?'

'I'd still have a pound! 'I'd give you the pound, though.'

'Why's that then?'

'So Nathalie can buy you a collar to put on you, and you can bark like the designer handbag pooch she wants you to be.'

I knew Miranda was right, and Nathalie's leash had always felt so tight I couldn't breathe. I just wasn't ready for Nathalie to thrust the prospect of marriage on me! We continued to delve, dive, joke, and jibe into the far-from-fairytale state of our so-called relationships. The positives of being married to one person forevermore was looking even more unappealing than it already was to me. Miranda was in a chapter of life that I didn't quite understand or, for that matter, was willing to understand even about my own life. She was going through 360° of emotions; her eyes were bright with tears.

'What am I going to do, Jay? I don't see a future for Lucy Kim and me any more. Hard as it is to admit, there's no more road left to walk with this marriage...I need to do something before we really rip each other to bits...before we really, really hate the life out of each other.'

'There's always an answer if you look for it, Miranda.'

We drank copious amounts of tea and coffee and dined on hummus and stuffed vine leaves from Ali's Kebabs. The topics of our no-holes-barred conversations had as many directions as an A-to-Z street map as they continued throughout the evening. We laughed a lot, Miranda cried a little, and in our weird but wonderful way, we were each other's comfort.

'My gut says it's the end of mine and Lucy Kim's chapter, Jay...what do you think?'

'Find another book.'

'What do you mean by that?'

'Well, if you go to a library, you're not going there just to read one book for the rest of your life, are you?'

We heard the beep of a car horn. Miranda had booked a cab to pick her up from my place just after midnight.

77 REBEL WITH A CAUSE

Jason,
Thank you for applying for our feature film, The Rebel. After watching your showreel, I would like to offer you the lead role of a Chechen rebel named Dukvakha.
Filming will take place at the end of the year in Mtskheta, Georgia, with specific dates and times TBC. We are nearing completion of the final draft of the script, but in the meantime, you can read the treatment I have attached.
I look forward to hearing from you.
Regards Bartosz Jankowski

Bartosz Jankowski, a Polish *wunderkind* filmmaker, had just made the bright start to my day even brighter after I read the attached treatment. The more I read, the more curious I became about the Dukvakha character. What more was in store for *The Rebel?* What about filming on location in Georgia? And What? Me? Another lead role? In a feature film? Abroad? I had more questions whirling around in my mind than in an episode of *Mastermind*, I had more bumble bees buzzing in my tummy than in a field of lavender in spring, and I had more thoughts about filming in Georgia than I knew what to do with. One of these thoughts skidding through my mind was about my old Georgian school teacher, Mr Khidasheli. He'd apparently retired and was back living in his home country, but what would have been the chances of bumping into him?

I needed to clear my mind. I felt like running and releasing this excited and nervous energy that had moulded into a bouncy ball of jitters inside me. After around half an hour of running in my local area, where the air was cleaner inside than out, I was pretty out of breath, pretty knackered, and pretty starved, so what better place to head to after a run than Ali's Kebabs; where I'd worked casually during my breadline days, preparing and serving slices of greasy chicken and lamb meat from the two swirling skewers.

'Jay my friend, how are you today? ...One minute, it's my wife on the phone.'

Ali quickly switched to Turkish.

'*Merhaba...iyi...akşa mlar...*' He muttered, his eyeballs rolling towards the heavens.

A portion of grumbling accompanied his smattering of Turkish words before he quickly ended the call with a sigh and then switched to English again.

'Sorry about that, my friend...women...I'm like Robert De Niro, you know.'

'You talkin' to me?'

'Yes, I'm talking to you; you're the only one in my shop.'

Ali clearly didn't get my De Niro joke, so I asked what he wanted me to ask.

'Have you been busy? And how are you like De Niro anyway?'

'I'm like a taxi driver! I take my wife here! I take my children there! I take them everywhere, school, shopping, friends' houses...you know...Then I have to take my wife to the hairdressers, her mother's, her friends, and Aldi. You ask if I'm busy...I'm always busy, my friend. I've now started to come to work at 7 am, because the wife wakes up at 8 am...Anyway, don't get me started on that!' Ali said, finishing his rant (that he didn't want to get started on) before adding a scoop of chips to the deep-fat fryer.

Ali Dogan was the middle-aged Turkish owner of Ali's Kebabs who had salt and pepper hair and a rotund build. His greetings were always as warm as the hot air that hit me every time I entered his toasty *kebab* shop.

'Who was that woman you were with last night? The one with lips like Angelina Jolie.'

'She's my friend, Miranda,' I replied, then continued by asking a simple question that opened a jar of hot Turkish peppers.

So how's things, Ali?'

'Ah. So-so... very tired, I couldn't get back to sleep this morning. I woke up at about 4 am for a piss. Then when I came back to bed, I just couldn't fall asleep...you know...I tried to hold it in, but I couldn't sleep anyway. It's the same every night...Then it wakes my wife up, and she can't get back to sleep...she told me that tonight I'll have to sleep on the sofa... but don't get me started on that!' Ali complained while taking his frustrations out on a Spanish onion.

Having clearly so much on his plate, he asked me to remind him of my drink and food order, which had gotten lost in his rant.

'...and no garlic mayonnaise on the chips, Ali.'

'Try this, new flavour, it's good, it's good.'

Ali put a small carton of *Ayran* in my hand as a gesture of friendship.

'On the house for you, Jay, my friend.'

'*Teşekkürler*, Ali, I'm not too far from poverty to accept a free drink.' I took a polite sip and then a big swallow. I just couldn't put my finger on the drink's flavour. It was much like the topics of the chats between Ali and me.

'Same as usual?' Ali's voice broke through the sound of the Real Madrid-Barcelona football game playing in the background on the shop's TV.

'Yeah, chicken doner and chips and no garlic mayonnaise please.' I repeated for what now was the third time before continuing.

'Who's your team?' Ali's eyes sparkled with interest.

'Sheffield Wednesday,' I responded (even though I'd told him this twenty times before).

'You were born in Sheffield?' Ali probed further.

'No, Bradford,' I clarified AGAIN.

'So why not support your hometown Jay?'

'It's a saga, Ali. As a kid, I was all about Liverpool. But as I grew older, I switched to Bradford City. Then, after they missed the big promotion, I was crushed and jumped ship to Sheffield Wednesday.'

'Changing football teams is like changing women for you, huh?' Ali chuckled, not missing a beat.

'Always root for your home team,' he smirked.

I was puzzled at Ali's comment, seeing that Ali Dogan, was born in Izmir, raised in Istanbul, lived in Peckham (whose nearest team was Millwall) but yet was a West Ham fan!

'Did you catch the game last night?'

'How do you miss a penalty, huh? West Ham's playing well this season, but last night, they were terrible, just terrible; you can't miss a penalty! But don't get me started on football, my friend.....large or small chips?'

'Large, please. I saw the penalty miss, shocking mate, shocking.'

'...and you made me in trouble with my wife too.'

'Me? Why, Ali?'

'Because of that free link you gave me for the sports streaming site...my wife saw the big titty ladies that kept popping up on my computer, and she now thinks I was looking at porn websites... I was only trying to watch football.'

In the midst of Ali heading down another path of spouting off about marital woes, he was interrupted.

'*Kebab,* get me a chicken *kebab* NOW,' spouted a drunk customer.

'I'm just serving this customer,' Ali replied, rolling his eyes at me.

'*Kebab*, give me a *kebab;* your sign outside says Best *kebabs* in London; your *kebabs* are naff bruv,' the drunk slurred whilst he stumbled over a chair.

'He doesn't know if he's coming or going, Ali,' I commented as I stepped out of the drunk's way.

'He's going,' Ali snipped as he came from behind the counter and opened the door and sent the *kebabless* drunk stumbling out.

'What were we talking about, my friend, prices? Yeah, prices, it's the government; all they give you is their lies, their lies about lies and their bigger lies. You know my electricity bill is higher than Mount Everest, but don't get me started on politics! Salad? So, how's the acting going? Are you getting a lot of work?'

'It's going pretty well. I have a new manager in New York, and, I got some good news today...can you put a few extra spicy Turkish peppers on there, mate, and no garlic mayonnaise on the chips.'

'You remind me of Al Pacino, same eyes...so your dreams of Hollywood have finally arrived?... Do you want these open or wrapped?'

God knows how our conversation arrived there, but the subject of my potential acting role in Georgia came up. Ali laid it on the line for me as he sliced greasy pieces of doner meat into the container.

'Georgia, oooooo, Georgia is next to Turkey, you know. Georgia is dangerous, my friend. Dynamite! Explosions! So when you're doing your big movie, you've got to be really careful, you know? You might run into trouble. I hope not. You see, it could be missiles or gunfire going off not too far from where you're doing your movie. Courage can't be bought; geography is destiny,' Ali concluded, putting the shit up me as he scooped my chips into a container.

'Salt? Vinegar?... For you, my friend, that'll be only seven pounds! I put extra *Aci Bibers* on for you.'

As my doner got cold, Ali continued rambling. But while one half of me tried to pay attention, the other part of me was wrestling with my thoughts. What lengths would I go to to be famous? How much did acting mean to me? What would I be willing to sacrifice? Would I die for acting? I needed to be brave but sensible in the same breath. I knew *The Rebel* was an excellent offer, and it sounded like it would be a great production. But did I want to enter a warring country surrounded by missiles, maybe gunfire? I clearly hadn't given this much thought until my former boss, Ali, brought me back to earth with a bump.

'I put another *Ayran* in the bag for you to take away. You seem a thousand miles away. Are you okay?'

I wasn't! My locomotion of thought wasn't a thousand but a million miles away from Ali's Kebabs.

Back at home, I couldn't ignore Ali's warnings, so before I could digest any dinner, I needed to be sensible and think logically. So, I emailed Bartosz to explain my concerns about the conflict and tell him I was prepared to be intrepid as I very much wanted the role.

As I ate my *Aci Biber*-filled dynamite *kebab,* I got an instant reply.

Jason,

We're glad you have accepted the role of Dukvakha. Also, just to let you know, the conflict in Georgia ended over ten years ago. I will be in touch soon.

Bartosz

As I opened my container of chips, Ali had drizzled my chips in garlic mayonnaise! He'd not only got my order wrong, he'd got the timings wrong about the Georgian conflict, AND I felt like a proper moron.

Thanks, Ali!

MY EGO SCREWED MY ACTING CAREER

78 SINK OR SWIM

'Bastards, they're crazy-mad! They tried to rob me blind,' Ali exclaimed.

His anger about the crazy-mad robbers was apparent by the steely look in his eyes. He, himself, was now as crazy-mad as a frog in a sock.

A gang of youths had attempted to rob him for his watch at 10:00am as he was helping to unload a delivery of doner meat from a truck.

Crime in Peckham had been slowly increasing, and no one appeared safe from it. Every week, on every street corner there was evidence of ripped blue police tape indicating that a serious crime had come and gone at those very spots. The neighbouring flat had been burgled a few weeks back, and that, alongside Ali's bad experience, made me question how much longer I wanted to stay in the gritty area that I had grown to know and like.

I'd grown out of my sofa surfing days; London had not become any cheaper. I didn't fancy a random room share with a total stranger, where I could either wake up after getting laid or not wake up at all after being murdered. I needed to feel safe and needed to feel more secure. It just so happened that I was to find that security with my good friend Miranda. Who was in the process of a very messy and ugly divorce from her long-term casting director wife, Lucy Kim. Miranda was fighting for the ownership of their townhouse in Church Road Wimbledon, a generous cash settlement and the only two things she would've fought tooth and nail for: the sole custody of their son Brandon and his black and white ginger eyebrowed crazy cocker spaniel Toby. Her soon-to-be ex-wife, Lucy Kim, was battling to keep their apartment in Ealing, their Audi car, and their two prized pedigree British short-haired cats, Samson and Delilah. Miranda shared photos of her lush pad on Facebook in a post that was captioned: *Housemate wanted. £110 per week! Anyone who loves tennis or The Wombles needs to read on.*

I messaged Miranda: *What a load of balls! £110? What a racket! But I'm game :)* An hour passed, and Miranda hadn't read or replied to my message, so I called her to check that she was okay. I could tell by her *sombre* tone that she clearly wasn't. We arranged to meet for what I envisaged was going to be a complicated coffee that same day.

At the Riverside Blend Café, a heartbroken Miranda was too upset to touch her soy latte and poured out her heart to me. Having gone through various breakups myself, I knew that words would not heal her void. I just listened, cracked some bad jokes, and shared some of my own experiences of when Cupid had misfired his arrow.

'You didn't do that, did you? Only you can cast a shadow on respectability!' Giggled Miranda, trying her best to hold her smile, as I began telling her about my experience in Greece as Roberto Verado. I nearly made Miranda choke on her latte when I told her about being a Sicilian target of the Mafia, and the woman I'd met, Sara, was far from happy when she walked past the Green Ocean Bar, where I was touting outside, and heard my non-Italian, gruff, Bradfordian accent. Tears trickled down Miranda's cheeks as she cried and laughed simultaneously. I tried to lift her mood by saying.

'Are you going to the Edinburgh Fringe this year? I heard you nailed it the last time you went.'

'That's just a rumour that I'm spreading,' Miranda quipped, looking down into her cup.

'I love *The Wombles*, and I don't mind watching a bit of tennis now and then!' I joked, hoping Miranda would catch my drift. Miranda looked up, finally clocking in and responded.

'As long as you don't tell any more appalling jokes, and you promise to use the recycling bin, I'd love for you to move in.'

'My Swatch stopped working, so I bought myself a new waterproof alarm watch...what do you think? How much do you think it cost me?'

'I don't know...You probably dived into a bargain bin for it?'

'Watch it, watch it, Miranda. You can't crack jokes like that; you'll do yourself an injury.'

In the comfort of my bear hug, Miranda laughed and then cried.

Two weeks later, I packed up my big yellow rucksack and moved out of my bedsit in the crime-ridden urban sprawl of gritty Peckham into the opulent surroundings of flowery Wimbledon with my good friend Miranda.

'See you when you get back then, Jay.'

No sooner had I moved into Wimbledon than I was on the move again. This time, however, it was only for a few days. I'd just landed my first TV commercial playing a Viking for a Danish Logistics company, *Gylden Pil*, and was heading to Denmark for filming.

The audition entailed three callbacks, and I had been desperate to bag this gig, AND I did. Although I preferred working on feature films, I wasn't complaining. I relished the opportunity to work in Denmark. Above all, I was walking on sunshine after being cast by one of the world's leading casting directors, Zena De Wolf.

I boarded a flight from Heathrow to Copenhagen, but my travel sickness hit me hard during the two-hour journey, making me feel nauseous and a bit green around the gills. Needless to say, I was glad when my feet were firmly on solid ground, and I was met with fresh Denmark air and the other four English actors, Laura, Max, Simon, and Thomas.

Thankfully, it was only a short minibus journey later that we arrived at our picturesque lakeside hotel in Kongens Lyngby Lake. Its decor had more wood than a forest. The fresh, earthy smell was a change from the polluted streets of London. After checking in, we each headed to our ensuite rooms. Mine was huge, with three beds, a balcony, a minibar and a big 50-inch TV. The works.

I had a shower and went to the bar downstairs. The other actors Max, Simon and Thomas, were already there, and we chatted and had a few beers. Laura came down sometime later, and we all spent a couple of hours drinking and getting acquainted. The bar was pretty fancy, with a vibrant atmosphere. Most of the other guests were chatting and laughing whilst downing the booze. The beer cost 7 *euros* a bottle, and with each of us having £45 *per diem*, we didn't have to worry about cost unless we guzzled more than seven bottles each. I didn't want to get drunk because I had to get into a boat the next day, and I'm not a great swimmer, even though I told the casting directors at the audition that I was.

After saying good night to the other actors, I returned to my room and chilled. I stepped onto the balcony, greeted by a sky ablaze with stars, starkly contrasting the polluted skies that cloaked many parts of London. The laughter and drunken, heavy footsteps of the jovial guests returning back to their rooms were the only sounds I could hear as I fell asleep. I slept so well I didn't even hear my watch alarm.

Fortunately, the honking Canada Geese woke me up at 7:00am, but I didn't have time to shower. But hey, I was playing a Viking; I was in character.

'*Hej, Hej*, Jason!' Said Klaus Jensen, the assistant producer tasked with caring for the actors while we were in Denmark. I followed Klaus to the canteen of the lakeside film set, where cold meats, cheeses, and coffee were part of the glorious breakfast spread. Once I had eaten like a Viking (well, kind of), it was time to look like a Viking, so Klaus took me and the other actors to the costume department.

'*Hej, Hej*, Jason, isn't it?' Said Claudia, the costume designer, who handed me my cumbersome Viking soft leather boots and Viking suit made of wool and leather.

'How is it?' Claudia asked, standing back to check for herself.

'Well, it fits better than my mankini!!!' I joked.

The other Vikings guffawed while Claudia smiled politely as I talked on.

'But there's nowhere to unzip my flies...am I missing something?' I asked the other perplexed Vikings.

Then Claudia said.

'Sorry, but that's the design; maybe don't drink too much!'

I and the other Vikings looked at one another, puzzled that we were being told without being told that we most probably wouldn't be able to use the toilet all day. I wish someone had told me that, though, before I had guzzled four cups of coffee for Dutch courage.

'Shock them! Startle them! Remember, you're all mean Vikings!' Directed Randy Larsen, the director.

The Danish commercial's premise was that we, three bold, rugged, battle-ready Vikings, Max, Thomas and I, would shock the dating couple Laura and Simon, who were picnicking on a riverbank eating cucumber sandwiches. The mean Vikings would steal their food and escape on a motorised boat, which had been tarted up to look like a sturdy, majestic and fearsome Viking vessel. Just before the cameras started to roll, Max, Thomas, and I climbed aboard. I was the only Viking that had to stand up on the boat. A Scandinavian frogman glided over, removing his snorkel before addressing me.

'Just a heads-up. When the boat sets off, there's a chance you might take a dip. For about 15 seconds, you might find yourself face down and go under for a bit. It may feel like you're in deep water. But don't worry—we've got your back. You'll be alright.'

Fuck! *Captain Nemo's* words hit me like a wet kipper, and I was horrified at the possibility of things going badly wrong and ending *twenty thousand leagues under the sea.* It may not have been as dramatic as that, but as the frogman had described, I would temporarily be drowning or dying, but they'd rescue me, so that was okay! Hmmm, this didn't sit right with me. I was trying to let it sink in. To be honest, this knocked the wind out of my sails because I couldn't actually swim. Then this *Volunga Saga* quote came to mind:

"Fear not death for the hour of your doom is set, and none may escape it."

Before the cameras started to roll, the director, Randy Larsen, who was watching the monitor screen, had a big problem with the frogmen as they were visible on camera. Randy then directed the disgruntled frogmen to go much further away from the boat. Reality then hit home for me. If the frogmen weren't nearby, and if I fell in the water, they couldn't rescue me within the original time of 15 seconds, then for sure I'd drown! They weren't Olympic swimmers, and they were dressed in heavy scuba gear, so when they had to move to the edge of the lake, there was no way they could reach me in the time that they'd initially told me. This was incomprehensible! I found this all very disconcerting! And feared whether I would sink or swim! I felt like I was up the creek without a paddle.

The boat had some motor problems, and it was leaking in water, which took an hour to fix. The clients from *Gylden Pil* complained about light disappearing, and the stressed Randy Larsen was trying his best to appease the clients. The tension was mounting.

Once the boat was fixed, we started filming. Randy called. 'Action.'

Although it wasn't travelling very fast, the motorised boat was listing from left to right in the wind. I had nothing secure to hold on to, just a flaming sword in my hand, no pole, *nada, niksen, nothing.* The other two Vikings, Max and Thomas, were pretty safe. They were sitting down behind me, ravaging the cucumber sandwiches that we'd just pillaged from the unsuspecting dating couple. I stood at the front of the boat, holding onto my sword with just one line to say in a Danish accent.

"Gylden Pil is the logistics company that will deliver."

My dialogue was not clear enough, as the Canadian geese honking in the lake made it inaudible. They were most probably peeved at the sight of Vikings and their vessel invading their waters as they honked, honked, and honked away. A frustrated Randy yelled. 'CUT.'

We had to redo the scene again. I feared for my life; I hadn't signed up for this. My agent hadn't told me how precarious the filming would be, and I hadn't been given any danger money! Fortunately, I lived to tell the story and managed not to fall and sink into the lake.

We wrapped up for the day and returned to our hotel bar for the wrap soirée. The atmosphere was buzzing; chatter and laughter mingled with the upbeat jazz music filling the room. There was a *Smörgåsbord* at the end of the room, with food I'd never seen before; after tucking into a couple of cold fish sarnies, it was time to get smashed and drink plenty. A few members of the Danish production team joined us, including the generously curved Danish costume designer Claudia. Her hair was in relaxed, loose black waves, which were pushed back elegantly; she carried an aura of mystery that I aimed to discover more about as I gravitated through the crowded bar to where she was at the other end. Her English words came out as smooth as the Baileys she had in her hand. Her words were garnished with notes of a Danish accent. Her eye-line seemed to travel south of the border when looking at me, but it wasn't my whisky cupped in between them that she was looking at!

'I couldn't help but notice your hands.'

'My hands?' I replied, with a curiosity that interpreted this as a flirtation, edging closer to her to appease her so-called interest in my hands. I went straight in without logic or strategy and showed my hand:

'So, how does an actor land a date with a costume designer? You could get to know me and my hands some more!'

'I'm sorry, but I'm happily married...and I'm not looking for anything more...really sorry.'

Her response, even though she'd tried to make it gentle, certainly stung a bit, and of course, I should've noticed the glaringly obvious, encrusted diamond ring on her marital finger.

'Drink?' Asked the rushed bartender, who looked like he was ready to finish for the night as he wiped down the bar.

'Whisky on the rocks...can you make that a double, please,' I replied, hoping the stiff spirit would remedy my bruised Ego.

'Care for another, Claudia?' I said, trying to swallow my pride before my double whisky arrived whilst Celine Dion's *Taking Chances* swelled out of the bar's pine speakers.

'No, I'm okay, thanks; I'm heading home soon,' she responded, delivering a second blow, but she showed an unexpected hand this time.

'...But there is one thing I wanted to ask, though...'

'What's that?' I asked curiously, holding on to the hope of this 'one thing'.

'Have you ever done hand modelling, Jason...?'

'...Hand modelling?...No, I haven't...'

I looked down at my palms and realised that it WAS only these babies that she was interested in.

'You should consider it, you know...I was looking at them earlier...I have a male friend who has been doing it for years, and he says it pays very well.'

After drowning my rejection in a few more glasses of hard spirits, I bid Claudia and everyone *Godnat* and resided myself to spending the rest of the night alone. All was quiet until I heard some noise from the room next door. The bed rattling, the faint moan of a woman, and a man's grunts suggested a couple were getting amorous. The moans became louder AND LOUDER, sounding like a pig's last moments in an abattoir. The sounds made me feel pretty horny, and I was toying with the idea of grabbing a cab to Central Copenhagen and finding a Danish beauty. But I had second thoughts; I was pretty exhausted, and the only Copenhagen softness I wanted to nestle myself in had four legs, a feather duvet, and a pillow. My left hand was the only company that appeased me that night just before I crashed out.

79 LANDED

'I refuse!!! I want to speak to my solicitor!!!'

My response. *'I want to see inside your bag…Have you got any sanitary pads?'*

At that point, I was stopped…ABRUBTLY.

I had been called in for a Vibrant Carpets music video audition with the well-established Northern casting director, Linda Barker, whom I'd auditioned twice for in the past. The first time was for a *James Bond* villain in *Casino Royale*, shot in Istanbul. And the second was for the lead role in *Lions at Dawn*, filmed in Saint-Tropez. But alas, my hopes for both roles took a nose dive in my Factor 50 sunblock, which, like me, wasn't at the time destined to see any light of day beyond England. I didn't land either part!

The Vibrant Carpets music video, which was due to be filmed in Slough, was less exciting than the feature films, but no one was going to pull the rug out from under my feet about the prominent casting director's promising interest in me.

It was a roasting day when I arrived at Casting Rooms, a location I had been to a few times before. The reception area was like Beardville, packed full of eager bearded actors hoping to be the catch of the day as they waited to be called into the audition room. I was welcomed by a hip brunette and her strong scent of spiced perfume as she ticked my name off a sheet on a blue clipboard. She directed me to sit down amongst the rest of the hopefuls waiting to be called in.

One by one, the actors took their turns for their chance to audition in front of the prominent casting director; each looked as desperate to land the role as the last. It felt like a pressure cooker, and it wasn't until about 45 minutes later that my name was called. I was the last actor to go in and was more than ready to impress.

The blackout blinds of the darkened audition room were pulled down to block out the sun's rays. A worn-out-looking Linda Barker was sitting at a long wooden table whilst her assistant was adjusting the camera. I walked across the grey carpeted floor, and as directed by the assistant, I said my name and my agent's name to the camera before Linda Barker asked me to start.

I had to play the role of a detective constable with a slightly aggressive nature. The scenario using improvised dialogue involved my character, the detective constable, walking into the house of a rock star's wife and talking to her about some missing jewels. Linda explained that she'd play the role of the rock star's wife.

'Show me the inside of your handbag!!!' I demanded.

Linda (the rock star's wife) replied.

'I refuse!!! I want to speak to my solicitor!!!'

I responded to this by saying.

'I want to see inside your bag, NOW!!! Have you got any sanitary pads?'

At that point, I wasn't sure if I'd caused her any offence as she raised her hand. 'It's been a long day. The role is yours, Jason,' she said as she shook my sweaty but grateful hand.

'Jason, you have fantastic hands. We would be very happy to represent you!'

I'd taken the advice from Danish costume designer Claudia. Surprisingly, a hand modelling agency, DHH Models, signed me up after weighing up my hands. Even though hand modelling wasn't in my long-term plan, the good pay it offered for perfect hands was certainly appealing. This would then allow me more space and flexibility to take my pick of the acting roles and auditions that I wanted.

On top of this, I had also landed a new agent, KJC Casting in Manchester, who, right off the bat, waved their magic by getting me the Vibrant Carpet audition. Alongside KJC, I had Elizabeth Grolle at Kipper Talent managing work in London and Europe and Verona Sanchez at VSZ Management in New York helping with American opportunities. I was certainly sizzling.

"You know me, don't you?"

"Yes, I know you, Luis."

"And you've cast me before?"

"Yes Luis, I've cast you before."

"I'm a good actor, and you know I'll be perfect for this role."

"Yeah, I'm calling you because I know you'd be perfect for this role."

'Then why do you want me to drive three hours in LA traffic to see me read some lines for a character you know I can do with my eyes closed?"

I had been tuning in to *Dinner for Five,* a TV series about acting hosted by Jon Favreau. One of his guests was the great Luis Guzman. Luis' anecdote about his alternative approach to a casting director reeled me in hook, line, and sinker, as Luis finished off.

"The casting director went quiet for a bit and then said. *Okay Luis, you've got the role!*"

Inspired by this story I wanted to know if I could use the same bait as Luis Guzman, so I tried my luck when an audition for a feature film opportunity arose. The invite was from an excellent director, Luke Smet, with whom I'd worked before. He had rang to express that he was interested in seeing if I was interested in auditioning, and I was interested in seeing if I had even a fraction of Guzman's pulling power.

'So what do you think about it, Jay?'

'Well, Luke, it's a great script, and I think I'd be perfect for the role.'

'Great, is Friday good for you for the audition?'

'Luke, you know me, you know I can act, right?'

'For sure, that's why I called you Jay.'

'You know I'm reliable?'

'100%'

'So why do you want me to come? I KNOW and YOU KNOW, that I can do the role! I KNOW and YOU KNOW, that I AM the ACTOR for this role.'

The phone call took a brief interlude lasting a few seconds as I waited with bated breath.

And then, TA-DA... he delivered his response to my bold attempt to reel him in.

'Jay, can you come to see me for the audition on Friday or not?'

Like a wannabe Z-lister, battling to be king on a jungle reality show, my Ego was showered with a tank of maggots, giving it a harsh dose of reality.

My Factor 50 sunblock, yellow Speedos, and flip-flops were packed, and I was ready to eat, drink, and be merry with the Atlantic Ocean by my side.

'...This is a call for all passengers for flight 1459 to Porto...Please go to Boarding Gate 11...would all passengers for flight 1459 to Porto...Please go to Boarding Gate 11...'

MY EGO SCREWED MY ACTING CAREER

My travelling companions on this pure pleasure and no business trip were my good friend Miranda and her son Brandon. I took the place of Lucy Kim on a holiday to Portugal, which had been booked for over a year, but the irreconcilable differences, as cited in the divorce, had obviously scuppered their plans for a happy family getaway. So, of course, it would've been rude of me to say no when Miranda had asked me.

'Fancy a trip to Porto Jay? I'd love you to join us.'

Miranda, Brandon, and I were at the boarding gates at Heathrow airport in a queue, just about to board a 7:00am flight to Porto, when my phone started ringing. It was a number I didn't recognise, but I answered the call just in case it could be for an acting gig after the holiday. On the other end of the phone, a flustered woman said.

'Hello, I'm Naomi, the costume designer.'

I was perplexed about what she was talking about, but before I could say a word, Naomi went on, telling me that everyone was waiting for me and they were on a tight schedule.

'How long will it take you to get to Slough station? I'll pick you up,' she said.

Now, even more perplexed, I started to say.

'Can I ask...'

But before I could finish my sentence, the loud tannoy blasted '...This is the final call for all passengers for flight 1459 to Porto.'

Naomi must have heard this and asked.

'Where are you, huh?'

'Who are you?' I asked, and I explained that I had to go because I was just about to board my plane to Portugal. However, the agitated costume designer reiterated who she was AND that I was supposed to be on location to film the Vibrant Carpets music video an hour ago. Frustratingly for me, I had to tell Naomi that there obviously had been a mistake, and I apologised profusely for the threadbare situation. I wished I had a magic carpet to do both the music video and the holiday, but alas, I had to turn the role down.

I had always kept my agents and managers informed about my availability. Someone at the Manchester agency had muddled up the dates of my availability that they gave to the production company. So, just like that, as my journey to Porto was about to begin, my journey with one of the best casting directors in the industry had just ended through no fault of my own. Obviously, I lost the role, and to date, Linda Barker has never called to cast me again.

80 LOST IN TRANSLATION

'Looking at it now, Jay, it wouldn't be my first choice but nor would it be my last.'

'Yeah, me too...Manchester United are playing and there's no football channel. Look, Mum,' Brandon said, plopping himself on the bed while flicking through the TV.

With its basic furnishing, the room at Porto Oasis, Esphino, didn't match its 4-star rating. It was more like a 2-star or, at best, a 3-star room, but even that would be flattering it.

In return for Miranda's generosity and the opportunity to bask in the sun with her and Brandon, I made an impromptu decision to go to the reception area to see if there was any chance for a room upgrade. Sure enough, after pausing to tap a few keys on his computer, the hotel manager said.

'Sure, come with me.'

The new second room had a view of the casino that Espinho was renowned for. The upgrade was a plush suite with three rooms, two bathrooms and two large-screen televisions. The works! Miranda and Brandon (who was only 11 at the time) were wowed as they gazed at the view of Espinho and the almost turquoise Atlantic Ocean from the wide corner balcony.

During our stay, we sampled fresh food in restaurants filled with locals, away from the main tourist traps that lined the beach. One place, Restaurante Do Mar, was recommended to us. However, it was more off the beaten track than we imagined.

'Where are the street names, Jay?'

'They don't have street names, just numbers.'

'How are we supposed to find it?'

'Instinct, Miranda instinct!'

'Huh?'

With Espinho being one of the only places in the world, besides New York, to have numbered streets, finding our way around was challenging. Being on the opposite side of the road from what we were used to in the UK while driving our rented Opel car didn't help much either. But eventually, after a car journey filled with lots of huffing, puffing and are-we-nearly-there-yets. We found the restaurant with as much ease as navigating our way through the Hampton Court Maze blindfolded and handcuffed.

The restaurant reflected rustic Portuguese charm, with its white and brown tiled floors, sunshine-washed walls, and cosy distressed wooden tables and chairs that we were now all parked on.

The cooks were huge, gangster-looking men, some of whom smoked while cooking the food and looked like they belonged in the *GoodFellas* mafia movie. The gangster cooks, who also didn't appear to speak English, were also the waiters.

Tiny bowls of shiny black olives and freshly baked bread rolls were placed on every table, tempting hungry diners, including Miranda, who tucked into an olive.

'Do you want one?' Miranda asked Brandon, who was distracted by the array of seafood on a platter of the diners next to us.

'Look at the eyes on that one!' Brandon said innocently but rather loudly as he made an impression of a crossed-eye crustacean, claws and all.

'Have an olive, Brandon. They're good!' Miranda said, intentionally swaying Brandon's attention back to our table as another waiter who looked like a character from *The Godfather* mafia movie walked past.

It didn't take long for us to decide on what we wanted, and after pointing out the pictures on the menu to the gangster waiter, it wasn't long before our order arrived.

'*Boa tarde*,' I said to the gangster waiter. My phrasebook Portuguese appeared to be to the gangster waiter's distaste as he rolled his eyes and placed my order of freshly grilled sardines (which spanned the size of my entire dinner plate) in front of me. The sardines were accompanied by a humongous bowl of boiled potatoes and a fresh, crisp salad that tasted like a bite of summer, drizzled generously with olive oil. Miranda tucked into her order a steaming bowl of traditional *Caldo Verde,* a soup with potatoes, olive oil, and finely shredded cabbage infused with strong onion and garlic. Brandon, who had ordered the freshly grilled squid on skewers, had found humour in me having to cover up the eyes of the poor sardines peering back at me, making me feel guilty about eating their delicious flesh.

The haunting, wailing-like sound of *Fado* music was accompanied by the powerful voice of a dramatic *Fado* singer and moved through the air like a beautiful storm accompanied by the just as dramatic guitarist, whose strings echoed the emotions of her tune. We ate, drank, and were merry even though the three of us seemed to be the only tourists in the restaurant full of locals.

'*Três bolas por favor*,' I used my smattering of Portuguese to order three *Leite Creme* desserts when the gangster waiter passed our table. The waiter looked perplexed, so I tried again.

'*Três bolas por favor.*'

'*Bolos,* not *bolas*! *Bolos* means balls!' An embarrassed Miranda explained.

After fixing my Portuguese, we tucked into the apple desserts, and I raised my whole hand with a smile to express my extreme satisfaction and show him that I needed the bill. He didn't return a smile but returned with another plate of five more gigantic sardines I wasn't expecting. I was already stuffed to the gills and didn't want to eat another plate of sardines that I didn't order, but equally, I didn't want to upset the gangster waiter. After Miranda, Brandon and I laughed nervously about the extra portion of fish, I decided to try my best to indicate I wanted to take the sardines away with me, but I didn't know the words for a doggy bag in Portuguese. So when the towering gangster waiter approached, I attempted to show my satisfaction with the food without offending, so I gave him a thumbs up, patted my belly appreciatively, and kissed my fishy fingers, trying to indicate that his food had been exceptionally good. Then, I pointed towards the plate of sardines and gestured towards the exit, hoping he understood that I wanted to take the food away. However, the gangster waiter's expression seemed more annoyed than understanding, and De Niro's iconic "you talking to me?" phrase flashed in my mind. Fuck! My attempts at communication were getting lost in translation.

'*Obrigada*,' I offered, hoping to express gratitude, though judging by his stare, this too seemed to irk the gangster waiter somehow. Miranda nudged me under the table, whispering urgently.

'O, *Obrigado*.'

'O, *ObrigadO*,' I awkwardly corrected myself, realising my mistake.

It appeared I had confused genders in my effort to say thanks, and I unintentionally offended him by expressing my gratitude in the feminine rather than the masculine form.

'*Ele é gringo, ele não fala nossa lingua*,' remarked our gangster waiter to his fellow gangster compadre who was serving customers at the opposite table. *Holy Sardines*, CLEARLY, my Portuguese needed improvement.

Thankfully, the gangster waiter eventually understood and scooped up my second plate of sardines with the vice-like grip of his huge, hairy hands. Then he returned with my sardines wrapped in foil. After settling the bill, including the extra sardines, we left the restaurant, satisfied with our meal and the sense of relief.

Miranda, Brandon and I spent the rest of the day breathing in the Esphino ambience. The salty sea breeze mingled with the smell of beach worshippers' sunscreen and the grilled food from other nearby restaurants as we strolled along the seafront. The sand gently tickled our toes, and seagulls were calling to each other overhead, looking for any potential tourist scraps left on the beach. I held my foil-wrapped sardines close to ensure I didn't drop them in front of a balding stray dog with a fish in its mouth, ready to enjoy its supper.

'I can't imagine it's any further...'

'I hope not; my feet are killing me; they're going to drop off.'

One hour and lots of steps later

'Miranda, I could have sworn it was this floor.'

'Jay, it's an Apple... A grey one, right?'

'No, Miranda, it's an Opel, and it's black!'

When the time came to head back to the hotel, Miranda, Brandon, and I found ourselves failing to find our rental car in the large car park where we had left it. We were like bewildered explorers in a jungle of metallic monsters on wheels as I pressed the panic button on my key fob. But *nada,* nothing. It wasn't until an hour had passed that we eventually found our GREY Opel.

Our mainly blissful day continued beside the hotel's outdoor pool. Brandon had found a friend a similar age to him who had challenged him to a game of table tennis by the side of the children's pool.

'You're amazing just the way you are, you know Jay?' Said Miranda, slightly tipsy from a cocktail of Portuguese sun, whisky and the chorus of Bruno Mars's *Just the Way You Are* that had floated across to us from the hotel's outdoor speakers. I turned my head towards Miranda as I lay on one of the hotel's sun loungers overlooking the sparkling Ocean.

'How exactly AM I then, Miranda?' I said, feeling slightly tipsy myself also from the Portuguese sun.

Miranda turned to me, pushed her tinted glasses down to her nose and said.

'You're handsome... you're talented...and... you're charming...'

'...And you're just saying that because...all of it is true,' I joked.

'There's a kids club downstairs, you know?' Miranda whispered, her face pinkening both from the sun and what she was forwardly suggesting. Brandon had no qualms about joining the kids' club, where he and his friend planned a friendly FIFA battle on the hotel's PlayStation. Miranda and I went upstairs and let out some steam in the hotel's sauna and then in our room.

The three of us on holiday in Espinho.

81 SOME YOU WIN SOME YOU LOSE

Goodbye and bad fortune to you!... I can't believe you're living with Miranda now. You're unbelievable!

Refreshed and energised from my Porto break, the last thing I wanted to read was an unsavoury Facebook message from Nathalie. She'd seen Miranda's posts and photos of Porto on Facebook, one which showed me on a boat going down the River Douro wearing the 69 T-shirt Nathalie had gifted me. I didn't respond to Nathalie's noise.

On a sweeter note, I received an email from my New York manager, Verona Sanchez. She had lined up a casting for me for the role of Omar Badir, a mysterious Middle Eastern man, in *Dollar Lady*, a TV movie set to be shot in New York and Hawaii. *Dollar Lady* was going to be directed by the multiple award-winning director Bryan Kopeka, who had also directed some major blockbuster movies. I felt honoured that I would be seen by him and Melanie Loveridge, another well-known casting director. They were both giants in the industry.

Slightly jetlagged, I opted to take a cab to the audition for the steep fare of £30. I still hadn't snapped out of holiday spending mode. It was an early audition held in Bryan Kopeka's office in Leicester Square, so I'd rather have gotten there without the stresses and strains that came along with public transport in London.

Fresh as a daisy and unscathed by any transport woes, I found my way up to the top floor and headed in the direction of Bryan Kopeka's office. A camera was already set up for recording, the directors were sitting on their plush leather seats, and my fate and the potential of Middle Eastern promise were in their hands. First was the formal introduction to middle-aged Melanie Loveridge, who was dapperly dressed in shiny silk, and then the older Bryan Kopeka, who was kitted out in an expensive and perfectly pressed linen suit. The posters of lead actors they had worked with were perfectly aligned on the walls, and as I prepared myself, I knew I was determined to show them that I, too, was cut from the same cloth.

As the perfectly arranged awards behind them glistened in my eyeline, I was ready to show the *Dollar Lady* directors that I was on the money as I read my lines of Omar, whilst Melanie Loveridge was ready to read the role of Special Agent Jackson. I knew that I had to keep my nerves undercover in front of these hot-shot directors whilst maintaining my poise.

Omar: *"I might have heard whispers of such dealings, but in exchange for my help, I need your assurance that the innocent of my country won't suffer."*

Agent Jackson: *"You have our word, Omar. We're not here to bring chaos."*

Omar: *"Very well. There's a hidden market in the old city, under the cover of night. It's where they meet to finalise their dark transactions."*

Boom!!! I left the audition like I could've burst with all the pride in London. The holiday in the sun had done my confidence some good because, boy, I was on fire! I texted Verona as I neared Leicester Square, which was abuzz with people. The mix of fried junk food, fresh sweet popcorn, tomatoes and garlic from the pasta house I passed floated in the atmosphere, as did the giant cloud of Disney helium balloons belonging to a seller that I nearly walked into.

'Sorry, mate,' I said to the balloon seller, who was preoccupied.

'Sling your hook before I call the police,' yelled the balloon seller, who was telling two lairy teenagers where to go, as he held the ribbons of the balloon bouquet in his fist. Not long afterwards, I received a call.

'You really went the whole nine yards, Jason, hun! Melanie Loveridge just texted me... they REALLY like you.'

'That's great to hear, Verona! So, where do we go from here?...'

'Well...I need to look into the union signatory process for you...but don't worry about that, hun.'

'It's not rocket science!' Miranda joked as we sat in our Wimbledon home. It was a rare occasion because she appeared to have beat me on the timed *Countdown* conundrum TV quiz before the buzzer rang. As we laughed about it, my thoughts went into their own conundrum when I saw an international phone number flashing on my phone screen. It had been three months since the audition. Was it finally the news about the prize I had set my hopes on?

'Hey Jason, it's Verona; how are you doing?'

'I'm great, Verona...just great, thanks...and you?'

'I'm all good, listen, honey, I've got some fantastic news for you. You've been heavily pencilled in for the role of Omar in *Dollar Lady*, and I wanted to let you know they're really excited about having you on board. This is a big deal, a massive opportunity, you know... Just wanted to remind you to sit tight. These things take time, honey, you know but they are worth the wait. Trust me when I say this could be a game-changer for your career. Oh, by the way, they will be posting you the script.'

I wasn't sure how much tighter I could sit, but it was as if I'd made it to the final round of *Countdown*, and Verona was right. I had to be patient and keep my eyes on the prize.

'Miranda, get changed and get your coat. Let's celebrate!' Miranda, who had overheard the call, had already gone to the fridge and returned with half a bottle of champagne.

'Forget about getting clothes on, Jay. Let's celebrate properly and take them off! Shall we take this upstairs?'

'Yeah, let's *Netflix and chill!*'

'Hand job?' Miranda enquired.

'Yeah, it just popped up in my inbox from DHH models, offering me a hand modelling job, no audition, it pays £1500 for the day...Get in there!... Double whammy!...What a day!... Am I on fire or what?'

'Lemonade on you later then, Jay?'

After a few days and nights of being in the warmth of cloud nine, I managed to convince myself to squeeze out of bed without disturbing the snoozing Miranda.

A freshly brewed Geisha coffee in one hand, mail in the other. Bills aside, a large, thick brown envelope piqued my interest. It was *The Dollar Lady* script.

Bang! This was when reality hit with the realisation that this could really happen.

So, from cloud nine to cloud eight, I jumped. Over the following few weeks, I read the script daily, I watched every Bryan Kopeka film I could get my hands on, I worked tirelessly hard to get my character down, and I had to say a lot of thank yous but no thank yous to some small time castings and scripts that continued coming my way including the three film offers and two hand modelling jobs I had to turn down. My appetite was being reserved for a bite of the big time, the Big Apple and the land that was big on hula dancing, so it was a waiting game and an endless countdown in those following months in anticipation of the elusive call.

Four months, five months, and then six months had gone by when D-Day arrived while shopping at Sainsbury's.

'Jason! It's Verona. I hope you're doing okay?....'

'I'm good, thanks, Verona and you?'

With my phone in one hand and trolley in the other, I swerved my wonky trolley just before two wayward children ran into it. They had been too caught up in the excitement to think about what was about to hit them. They were running and giggling during their game of chase to grab the multipack of gobstoppers that one of them was holding whilst their distracted mother looked at a packet of *Quinoa*.

I didn't sense the electric energy from Verona's initial words that she had set me alight with in her previous calls. The hope that I was wrong about this became wedged in my throat like a hard gobstopper as I awaited her words.

'I have some tough news, honey, and I wish I didn't have to be the bearer of it...'

As I had thought, I was right, and my heart sank as I stopped pushing the wonky-wheeled trolley, narrowly avoiding the tins of four-foot-high Green Giant sweetcorn that had been neatly arranged in a pyramid.

'It's about *Dollar Lady*. I'm sorry, Jason, but there is no easy way to say this. Unfortunately, it's not happening.'

'What? Why? What happened?' I voiced so loudly that an elderly man who was putting the third tin of marrowfat mushy peas in his basket looked at me as if I was talking to him.

'Listen, honey, I'm as shocked as you. The investors got cold feet and backed out at the last minute.'

She paused momentarily for a response before continuing.

'I know it's incredibly frustrating, especially after all the preparations we've made. Your artist visa is ready, and you've been patiently waiting for the dates, the flight times...everything.'

It felt like the pyramid of tinned vegetables had come crashing down on my big toe. A shelf stacker glanced over at me, making it obvious that I was rather loud as I said.

'...Verona, this is a huge blow. Do you know I've turned down three feature films to focus on *Dollar Lady!*'

'Jason honey, I hear you, I really do, but it's just a setback; we're not giving up. I'm already exploring other opportunities for you. You're a talent, and we'll find another production that's just as promising, if not bigger. I know it's disappointing! It's the nature of the industry, you know. We'll get through this together, and I'm here to support you every step of the way. Just hang in there!'

The call ended in the tinned vegetable aisle as the shelf stacker's digital pricing gun continued to beep. I picked up the sign that had dropped from underneath the tinned spinach and handed it to him...There was an irony to what the sign said: A Knockout Price!

It was another tough blow to take, and this was one that I thought some time off from acting might heal. I was to-ing and fro-ing about what would be best for me. To carry on this game? Or quit altogether? I finally came to the conclusion that I didn't like the taste of dust in my mouth, so even though I bit the dust this time, my pure Yorkshire grit hoovered up the remnants of my lost dream and made way for me to start again.

'...Sometimes, it takes a storm to clear things up...!!!! Ha...I got it...I got it...Get in!!!'

'Hey...I was going to say that Jay...!'

'...Who's the master?...'

'... Let's watch who'll win the next round, Jay.'

'You win some, you lose some,' I said as Miranda and I sat in our Wimbledon home watching another afternoon TV quiz together, *Eggheads* this time.

'Jason, are you sitting down? Zena De Wolf just called. She wants you for a Tobias Rodrigues, *Aurelia* TV commercial.'

'What, really?... When's the audition?'

'Wait, Jason, there's more?'

'More?'

'Yes... there's no audition!'

My UK agent, Elizabeth Grolle, couldn't contain her excitement on the other end of the phone as she told me that the last-minute gig was being cast by one of the world's leading casting directors, Zena De Wolf, who'd previously cast me for *Gylden Pil,* the Danish Viking commercial.

'Elizabeth, you're the best,' I chimed as I hung up.

In a few decisive gulps, I finished the rest of Lucy Kim's Mortlach whisky she'd left in the cabinet; at that moment, the world seemed to mellow up. I knew this would be my last drink for a while.

'*Espresso* good for you, Jason?'

'That would be great, Tobias, thank you.'

Eight months later (my longest stretch of sobriety), I was filming the commercial in Malta.

The director was Tobias Rodrigues, who had directed several other TV series for EmpireFrame Productions.

82 JE NE SAIS QUOI

'*Bonjour* Jason, it's Alfred here, how are you?'

'Good Alfred and you?'

'*Ça va bien, merci!*...I wanted to speak to you about the showreel you sent.'

My ears pricked at Alfred Rambaud's promising tone, eagerly awaiting some ray of hope in the form of a role. As I found a quiet shop doorway, I held the phone close to my ear as Alfred continued.

'Jason, after looking over your showreel and acting resume... I want to ah...offer you the role of Le Mari...'

'That's great news, Alfred...I would be honoured to be part of the film.'

'*Parfait*, Jason! You and the other French lead actors, Hadrien, Flore and Antonia, have distinctive faces and are well suited...You said you know some French ah?'

'Ahem...*Oui*...*Oui*...Alfred.'

'*C'est merveilleux!* Le Mari will have uh...ah *une barbe*......how do you say a...beard...he'll have a beard in the film, could you grow your beard before the filming dates?'

'Sure, *oui, oui,* no problem.'

'*Fantastique,* welcome on board Jason ah; I will...uh...email you the script, and I will be in touch ah. *Au revoir.*'

I'd not long returned from Malta, and I was on the move again, heading to Paris this time, after being cast by director Alfred Rambaud in a new role as Le Mari in the upcoming French film *White City Spleen*.

I was excited; however, the fact that my character had to speak some French meant that it would be pretty challenging, given my limited proficiency in the language. The only smattering of the most romantic language in the world I had was from reading *Astérix* comics, failed French lessons in school and my on-again-off-again relationship with the French siren, Nathalie Dubois.

I spent the hour-long *Eurostar* journey from London to the City of Light, immersing myself in French by flipping through a French phrase book I'd gleaned from the library and tuning into French music on my iPod in the form of Vanessa Paradis's *Divinidylle* album.

Before I knew it, I was stepping off the train at Gare du Nord and was warmly greeted by the cheerful tunes of an accordion player and Pascal, the film production driver.

'*Bonjour Jason, Ça va?*'

'*Bonjour*, how you doing?' I returned as I hopped into his people carrier, and he heaved my big yellow rucksack in the boot and closed my door.

As we embarked on our journey, the city's beauty took my breath away, as did the awkward pauses that hung in the air as Pascal and I fumbled through expressions that we both could understand because, like my French, his English was, at most, pocketbook level.

As we drove through the streets of Paris on a journey that took just twenty minutes, a swell of anticipation swept over me. Then we arrived at the vibrant multicultural thoroughfare of Boulevard Barbès, my residence and the filming location where I would be staying during the two-day film shoot.

Alfred Raumbaud, the director of *White City Spleen*, emerged from a large stone building. His untucked cottoned pink shirt with a few buttons was left open, and his denim ensemble was indicative of the director's laid-back and relaxed charm. He reached out to me for a hug and a kiss on both cheeks.

'*Bonjour Jason, Ça va?* Good trip?'

'*Bonjour* Alfred, how are you doing? My journey was smooth, thanks.'

'Here, let me help you with that.'

Alfred offered as he held out his hand to help with my rucksack, and we walked towards the side entrance of a ladies' boutique.

'It's on the top floor of the building...and no lift, so sorry, Jason,' Alfred said as he led me up the four flights of stairs.

Having felt like I had done a workout as we arrived at the room, Alfred opened the door to a room soaked in Parisian charm, which was a far cry from some of the hovels I had stayed in in England.

'You will be staying here...I know it isn't much, but I hope you like it, uh?' Its rustic vibe was chic rather than cheap, and Alfred placed my big yellow rucksack next to a wrought-iron bistro chair.

'You want thé or café Jason?'

'I would love a cup of tea, thank you.'

'Ah, very English.'

'Milk? Sugar? Cream?'

'I'm sweet enough,' I joked, hoping that Alfred would catch my gist. His polite laugh suggested that he did before he headed towards the whistling kettle in the kitchen. As Alfred went to make tea, I made myself comfortable by the casement window and took a second to glimpse down onto the bustling Parisian street. A child opposite the road was coming out of a *patisserie* with an elderly lady with coal-black hair who looked very much like Nana.

'You see...the light here is *parfait*,' Alfred said, showing me the film set after our tea. As he had said, the natural light bouncing in from the balcony window made for an excellent shot. The sun shone onto the film equipment and the backs of the busy crew who were setting up the cameras. The young French crew looked up to greet me with a flurry of warm smiles and *bonjours* as they heard Alfred Rambaud's voice enter the room.

Other cast members conversing in unfamiliar French made the feeling of being an outsider more apparent, but when they saw me, they welcomed me in English to sit with them at their large wooden table. I settled at the table and flicked through the first pages of the script that was in front of me. I turned page after page of the script, having myself on that I may find a hint and hope of English dialogue, but alas, it was almost all in French. It was all *In vogue en vogue* to me.

'*Votre attention, s'il vous plaît!*' Alfred Rambaud said, drawing all eyes to the scripts in front of us as we prepared to begin the read-through rehearsal. My intense focus was centred on following the French dialogue with my fingers on the text, just like when I was learning to read at the tender age of four. As the actors read their lines, I had to ensure I didn't miss the cue of my character, Le Mari. When it did come to my part, my attempts at French sounded broken and butchered amongst the other actors' smooth dialogue. I was never a man usually lost for words, but on this occasion, I clearly was. Still, I felt the kindness and understanding of the actors in their quietness as I continued to leave out key intonations and mispronounce many of the words. Getting my French dialogue down was becoming like peeling pineapples, near impossible. As I struggled and stumbled, I began to wish I'd listened more in Mrs Caron's French class at school rather than staring at her breasts! The difficulty of the French pronunciation hit me more and more as I continued to fluff my lines. I sounded as French as a *croissant* singing *La Marseillaise:* Ridiculous. I wished very much to get the reading of my scenes out of the way, and I knew I had a big challenge on my hands.

'*Pas de souci, Jason...répetez s'il-vous-plait.*' Alfred voiced testing my waters.

Zut alors! It was one thing being able to read a script while sitting at a table during rehearsals, but delivering the French lines convincingly in front of a camera was going to be a different story. I needed to get this right, but how?

We spent a couple more hours reading through the script while the crew was finishing setting up the cameras, lighting, and sound. I wasn't becoming any more fluent, and I was feeling increasingly self-conscious. I didn't want to fuck up this great opportunity. I needed to think of something, then the euro dropped; I had an idea!

I had read about Marlon Brando using a technique in *The Missouri Breaks*, in which the great actor used cue cards during scenes with Jack Nicholson. During a brief coffee break amidst the hustle and bustle of the film set, I cornered Alfred and casually brought up an idea that had been lingering in my mind.

'Alfred, do you have a minute?'

'Sure, Jason, is everything Okay?'

'I've been thinking about Le Mari's dialogue.'

'Uh huh, is everything Okay?'

'To be honest, Alfred, I'm finding it a bit tricky, and I'm concerned about getting the pronunciation and intonation right...'

'Uh huh...'

While sipping his coffee, Alfred looked at me with a hint of reluctance, not knowing what I was going to suggest and whether he would have to politely decline. I myself wasn't sure how he'd react to my next suggestion and hoped he wouldn't vent his spleen. I asked anyway because, as the Yorkshire saying goes, If you don't ask, you don't get. I cleared my throat and my nerves and went for it.

'Do you think it would be possible to write down my lines phonetically on some prompt cards?'

Alfred looked at me, slightly confused, like I was a double-glazing salesman on commission trying to blindside him with a spiel. But what other choice did I have?

'What about this Alfred?... We could discreetly place the cards just out of the camera's view when we start filming.'

I got hands-on with my demonstration, hoping that I could see a glimmer of a potential sale in his eyes. With a thoughtful expression, Alfred paused.

'Elodie.'

Alfred Rambaud called across the busy film set room; the script editor, Elodie, appeared. I was better at trying to understand body language than I was at French as I tried to grasp Alfred's gesticulations a few metres away and the puzzled look on the script editor's face. From her going off and coming back with paper and a marker pen, I assumed Alfred agreed. *Parfait!* I wish I could've said the same for my French.

Alfred called. *'Action.'*

As the cameras rolled, all eyes were on me as I played my character, Le Mari. Years ago, I had perfected the art of subtly looking at things and not making it too obvious, so looking skillfully at the cue cards whilst trying to perform in front of the camera was not the problem.

"Les fourmis, on croit qu'elles chantent juste: We are the Vikings of the night, alors qu'en fait c'est pousse, pousse. Nous sommes les Vikings de la nuit!" I delivered (albeit a tad butchered).

Alfred called. *'Couper.'*

'Good Job Jason! Now you breathe!' He joked.

After I delivered my broken French, the palpable tension in the air had now subsided. Alfred smiled kindly, and I smiled with relief. My unorthodox technique had caused a ripple of laughter around the room.

'Did I mess up?'

'Bien au contraire, Très bien, Jason! It is the cue cards and not your French that they are laughing at, uh!' Reassured Alfred.

His comment was pillowed with a round of light applause and warm smiles from the cast and the crew. I welcomed Alfred's reassurance, and though I didn't puff my chest out like I may have done in more familiar surroundings. The pressure had eased, with only a few more non-dialogue scenes to do now. On that day, Paris smiled on me. Okay, by no means was I Gérard Depardieu, but I'd bloody done it! I was as proud as a cockerel that I'd pulled it off.

I was momentarily distracted by the cooking aroma of meat and red wine oozing through the room, which indicated that wrap time was nearly in sight.

After we'd finished the first day's shoot, Patricia, the assistant producer, took the cast to the next room: a large kitchen and the source of the sizzling smells. Weathered oak tables, wrought-iron chandeliers, mismatched chairs, and vintage ceramic tiles added to the charm of the room, where vibrant-looking small dishes of food were laid out on the table. Maurice, the tempestuous chef they hired from Normandy, came out and grunted in French as he placed his main dish on the table: *Tourte au bœuf* — beef pie!

Maurice's pie tasted miles better than the reduced-priced beef pies I'd tasted in the past. The succulent beef was soft and flavoured with *Burgundy* red wine, the shortcrust pastry melted in my mouth, and the beans were not baked from the tin but ones that were fresh, green and crisp. Alfred Rambaud said.

'It is...how do you say...humble offerings.... to what you probably have had on the bigger films you worked on, *non?*'

'Not at all, Alfred, this is *fantastique*. It's like the food of the Gods,' I replied as I scooped up another helping of pie.

The grimace on Maurice's face suggested that he didn't quite get the jist of my compliment, though, as he went away, then returned with more plates of delight in the form of French *crêpes*. Just one spoonful of the soft, sweet, buttery *crêpe* hit parts of my palate that had never been ventured into.

As we ate and drank, the cast and crew appeared more relaxed; some welcomed me into their meal conversations by speaking *Franglais,* and we created an *esprit de corps*. Laughter and lively conversation filled the rest of the evening as I savoured the rest of Maurice's soul-warming dishes. After a few beers, I wished everyone a *bonne nuit* and headed to my room feeling full to the brim.

'*Bonjour, Ça va?* You like rabbit Jason?'

Enquired Hadrien Mekki, one of the leading actors; he was looking at the next meal offering for our characters.

'*Bonjour* Hadrien... um...kind of... I've eaten rabbit once before...' I said, slightly dubious about the cooked white meat sitting underneath the hot film set lighting and unrefrigerated.

I was experiencing a *Deja Vu* food poisoning moment from a student film years before when I got really sick from eating unrefrigerated chicken left under the film lights. So, I figured the best thing was to warn Alfred that none of the actors should eat the rabbit. Alfred was grateful for the advice, but I wasn't sure Maurice was though.

Following the smooth last part of filming and the lucky swerve of potential salmonella poisoning, the film set equipment was packed away to make room for our wrap party, where Maurice had put on a spread of more amazing *soirée*-type food, *soirée*-type alcohol, and French pop songs so we could *soirée* the rest of *le nuit* away. A *joie de vivre* filled my soul as I soaked up the ambience. The cast and crew had invited some of their friends and partners. Now living in Paris, Nathalie had seen my Instagram post showing behind-the-scenes Paris shots of me on set. She cheekily messaged me to see if I was free for a rendezvous. Influenced by the copious glasses of red wine and by my levels of horniness, I did the most sensible thing I could think of. I ignored her.

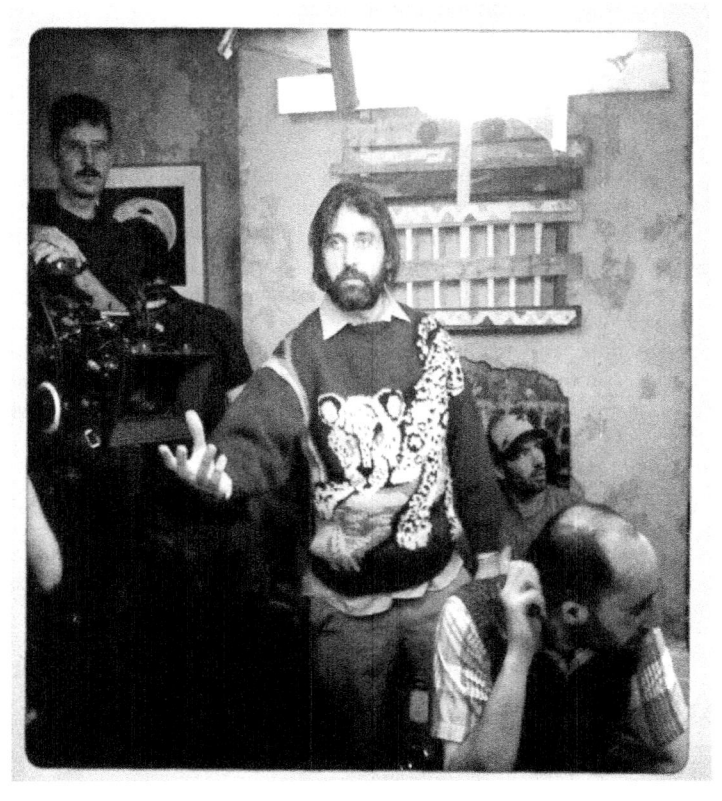

Me as Le Mari on the set of White City Spleen.

83 BLUES BROTHERS

'Jaaaaayyyyyyyy! You should've told me you wanted barbecued toast for breakfast! I prefer toast that you can eat, not sketch with.'

Back in Wimbledon, I heard the smoke alarm become alarmed, having detected my toast burning to smithereens. I went downstairs; Miranda was screeching and clearing out the toaster.

'Where did you graduate from, Jay, the school of haphazard cooking techniques?'

'Sorry Miranda, I just got caught up on the toilet.'

'No problem, disaster averted. There's some bad news though.'

'What's that?'

'I tried to resuscitate it, but unfortunately... I'm sorry to tell you this...but your toast couldn't be saved. Want another slice Jay?'

As Miranda proceeded to get another slice of marbled rye bread from the cupboard due to my absent-mindedness, I shared the news that had distracted me and nearly caused an almighty inferno. 'Miranda, I got an email from Pete Hunt. You know the filmmaker I'd met two years ago?'

Two years earlier

My agent, Elizabeth, received a call from a York-based director and writer, Pete Hunt, who'd expressed an interest in me being in his feature film *Elevator Gods*, a film based around life in my hometown of Bradford, and modelled on tribute bands from the 80s. Of course, I was *hungry like a wolf* and jumped at the chance, so I booked a train ticket straight away to travel from London to York to meet Pete Hunt.

It was in the studio of York 88 FM radio station where I auditioned for the leading part of Bry Teasedale. Pete Hunt read for the other character, Bry's brother, Adam Teasedale. In between our dialogue, Pete Hunt stopped reading, and I wondered why he appeared to be weighing me up through squinted eyes. He lowered his script, and the straight-talking filmmaker blurted out.

'You don't have blue eyes?'

'No, they're olive,' I replied, my face matching the film director's puzzled expression. At that point, Pete Hunt put his script down.

'Sorry pal, it was just that I was told you actually had blue eyes. That's what I specifically wanted for this character, Bry Teasedale. When your agent sent me your black and white photos, I was under the impression she'd understood what I was looking for. Sorry to waste your time, pal.'

It turned out that the director, Pete Hunt, didn't give me the leading role of Bry Teasedale, which I was sitting in front of him auditioning for, and I was absolutely gutted.

Before I left, I asked Pete Hunt where the toilets were and if he could keep an eye on my rucksack while I went to the loo. I returned to pick up my dented pride and belongings from the corner of the floor when Pete Hunt looked up from the script in his hands.

'Hey up. Before you go there is a role still to be cast, playing alongside Stuart Wolfenden, you know, from *Dead Man's Shoes,* you know, the Shane Meadows film... Anyway, the role I have in mind for you is Cobra. I think you'd be great. He's an 80s throwback...a whacky character...very out there...just like yourself. What do you think, huh?'

To pick myself up from the mishap of mistaken identity, rejection, and being likened to an 80s throwback, all in the space of three minutes, wasn't easy, but the wise words of my friend and director Dave Antonelli replayed in my head: A cameo role in a feature film is better than no role. So, after licking the wounds that deeply dented my Ego, I held out my hand to the director with a smile.

'That sounds amazing, Pete. I'm in!'

I was packing my bag to set off for York again two months after agreeing to take the cameo role. The last of the items on my list to pack was the rather large gold belcher chain for my character, Cobra.

Cobra was a 30-something guy stuck in the 80s era and self-tanned to the nines, with the aim of emulating every essence of his idol Detective James "Sonny" Crockett from the 80s American TV series *Miami Vice*. Cobra, however, was blissfully unaware that he didn't resemble his idol much. To add to my prop ensemble was a white polyester suit I had neatly folded and some Ambre Solaire self-tan mist to top off my sun-kissed look.

'Have you got any *brie* and cranberry sandwiches?'

'No Sir... I'm sorry...we have...' she explored her trolley before the flinty-voiced, Asian food and beverage trolley service attendant shared what was on offer.

'...Ploughman's Lunch...Coronation Chicken...Ham Salad?'

'No, I'll leave it then, cheers.'

She rolled her eyes and rolled her trolley forward as my two-hour train journey from London rolled on its way. Nestled in a far corner of the train carriage, a lanky teenager sat opposite me and had fallen asleep against the window, lost in the lyrics of the Crowded House track *Don't Dream It's Over*, escaping from his headphones and playing on a loop. The music was loud enough for the people in the several rows of seats behind to hear and tut-tut about...

Nearing the end of the journey, I was flicking through the script when the strong stench of cow pat drew my attention. Looking from the train window, I could see the sullen-looking small cows being cornered by significantly bigger ones, and they all aimlessly chewed their cud in the browning field where the train had stopped. The loud tones of Red Hot Chili Peppers, *Can't Stop* cut through the relative quietness in the carriage, the lanky teenager who had awoken from his two-hour slumber, said in a rather loud voice.

'Sorry, mate, excuse me. Can I just get my bag up there?' I swung my knees out of the way to make way for the teenager to get his tethered rucksack that he'd placed in the overhead storage.

'You got the time, mate?' He asked.

'12 o'clock, mate!' I replied, picking up my big yellow rucksack as the train pulled in at York station. Having sailed smoothly through a bunch of ticket inspectors, I meandered through the dash of passengers that were coming and going on the concourse. As I looked for the exit, I narrowly avoided an advertising board for WHSmith's promoting any sandwich and any drink for £4.99 before stepping into the Roman ground, which was encrusted in mediaeval 13th-century architecture. It was a refreshing contrast from the concrete jungle and high-rise buildings in London, where I had come from a few hours back. York was a city that, in its splendour, took my breath away in a way that London never could. It felt good to be back on my familiar, wholesome stomping ground of Yorkshire, amongst the clean air and the people who said it as it was.

'Hey up lad, didn't you sleep last night? You look like crap!'

Pete Hunt greeted me with a slice of Yorkshire charm as he wrapped me in an awkward, manly hug.

The laid-back Pete Hunt, who was dressed in a Kaiser Chiefs T-shirt and stonewashed jeans, drove us to the purpose-built film set that Pete's dad, Ron Hunt, had skillfully helped to put together. The film set was spread out with glistening trimmings, which made it look like a nightclub. After two hours of my make-up being done and my costume sorted, it was my time to take a bite of the action.

Pete Hunt called. *'Action.'*

Cobra (I) walked into the toilet...

Socket (Stuart Wolfenden) was checking himself out in the mirror.

"Hey up, Cobra, you got any gear to calm my nerves?"

Cobra took off his shades, slipped Socket some paracetamol, exited the toilet and hit the dance floor... A tribute band, Spandau Cafe, blasted out the timeless rendition of *Gold* as they performed on the big wooden stage. The club was full of actors playing 80s clubbers with big hair, spangled dresses, sequined and shoulder-padded jackets, and neon-coloured tops. The dance floor was a kaleidoscope of retro fashion. The swirling disco ball and flashing disco lights made the clubbers shine as they busted out their best dance moves to the 80s pop music. I, in the role of my character Cobra, (donned in my white suit and false tan, which seemed to make me look like I'd fallen in a vat of turmeric), cruised cooly across the heaving wooden dance floor, emanating an aura of effortless cool as I arrived at the stage. I was ready to bring my own brand of 80s swagger to life. I looked around the crowded stage and delivered my dialogue.

. "No one puts Baby in the corner."

Pete Hunt called. *'Cut!*...well done, Jay!' And just like that, my Cobra cameo role came to an end.

Cobra (Me) and Socket (Stuart Wolfenden) on the Elevator Gods set.

84 ELEVATOR GODS

'Jay, I can't reach to turn the smoke alarm in the living room off. Can you please hurry up?'

The pint-sized Miranda called, in a shriek nearly as high-pitched as the shrill fire alarm in our Wimbledon home that had been set off once again whilst Miranda toasted my marbled rye bread.

'I think this toaster is a goner now...it's beyond me why men always take their phones to the toilet. Anyways, read me Pete Hunt's email...sounds exciting.'

I continued to read out loud the out-of-the-blue email from Pete Hunt titled Feature Film.

Hey up Jay; I hope you are well. Elevator Gods is undergoing a reshoot. I've decided to scrap the character of Cobra, BUT don't fret! Instead, I want to offer you the leading role of Bry Teasedale in my film. Please find the script attached to the email. Let me know your thoughts. Cheers, Pete

The concourse of King's Cross was heaving and a busker was doing his best to entertain, but his talent was being swallowed up in the busyness of the London crowd as he sang *Caravan of Love* by the Housemartins. I scanned the station's main destination board to check which platform my train was leaving from, and shit, as I thought, I only had a couple of minutes to belt it before the train departed. Puffed out and pooped, I managed to get on the 7.00am train from London to York before its doors snapped shut. I had just managed to find a comfortable seat far away from the antisocial bleach smell of the newly cleaned toilets.

Tickets! Tickets! Tickets! Please!'

I could hear the holler of a grumpy train inspector who looked like he got out of the wrong side of the bed.

I picked up a glossy Country Life magazine that someone had left wedged between the seats and had been missed by the nighttime cleaners. The magazine had been folded back on a page written by a charity founder. Accompanying the article was an idyllic picture of a country field with a rogue black and white calf that had left most of the herd and was edging near the field's fence. Interrupting a daydream that I'd fallen into was a food and beverage attendant parading his fully stocked trolley and inviting any takers for his teas, coffees, sandwiches or snacks to speak out or forever hold their peace.

'Mummy, I'm hungry... I'm hungry, Mummy...can I have some Rolos...?'

'...Me, Mum, me, me, pleeeeeassse, I want a Kit Kat...I want a Kit Kat!...'

A family of five with two young, eager beaver brothers sat in the row of seats opposite, already high on the cartons of concentrated orange squash they had in their hands. Their family labrador was trying to snooze under the seats as the siblings began to bicker. The mum looked aggravated as she looked sternly at the dad, and she said.

'I can't believe you forgot to take the sandwiches out of the fridge.'

The dad looked embarrassed as he looked at me, looking like he himself needed a Kit Kat and hoping I'd let him sort out his pressure cooker of a family first.

'It's okay...you go first!' I said, nodding to the dad of the family as he proceeded to buy some tempting-looking croissants and bits and bobs from the attendant's trolley, lightening his load. I took out my script and fumbled around my rucksack pockets to look for any jingle money; after finding a few shekels, I fingered through the script as I waited for the attendant. I thought about what it would be like now that I had been given the leading role of Bry Teasedale two years after I initially was auditioned and rejected for the role.

A set of photos of Mum and Dad fell out from between the pages of the script where I had clipped them. I reattached them as I skimmed through the scene with my character's parents. A pang of yearning hit where I hungered as I thought about how Pete was planning to cleverly incorporate archival footage using pictures of my parents, Alice and Dennis Croot, and intended, through smart editing, for them to be the on-screen parents of Adam and Bry Teasedale.

'Sir, would you like any tea? Coffee? Sandwiches or snacks?'

'I'll have one of those apple danishes, please, and a tea,' I replied to the seller.

'Right, have you zipped up your coats, boys?...and don't forget your scarf Sebastian! Right boys, remember what I told you?' the Mum said.

'We're going to give grandma a big hug when we see her?' said the younger brother, as proud as punch that he remembered.

'No, I am,' retorted the older brother.

'No, I am...' the younger one returned.

Whilst the brothers bickered again, the mum of the family threw a look to the dad of the family as he picked up his cable-knit scarf from the space next to him and tied it around his neck as his clan prepared to disembark from the train.

'The next station is York Station, York is the next station,' the automated voice announced loudly over the train's tannoy.

'Does the King live there?' asked the younger child, who was all wrapped up and looking at a leaflet of York's magnificent Romanesque walls that encircled the historic city.

This was it; I rolled up my script and wrapped myself up before lifting my big yellow rucksack from the overhead storage shelf.

'Hey up lad, good to see ye again. Did ye have a good journey?' Pete's charming dad, Ron Hunt, said as he met me at the entrance of York station before driving us to Pete's house, my place of residence that week while filming.

'Aye, he's excited...I can't even remember how long he's been working on this film for, lad...but I tell ye what, lad, I'm over the moon for him that finally he's getting it on the road again.'

As I chatted with Ron, I felt his overwhelming support for Pete's dream. Ron had been helping *Elevator Gods* get off the ground and working tirelessly on technical set-building and behind-the-scenes stuff, as well as recording the sound on the film. Ron's love and dedication to supporting his son's dream were evident through his enthusiasm and showed that Ron was cut from the cloth that only legends were made of.

'Hey up, Sergio.'

'Sergio?'

'Yeah, Sergio Pizzorno, from Kasabian, you look exactly like him...like twins...let me show you your room,' Pete said enthusiastically.

After putting down my big yellow rucksack and quickly changing, my nose led me to the beautiful aroma coming from the kitchen.

'Great scran, Pete, compliments to the chef,' I chimed.

Pete's mum had made some delicious lasagne and a surprise Yorkshire Parkin for pudding. Pete, Ron, and I tucked into the yummy food, which we washed down with cups of fresh Yorkshire Tea. Pete's mum's dessert wasn't my only surprise after the evening meal.

'Hey up Crooty lad, how's it going? Long time no see.'

It was my good old school chum Steve McAleavy, who had arrived at Pete's house. Steve was now a filmmaker who was working as a camera guy on the film. Steve joined Pete, Ron, and me for a brew and dessert at Pete's dining table as we filled the evening chatter with future plans for the film and past memories of our Yorkshire school days.

Just one Cornetto

The feral pigeons of York hooted loudly, the York locals went about their business, and the Jack Frost October chill was deciding whether his time in York was to be a long or short spell. The serene quietness was met with echoes of...

"Engines nearly on fire! We are out of bloody oil."

Pete had borrowed a 35-year-old banger-of-an ice cream van, which aesthetically looked cool, but it was noisy as hell. It was continuing to backfire, and needless to say, it hardly had the engine of a Ferrari.

'Chuffing heck,' Steve McAleavy said.

'You'll be alright, lad,' Ron Hunt said..

'You alright back there, lads? Howard Harling, the driver, said.

'I didn't sign up for this,' I said.

'Ready guys?' Pete Hunt said as he called *'Action.'*

The scene was challenging, to say the least, as there was no room in the moving van to swing a skinny cat. Four strapping, intrepid Yorkshiremen in the back of a tiny ice cream van felt more like four giant sausages in a Yorkshire pudding. The cameras and sound rolled, and Pete and I acted in the shoebox space. Howard tried his best to keep the ice cream van on the road. To make things even more challenging, the filming equipment wasn't small. Ron was trying to hold the sound boom steady and out of view of Steve's £4000 Sony camera, which Steve was clinging onto for dear life whilst Pete (Adam) and I (Bry) were trying to remain upright and in the camera's shot as we all wobbled in the back of the careening ice cream chariot. I thought to myself, it's a good job that Romans built straight roads. We had to swerve several Cornettos and ice cream cones, flying out like balls in a Screwball Scramble game, one after another, first onto our heads and then onto the floor. Howard Harling (Vin) was at the wheel, and my character Bry had to climb from the back into the front whilst the ice cream van was in motion. I could've gone flying out of the unlocked doors at any time. Boy, oh boy, the lengths I would go to to become famous. As I clambered over the seats, my head dropped dizzy. I managed to climb into the driver's seat and grab the wheel from Vin, who shouted.

"Engines, nearly on fire; we are out of bloody oil."

The oil gauge wobbled, and the gears crunched and produced a distinctive unhealthy mechanical sound. This was raw "Guerrilla filmmaking" at its best, the type I relished the most. As we sped down the York country roads with our smoke-filled exhaust billowing out onto the clean Yorkshire air, the backfiring vehicle grabbed the attention of the pedestrians looking on and the blues and twos of a passing police car. Fortunately, the police stopping us was part of the film and one of a multitude of scripted and improvised scenes.

Improvisation is one of my fortes, and this was a technique we used during the next scene. Bry (me) was enraged at his on-screen brother, Adam (Pete), who had run off to Bulgaria without telling anyone. Upon returning to Yorkshire, Adam entered the old, small two-berth caravan, where he said nonchalantly.

"Tea? Coffee? Chocolate Digestive?" Adam hadn't realised that he'd just pulled out a key to a live grenade as his outraged brother exploded at Adam's prodigal son's attitude. Adam faced the music when Bry (me) wrestled him to the ground, and whilst on top of him, Bry delivered a few hard blows to Adam's head with a plastic milk bottle, which was topped off with a kilo bag worth of sugar over his hair. The commotion made the caravan rock from side to side as a fuming Bry yelled.

"Cupppppp of teaaaaaaa? Do you want a fucking cup of teaaaaaaaaaa? Where were you? Where have you been? Why did you fucking leave without telling anyone."

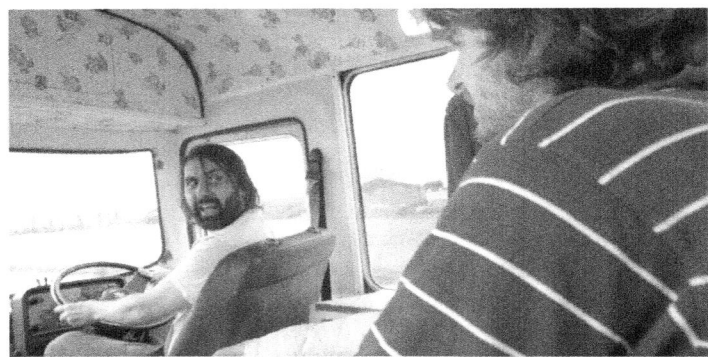

Above me, and Pete Hunt on the set of Elevator Gods, during the Ice cream mayhem. Photos courtesy of Steve McAleavy.

85 MOVING ON UP

'...Sorry, Jason, the cat has just pressed something on my laptop...I need to find the email I'm talking about...I'll be with you in a sec.'

I waited whilst taking a sip of my Earl Grey, sitting on my sofa in Wimbledon as Elizabeth continued to talk to herself.

'...No I don't want that update...no...close...close...close...I've got about a hundred tabs open...arrgghhhh...no wonder this computer is running like shhhhh...Sheeba, get away from there...'

I continued to wait and wait. Every second, which seemed like an eternity, I could hear the loud meowing and Elizabeth tapping, clicking and venting her frustration out on the keys of her laptop. After managing to sort out her temperamental laptop and the even more temperamental feline, my London agent, Elizabeth, came back to me....Ffff...found it now, Jason. It's from Tobias Rodrigues...you know, the one from the Malta commercial?'

'..Oh really...I know Tobias...'

'Well...Mr Rodrigues wants you to read for him... it's for a TV production...he wants you to read for a role in *Roma Nights*... it's produced by...EmpireFrame Productions...he seemed to be pretty impressed with your performance in the *Aurelia* commercial in Malta....what do you think, Jason?... The only stipulation is that you need six months of validity on your passport... Jason, are you there?'

I walked into The Gold Bridge Hotel, Central London, the venue for the casting, where there was a welcomed lack of actors. I was met by a plain-faced but alert Muriel, a casting assistant who asked me if I wanted tea or coffee. An *espresso* was my tipple of choice.

Jessica Simons, the renowned casting director, had a coffee in her hand when I introduced myself to her. She was sitting next to Tobias Rodrigues, a man with spectacles whose age had looked upon him favourably; his complexion had a Mediterranean sun-kissed glow, and his suave charm radiated through to his polite and friendly manner. Both Tobias and Jessica appeased me with routine niceties, speaking about how my journey travelling to the audition was and how the weather was due to be a scorcher that day. When Muriel indicated that the camera she had been adjusting was ready, Jessica Simons smiled (as I was finishing off my sentence about being stuck for ten minutes on the train in Battersea because of some sort of intrepid animal on the line). Jessica's bright red lipstick spanned from ear to ear, and she managed to find an opening between my *espresso*-fuelled gibberish to ask me to start.

I started reading for the part of Italian Mafia leader Riccardo Gallo, and five minutes into my reading, as I got to the end of one of Gallo's sentences, Tobias Rodrigues held his hand up and asked me to stop.

'A bravura display of acting, Jason, executed with precision, well done... I'd like you to read for another character, Lucca Bombello,' he asserted whilst adjusting his Ray-Ban specs. He flicked through a small pile of papers, licking his index finger to separate the sheets stuck together, then passed me one of the pages.

Bombello was an Italian assassin. I hadn't prepared for this, but because the characters of Gallo and Bombello were both members of the Mafia, I didn't have to drastically switch personas. However, given that Bombello didn't have much dialogue, the role, as Tobias explained, was more about the nuances of Bombello and being convincing through movement to portray a hardened badass. Tobias directed me to walk around the room menacingly, fueled by *espresso* and my drive to make an impact with both directors. I kept my cool under pressure and paced up and down the room like Bombello, the sinister hitman. In front of Tobias and Jessica, I took a moment and stared right into their eyes. I was close enough to see the caramel brown eyes of Tobias were slightly bloodshot, and part of Jessica's left eyelid had missed being touched by the black eyeliner pencil that morning. The few seconds of silence whilst I glared at them as Bombello created an uneasy atmosphere, which was only interrupted by the voice of Tobias, who held his hand in the air and said.

'Okay, Jason, thank you. I've seen enough.'

I was dropped off at the airport by a driver named Billy, who had picked me up at noon from Wimbledon to take me to London Heathrow Airport, where I caught the two-and-a-half-hour business class flight to flaming hot Fiumicino Airport Rome. I was met at the airport by another personal driver, an olive-skinned elderly man who seemed an expert in his role. As I headed towards the airport's exit, the personal driver was well placed behind the barriers among the other elite group of drivers waiting patiently for their clients. De Luca, Caruso, Takahashi, Armstrong, Wang and Crot were some of the various names held up, waiting to be recognised by their rightful owners. I spotted my surname straight away, not only because it was misspelt but also because my driver was the only one amongst the group who was suited and booted in a navy blue driver's uniform.

The driver greeted me in English with a hint of a Sicilian accent. The silver-haired man offered his hand for my sweaty palm to shake.

'*Buongiorno, como stai?* Welcome to Roma. I'm Guiseppe, your driver. I will be looking after you for the next three days.'

'*Buongiorno*, how's it going?'

I replied, not mentioning anything about my misspelt name.

Guiseppe took my big yellow rucksack as we walked to his black stretch limo, where he opened the rear door to let me in.

We set off slowly, driving through Rome's bustling narrow streets, where the cacophony of car horns beeping seemed louder than live music from a heavy rock band. The ageing chauffeur's strong, citrusy cologne was overpowering, so I pushed the buttons to open the window next to me. What I hadn't realised was that this was the button to put up the blacked-out divider between the backseat passenger and the driver. I pressed it again but couldn't get it back down, which was rather embarrassing because it appeared like I was already a prima donna before my Italian journey had even begun.

The divider was still up when I found the button for the window next to me. When the window slid down, the scorching heat hit my face instantly. For the rest of the journey, I soaked in the magnificence of the city's architecture. Fifteen minutes later, we arrived at Hotel Valentino in the Testaccio region, near the River Tiber.

Guiseppe maintained his professionalism and didn't react to what could've been misconstrued as me being rude. He took my big yellow rucksack out of the boot and offered to take it inside the hotel for me, but I told him I could manage and gave him a five *euro* tip.

'*Grazie*. Have a good day, sir.' Guiseppe walked back to the limo and set off.

My lumberjack-style checked shirt, ripped jeans, and memory foam Skechers made me feel a touch out of place as I stepped into the marbled floors of the swanky and stunning lobby, which was picture-perfect, just like the posh and glitzy hotels in the Hollywood movies. The chandeliers sparkled from the ceiling with elegance, the same type of elegance that the clientele dotted around the lobby area had. Scents of expensive perfume lingered in the air. I tried to keep my arms glued to my side because my flannel lumberjack shirt had created an aroma of its own as it clung to my armpits with sweat courtesy of the Italian heat.

The 5-star Hotel Valentino I had just stepped into was to be my base whilst I was filming. Tobias Rodrigues and Jessica Simons had hired me on the spot for the role of the Mafia assassin Luca Bombello for the major TV production *Roma Nights... I'd arrived!!*

86 TO ROMA WITH LOVE

'It's a common feature in most hotels, sir. The key card activates the electricity in the room, including the air conditioning.'

I had gone down to the hotel's reception to enquire about the dicky air conditioning in my room. But it turned out that it wasn't dicky after all, as pointed out by a well-groomed hotel manager behind the reception desk. She expressed a tone of impatience and took about ten seconds to explain to me in layman's terms that I needed to actually put my plastic key card in a slot in the door to get the electricity to work. My face went slightly warm as I thanked her and went back to my room.

Back in my snazzy hotel room, I perused the extravagant choices of the minibar, but when I saw the prices, I changed my mind and shut the fridge without a drink. Even though my *per diems* were included, I wasn't sure they covered the minibar. Being a tight Yorkshireman, I wasn't going to fork out eight *euros* for a *Birra Moretti!*

The edges of my script poking out of my rucksack reminded me that I needed to pick it up and get reading. So now, with lights and air conditioning on, I needed to get my head back in the game and study the nuances of Lucca Bombello.

My character, Bombello, was mainly silent, like most hitmen. As I read, I envisaged his movement as I walked around the hotel room. I wasn't feeling the character in my movement. I suddenly remembered what Perry Rivera, the drama coach who gave me a massage, had advised me a few years back about an actor's footwear making the character. I dug into my rucksack to look for the heavy boots I brought with me. As I emptied my bag and found the boots, their price tag was still attached, reminding me that I hadn't even tried them on. When I squeezed my feet into the boots, I was horrified to find that they were, in fact, too tight. I tried the lighter hi-tops I had packed for walking around Rome, but they were no good. These Converse hi-tops didn't give me the weight I needed for the assassin's movement, and as far as I could fathom, hired hitmen didn't wear Converse hi-tops!

Now, in a panic, I typed in the hotel's wifi code on my smartphone to look for local shoe shops, but all the writing was in Italian, so I couldn't make head nor tail of what I was looking at.

Back at the reception desk, I asked the mardy manager where the nearest shoe shop or shopping mall was. She indicated on a map with a Hotel Valentino gold pen how to get to the Centro Commerciale and explained that there was a hotel shuttle service in half an hour if I wanted to wait.

I decided not to wait for the shuttle and to take the 10-minute walk to my destination so that I could soak up the city's thriving ambience.

I eventually found the mall, which was pretty standard, like most of the malls I had been to on my travels. It was air-conditioned with an array of chain shops and a food court at the centre, which played host to a few pizza places and small, well-known burger joints. It lacked the soul and tradition of Rome that I was expecting and seemed to lack the shops that sold the heavy-soled boots I was looking for. I left the Centro Commerciale with nothing but two I Love Roma T-shirts that I had bought for the bartered price of three *euros* each from a West African street seller who was standing outside the shopping centre.

Back at the hotel, I thought about what I should do. As I carefully put my I Love Roma T-shirts in my rucksack, I thought about my boot dilemma. I considered leaving it to chance and holding on to the hope that the costume department would have a suitable pair of boots, but it bugged me to leave the issue unresolved. I didn't want just to wait for the other shoe to drop. I knew I needed to have my own pair of boots, just in case. The character needed to walk heavily, so unless I ate 25 pizzas and gained 10 kg by the morning, I had to think on my feet and do something.

I remembered, as a boy, to make my new boots bigger, Gan Gan would put in pages of scrunched-up wet newspapers inside them and leave them overnight, either that or potatoes, and this technique, as I remembered, seemed to work, but where was I going to find a King Edward potato now? Maybe not in Piazza del Popolo. I remembered bagging a couple of glossy magazines that I had flicked through on the flight from London because they had a few samples of a vitamin C moisturiser I wanted to try. So, I got the magazines out of my bag, removed the moisturiser samples, ripped some of the pages out, soaked the papers under the shower, and then stuffed them in my boots. While I left my boots to soak, I picked up the menu of the day, which was placed in a smooth leather-bound folder. The menu items included snail *caviar, veal broth ravioli, tortellini stuffed with rabbit, and steamed oysters with squid ink pasta,* and unsurprisingly, the majority of the overpriced menu with dishes ranging from 45 *euros* was as appealing as the soggy paper in my boots.

I headed back out to see if there was some local food that actually appealed to me. As I strode further and further down the side streets, it appeared that I was spoilt for choice. My senses were treated to a delightful array of aromas from the small cafés, humble *panetterias* and quaint *trattorias.* The air was filled with the smells of roasted coffee and the aroma of fresh basil, oregano, fried garlic and freshly baked bread, which made my mouth water. I noticed a massive queue of Italians lining up outside *Trattoria Trapizzino*; seeing that I was in Rome, I needed to do as the Romans did. Thirty minutes later, I understood why it was so popular with the locals. The divine meatball *Trappizino* that I was devouring was to die for. I hadn't finished yet; a pistachio *cannoli* stared at me from the *panetteria* window opposite me, daring me to buy it. Once I had wolfed down the meatball pocket pizza, I treated myself to a *cannoli.* I debated with myself whether the idea of getting an Italian coffee was sensible considering the time, and I knew if I drank coffee so late, I wouldn't be able to sleep. *Caffè Macchiato* was in hand, filled and satisfied. I was ready to tackle my script, so I went back to my room, took my crumpled script off the bed, and took it in the jacuzzi tub. I realised that it was hard to think like a killer hitman, get into character, and find my motivation in a tub of bubbles, so I got out after a few minutes.

I put on the soft white Hotel Valentino robe hanging in the wardrobe and put my feet up on the bed. My Ennio Morricone's *Once Upon a Time in America* soundtrack filled the room as it played on the hotel's iPod speakers. I searched for inspiration.

I tried to think of people I'd met, and even though I had met a few unsavoury people in my time, murder had never crossed my mind. So, it was more challenging to get into character than I initially anticipated. As I continued to dig deep for inspiration, I eventually conjured up an imaginary persona—one who force-fed me custard and made me drink cider. Though the thought made me feel queasy, this became my motive. I imagined the headlines:

Assassinated for feeding a guy custard and cider.

After a few hours of going through the script, it was getting late, and a good night's sleep was imperative as this was my biggest, most demanding role to date. But on this night before the crucial morning after, the consequence of my 'giving in' to the temptation of a *Caffè Macchiato* had now kicked in.

87 BOMBELLO

After a fitful night's sleep, tiredness pulled my eyelids down like a 100-kilo weight. But the intrusive ring of the reception early morning wake-up call forced me to raise my head from the comfort of the Egyptian cotton pillows; even the rude awakening of the power shower did very little to help my tiredness; in fact, the complicated motion sensor shower stressed me more than revitalise me, to top it all off, my boots were still soaking wet.

'Buongiorno, como stai Jason?'

'Buongiorno, how's it going?'

I replied as Giuseppe courteously swung the rear car door open. I settled into the plush confines of the chauffeur-driven car before we set off.

This was our only interaction during the 30-minute drive to the filming location: The breathtaking and iconic Spanish Steps of Rome. When I arrived at the 138 steps, it was already beginning to bustle with adoring tourists and locals marvelling at the pink-blooming azaleas.

The film crew had cordoned off a small area around Piazza di Spagna at the base and Piazza Trinità dei Monti, which boasted the magnificent 15th-century church at the top. One stipulation hung over the production like a blade on a raised guillotine: the local authority had only granted the production team two hours to film the scene on the Spanish Steps.

I was met by a man with an untucked shirt, get-out-of-bed hair, sporting a scruffy beard; he greeted me with an overly warm welcome of a kiss to both cheeks and asked with genuineness how I was and whether I slept well. I said I was good, and my sleep was great because I was hardly going to say how I actually felt: nervous, shitting myself and exhausted. The man was Angelo Conti, the assistant director.

Angelo took me to the small caravan-style trailer to have my makeup and hair done by Fia, an energetic makeup and hair stylist who was glamming up the Italian siren lead actress Sophia De Mornay, who would play the Italian secret agent Sophia Bianco and who would be acting in some scenes with me as hitman Bombello.

As I took a seat, Sophia appeared to pretend not to have noticed me. She looked down at her phone as her hair was being styled and sprayed. The strong aerosol nearly made me gag, so I had no alternative but to waft the smell away with my crumpled script. I caught Sophia in the mirror, rolling her eyes, and the buck stopped there in terms of her acknowledging me. During the rest of the forty-five minutes that I sat beside her, she didn't afford me as much as a hello. After Sophia was done, Fia was a couple of minutes into caking on my makeup when Angelo came into the trailer, blurting out.

'How long, Fia? How long?'

With time not on our side, Angelo looked rather stressed out and paced up and down like an expectant father as Fia masked the tiredness in my eyes with concealer.

With makeup done, I went into the costume trailer. Hagne, the head costume designer, couldn't find any suitable heavy boots to fit me. Great, I had to wear my soaking ones.

Hagne handed me a pair of chinos; after trying them on, they felt so tight that I could have sang soprano.

To top off, my ensemble was a long black trench coat, which Hagne was trying to find. She was going as nutty as a squirrel because she couldn't find it anywhere.

My body stunt double Enzo Caruso, who had filmed some of Bombello's pivotal death-defying dangerous stunts the day before, had worn it and apparently given the trench coat to Hagnes' younger costume assistant Claudia.

Hagne's fiery Italian temper matched the engine-red tips of her hair. She retorted something in Italian at Claudia, who was fiddling with her phone while Rome burnt all around her, but now she was feeling the wrath of Hagne's volcanic temper.

The tension was mounting as precious time ticked on, and by now, eight film production crew members were looking high and low for the coat in the cramped trailer. I was helpless and felt more underfoot than anything else, so I got dressed in my chinos that

Hagne had got ready for me and put on my sodding wet boots.

I left the trailer so as not to get caught in the crossfire of the fraught Italian crew as they continued their search for the elusive trench coat. I took the short walk across Piazza Trinità dei Monti, where we would be filming my scene at the top of the Spanish Steps.

The time to do the scene was ticking down as the bombshell Sophia, who was as bold as her figure-hugging cream dress, strutted towards Angelo like an award-winning peacock; she billowed.

'I'm not standing here all day. I have better things I could be doing, you know! And I don't like this microphone stuck down my pants!!!'

A stressed-out Angelo paused momentarily from his puffing and snapped back at her in Italian. They then had what seemed like a heated exchange. Their hands flew in the air as did angry Italian words, and all the while, I stood awkwardly beside them, not understanding a word. It was evident that Sophia had emerged triumphant in the heated argument because she stormed off, taking her entitled attitude with her and leaving Angelo looking bamboozled.

The moment's awkwardness was cut short by a cheer from across the busy Piazza. It seemed to be coming from the direction of the costume trailer. Hagne came out of the trailer holding the trench coat like a golden Oscar. A relieved-looking Angelo stubbed out his half-smoked cigarette on the floor and ran over to the trailer through the crowds in the Piazza.

Angelo brought me my coat. Apparently, it was hiding on the same hanger underneath a long mink fur coat. I was ready for my scene.

Several curious tourists had gathered to watch us film the scene. Due to the trench coat saga, we only had 30 minutes remaining to get this scene done. The cameras were set and ready at the top and base of the steps, and the director, Tobias Rodrigues, called. *'Action.'*

Agent Bianco carefully walked down the narrow Spanish Steps in her kitten heels, closely followed by my character Bombello. She turned around, but as she did, Tobias called. *'Cut!'*

I thought fuck, had I got my acting wrong? NO! There seemed to be an issue with the sunlight affecting one of the cameras. *Mama Mia!* Tobias was stressed. Angelo was stressed. Sophia was stressed, and honestly, I, too, was fucking stressed. After ten minutes of technical testing, the camera guys put a filter on the problematic camera. We started again from our first positions. I was Bombello once again, as *'Action'* was called by Tobias.

Bombello followed his target secret agent Bianco down the steps.

Sensing someone was behind her, she turned to see the hitman following her. Bombello bent down to fasten his shoelace, and Bianco took this as an opportunity to run. In the process, she managed to shake off Bombello amongst the heaving crowd.

Tobias called. *'Cut.'*

After the morning drama, filming was complete in the nick of time. Day one was in the bag, and the rest of the day breezed past.

The following day, my driver, Giuseppe, picked me up and dropped me off at the next filming location—Maestoso Plaza Hotel Roma. The production had hired this 1960s grand Italian 5-star hotel for filming.

I was greeted by a calmer-looking Angelo, who directed me to go straight to costume, where I saw a different side to Hagne than I had done the day before. This time, the costume designer was very chatty and bubbly and evidently a morning person, the type of person who talked like there was no tomorrow. I'd never been a morning person, so I had to force the upbeat energy out of me as she relayed the tale of her finding the trench coat the day before and highlighted the clumsy mistake of her assistant Claudia, who was nowhere to be seen. She kitted me out in the long black trench coat and chinos that she'd obviously stored carefully. Then she sent me off to Fia in hair and makeup.

After Fia touched up my face with foundation and sorted my hair, Angelo came in and asked Fia something in Italian when Fia replied.

'Dieci minut.'

I gathered it was about how much longer it would be before I was ready. Angelo waited and then took me to the set.

This was my final scene, a death scene and one I wanted to look convincing. So I found one of the stunt coordinators and ballistics expert, Phillipe, who was having a coffee, to ask him about the stunt. Phillipe put down his coffee and demonstrated through his movements how the force of the body would go backwards.

'Have you ever been hit in the stomach by a football?' Philippe enquired.

'Yeah, many times.'

'Okay, Jason, imagine that impact, along with someone stronger than you pushing you with force... this is how it would feel to be shot close range in the torso.'

In the final scene, unbeknownst to my character Bombello, Sophia, A.K.A. Secret agent Bianco, in fear for her life, was due to shoot and kill me through a hotel room door. The door was loaded with ample expensive special effects and gunpowder attached to it and would explode on impact from the gunshot. We only had one crucial shot to get the scene right, and if I got it wrong, they wouldn't be able to refilm it, so the pressure was on. The stakes of my acting game were the highest that they'd ever been, and I didn't want to blow it, as Tobias Rodrigues called. *'Action.'*

My character, Bombello, was dressed in a long black trench coat, and hidden underneath my coat was my assassin pistol with a silencer attached to it. I was armed with a weapon and the expert knowledge of Phillipe, the stunt coordinator. The pressure to get it right in one take had forced me to swallow the hitman character and embody him into my performance, which I did from the moment I was living as Bombello (I) entered the hotel lobby through the revolving doors.

My sinister-looking character stood out a mile as he set foot in the spacious and tastefully designed lobby with high ceilings adorned with elegant chandeliers and beautiful hanging artwork. Bombello looked around and strode over to the elevator. He hardly looked inconspicuous.

Bombello noticed a tall, thick-set concierge walking towards him. The hitman kept his cool, walking through the lobby full of classy guests, and entered the elevator, followed by the cautious concierge, who stared at him suspiciously. As the elevator travelled up towards the 16th floor, Bombello took no chances. He didn't like the way that the concierge was looking at him, so he whipped out his pistol and, in an unplanned move, shot his first victim right between the eyes. Bombello then removed the dead concierge's jacket and swapped it with his trench coat. He wrapped his coat over his arm to conceal his pistol.

As the elevator made its ascent to the 16th floor, Bombello neared closer to his intended target. He exited the elevator with an eerie calmness and jammed the elevator doors open with a fire extinguisher to make sure nobody could find his bloodied victim. He stepped over the corpse and wiped his heavy blood-stained boots on the grey floral patterned carpet as he walked towards room 181. As he approached room 181, Bianco, the planned victim, received a text (unbeknown to Bombello). The text was a tip-off, which informed her that she was about to be attacked. Bianco, half-dressed, grabbed her gun out of her pocket and, with her special-agent instincts, moved with her back to the wall. By the twisting door handle, she saw that someone was trying to enter her room. Through the spyhole, she saw Bombello dressed in the hotel uniform. The blood splatters on his cheeks gave away that he was a killer, not a concierge. She coolly raised her pistol, aimed and shot Bombello through the locked door.

At the same time as Sophia shot me, the special effects came into effect and boom, the explosion happened. I flew back against the wall with a considerable force that I felt throughout my whole body. I had little time to think about the pain in my back as I had to slide down towards the floor and play dead convincingly. I tried my best for the life of me not to inhale the surrounding smoke and gunpowder; otherwise, I'd break out in a fit of coughing. I was dead for about ten seconds before Tobias called. *'Cut.'*

And once he did, the unsuspecting Yorkshire lad and hitman received a welcomed surprise. My energy felt plugged in with electricity as I stood up and showered in the recognition, the cheers of bravos, and the round of thunderous applause from the cast, the crew, Tobias Rodrigues, and Angelo. I wouldn't have changed this feeling for all the art in Rome as the roar reached a crescendo, my heart thudded as hard as the momentous explosion that had happened a few seconds before, AND that, Ladies and Gentlemen, was MY moment.

88 THE CONVERSATION

'Move your finger up a bit, Jason...a bit more...just a tad more...steady...steady...you've got a very steady hand, haven't you, which is good...ah yes THERE...right there...lovely...hold it!'

After a few hours of posing for hand positions that looked easier than they actually were to do, the director was satisfied with what he'd got for that scene. DHH Modeling had lined me up with a mainstream TV documentary: *You're Whose Body Double?* It was about, yes, you guessed it, body doubles and featured me as myself, Jason Croot, The Hand Model. Okay, it wasn't an elusive acting role, but a bird in the hand was worth two in the bush or Shepherd's Bush, to be more precise, which was the location of the film studios where the TV documentary was taking place.

'Let's take five guys,' voiced the director.

I headed over to the water cooler, and from another room, I overheard the voice of a hand modelling agent, apparently renowned in her field, who was being filmed as part of the documentary.

'... It's more than just having pretty hands...because, most of the time, hands are not just modelling. Their hands are actually acting.'

I slowed down my pace so I could hear as she continued.

'...Yes, for that commercial, I was commissioned to do the entire casting, which wasn't easy! I had to trawl through London searching for the best finger that could do the walking and the dancing...I think I had something like 100 models and actors...but 100% I had to go to actors...because I needed the dexterity of fingers...' the agent explained.

I was on a tight rein and directed to talk only about my hand modelling career, BUT after overhearing the agent's interview, I saw this as my way in to talk openly about my acting career tool alongside my hand modelling career. My pocket began to vibrate to alert me to a voice message on my newly purchased iPhone. It was from KJC Casting:

'Hello Jason, It's Tina. I have some news for you. It's urgent. It's exciting news. Call me back ASAP, okay? Ciao for now.'

Before I had a chance to return Tina's call, the director bellowed for all hands to come back on deck.

During the remainder of the filming, I tried to weave in the highlights of my acting career into the conversation, but trying to steer the topic in this direction was more difficult than it appeared.

'Maybe If I mention my name and what I've acted in, it will bolster your TV ratings?...'

The sharp director steered the conversation back to the script while my hands got the limelight as the camera pointed to them.

After hanging up my gloves for the day, I headed towards Deptford, where Cosmo had invited me for a beer before he left England to return to Athens in the morning. On the way, I tried to return Tina's call, but frustratingly, I was continuing to lose connection on the tube, and annoyingly, I had to wait.

As soon as I stepped out of Deptford station, I was welcomed by the ideal weather for sporting my new Adidas London Malmo's, NOT!!! It was pissing down Persian cats and pit bulls when I arrived, but I had to brave it through the daytime shoppers to the other end of the high street anyway because I needed some cash to get a leaving gift for the wisest friend I'd made in London.

Deptford High Street was more like Las Vegas with all its bookie shops, and it didn't boast many places to buy a decent gift unless, of course, I wanted to give Cosmo a five-day-old fresh-frozen red snapper. Fortunately, some local artists had opened Bearspace, the only art shop I knew of in town.

Though I hadn't yet saved enough to merit a Swiss bank account, the money I had saved, courtesy of how fruitful work had been, was locked up in the vault of Nationwide Deptford High Street. Irritatingly, the only way to withdraw it was to join the midday peak-time queue at the bank. I sandwiched myself in the middle of the queue that reached all the way out to the entrance and looked like it was moving nowhere fast. I was hot, I was tired, and bothered because a long queue was the last place I wanted to be standing, and my iPhone had only 1% battery clinging on to dear life. Great! I returned Tina's call.

'Jason, I'm glad you called back. Great news! EmpireFrame

Productions...you know...Tobias Rodrigues's office. You've worked with them before, right? Well, They've been in touch. They loved your work on *Roma Nights* and were thinking about you for another of their productions, a TV series called *Black Mist*.'

Tina's words were like a jolt of electricity that hit...I took a few seconds to compose myself before Tina began again.

'Hold on, hold on, Tina, let me get something to take the audition details down; I've only got 1% battery, so if it goes off, I'll have to call you back.'

While reaching for one of the complimentary bank pens and a paying-in slip, I leaned on the stand to take down the time and place of the casting, and I put Tina on loudspeaker. With the background noise of the bank and Tina's loud and fast chatter, I could vaguely hear her words,

'It's for the part of Frederich Volkov. By my understanding, he is a clothes shop assistant and undercover spy. Sounds exciting, doesn't it, Jason? What do you think?'

'That's great Tina, where's the audition? I'll be there,' I asked while still holding the branded bank pen and paying-in slip in my hand, waiting for the important information. Tina always had a hundred things on the go, and I could hear Tina's office music, the tune of *Time Warp,* playing in the background. She was tap, tap, tapping away on her computer as she continued to fill me in. I hadn't noticed that there was now a huge gap between me and the person in front of me. An aggravated Carribean woman with a bag of fresh fish behind me appeared vexed.

'Weh dem get dem manners from? Move forward, man!!! Stop wasting mi time!' She grumbled, in her Patois, as she kissed her teeth loudly. A bald-headed, brutish-looking male with a swallow tattoo on his neck backed her up.

'Yeah, move forward, bruv, will you...?' He grumbled with a voice likened to *Droopy Dog*. I moved forward as I waited for Tina to give me the information that I needed. I asked her to clarify the information again to make sure I heard it right:

'There's no audition, hun. You're a star now. They've given you the role if you want it. The production company has confirmed...hold on...let me just check that email...yes Jason, they've said that they'll send Episode 5 of the *Black Mist* script to you in the morning via special delivery once I've...'

Having arrived at Cosmo's, he'd already ordered us some fine dining in the form of two lamb Kebabs from Ali's. Ali was still at the helm of the kebab shop, slicing doner meat day after day because there had been no takers to buy his business when he put it up for sale.

'Hey sugar...I want...to give you... £1000!' Cosmo said aloud while browsing on his laptop and downing his third bottle of Hells lager I'd brought.

'Huh?' I replied, whilst wolfing down a slice of doner and chewing on some gristle that I hoped wasn't a piece of lamb's testicle.

'Look at this here, Jay...can you see?... I've just been offered £1000 from this stranger on Facebook!'

We laughed at the hook from the Jennifer Lopez-look-alike scammer trying to reel Cosmo into a conversation and ultimately get his bank details.

'Hmm, these catfish are trying every trick in the book to scam you these days...I had one message last week offering me the path to fortune!!!'

We spent the rest of the afternoon putting the world to rights before hugging out our awkward but emotional farewell.

'Ha ha...very funny!'

I made this for you,' Cosmo said, handing me a piece of his artwork. I almost cried when I saw a three-inch handcrafted actor on stage that he'd created intricately from recycled wood.

In the shadow of Cosmo's kind gesture, I placed a thank-you gesture on Cosmo's lap while he scrolled the World Wide Web to show that his kindness had meant the world to me.

'Cheers, Jay, you really shouldn't have...but I'm glad that you did.'

'Don't mention it...I thought that would be perfect for you...right up your street...being an artist and all...it's only a 'painting by numbers' set.'

'That'll be £60, please, mate.' Ouch! After handing the cab driver the fare money, I crossed the road to The Fox and Goose to meet Miranda and admired how the streetlamp reflections glistened on the rain-slicked pavement.

I wanted to share my news of the upcoming TV role on *Black Mist,* but before I could tell Miranda about it, a barman collared me as I headed towards where Miranda was sitting. He held a tray of empty wine and pint glasses. With his hands full, he started to converse.

'Whatcha...oh yeah, I was hoping I'd catch you...the missus asked me to ask you, like...er..how does Stacey... Stacey's my daughter, see...how can she get into the acting game? She's 16 and just finished her GCSEs...and has been goin' on about becoming famous like, and goin' on and on about the acting lark every bloomin' day...my missus who's also been rabbiting at my chewed off ear let the cat out the bag that I had a good friend who was an actor, meaning you!...I told her that you might be busy...but I would try to get some info! And the lowdown. So what do you reckon? Can you help our Stace?' Trevor foghorned. Trevor was the beer-bellied barman whom I'd spoken to all of three times.

'Do you have a pen and paper? I'll write down some tips and websites for you to pass on to your daughter.'

'Cheers, geezer. I thought about acting myself when I was younger, but I was born on the wrong side of the bar...'

'That's so good about the *Black Mist* gig. I'm so happy for you. You know that I know how it feels to yearn for that big part, that big gig. We just talked about it the other day, didn't we? It's very much like fishing. Not knowing when the big one is going to come along...But you've managed to land a whopper there.' Miranda expressed her delight for me with the tightest hug after squeezing me like a bear. She handed me a whisky that she'd pre-ordered for me.

'Now that you're going to be famous, do you mind signing my beer mat? So I can flog it on eBay,' she joked, handing me one from a nearby empty table.

'Let's take a snap; I'll post the photo on Facebook and Instagram. I'll make the harlot *Mademoiselle* Nathalie jealous...'

'Try and get my new Lacoste sweater in the shot.'

After Miranda posted a photo of her and me together, she put her phone down and said.

'Whatever did you see in her?... I always thought she had the personality of your Deptford freezer on most days, Jay!'

'What do you mean?'

'Cold and empty, that's what I mean!'

'She's damaged her neck.'

'Hmm, I wonder how she did that, Jay?'

'Not sure, but she's under the chiropractor, apparently.'

'I bet she is under him,' Miranda quipped as the pub pianist played in the background.

'Are you musical, Miranda?'

'No, my mum put me off playing the piano after forcing me to do it when I was little. I'm sure if she hadn't, I would have enjoyed it.'

'I had the same problem when I was forced to play the triangle.'

Miranda burst out laughing.

We finished our drinks and took the five-minute walk home across the park. That evening, there was a refreshing autumn breeze, and it felt good.

My mind was working overtime; I lay in bed thinking undercover thoughts, and it was almost midnight when Miranda emerged from under my cotton blue bed covers and wiped her mouth.

'I know you've got a big day tomorrow and lots of reading to do. So I'll let you sleep...goodnight Jay,' Miranda said, kissing me on the lips before getting up to leave my bed.

'...By the way, Jay...I know you're going to smash the part...because your grrrrrrreat!' Miranda smiled, impersonating *Tony the Tiger*.

'Well, Miranda, I'd argue if I could, but I simply can't.'

After tossing and turning with my thoughts on the most important delivery I was ever going to receive...Two eyes were alert. He panted heavily as he lay undercover in wait. Then he spied his target and made an almighty noise loud enough to wake the whole of Church Street.

'Hello there you...'

The four-legged cocker spaniel spy wagged his tail profusely in surrender before accepting a pat on the head and retreating from the long-awaited postman who chimed.

'...Morning, Special Delivery, can you sign here?...'

89 WHAM

My heart pounded hard as I opened the rest of the package, and finally, there it was, in my hands. I flicked through each page of the *Black Mist* script as if the script was gold, slowly panning the dialogue for the nuggets belonging to Frederich Volkov.

Frederich Volkov was my character who had a pivotal role. My luminous highlighter identified where he would fit in the whole scale of the episode.

I wanted to get this right. I needed to get this right. It was paramount that I get this right. If I hammered the lines and nailed Volkov, then quite possibly, EmpireFrame productions could expand my character, expand my opportunities and expand my acting horizons. Then maybe, just maybe, I would possibly appear in episodes 6, 7 and then 8.

For the next three weeks, in preparation for filming my scenes for *Black Mist,* I locked down, knuckled down and tried my damndest to get my lines down.

'Jason, it's Tina here; I don't know how to tell you this, hun...but *Black Mist* is not going to happen as originally planned....'

After the *Dollar Lady* fiasco, Tina's news was like a harsh, hard jolt of electricity to my gut with a sharp, metal fork. This poo-pooed the saying that lightning really couldn't strike twice...because it did!

'Jason...are you there?.... But I do have some good news for you...I got an email this morning from a...Jitendra Ahluwalia.'

'...Right...' I said with a hint of uncertainty that Tina must've detected.

'... He's an Indian filmmaker, hun...he saw you on *Roma Nights*...and he wants you for a lead role...'

With my hopes momentarily elevated with this sort of, kind of, consolation prize, I continued to hang onto Tina's words.

'Hold on...let me check the details...yep... it's for a short student film project...'

The rest of Tina's words disintegrated into the air like cigar smoke and must've ended up in the same place as my hopes and dreams. I had no choice but to interrupt Tina's jabbering with:

'...Look Tina, can I call you later!'

Arrrrghhhhhhhhhh. I mean, a fucking short film, COME ON!!! How would a short student film look on my public image? Having hung up on what seemed like some sort of horrible joke, one of the loose gaskets in my mind felt ready to explode, that is until my only companion in the house nestled his head on my lap and conveyed how dogs really did have a sixth sense for human emotion. What choice did I have anyway but to let sleeping dogs lie with this one?

After a week of doing the backstroke in my whisky ocean of self-pity, a voice message buoyed my spirits.

'Jason, Tina here again. Did you have the chance to think about the short film? I need to respond to Jitendra...oh and I forgot to inform you Jessica Simons, the casting director from *Black Mist* production, contacted me. The new filming dates are on the 29th of November. Call me back, hun.'

The voicemail from the heavens that resurrected me was from Tina. *Black Mist* wasn't cancelled after all; it was just postponed, a minor detail that the hundred miles-a-minute Tina had neglected to clarify on the first call when my own mind was working a hundred miles-a-minute. I called Tina back. Tina's greenlight put a catapult up my arse and signalled my cue to start working like a dog.

The words of the iconic Beatles became entrenched in my being as nights became days, and days became nights—day after day after day and night after night after night; I slept like no log, and instead, felt, thought, and breathed Frederich Volkov.

'Fancy a drink at the Fox Jay? You need a break.'

I jumped in the shower, scrubbed off three days' worth of my epidermis, and shouted.

'I'm ready!'

'Just give me a mo to get changed, Jay; I look like a porkchop with jeans on.'

In the corner of The Fox and Goose, Miranda and I settled ourselves at one of the vacant tables.

'I'll get them Miranda...it's orange juice you want, isn't it? I said, double-checking before heading to the bar.

'What can I get you?'

'An orange juice and a whisky, please.'

'Is Britvic okay?' asked Trevor, the barman, who I'd just temporarily distracted from watching the *Match of the Day* Arsenal v Manchester United game on the pub TV. He opened a juice bottle and poured it into a glass.

'Take a seat. I'll bring them over to you.'

'It's okay, I don't mind waiting.'

'I saw you on TV last night, Jay; you don't mind if I call you Jay, do ya?'

Trevor had poured the harder stuff into another glass and then turned to another pub regular, Gary, who was propped up as he usually was like a permanent fixture of the pub; he was also watching the football.

'...Gary. Did you see Jay on TV last night?'

'...Nah Trev, I missed it...do you mean the Viking advert?' Gary replied, genuinely curious but not starstruck.

'...No, not that TV advert Gary...our man Jay here has moved on from that!...it was that documentary....this dark horse...kept it under wraps...Didn't you know that this guy standing here...is only a bloody hand model by all accounts.'

'I really don't understand this conversation at all. How pissed up am I?' Gary slurred whilst Trevor continued.

'My wife was watching the documentary, and she said to tell you...you need a haircut...it was called...hmmmm... *You're Whose Body Double?*... weren't it? Or summat like that... that'll be £5.75, please.'

...And, just like that, my Ego fell into Miranda's orange juice and sank with its pulp. I paid, took the drinks and left the bar to join Miranda.

Crunch time

The 29th of November came around in a flash, and the first evidence that crunch time really had come was the production driver Billy's text saying he would be arriving to pick me up in 15 minutes. I'd been ready; my yellow rucksack had been packed with essentials, and I had been armed with my script, waiting since 5:00am, ready for the biggest day of my acting career to date. No sooner did I know it when, out of the window, I saw an arctic white Mercedes-Benz doing a U-turn, which then pulled up outside my house.

'Good morning, Mr Croot. It's a chilly one today.'

Billy said as he opened the rear door so I could get in. Despite the cold, foggy morning, a kaleidoscope of emotions swirled fast and furiously inside the pit of my stomach. The adrenaline was fuelled by my excitement and the mint Affogato I had been sipping on, along with the continuing flutter of trapped wind and nerves which were wanting to escape; rolled into all of this was a pressing doubt that came along with the responsibility to deliver a performance that met my own expectations of myself. Between sips of the sweet, minty coffee, I tried my best to get into the zone, closing my eyes to lock in my lines and secure them in there for today, at least. Billy hadn't sensed these vibes and had other ideas. His bid to strike up a conversation with me started with the topic of a visit he took to Wimbledon over the summer with his wife Tracey to watch the tennis. It seemed he almost wished, almost like he wanted me to engage with him, but I cut him short when I told him I never liked tennis and held my script up to my face to get my head back into my own game. I'm not sure if Billy appreciated the attitude I inadvertently served him, and we spent the rest of the forty-five-minute journey without a word.

On arrival at the filming location—Silkano, a famous London clothes store in Chelsea—I was met by MY VERY OWN chirpy personal assistant. She showed me to MY VERY OWN trailer parked nearby, with MY VERY OWN name engraved on a gold plate...well not really...My name was printed on a piece of white A4 paper, inserted into a slippery fish wallet and temporarily blu-tacked on the trailer's PVC door window, as I wasn't quite Al Pacino YET!

My personal assistant asked if I needed anything from Starbucks. I ordered a mint Affogato and a fresh orange and cinnamon croissant.

As breakfast, hair, and makeup were delivered and done in a style I could've easily gotten accustomed to, teasing drops of light rain bounced on the roof of my trailer coinciding with the tick-tick-ticking down of time as I neared my big moment. I was focused on my script trying to digest the last essence of Volkov, when, knock, knock, knock...

'Jason, Tobias Rodrigues has asked all actors to go to set to block the scenes.'

As we neared the set, my personal assistant took down the Godly-huge Breton striped umbrella she'd been holding over my head to shield my hair, makeup, and Ego from the threatening rain droplets as I entered the set.

'Tobias will be with you in a second, Jason.'

The scent of brand-new clothes came from the beautifully arranged designer garments spread around the store. Silkano's was the kind of store many working-class Londoners only ventured into to gawk at the extortionate price tags before walking out again. On special occasions, they might consider treating themselves to a designer scarf at the hefty price of £400. Silkano's catered not to the everyday Joe, but to the elite whose names belonged on the Sunday Times rich list. For them, price was no issue with their worries and woes appearing to just float within the bubbles of their ivory tower toy sets.

With my own feet, grateful to be treading the ground of this filming set, this was no game, no time for play or pleasure; my mind and train of thought were firmly fixed on Volkov.

Volkov worked at Silkano as a sales assistant, but this was a front for his real job as an undercover spy. His real bosses were a Russian organisation, RI6, targeting high-end customers for an embezzlement sting. Volkov was indistinguishable as a spy, wearing black cotton trousers, brown brogue shoes, and a pastel Oxford cotton blue shirt with Silkano's logo embroidered in cursive on the right breast pocket. With his beard shaved and hair styled, he almost fit into the high-flying environment. As Frederich Volkov, I had to ignore the twenty or so crew members, the cameras, lights, monitors, wires, sound equipment, etc. I had to lock my brain to the job at hand and nail this scene.

Tobias Rodrigues called. *'Action.'*

90 THE SPY WHO SCREWED ME

I staked out my unsuspecting target, the actress Chantelle Ellis-Khan, who was playing Aria, an agent specialising in espionage. Aria's attire reflected the typical clientele of the store as the elegantly decorated woman browsed the rails of Silkano's designer clothes.

I, as Volkov, subtly absorbed her every movement. My eyes were fixed on her intently, and my movements aimed to be like those of a silent but deadly panther stalking his prey.

'CUT.' Tobias bellowed, and I wasn't sure why.

It was about five minutes before the second unit director came over to me and told me that there appeared to be a technical problem. I thought that was the case, as I was pretty certain it wasn't a flaw in something I'd done; I continued to listen to the flustered second unit director.

'It may take another 20 or so minutes to fix, so your best bet is just to take five and grab a coffee or something. It shouldn't take too long.'

My personal assistant bounced over to me and asked me.

'Would you like to grab a coffee, Jason? Or do you need anything else?' Maybe a make-up touch-up? Your shirt looks a bit creased as well...'

'Forget it. I need to work on Volkov. AND If people are looking at my make-up and shirt, my acting can't be up to scratch.'

I decided to stay for the time being and practise my Volkov stalking techniques by pacing between the aisles.

It turned out that I wasn't the only one who was stalking the moves of the unsuspecting. When an upper-class man dressed in a grey perfectly fitted blazer came over to me, only his small gold name pin gave away his importance. It was Richard Sanderson, CEO of Silkano. He adjusted his designer spectacles and pulled at the strings of my Ego immediately when he told me that he had been watching my performance.

Not remembering that I had intended to stay in character, we got to talking about my acting experience, which significantly inflated my Ego.

'I have two agents and a manager in New York... I have thousands of followers online... You've probably heard of me, JASON CROOT.'

'I can't say I have, but I tend not to watch much these days.'

'...I've worked on TV and film, mainly bad characters like assassins or hinky cops, you know.'

Then Sanderson went in for the kill by asking more questions about my role. Someone obviously had forgotten to update this man of importance about the plot of *Black Mist,* and I was getting carried away with the interest he was taking in me playing a spy, so I thought I'd give him the lowdown. What I didn't realise is that he had his own lowdown intention, which was a million miles away from singing my praises.

'Spy, did you say? Hmmmmm...okay!... Thank you!' He hissed.

His furrowed brow and newly crossed arms suggested he wasn't Volkov's number one fan, as indicated by his marching off abruptly towards Tobias after having caught a glimpse of my spy performance. His abrupt departure suggested to me that...shit was about to hit the fan.

My stalking eye gaze was put into full swing practice as I watched Sanderson, like a hawk, move across the floor, making a beeline towards the obviously busy and obviously fraught Tobias Rodrigues, who was standing by the filming equipment. He himself had his arms crossed as a small group seemed to be making adjustments to the sound equipment.

Oh, how I wish I could've been a blue bottle fly on that sound boom as the cloak-and-dagger atmosphere began. I could have sworn, by the gesticulations of the snake Sanderson towards Tobias, that the CEO was suggesting that there was no way that Silkano would want a spy to be wearing the elite and prestigious Silkano emblem as it could risk the reputation of damaging the brand name. I spy with my little eye something beginning with T. Traitor!

It was like a game, trying to figure out Sanderson's gestures, but this was no party game to me. My messing up could affect everything; I had worked my mind up to quite a frenzy, but as I moved out of the way of a runner rushing towards another direction with a script in her hand, I had to remind myself where I was. I had to stay focused and couldn't freak myself out of the game at this crucial and pivotal time. I had to tell myself that I possibly was being paranoid, but then it hit me hard; I realised that this might not be the case when Tobias Rodrigues looked over to me as if I had sold my soul to the devil incarnate himself. That was STRIKE ONE.

Tobias's normally relaxed demeanour appeared to disappear amid the strife; his disgruntled look now mirrored that of Sanderson's. I was gutted. It seemed that I had gone from saint to sinner, and I'd disappointed the very man who had helped me reach my summit on *Roma Nights*. When my personal assistant bounced over to me again to check if I needed anything, she made it worse for me without realising it when she confirmed my worst fears and told me that she had heard that Sanderson was making things so awkward for EmpireFrame Productions because in the personal assistant's words.

'Sanderson had a beef about something.'

So much so that Tobias was debating whether to continue filming. *Fuck!* I didn't know how to fix the situation; it looked like I was cooked. With my brown brogue shoes feeling as if they were superglued to the spot, approaching Tobias without a plan of what to say without saying that I messed up was not an option. I'd inadvertently sent Tobias a curveball. My solution to fix this would be to smash an outstanding performance out of Silkano's park when filming recommenced to regain Tobias's belief in me.

Tobias Rodrigues called. *'ACTION.'*

With sound sorted and Sanderson out of sight, we started filming again. My head was now in a different space as if it had been locked in a sinking submarine. My heart had followed it, too. We completed the scene and moved on to my final scene, where I would be working on the tills. However, we were constrained by a tight schedule due to the clothes store opening to the general public and members of high society in 30 minutes.

Tobias Rodrigues yelled. *'ACTION.'*

I tried my best to get back into my character Volkov as the elegantly dressed Aria approached the counter. I, as Volkov, took the gold credit card Aria handed me and rang the high-priced designer items through the tills. Aria didn't flinch as the total shown on the display continued to go up into the thousands. I then swiped Aria's card. A text message notification temporarily distracted Aria, and a few seconds later, she said suspiciously to my character, Volkov.

"I just received a transaction alert for a much higher amount."

It was my cue to deliver my lines when the snake in the grass

CEO Sanderson came into the line of my vision, his beady eyes leering as he slithered next to my personal assistant. Sanderson's presence rattled me, and his fangs took a deep bite into my concentration.

"*Hmm, my apologies, madam. There must be a mistake,*" I said as I hurriedly printed out a receipt and tried to rip it off the till.

Tobias Rodrigues called. '*Cut.*' He walked over to me.

'Volkov, can you look around the store whilst Aria receives her text message...Okay, let's go again.'

Tobias Rodrigues Screamed. '*ACTION.*'

My next line came out skew-whiffed as I fumbled for the receipt.

"*Hmmm, I'm sorry, madam...um...um...it must be a technical glitch...um, let me correct it for you.*"

As I performed, I could feel my frustration lingering like a poisonous ache deep in my gut. I was frustrated that I had fumbled my scene and forgot to look around the store as Tobias had directed. My immediate thoughts that I could've done much better plagued the mistiness of my mind. My words had come out of my mouth, but my thoughts were on what I had told Sanderson. Obviously, I wasn't a real spy, for goodness sake...why didn't I stay in character, inconspicuous, and *schtum* like a spy?

Tobias Rodrigues called. '*Cut.*'

The atmosphere was off, and it was a huge contrast to the elated and vibrant mood of *Roma Nights*. I could see that Tobias's feelings towards me were different too.

I wanted to do the scene again. However, I simply ignored the fact that I wasn't in a position, like a big Hollywood star, to call the shots and ask to do another take of the scene, but Ego driven, I went ahead and asked Tobias anyway. He answered my almost plea with a firm 'NO!'

That, in my eyes, was STRIKE TWO.

My request to Tobias was met with a glance like that of a disappointed parent, where without further words being spoken, you know that you have truly messed up.

We wrapped up the day's filming, but I wanted so much to rewind the clock and start the day all over again. I felt like a champion boxer who had just been walloped, lying on the canvas, not able to climb up.

When my driver Billy dropped me off in Wimbledon, it was 10:30am. I poured a swig of whisky from a bottle into a mug in my room. Like a brewing storm, the sadness in my mind quickly evolved into a wild impatience and then a frenzied frustration in the space of a couple of hours. I should have followed the phrase: Wait until the fat lady sings. But instead of being patient and just putting this experience down as a non-planned lesson in life and moving on, I did quite the opposite.

It wasn't only the whisky I'd downed that'd got to my head when I got on my laptop. My overinflated and self-obsessed thoughts of my own potential rise to fame did, too, as I waxed lyrical online on my social media pages, telling all and sundry I JASON CROOT was going to be on the TV series *Black Mist* and that I was the next big thing; I was a big star, even before the show had been aired.

This Shakespeare's *Lady Macbeth* line came to the forefront of my mind, *"Out damned spot, out!"* more like, *"Out damned Ego, out!"*

What was I thinking? Going on social media and gasconading. My tank of fuelled Ego drove me forward with speed, and I'd blown my head gasket with my sensible logic and rationale being empty.

I was thinking like a drunk being asked to walk a straight line. I was out of control. I couldn't leave it be.

Six weeks later, I was still trying to hit a home run to fame by broadcasting to the online world that I would be on *Black Mist*. I hadn't realised that this action was *taboo,* that I'd broken the rules of my contract, and that I'd sabotaged my own acting career. Looking back, I guess this could have been STRIKE THREE.

I had convinced myself that holding onto my appearance on *Black Mist* would give me the solid recognition I craved. I made myself believe that my appearance would mean even more prominent TV productions and long-term roles where I wouldn't have to audition. I convinced myself that there was still hope. Fueling my bubbling impatience, however, was that after several weeks, I still hadn't been paid for *Black Mist.* Rather than be patient and wait, I called EmpireFrame Productions.

'I'm JASON CROOT.. you must know who I am. But I've worked for your production company before. My photograph is on your wall...I know the director, Tobias Rodrigues! So can you tell me why I haven't received my money?'

After taking down some necessary details, the patient and polite lady from the human resources payroll on the other end of the line (who most probably thought I was a right arsehole) told me that she would look into it.

Thinking that the incoming phone call on my mobile was from an unknown number, I thought maybe it was EmpireFrame Productions calling me back. I answered. But it wasn't them; it was the familiar chirp of Tina, inviting me to a film industry networking event that was to be held in Manchester. I had attended a few such events before with the aim of networking with film and casting directors and hoping for the possibility of connections and exposure. I had to tell her, however, that I was NOT interested. When I could finally squeeze a word between Tina's chatter, I told her about my delayed payment for *Black Mist*.

She asked me to hold on while she checked her computer. Her mobile phone rang in the background. The *Hit Me, Baby One More Time* ringtone was shrill; it continued to ring as she came back to the office phone and voiced casually.

'I'm sorry, hun. I forgot to submit the invoice to EmpireFrame Productions. I'll do it right away. I was meant to do it just before going to Magaluf with the girls, but I didn't get around to it. I promise I'll do it as soon as we finish the call...'

I was furious, but rather than say anything, I just hung up the phone and threw my mobile at the wall. If I had known that Tina had forgotten to submit my invoice, I would never have called the EmpireProductions in the first place.

Two weeks later, inked in the week's edition of TV Times, I saw that *Black Mist* episode 5 was due to be aired on mainstream TV....woah this was it! Seeing this, I decided to take the path of sense and sensibility as I waited. NOT!!! I took to social media once again. I followed more people to increase my reach and reminded family members, friends and acquaintances on my social media network that I was due to be on TV.

On the night of its airing, Miranda and I tuned in and watched the prime-time series. My scenes were in the middle of the episode; 15 minutes into the show, scene by scene had gone by, and my heart thudded hard against my chest when the external shots of Silkano appeared. This was it. These were opening shots of my scenes.

The unsuspecting target, Aria, who was played by Chantelle Ellis-Khan, walked into the clothes store and browsed the designer garments. I waited with bated breath. Waiting for my part in the scene felt like an eternity. There was still no sign of Volkov. The fear of being cut from the series was hanging over my head like a sword of Damocles. When the Silkano scenes ended and moved to a completely different external shot of Piccadilly Circus, I realised that I was like the arrow of the world-famous statue Anteros: missing. There was no doubt about it now that my character Frederick Volkov had been completely, well and truly, most definitely, CUT OUT of the episode. And that, ladies and gentlemen, was the result of *My Ego Screwing My Acting Career*.

Photography by Slater King.

91 COUP DE GRÂCE

I wasn't the first nor the last actor to fuck up. Yes, I screwed things up, but everyone screws up at some point or other. *Even monkeys fall from trees.*

'You know I'm grateful, don't you?... But right now, I need some solitude.'

I could hear in her sniffle that Miranda was crying but trying to hold back her tears behind our hug.

'But...but Jay...Jay, please don't go...is there nothing I can say or do for you to change your mind?'

It tore me up to say goodbye, but I just had to. I packed up my big yellow rucksack and moved out of Wimbledon, and before I left, I gave Miranda my spare I Love Roma T-Shirt. Brandon gave me a hug, Toby gave me a lick, and Miranda gave me her spiritual self-help book, *The Road Less Travelled*.

'You are a hell of an actor when you're on your game, Jay. Please don't quit now; you must keep going.'

She tried to convince me to stay in Wimbledon, rent-free, but my mind was made up. I needed my own space, and I needed serenity. I didn't want to put Miranda through any more of my turbulent and capricious moods. I didn't want to take her with me on my descent, so I moved back to the sprawl of Deptford.

I had contacted Cosmo, who was still in Greece, on the off chance that his bedsit, which he'd been subletting to transient tenants (and an opportunist squatter), may have been vacant. It was, and Cosmo offered it to me to stay for six months.

On my way from Wimbledon to Deptford, I thought about people in London, some on the way up and others on the way down, but all living alongside each other, most unaware of each others' struggles.

Exiting the tube, I saw a dishevelled man coming towards me. By his raddled appearance, he looked tired of life. His weathered face told a tale of a rugged past. I dug into my jeans and found a crumpled £5 note; I figured he needed it more than I did.

I'm walking around in some kind of ink-black mist.

Raindrops are running down and seeping in through the cracked window panes of this rundown bedsit.

Even the fucking cream that has risen to the top of my coffee is fucking sour.

The rain and coffee reflect the turmoil, pure and utter turmoil, in my heart...my mind...my soul.

It was the dead of winter, a brutal winter, at that, and I'm Looking out of my window into the wet, dreary, black, starless sky. My survival instinct has flown out of the window and crashed head-first into the pavement, seeing the status quo of life continuing. Happiness, what the fuck is happiness? Happiness is an elusive commodity.

The rage against the machine of my very being is so apparent inside the window to my soul.

My only friend and my only sunshine, my only comfort is whisky. Whisky can't mess me up, not any more so than I am anyway. A messed up, screwed up, fucked up actor.

Funny how I thought acting was what the stars wanted me to do, but I'll be damned if I see any stars in my sky right now.

I screwed up the pain I had just poured out onto the scrap paper, tossing it toward the waste paper bin in the corner. Just as I had missed the opportunity, *Black Mist* presented to me... I missed the shot. Just like that note... I was screwed.

I lost my confidence to write or audition for acting jobs. I stopped taking care of myself, hardly showering and wearing the same coffee-stained I Love Roma T-shirt for weeks. I stayed locked away in my bedsit, bingeing on junk food and using my almost-maxed-out credit cards. Over a few months, I gained three stones and became an overweight recluse. I was put on the blacklist and restricted from social media for over-promoting *Black Mist*, but I didn't want to be part of that artificial world anymore anyway. I withdrew from socialising and hardly spoke to anyone, which worsened my mental and physical health. My life felt like it was going nowhere at all, as if I was stuck in a blind alley.

Thoughts of my heyday and the golden moments of my acting career just a few years back stomped into my peppered mind. Just before walking into a casting for Zena De Wolf, I stumbled across the back end of a conversation between the directors in the room.

'We have Jason Croot next. He's an excellent actor.'

In those next few seconds, I had to yank out the composed version of myself, take a huge leap over my swollen Ego before I walked into the casting room and pretend I had never heard Zena De Wolf's golden words.

Excellent! Excellent! Excellent!.... That flashback of that golden yesteryear contrasted starkly with how it now was. What had become of me?

A few months passed, and my phone's shrill tone disturbed my darkness. The caller was Zena De Wolf's assistant, Gabrielle, asking me if I was available to film.

What? Me? How? I couldn't believe it. I couldn't believe that after all this time Zena De Wolf still believed in me.

Gabrielle's words did to me what Barry Manilow and several others had famously sung about. The relit fire seemed to be melting the iceberg I had isolated myself on. I was ready to run, storm and blow like the wind (whatever it took) to take this opportunity. This was massive, this was humongous, and this was probably one of the most famous TV series of modern times.

'Excellent! Just to reiterate, we would like to offer you a role in *G**E O* T*****S* for season two.'

I took all of 15 seconds before accepting the role. And this was no flashback.

Putting the cherry on this unexpected cake was the fact that I was being offered the role without an audition.

Gabrielle continued, explaining that I had to fly to the Czech Republic and that the filming dates were in two days' time. The only requirement was that my passport had at least six months of life on it before the expiry date. I told her I had a valid passport, and she said she'd email me all the production and flight details later that day.

The truth was, I wasn't sure how long I had left on my passport, and to top it off, I couldn't find the bloody thing. Stressed out, I had the bedsit upside down, looking everywhere. It was nowhere to be found.

It would take two full working days to get an emergency passport—which was time I didn't have!

Hoping I'd left it in Wimbledon, I called Miranda, and she stayed on the phone while looking for it. But no joy. So I turned to the heavens, praying to the patron saint of lost things, Saint Anthony.

Just as I hung up the phone, in the corner of my eye, I saw a small wooden box that I used for putting in small nostalgic memorabilia from my filming, flight tickets, photos on set, etc. I ran over and opened it. There at the bottom was my passport. YEESSSSSSSSSS, I celebrated...

This was a once-in-a-lifetime chance given to me, BUT with a twist of cruel irony, it slipped through my fingers in the blink of an eye. The jubilation of finding my passport was short-lived, and I found myself with no option but to turn the huge career-changing opportunity down because my passport had, by the great law of Sod, EXPIRED! As quick as the glory had come, it then vanished like a rainbow shining inappropriately on a condemned prisoner's day of execution. It felt like the blade for my own guillotine had taken its final, twisted, cruel and ironic plunge. I turned to my full-length dusty mirror, looked at my reflection, and roared with rage.

Ahhhgggg Fuck!

Down, out and defeated, bad luck hadn't just rained on me; it had poured and pissed all over me. My gut was wrenched, my mind was dark, and my heart was shredded. The BEAST of the passport fiasco had ripped the heart right out of my chest. This event triggered the downfall of my life's nadir and acting career.

The straw had finally broken the camel's back. The ship had finally sailed. The *coup de grâce* had cut me deep, deep, down.

THEN...

My decision made, and my...

Ego smashed to smithereens...

Screwed and savaged by my bad fortune...

My mind was blown.

Acting, which was once my one pure love, was now a

Career, that was now sunken to the gutter...

I vowed I would NEVER ACT AGAIN... I couldn't take any more of my beloved passion continuing to destroy my soul.

There wasn't a word strong enough, painful enough, or apt enough in the English language that described my feelings at that moment in time.

To all those I love...I'm sorry, but I don't think I can do this anymore...

MY EGO SCREWED MY ACTING CAREER

92 WUTHERING HEIGHTS

The start of 2010 was the decade in which the YouTube sensation Justin Bieber reached one million followers on Twitter and *X Factor* formed the boyband One Direction.

While millions loved the rising of the reality stars, I lay in the gutter, drowning myself in enough whisky to sink a battleship. My days were usually filled with a daytime playlist of police sirens, drunks grappling on the street, pit bulls barking, and neighbours' domestic argy bargies. AND every man and his dog talking about *G**E O* T*****S*.

I wasn't starring in Hollywood, more like starving in Deptford.

I drowned out this whole world with plaguing thoughts and festering regrets, and Amy Winehouse's *Back to Black* played full blast on repeat as I sunk deeper into oblivion.

My nights were now filled with more whisky, more chicken jalfrezi ready meals and fast food, and more nightmares. I locked myself away in my fortress of solitude in exile in my Deptford bedsit, which, alongside my mind, appeared to be in an even more rack and ruin state than ever before. I avoided the world and all its negativity.

Acting had been my life; it had meant everything to me, and choosing to turn my back on this world and being unable to perform for such a long time was slowly killing me inside. During these darkest days, my mind felt like a wuthering storm was passing through it, and it'd become entangled in a maelstrom of emotions.

My verve for life had sunk, and my depression seeped so deeply as I drowned slowly in the deep lagoon of my crying game. My outlook on life became distorted. All the hopes and ambitions I once had to make it in the acting world became stagnant and lay dumped in the skip of all I thought had been good in my life, all the things that I now didn't want anything to do with. I started questioning my decisions, which led to the blame game, beating any rationality I had left in my soul to a pulp. I blamed all and sundry: the industry, the agents, the producers, the directors, the lack of opportunities and the country. I told myself the industry was sewn up. I told myself it was about whom you know and not what you know. I blamed everything and everyone I could, and most of all, I blamed myself. The beast ravaging me inside was uncovering even more self-pity, not only about my recent fuck ups but the fuck ups from yesteryears.

'It's not only the acting, Miranda; I've fucked up my WHOLE life, through drinking, through gambling and through sex.'

As I poured out my pain to Miranda, she offered solace through the words of the great poet *William Blake*.

'You know, Jay, *"The road of excess leads to the palace of wisdom."*'

Miranda brought me chamomile tea and sat next to me on her sofa in Wimbledon. I had escaped from my Deptford room and braved the crowds of London and the bustling trains to accept the helping hand of a good friend.

'Jay, sometimes, out of the worst comes the best...'

I found it difficult to look up from the swirling teabag of chamomile but was listening as she continued.

'You've gone through the wringer, but you're a fighter; you must keep going.' Her words alone comforted me more than I had felt in a very long time.

'Halt the world. I need to escape...'

'...I will help you, Jay, don't worry.'

Miranda's heart was always in the right place. She knew of a psychotherapist that Lucy Kim had recommended to many actors. Miranda called the therapist and booked me in for my first month of therapy sessions. The shrill ring of Miranda's doorbell interrupted the fragility of the moment when she got up to answer the door.

I wept.

Therapy

Never before had someone attempted to unpick the details of my life through a magnifying glass until my therapist did. During our sessions, she started to unpeel the layers of past pain, just like the layers of an onion, and she began to dig into roots, which stemmed much deeper than acting, much, much deeper.

'Childhood traumas can often cause you to ignore those who offer you love and seek ones that will make you work hard for love.'

The first port of call we arrived at was the women in my life. The therapist reflected on several factors, including the many short-term and long-term partners I had been with, many of whose non-committal outlooks, just like my own, had apparently made it all the better and easier for me to up and depart the relationships.

'Ladies and gentlemen, we apologise for the delay. We are experiencing a brief interruption in service due to signals in the tunnel.'

Every fortnight, I ventured from Deptford and made the one-hour journey to Richmond, South West London, to my therapy sessions, where I talked at length about my depression, my reckless decisions, and my iniquity. The sessions helped me to begin to understand more about myself, about my emotions and about the triggers that took me to dark places.

My therapist told me she had many actors as clients, explaining that the main common problem they had was rejection. She touched on a delicate nerve of my early childhood and my separations and losses as a very young child. Then the conversation meandered towards a suggestion that I didn't foresee: I should forgo acting FOR GOOD because of the rejection I experienced each time a casting director or director said 'NO' to me. The problem with that advice was that acting had been my passion. I had chosen to quit acting, which was one thing, but being strongly advised to do this by someone else was another! It was the forever part that made me uneasy.

Acting had been nirvana to me. I had tasted how it felt to perform on stage and on the big screen, receiving cheers, bravos, and rounds of thunderous applause. Though there had been huge bumps in my road, there hadn't been anything else I wanted to do as much as this.

In some ways, acting had been cathartic. It helped heal pain, fill voids, and provide escapism from the real world. It tested my patience, kept me constantly learning, and drove me. Even though my therapist highlighted the mental harm of the numerous rejections I'd experienced being part of the industry, I just couldn't grapple with the reality of quitting acting forever. But of course, there was the good, the bad, and the ugly side to me having taken this journey less travelled.

'Attention passengers, we regret to inform you that our service is currently delayed due to a signal issue in the tunnel. We appreciate your patience and will provide updates as soon as possible. Thank you for your understanding.'

I was sweating and feeling like I could keel over in agony from the spiky bouncing ball of metal nails that was ping, ping, pinging like a game of Frogger around my stomach.

The train delay was prolonging my already prolonged agony and making my visit to the feral train toilet even more imminent before my stomach actually exploded its spiky contents.

I had delayed my trip to the toilet for a few more minutes longer than I should have, not wanting to barge past the standing passengers with my obvious desperation. But waiting it out was a big, big, big mistake I made, AND the ball of bouncing nails that leapt around my stomach made sure I knew this was so.

As I shuffled as quickly as I could towards the train toilet at the end of the carriage, I noticed the polite British grimace from a woman who had a few minutes ago, from a few meters away, shot a quick smile at me as well as one coming from a man who was sat down reading the Metro. It indicated that a truly unpleasant smell had dangled past their nostrils. How I wish I could've said it was one of the small children sitting down playing on their Nintendo DS, oblivious to the world, but I couldn't. It was me who soiled myself.

I reached my place of safety to find that the door was locked and the toilet was OUT OF ORDER. Fuck!

My stomach cramps still felt like they were knocking my insides out for six. The smell, though my own, was making me even more nauseated. As we neared the next stop, I could feel passengers' eyes darting in my direction. Coinciding with the continuing loud murmurs my stomach was making were the passengers' murmurs of disgust.

In the Clapham Junction station toilet, I binned my soiled underwear, binned my self-esteem, binned my evening's slot of therapy and made my way home.

After that incident, I never went back for my final three therapy sessions.

Dark Days

In the grand scheme of things, one year of therapy sessions helped me in some ways, but ultimately, after the sessions had ended, I locked myself away in Deptford and continued to battle through the dark days of my deep depression. I would lay in my bed, staring at my ceiling as thoughts ate out my mind. Thoughts about when I started my acting journey. Thoughts about my naivety about acting, and thoughts about my rise to the mountain's summit and the hard and bitter fall. Thoughts of the ruination of my acting career tortured my very soul. This time, I was at a dead end in my life. I felt an overwhelming sense of emptiness. And it seemed that there was no light at the end of this tunnel. My acting world's once vibrant and silky colours felt like they had now faded to a lustreless grey.

I had now reached a stage in my life where I realised that I was struggling to truly understand where I belonged in this world. I wanted to know who the fuck I was and why the fuck I was here.

No Caption required.

93 BREAKFAST AT MIRANDA'S

"My honoured father in the shades below,
or my unhappy mother, both destroyed
By me? This punishment is worse than death,
Or them, or this fair city, or the palace
Where I was born. Deprived of every bliss."

'Excellent, Jason. Great monologue. Well done...very well done. Are you available early January for rehearsals?'

My therapy sessions led me to a point in my life where I realised that I was struggling to find my place in the world.

One year later, I found myself on a new stage—the Wimbledon Hall stage—auditioning for a small theatre drama production of *Oedipus the King*.

I still had a long way to go to discover who the fuck I was and learn more about myself. But what I had become more definite about, now more than ever, was my stance of turning my back on the acting and film industry.

Though I was going against all advice, packing it all in was simply not an option—not yet. In fact, I felt getting back into the industry was the only way forward for me.

My mind swirled back again to my golden moments in acting, thoughts of how being on a film set or stage made me feel in the moment. Being in the almost beautiful zone that I got into when amongst the lights, the cameras and the action.

I remembered the unbeatable spark it gave me, making me feel so alive. These were the types of thoughts that drove me.

I had to start liking myself again. After all, I would be waking up every day with me, and the sooner I got to grips with that, the better things would become.

Slowly, day by day, I became mentally stronger. Watching *Seinfeld, Taxi,* and *I'm Alan Partridge* fuelled my dopamine. My Jeans fit me once again, as my barrel belly was disappearing, and my self-confidence was coming back.

My acting career was like a book that was never completed, and I wanted so strongly to finish the story. It was the end of an old road and the beginning of a new one. My next chapter was the road to redemption. Which led me to the fresher climes of Church Road Wimbledon. An Australian couple renting my old room in Miranda's house had done a bunk and left without paying. My offer to stay with Miranda for a few days naturally had turned into a longer-term arrangement as I decided to turn my back on my days of isolation on my island in Deptford, pack my big yellow rucksack and take up Miranda's offer of a free room.

Toby was, of course, the first one to welcome me at the door with a big dog lick to my face. He was now greying and less crazed in his movements after an accident resulted in a spine injury, but this didn't stop him from sniffing my pockets for a potential sweet treat. Brandon welcomed me with a fist pump courtesy of Skype whilst on a ski trip in France, and Miranda welcomed me back home with a golden crisp, fresh vegan Belgian waffle, which fuelled my energy and tasted much better than any greasy English breakfast I'd ever had. Miranda was putting her I Love Roma T-shirt back on awkwardly when she got her hair clip stuck.

'Don't you just hate it when you get a new T-shirt and the instructions are in Italian,' Miranda said, smiling.

We sat and chatted for a couple of hours, and over copious cups of steaming soya hot chocolate Belgian style, Miranda filled me in about another Belgian indulgence: Lucas, a professional chocolatier she had met during a gig in Winchester.

'Ménage à trois maybe?'

'I don't think I'll be seeing him again, but you can wrap your lips around one of these though. Try the *Van Dender;* it's delightful,' said Miranda, offering me to choose from her box of half-eaten vegan luxury chocolates.

'I'm glad you're here, Jay. It'll be a new start for us. A rediscovery of what makes your soul actually sing.'

'Hopefully Miranda! Me getting back out there, and you get a million more laughs.'

'Pah, me a million laughs! You're making me chuckle already!'

Miranda swelled up Adele on her CD player, and we danced

before we hit the sack.

That night, with Toby warming my feet, I slept the sleep of many sleeps. With my battery on full charge the next morning, I woke up early, had a quick shower and headed out for a walk. I had very little money, but I wanted to buy some food to make a meal to show my appreciation for Miranda's kindness. I headed to the local organic shop, thinking the trip would be my preferred way to shop (whistlestop style), but I discovered that buying vegan food wasn't easy as it took me over an hour to check the ingredients of each item. What was even harder to swallow was the £60 bill for the handful of food that I bought.

On the way back home, a group of teenagers were using a digital camera on Wimbledon Common; they were making what I assumed was a home movie. The guy holding the camera was looking aggravated as he was directing his friends. It got me thinking of my own experiences in front of and behind the camera, the highs, the lows, the calamities. It got me looking at my film career through a new lens and from a different angle. I got thinking about making a feature film of my own, a thought that had peppered my mind since living in London, but my focus had solely been on being in front of the camera.

What was I waiting around for now? A myth to come alive?

94 THE ROAD TO REDEMPTION

On a mission, I sat on Brandon's gaming chair with ideas that whirled, spun, shaped, and reshaped in my mind. Just like the characters and tunes of the classic *Mario Bros* video game, I couldn't stop seeing and hearing them. It was as if I was navigating through my own version of the Mushroom Kingdom, dodging obstacles and collecting power-ups along the way.

My adrenaline was pumping, and within several hours of writing down ideas and contemplating different options non-stop, I was ready for the next level. I had completed the first mission, used the memories of experiences that I had and had heard about on productions, and bagged an outline of scenes, possible characters, and ideas of possible storylines of a film. I was ready to turn it up a gear.

Mission two intensified, where the ideas now had to grow from novelty to reality. My mind was now operating on several levels at once.

I phoned people, emailed people and reactivated all my social media accounts in the bid to get in touch with people, viz my actor friends, some of whom were wondering if I'd dropped off the face of the earth given my exile from social media and the world itself. Of course, not everyone I asked on social media to be in the film replied. Some people had unfollowed me, and others blanked me. However, there were those who, despite my hiatus from everything that was considered social, stuck by me.

Jay, can I WhatsApp you?

Sorry, Lance, I don't have WhatsApp. Let's Skype.

'Jay, you never returned my calls, you disappeared off the face of the earth... I even had to resort to Googling you to see what you were up to... how's the hustle, how's it been going?'

'Life's been a real picnic for me, you know!'

After 30 minutes of talking about this, that and the other, and listening to Lance's Freudian analysis of me, he brought up what I had been swerving: My Acting Career.

'Jay, I saw you on TV...on what was it?... that's it...*Roma Nights*...I recorded it as soon as I saw you...you know, the one you played that real badass... like Javier Bardem in *No Country For Old Men*. That shooting scene you did was absolutely fucking brilliant...you must've been chuffed with that!'

'Cheers, Lance, Bardem, that's a huge compliment...that was a pinnacle for me...filming that was amazing...I was shitting myself to get it right on the first and only shot they had for that scene...Lance...I wish you could've been there...'

'I felt it for you, buddy; I really did...I know how hard you've strived...I know how hard it is to try to get there, remember?... It's gut-wrenching sometimes... I've had my fair share of rejection, you know; that's why I decided to take a hiatus from acting...And when Genoa to Roma never saw the light of day....'

'...I get it, Lance...I get it...It's a jungle out there! It's as if you need the hide of a rhino to survive in the big acting game! Tons of films with big budgets are never released, like *Black Water Transit,* which cost a whopping $25 million. And *Divine Rapture,* with Brando and Depp, which was never finished... It's the industry, it's what I've learnt myself, and it's just life...*C'est la vie*... Anyway, what about your book? How's it going?'

My monologue stirred Lance into his very own monologue.

'I'm attempting to write, but the construction noise racket outside my door frustrates my every thought. I'm dreaming of the tranquillity of a desert island right now. Those thoughts seem fruitless as each jackhammer blow puts the *kibosh* on that...oh, Jay, the book, the writing, the frustration...don't ask Jay, just don't ask.'

'I'm actually writing too, but not a book, a script, and that's why I contacted you. I want to offer you a cameo...in a feature film that I'm making...'

'You're writing and making a film? When are you thinking of filming it?'

'Soon, very soon, I want to do this. I don't want to procrastinate. I just want to do it.'

'Look, Jay, thanks for the offer, but I think I will stick to my guns...this pause from acting is doing me good... it's giving me the time I need to finish writing my book. I just wish these bloody builders would piss off.'

After ending the call with the frustrated Lance, I spent some hours more jotting down ideas, but I knew that I had to rustle up some food for Miranda before she got home. I was keen as mustard to tell her about my film idea.

'Dinner's ready, great... I'm starved.'

Miranda had arrived back after rehearsing with Joe Tarney, the other half of their double act Nip and Tuck. They had been recently booked for a stand-up gig in Blackpool, and she had been hoping to get recognised and eventually have her name on Blackpool's comedy carpet, where anyone in the world of comedy had their name immortalised in the granite.

'What do you think, Miranda?'

'Jay, It is a brilliant idea, a film-within-a-film...only a genius could have come up with that idea!.. You've got bags of creativity that's worth millions...'

'...When you figure out how I can put it in the bank, let me know, won't you, Miranda...'

'...I'm so excited for you...you know the offer always stands should you ever change your mind.'

Miranda's belief in me was reflected in her more than generous offer of money to help me achieve my dream, but I did not want to impose any more on her love and her soul of kindness.

'I'm pressed for funds, I'm pressed to get the right people, and I'm pressed to get this film on the road! But you know what, Miranda, I'm loving it.'

'What did you put in here, Jay? It's an...interesting...fusion... it's like a rave in my mouth.'

Miranda pulled an unidentifiable morsel of food out of her mouth, and I could tell she was politely trying not to heave.

'Lots of things...*harissa*...chickpeas...dried *Shiitake* mushrooms... and some seaweed...oh, and I added a bit of *chipotle* sauce...and tinned tomatoes.'

Okay, so a *Michelin-star* vegan chef may not have been my next calling, but I was determined to try to cook up a storm and turn up the heat to complete the next level of my film mission.

Being near to broke meant that I'd have to beg, steal and borrow to make it happen. Filming on a shoestring budget would be a real challenge, and it was going to be nearly impossible to make the film for zilch. I wasn't just broke; I was also in debt, and the bank wouldn't likely give me an out-of-work actor a loan.

One thing I was doing wrong was calling it a production, not a project. Calling a film a production usually meant payment, and calling it a project usually meant low or no pay; I'd done many of both. I wouldn't be able to afford to pay anyone, so everyone who agreed would have to work on a percentage of any profit the film project would make. Plus, it would be virtually impossible to find an investor, given that all I had were ideas. I had no actual script and no title for the film; the realisation soon hit home. I was going about this completely arse-about-tit.

Some sleep and digging deep into what I had already was a much-needed reboot that I managed to grab hold of. When I rose, I thought about *Two Faced*, the micro-budget short film I co-created years back with Mohsan Qureshi. I realised that way back then, I was armed only with the fire and determination to get the film made. Back then, I was green to the filmmaking and acting world. But my first ever short film was born despite being ignorant about the pitfalls and hurdles. I made it happen back then, so why couldn't I make it happen now?

Seeking inspiration, I submerged myself in a daily ritual of movie-watching. Jim Jarmusch, Spike Lee, Woody Allen, and John Cassavetes' films made my creative juices flow. I loved their unique approach and their passion for filmmaking, which became tattooed on my mind.

I had the DYNAMITE I needed to get back into action, and I played on to win the game. I continued to do what I could with the tools I had to manage the intricacies of producing a film. My unconventional approach and my gift of the gab helped me sell the strong film plot idea I had in mind to various people.

Maria de Lima asked whether I would be doing a London screening for the cast and whether I was hoping for film distribution or aiming for the film festival route.

Spencer Austin advised me to put a bloody hammer through my laptop and get myself an Apple (not the fruit). Then, asked me to forward him a script.

'No script, no location, and no budget sounds terrible, but count me in, Jay. Just tell me where and when,' said Tony Resta.

Though film distributions, screenings, and Apple computers were hundreds of miles away from where my budget could reach right now.

MY EGO SCREWED MY ACTING CAREER

I was hooked on making this happen, and so were several other actors who responded to my plea for help.

With only £37.50 to my name, I did what I thought was the most sensible thing to do. I decided to take a punt on the day's declared horses.

I stepped into the local betting shop, full of middle-aged men holding onto the hope of winning, with betting slips in their hands as they watched multiple screens. Laying around their feet and strewn across the floor were the mounds of screwed-up let-downs in paper balls. A group of middle-aged men who initially were chatting amongst themselves were sitting like stockbrokers in a swanky Mayfair office, looking at my long hair, unruly beard, and scruffy jeans as if I was *Donkey Kong* who had suddenly walked into their world on dress-down Friday. Nonetheless, I was on a mission as I walked with purpose through the betting shop.

Slot machines jingled with tunes of temptation and promise, which battled to be heard amongst the fast-paced voices of horse racing commentators screaming like they were nearly going to burst a vessel. I was in search of some hidden gems and some much-needed inspiration, which I found in the racing newspapers that hung on the wall. I picked three horses for my Round Robin bet: Safecracker, Pawn In Life, and Movie Star.

'Go on...go on...go on...Safecracker...you beautiful bastard!' I shouted, wishing the stallion horse to the finish line first...and wouldn't you know it...he only bloody won!

95 AGAINST ALL ODDS

'Come on baby, ride it, baby, come on, come on baby. Yes, hell YES,' I howled.

This wasn't me rolling around the hay, having rumpty-tumpty. This was me back in Church Road, tuned in to the TV horse racing channel, and I'd just watched Pawn In Life romp home at 6/1. Safecracker had already won at 33/1. And it was looking like it was going to be a very, very, very GOOD DAY.

My final selection, Movie Star, wasn't running until the evening at Wolverhampton, and the TV wasn't covering that race meeting. If this mare won at 22/1, I would win almost 11 grand. I kept myself busy for a few hours and didn't check the results till later that evening.

It wasn't until about an hour after the race had finished that I dared to open my laptop for the results. There were 11 runners. As I slowly got from the bottom to the top of the results page, my final selection, Movie Star, was not on the screen. I thought that there was some kind of mistake. I checked my betting slip and the time of the race, and then at the bottom of the page, Movie Star was declared a non-runner. I was relieved she didn't lose, but I knew my hope of winning 11 BIG ONES was not to be.

The next day, I headed out to the betting shop, not certain about how much my winnings would be. The betting shop elite looked down their noses at me once again as I entered, but I didn't care. I handed my betting slip to the grumpy cashier, who looked as tired of life as his stray and straggly strands of greying hair did. He looked at me and left his seat to go into the back. A few minutes later, he came out with a big wad of £20 notes. After he counted out my winnings of £1139.16. I gave him the £9.16 as a tip and turned around to see the envious locals gawping at my big wad of cash.

'I've had better days,' I said with a smile as I left.

I was hardly swimming in money but I had enough to make my film. I treated Miranda to a vegan takeaway.

'I expect you're wondering?'

'What gave you that idea, Jay? I already half-guessed it when I heard you shouting at the horses on TV yesterday.

In just three weeks and with no physical script and a lot of pushing, and pushing and pushing, insofar as humanly possible, with the endgame in sight, I managed to make it to the next level; I had secured a location, filming dates, a crew, and equipment, including two excellent £30,000 broadcast cameras for free from a film school. Some talented actors agreed to jump in the deep end with me and do the untitled, 100% improvised comedy horror B-Movie.

After weeks of tirelessly trying to organise the schedules and as crunch time neared, I was hoping that the cast and crew had had a chance to recover from the frivolities of Christmas. I was hoping that their spirits were still high. I was hoping that Santa would grant me this belated wish of getting this feature film, my directorial debut, done.

December 28th was the day of reckoning, and it had arrived in the blink of an eye. I had heard snow was expected, and I thought that it would only be a light blanket of sleet, which is common in London. When I looked out of the window, it was like a feather down, 15 tog duvet of thick, white snow that was covering the entire street. Opposite my bedroom window, only the tips of the bare tree branches, shaped like fingers, were peeking out from under Mother Nature's cold duvet, daring me to come out. In all my planning and organisation for this day, I hadn't envisaged that I would be met with a potential avalanche.

'Good morning. The sun has risen over London and the southeast of England. We're waking up to a blanket of snow that has fallen overnight. Temperatures remain well below freezing at around -5 degrees Celsius. If you're heading out this morning, please take extra precautions. Allow plenty of time for your journey, and be prepared for severe road and public transport delays. Stay safe and warm. This is South London Radio 103.9FM. Keep tuned in for the traffic updates. Let's warm up your day with Black Eyed Peas, *I Gotta Feeling*.

The morning radio weather report reinforced that it wasn't just Church Road in Wimbledon that was covered in snow; it was, in fact, the whole of London! *Fuck!*

Londoners were resilient people who'd been through a hell of a lot as a city, but it somehow seemed to be that snow sent everything and everyone in the city into a tizzy. I knew this would cause havoc to London's transport system even though it is known to be one of the most efficient public transport networks in the world. The snow was due to put a spanner in the works for the city AND my plans for my debut feature film.

I armed myself with three layers of socks, two thick jumpers, one fleece, my thick duffle coat, my cable knit scarf, my deer hunter hat and my mountain hiking boots. Miranda wrapped her support around me in the shape of a bear hug and joked.

'Blimey Jay, your outfit will come in handy if you go to the North Pole. You've got more clothes on you than a rack in a ski shop.'

Stepping out was like entering a freezer with an attitude, making me question my madcap idea and my decision to venture beyond the cosy cocoon of my blankets.

I said to myself, 'Let's do this, Jay!' I left armed with my plans, and I trod carefully on the deep snow, ensuring that I wouldn't fall flat on my arse. As the only one venturing out on my street at that time in the morning, it was only my trail of footprints from the house to the station that was prominent in the thick duvet of snow.

My phone was pinging messages from the cast and crew asking if filming would still happen. I was determined that nothing was going to stop me. I was determined that no snow was going to scupper my plans. I was determined to get to my filming location by hook or by crook and could only hope that everything else would fall into place. I had to remain confident that everyone would still turn up. So to all who messaged me about the film, I replied.

YES, WE ARE STILL SHOOTING.

I had to travel from South West London to the North East part of the city to get to the filming location at Palmoak Film Studios, New Barnet North London. Only the fresh smell of cold air followed me into Wimbledon station. I felt like I had been hit with an icy water balloon when I saw the blank, black digital boards, which explained the long queue of disgruntled-looking people trailing from the ticket kiosk who wore their frustrations of the morning around their necks. The waiting passengers whose morning starts had been kicked out of sync like mine remained very British and reserved about the chaos. They kept *schtum* in their orderly queue, waiting for clarity about the start of their days. Knowing if the trains were working for me to get to the location was one hurdle, but whether any of the cast and crew could make it to the set was another.

'How can I get to work, then?' Inquired a softly-spoken man in a pinstripe suit, obviously thrown off by the snow disrupting his routine.

He resembled a lost sheep, much like everyone else in the queue that morning, including me.

It was now questionable whether the filming would go ahead, but cancelling and rearranging would mean that I may not have access to the same equipment, the same location, and the same cast and crew who had kindly offered up their valuable time. I needed a backup.

I called Lance to see if he could drive me up to the film set. He didn't answer his phone. He was a night owl and more than likely had been up burning the midnight oil, finishing off his book. I wanted to know that at least we would have the filming equipment.

I called Mike Berwick, the camera operator who was travelling from the south coast, but there was no answer. One by one, I tried ringing other members of the crew, including Jon, Matt and Oli, but once again, the phone rang and rang, as did my own alarm bells. Another actor, Lucinda Rhodes-Flaherty, texted me to see if the filming was still on. I texted her back to say yes, but the chances were looking as thin as the ticket seller's comb-over on his bald head, hanging on to hope. I asked the question that the balding seller had probably heard for the 850th time that morning about whether the trains were running.

'It's a limited service...where are you travelling to?' he enquired dispassionately. I told him, and as he checked his computer, Lance called me. I took the call in 20 seconds and was ready to discuss my dilemma with Lance when he said.

'Jay, do you know the bloody time, huh?'

'...Sir? Sir? Sir?' the balding ticket seller was calling out to me.

96 LE FEAR

Lucinda Rhodes-Flaherty (Debbie D), Dave the Werewolf, and Spencer Austin (Leon).

'Jay, are you kidding? Have you seen it out there? Your hopes of making your film today have as much chance as a snowman seeing summer! I mean, I know you're from Yorkshire and all, where every man drives a Land Rover or tractor, but in London, things are different; here, everything comes to a standstill.'

'Lance, you know I won't stand still when it comes to something I need to do... I will make this film happen, even if it kills me.'

'Not even Dynamo the Bradford magician could make this happen!'

'Lance...please mate... I'm begging you... I'm in a real jam, and remember you still owe me one from the Cheesed Off gig...remember?'

After ten minutes of convincing him, Lance, though slightly cheesed off himself, agreed to drive me to the film studios.

Phew! At least I could get to the set. I stood and waited, feeling like an expectant father. Lance eventually arrived panda-eyed and looking like death warmed up.

'Are you planning to climb Mount Everest, Jay?'

Lance commented on my Michelin Man winter attire. I granted Lance the panda jibe without retaliating because, in my congested mind, there was no room to respond to jokes.

Lance's car was like a landfill on wheels with empty and scattered pizza boxes, KFC packaging and mini aluminium meat pie trays covering his car floor. I had to move an empty glass bottle of Appeltiser alongside the other rubbish out of the way for my Michelin-Man legs, and we set off on the 50-minute arduous journey on the icy roads.

Besides the annoying drumming of his fingers on the steering wheel, Lance was quiet at the start of the journey, which is more than I could say for his old car. The Fiat sounded like it had had better days and was in much need of a Lemsip equivalent for cars. The unhealthy banging and rattling noises it was making made me begin to question whether we were actually going to make it to the studios or be left stranded and freezing on the hard shoulder. Through texts, I reassured everyone that we would still be filming, but I wished that someone could reassure me. I remained at the edge of my seat because there was still no answer from Mike, the guy who had the crucial component to the whole production: the cameras! As Lance drove, I thought about a lot of ways around the various pitfalls ahead. If Mike didn't arrive, could filming the film on my camera phone be a possibility?

I'll be there if we're still shooting today, buddy. Are we? Texted fellow actor Spencer Austin and the lead actor in the film.

At the very least, I would have a lead actor and someone who hadn't succumbed to the terrors of...snow! The traffic moved like a sledge on concrete, but somehow we made it.

'You're a lifesaver, Lance mate!...are you sure you don't want a cameo?' I asked as I salvaged my big yellow rucksack from the pile of rubbish.

'Cheers, Jay, but I'll take a raincheck on the cameo. I've started my next chapter, and I'd prefer to just crack on with it, to be honest.'

I arrived at the set but was one hour late. I gave my name to the elderly, wrinkle-faced security guard. He gave me a small map and pointed me towards Studio 3, where we would be filming.

I knew somebody who knew somebody else who was able to secure a room in the well-known Palmoak Studios for a discounted £100. We had only two stipulations, the first of which was that we could only have the room for eight hours.

I walked up the two flights of stairs, and there, to my relief, were Mike and the crew setting up the lights and cameras. The room was freezing, so much so you could see the steam coming from people's mouths when they talked. One by one, the actors turned up, but we were still waiting on a few. Many of the actors present were shivering as we did a quick rehearsal whilst the crew were setting up.

We were allowed to use the discounted room for filming at a discounted cost as long as we abided by the second stipulation: NOT to turn on the heating. There were, of course, exceptions to every rule. Before the actors turned into icicles, we had no option but to break this rule without telling the security office. After half an hour had passed, the room was toasty and warm, which was more than could be said for the stale expression of the security guard who had arrived asking rhetorically.

'Excuse me, do you have permission to turn on the heating, huh?' We told him no, so he warned us that unless we paid £80 per hour, we'd have to switch it off. So we turned it off.

'It also looks like you haven't paid for the room,' the guard stated. In my haste of getting to the studio, I'd forgotten all about it. It would have been too embarrassing to ask any cast or crew members, but the guard was not budging.

An old friend from Bradford, Tawi, who now lived a few miles away from the studio, stepped in.

'Here you go,' Tawi said on his arrival, handing me £100.

'I'd love to stick around mate, but I'm afraid I might turn to ice…but keep the excess from that for the film budget.'

Tawi was another lifesaver that day who helped keep the wolf from the door.

The Beast from the East had my arse on the edge of my seat, waiting and waiting and waiting for the actors who had committed to the film to battle their way through the stormy howling winds and the worst weather we'd seen in years to make their way to the set. This meant we were three hours behind schedule and running out of time. This was challenging, but this was my directorial debut, and I was determined. Eventually, all who were meant to turn up turned up, and with the weather changing in our favour, everything began to fall into place.

The room in the studio let in natural light and was designed to look like a living room; a small coffee table, a side table lamp, and a fake TV were the centrepiece in the middle of the room, facing a floral upholstered sofa.

The cameras were set, the lights were set, and I was set.

I called. *'Action.'*

The first scene kicked off with two lead actors, Lucinda Rhodes-Flaherty (Debbie D) and Spencer Austin (Leon), who were snuggled on the upholstered floral sofa, trying to have an evening in front of the box and trying to reflect two people who were acting out dialogue from a badly written script.

Debbie D said.

"*Oh, Leon, where have you been?*"

As they sat watching TV. An over-emotional Leon poured his heart out to an oblivious Debbie D.

While Leon was having a mini-breakdown saying,

"*My life's a mess, my life's a mess.*"

A grey furry, pointed and sinister set of ears appeared from behind the sofa. The ears belonged to an unconvincing and gormless werewolf which Debbie D abruptly told to.

"*Fuck Off!*"

I called. *'Cut.'*

The man behind the werewolf mask was an actor called Dave dressed in my long black trench coat, a grey werewolf mask and furry hands that I'd bought at an online fancy dress shop for £15.

The genre was a film-within-a-film, and many of the cast members played roles as actors, crew, a producer, and a director.

In the next scene, Spencer Austin (Leon) summed up the chaotic vibe of the film with one of his lines:

"*...Booms are hitting me in the head...imaginary planes are flying over us... it's one thing after another!... it's like working on a fucking student film.*"

The character of Carlos Revalos, a hapless film director, was played by another leading actor, Kyri Saphiris. Revalos was a man who was pretty hard to take seriously by everyone as his character tried in vain to iron out the frustrations of the cast and crew that were mounting like a Jenga Tower.

"*Lets...All...Calm...Down...Everyone? It's not too much to ask, is it?*"

In the few hours that we had, we filmed about 30 scenes in total. However, by that time, I felt like frostbite had found its way past my three layers of thermal socks and had clung for dear life like leeches on my toes. However, the fire inside me was alight and roaring.

'That's a wrap, guys,' I smiled like a wolf who had had a roast pork dinner.

I couldn't have done it without the dedication of Kyri, Spencer, Lucinda and Dave, who, like all the other actors and crew that got on board with the film, were top-notch, and to them, I was truly grateful for helping me get my first feature film up and running.

The film wasn't perfect by any means, but the determination and dedication from all involved was as solid as the snow that had settled that day. We made it. We cheered, we clapped, and we hugged, and my whole body flushed with a cry of triumph which ran through my veins. We'd managed to carry the film to its conclusion together. It felt like I'd been awarded an Oscar.

I thought I'd bitten off more than I could chew with the tasks of having to act in the cameo role I'd given myself as Rasputin, a werewolf tamer, and ensuring that I had the beasts of producing and directing under control.

Many times during filming, I had my heart in my mouth with problems such as running behind the intended schedule and experiencing many issues with the equipment and lighting. My blood pressure rocketed to the moon and back again when, after getting home, I realised I hadn't asked any of the cast and crew to sign contracts, which I eventually managed to sort out! I'm sure I made thousands more mistakes that I knew of and thousands more that I didn't know.

I now had the mammoth task of editing the film. Its title, *Le Fear,* was aptly named after the rock-bottom fear that I had faced with the prospect of turning my back on the industry. It was the fear that helped me push my way out of my darkness. It was the fear that helped me find the new fire in my life in front of and behind the cameras: filmmaking against all odds.

Like a phoenix from the flames, I was back!

97 TOP DOG

'Jesus Christ!...aye...sounds lovely...where...and how far is that from where you live?...'

'Not far, Mum...look, Mum, can I call you back later... makeup is ready for me now.'

'Okay, luv, call me when ye get in, won't ye?... Give Miranda and Brandon a big kiss from me.'

'I will Mum.'

'...We thy children place all our trust in thee...for those that shall see God...Luv ye Jason...'

'You too, Mum...'

'...Can you go to makeup please? I'll bring you up an...Earl Grey...was it?...yep, I'll bring it up to you,' said a pushy runner on a schedule who was urging me to up my pace as soon as I hung up on Mum.

I had stepped back into the light of acting following the success of *Le Fear*, which lit a flame inside my gut that continued to shine. I started running weekly acting workshops, with one of my students being the Moroccan actress and Instagram sensation Sahar Seddiki before she graced the heights of fame in *The Voice*.

With my good friend Dave Antonelli's wise words still gelled in my mind, I took on some cameo roles, including a Western short film called *Kentina* and three feature films: *Umbrage, My Horrible Love,* and *Life Just Is.*

Alongside these, graced upon me was a role I landed in a biblical TV commercial for a religious Channel, as Jesus Christ, and I was ready to be donned with imitation holy garments.

We rehearsed scene after scene on a set taken over by a huge green screen, which aimed to link our performances as actors standing in a studio on the outskirts of London right back to biblical times with special effects during the post-production phase.

During the final rehearsal, as the actors waited for the director's next call, cameras, lights, and sound were nearly ready; the hair and makeup people had just come from behind the set and were asked to add a few final touches of blusher to the Virgin Mary's cheeks. Then, an almighty commotion started right behind me and caught me totally off guard, making me jump and spill my Earl Grey on the floor, only just missing my immaculate blue holy attire. The ruckus was caused by a four-legged actor of the canine species, a pointer breed to be exact, who, for some unknown reason, had taken a more than intense disliking to me, and at the time, I had no idea why.

'That's why you should never work with children or animals!'

One of the wise kings said, trying to adjust the uncomfortable fitting crown he'd been given. He was referring to the out-of-control, huge white and brown-trained canine actor that was transfixed on me. The dog's incessant barking left his elderly handler red in the face. Perplexed but not phased, I turned the other cheek as it continued to become glaringly obvious that the canine was not prepared to share the stage with me and appeared to be insisting that there was only room for one top dog on set. I soon came to realise that the prima donna pointer had probably picked up my best canine pal Toby's scent on me and wondered why I probably smelled like a spaniel.

As it turned out, the prima donna scene-stealing pointer managed to get his way with the producer, who was left with no option but to decide that we would film our scenes separately because we simply couldn't be in the same scenes together. I went along with the producer's decision; I mean, I was only playing Jesus; who was I to judge?

'Bring that back here, you food monster!'

I called, smiling and giggling much more than I was cross.

My plea to Miranda and Brandon's dog Toby had fallen flat on Spaniel's ears as he continued to ignore me and squeezed himself into an unreachable spot with the other half of my Ploughman's sandwich. Toby was a tri-coloured crazy cocker spaniel, a proper food fiend, who had grown to be one of my best friends over the years whilst I lived in Wimbledon. He had the crazed spirit of my childhood pet spaniel, Beulah. It was Toby's loving and loyal nature that helped me through some very dark days.

It was in those very last weeks before he left that we noticed he had slowed completely down. It was in those very last days that we knew that a goodbye was imminent when he lost the use of his back legs and he wouldn't eat. It was in the very last hour that I whispered in his soft, grey, floppy ear as he lay in the vet's clinic:

'I love you Toby boy. We'll meet again...one sunny day.' R.I.P Toby, my best friend.

98 HOLD YOUR HORSES

'You have the right biblical look I'm looking for...can you ride a horse?'

After spotting a peculiar casting call on an acting site, I threw my hat in the ring. I stumbled upon Stephen Southouse, an indie filmmaker who was working on a masterpiece, *Song of King Solomon*, a film in which the lead role, *King Solomon,* was up for grabs.

'Okay, Jason, the role is yours,' Stephen Southouse said whilst we sat drinking coffee underneath a trellis of fragrant Wisteria in Perk Up's garden café. He'd been impressed by my experience, my look, my presence, and our connection in our love of film.

After accepting Stephen Southouse's offer, I was faced with a scenario where I remembered the wise words that another wise king had said to me: Never work with children or animals!

Song of King Solomon was my second feature film lead role, and the responsibility that came with this was the Herculean task of tons of biblical dialogue to learn and deliver. It also came with the great opportunity to film outside of the UK, the enchanting island of Rhodes, Greece, to be more precise. Once the organisation of the filming locations, props and cast were in the bag; we got stuck straight in, that is, until things had to come to a halt, as a giant white horse came out, led by his Greek handler, trotting in my direction (the horse that is!). *Fuck!*

Stephen Southouse had inquired about my equestrian skills during our initial meeting before he actually gave me the role, and without thinking, I, of course, said. 'Yes, I can ride a horse!'

The reality hit me when I came eye to eye, or (eye to nostril, to be more exact) with Victoras, the great white stallion of a horse; I knew full well that the only four-legged creature I'd ridden was Beulah, the donkey I worked with as a child, during my holidays in Bridlington. I foolishly fooled myself into thinking that was a sufficient qualification for horseback riding. But in reality, there was a vast difference between the size of a small donkey and this huge stallion. Not only that, but I was also expected to ride bareback with no saddle to keep me upright! *Holy horseshit!*

It was a ten-minute struggle to climb onto the seven-foot horse, which was starting to get agitated. The cast and crew members, including director Stephen Southouse and the horse handler, wondered why I, an apparently experienced horse rider, looked like a fourth member of the *City Slickers* comedy cowboy movie, which Southouse certainly didn't sign me up for.

'Jason, you did say you could ride a horse, didn't you?'

'Yes, Stephen, but I've never ridden bareback...well, a horse, that is!' I was hoping my joke would compensate for my blunderous attempts at trying to mount the white stallion, and he hadn't seen me riding yet, but Stephen Southouse's expression clearly showed that my humour hadn't won him over.

'You say you've ridden a horse! No?' enquired Rasim, the horse handler, who was right to be suspicious as I did my best to remain upright on the horse.

I didn't have a chance to answer him, though, because Victoras, being the smart horse that he was, realised that I was far from the *Lone Ranger.* Then, Victoras decided to rear up on his hind legs to make matters more interesting, and I clung to his mane for dear life. It felt like a rodeo in biblical times, and I prayed I wouldn't end up in a different era altogether.

Luckily, the stallion's handler promptly calmed the horse down and brought his four legs and my dear life, which I had been clinging to, back to earth as I caught my thudding heart before it rocketed up to heaven.

Now dismounted, I caught the eyes of the aggravated stallion looking at me with a don't-mess-with-me-again-or-i'll-mess with-you-again-look. Between us, we knew that I was fortunate that neither the horse nor I had been injured in this process.

With the horse distracted by some raisins fed to him by his handler, Stephen Southouse came over and asked.

'Jason, are you sure you can ride a horse?'

'Really? Jay, How? Did the horse have some sort of sixth sense, then?' Miranda said that evening after filming, during our FaceTime.

'No, Miranda, it's because I accidentally knocked and kicked its side about 85,000 times when trying to mount and stay on it...and eventually, it figured out that I wasn't horse rider of the year!'

'Jay, by the sounds of it, you hardly showcased your daredevilry as an actor. The moral of the story is that when anyone asks you if you can ride a horse, don't get carried away....'

The following day, we continued filming the horse scenes. I wasn't exactly chomping at the bit to get back on Victoras, and I'm pretty damn sure that he wasn't thrilled to see me either!

Much to Stephen Southouse's dismay, it took an extra 100 *euros* to convince Rasim, the horse's handler, to guide the horse around the limelight while Rasim stayed hidden from the elevated camera's view, and we continued the rest of the filming. Stephen had no choice but to pay the 100 *euros*. After all, the film couldn't have the magnificent *King Solomon* riding a tiny donkey—it just wouldn't have the same *je ne sais quoi!*

Me as King Solomon and Victoras tempted by raisins.

99 SONGS OF PRAISE

'I'm not being awful, Jason, but how long are you going to watch this for? *Songs of Praise* is on at 6 o'clock, you know.' Mum snipped.

Going back to Yorkshire is usually a wonderfully rewarding and exciting time. However, this wasn't entirely the case one weekend when I went back home to spend time with Mum. In between Mum's day-to-day chores from which, she hardly ever took a break. I planned to watch the *Le Fear* film scenes and timeline them for editing. Mum knew I'd made a film, but she didn't know much else about it and hadn't asked.

She had just finished sweeping the kitchen floor for the 85th time and was making a cup of tea while I was in the adjoining living room, putting the first DVD of the unedited *Le Fear* scenes into the DVD player. After passing me a cup of a much-needed strong Yorkshire brew, Mum sat beside me on her newly dusted leather sofa while I watched the first minute of the scene. I was deep in focus, and I hadn't thought to tell her it was the film I had recently made. As she sipped her tea, Mum looked at the 56-inch screen. She didn't realise that it was my film that was playing on the TV. She watched as the gormless *Le Fear* werewolf tried unsuccessfully to be inconspicuous. Mum assumed it was a programme on one of the TV's mainstream channels, and after about five minutes, Mum picked up the remote control.

'Jason, did ye hear me, eh? *Songs of Praise!* I'm missing it. What time does this finish? Can I turn it over? Jason, it's one of the two joys I have in life. Can I turn it over?'

'No, mum, not yet, I'm still watching.'

After a polite and quiet groan, Mum looked back at the screen where the *Le Fear* werewolf scenes were playing out. Mum's restlessness and irritation awakened her voice of dissatisfaction, which was reflected by her curt comment.

'They do put a lot of rubbish on telly these days.'

I kept *schtum*. Before I could explain that I needed to watch it, Mum tutted and muttered.

'Terrible, who makes these things, eh?'

'Mum, you know I told you I made a film.'

'Aye, Jason. Ye did.'

'Well, Mum, this is it, this is my masterpiece!'

I could tell Mum was a little embarrassed as she'd changed her tune.

'Oh really...oh.... it's lovely, Jason!' she chimed.

There was some irony in Mum's comments, given my initial thoughts for a title wasn't *Le Fear*, but it was: *This Film is so Crap it went Straight to DVD*.

I knew *Le Fear* obviously wasn't her cup of tea. My first film critique from Mum matched the veracity of a panel judge working for the Golden Raspberry Awards, but I didn't take it personally.

The following day, I woke up early to do more timeline editing. While sitting in the living room, I was met by.

'Who's in it, Jason, eh?' Mum shouted from the kitchen.

'In what, Mum?'

'In yer film, I'm on the phone with Patrick O'Leary from church... and I told him about yer little film...and he asked me to ask ye who's in it? And when will it be on TV?'

One Year Later

Once the editing of *Le Fear* was in the bag, I had a feature film. Now, though, I was unsure what to do with it. I knew that in the creative world, things were sometimes more about the process and the experience rather than the end goal. But insatiable as I was, I couldn't just leave it be. I wanted the blood, the sweat, and the tears that I put in to equate to something, an end goal, something to show that it was all worth it, something to show it had been recognised, and something to show it had been seen. So, on a new mission, I tirelessly sent it to various places worldwide to get reviewed by different distribution companies. After a few months of hitting hard brick walls with rejections and emails along the lines of...*Thank you for your interest but...we're primarily accepting films with NAMED actors who can get bums on seats...we're looking for films with Dolby sound AND are filmed on 4K...we don't believe a film-within-a-film genre is sellable... Werewolves in raincoats aren't our thing...*

It was looking like nobody, but nobody that I sent the film out to, seemed to actually give a ruddy DAMN about it.

Then... Hallelujah...Hallelujah...Hallelujah...

Jason,

We feel the best market for Le Fear is going to be online streaming and video on demand, and we will place that as aggressively as possible for you. However, I will be frank—it will have more promotional value than financial reward. Online sales are generally revenue sharing, and the dollars are modest.

Randy Van Pelt

(Blue Squared Films)

I had slowly built up a *Le Fear* audience on Facebook with 1505 followers, one of whom was Randy Van Pelt. He had seen something in *Le Fear* that he liked. And, despite its humble beginnings, the film secured a distribution agreement with Blue Squared Films in America. Despite Le Fear's opening song being titled Woody Allen, I was under no delusion that I would be the next Woody Allen, who would grace the red carpets of the Cannes Film Festival in my stretch limo or make the Hollywood Walk of Fame just yet. But after securing a distribution deal, for that moment in time, at least, I was over the moon that the fruits of my labour had actually been recognised by a company that wanted to take a leap of faith with my creation as a filmmaker, and I had a DEAL!

Filming Le Fear in Leicester Square, with the raincoated Werewolf and Kyri Saphiris.

100 THE TRYING GAME

...Have you ever felt like making a movie or even investing in one? Maybe after watching this, you'll have second thoughts...A hapless film director who embarked on his biggest film yet, "Le Fear," and in the process, he managed to hire the worst cast and crew ever to walk on this planet, including a colour-blind electrician, a hysterical glamour model, a temperamental lead actor and an overcoat-wearing werewolf.

Now hungry for more, the film director was back again, ready and raring to go and make yet another film, which he aimed to be even more explosive than his first...

'...Hold on, let me pause this thing...'

'How did you ever make a feature film like that, Jason?' Julian Lamoral-Roberts enquired after watching the trailer of *Le Fear* on my laptop at one of the Riverside Blend Café tables.

The charming and very refined English gentleman, who was also a film enthusiast, reached over for the cream and asked.

'You actually made this for £1000?'

Our meeting place overlooked the River Thames, where we discussed the possibility of Mr Lamoral-Roberts coming on board my next film as an executive producer. He wasn't short of questions.

'What cameras will you use?... How about the lighting? Lighting is very important! And what about the sound?... Would you like more tea?'

The climax I had tasted, from creating, producing, directing and editing my first feature film and landing what seemed like a promising albeit modest distribution deal, was as satisfying as the well-brewed Earl Grey I was being offered.

MY EGO SCREWED MY ACTING CAREER

'I don't mind if I do,' I said as Mr Lamoral-Roberts poured some more tea into my now empty cup.

My meeting with Julian Lamoral-Roberts, an actor, director and producer, had come about from my efforts trying to explore each and every angle, searching every nook and cranny and posting on every social media and film site, including Facebook, Instagram, Twitter, ShootingPeople, StudentFilmmakers and FilmCommunity. I messaged, called, and emailed multiple producers in the UK and across the globe. No one could've faulted me for reaching for the stars, even though I seemed to be getting only a handful of clouds.

After watching Roberto Benigni in Jim Jarmusch's *Night on Earth*, I loved his way of acting. I wanted him in my next film, but I doubted that an Oscar-winning actor wanted to be in my low-budget movie. So, I did the most sensible thing I could think of: I contacted Roberto Benigni's agent.

Meanwhile, my efforts on Facebook to involve producers and investors were also noticed by my old-school chum, Steve McAleavy, who commented on one of my posts:

Remember what I said Jay? Making a blockbuster film when I make my millions is still at the top of my life's list of to-dos.

'May I have your attention, please! This is a customer announcement. The Southern service to London Victoria, calling at Gatwick Airport, East Croydon, and London Victoria will depart from platform...'

My attention had been temporarily diverted from listening to my platform number to a well-dressed man standing merely a few metres away from me, amongst the hustling crowd at Brighton Station. I was heading back from an unfruitful meeting with a potential investor and had just found my return ticket to London when I had to do a double-triple-quadruple-take at a man who was reading something he held in his hand. Blooming heck, It was ONLY the British TV extraordinaire, Steve Coogan. In those few seconds that I stood next to the star whose acting and creative endeavours I had watched, from *Alan Partridge* to *The Trip*, I contemplated how I could make the most of the opportunity and what would be the most sensible thing to do. Maybe give him a copy of *Le Fear*? Maybe strike up a conversation? Maybe get some infinite words of Coogan's admirable wisdom? Unfortunately, although (for the record, I refuse to let this happen normally) in this situation, during rush hour at Brighton Station, it did: I got starstruck! My Karrimor boots felt as if they were superglued to the station concourse. My voice had disappeared, and my nerves well and truly had gotten the better of me. I said and did nothing! *Nada! Nulla! Nichts!* Consequently, I missed my train and caught a short case of the could haves, should haves, and would haves.

I had pushed and promoted *Le Fear* to the high heavens since its release, its social media pages had a healthy following, comments received were overall positive, it was making people talk, and I was certainly hoping that all the work that was put in by me online would be a springboard and a selling point for what I could do as a filmmaker, and a hook to gain all the interest I could for my next film.

Like with *Le Fear,* I had an outline, a plot, and characters. This next film would also be a 100% improvised film-within-a-film. I would give *carte blanche* to the actors to act how they wanted to. I just needed to convince actors that I knew, to believe in my methodology, believe in my film and believe in me.

Andrew Tiernan, Ephialtes from the epic movie *300*: YES.
Actor A. Sorry, Jay, I don't do improvisation. I need dialogue: NO
Aiko Horiuchi Kayako from the horror film *The Grudge 3*: YES
Actor B. Jay, I like your ambition, but this film is not for me: NO
Ian Cullen, D.C Skinner from *Z-CARS*: YES
Roberto Benigni's agent: NO REPLY

One by one, the characters that I'd written and developed were cast.

But for each step forward, there were five steps back. My good acting friend and restaurateur Tony Resta agreed for us to film scenes in his charming Italian restaurant, and another acting contact had agreed to lend me The Gremlin, her canal boat, which was her home on London's Grand Union Canal. Having secured these, other integral cogs were either not in place yet or had become loose, and messages were coming in thick and fast along the lines of:

I'm filming that week...I have another gig on those dates...Sorry, we can't allow you to film during the day...The location is booked up on that date... I'm sorry we sold our last inflatable alien on Tuesday. Each message was like a solid brick that formed an obvious brick wall between me and making the film happen. Setback after setback after setback, it felt like the heavens were conspiring against me.

'So you're dating Uganda's Top Supermodel, Jay? You never said.' Miranda commented as I ate my porridge topped with fresh blueberries, one of which, following Miranda's random comment, nearly went down the wrong hole.

'What?'

'Here, look, Jay,' Miranda chuckled as she passed me her iPad. Although it appeared like one big joke, it was not one of Miranda's. I wasn't finding it very amusing that my *Le Fear* Facebook group had been hacked, taken over and changed by somebody claiming to be, as Miranda had rightly described, Uganda's Top Supermodel. This, even more frustratingly, was something I found I couldn't change because the canny hacker had disabled my admin access.

It was 3:00am, and I was in my bedroom in the dark with a naked flame beside me. I'd been at it for a few hours. A power cut had hit the area, and I only had a lavender-scented candle as my form of light. I had gone through the mill with hitches left, right, and centre, but the springs on my keyboard bounced hard and fast as I made the final arrangements...

101 LE SEQUEL

'Shall we call the police?'
'I think they might be the police!'
Looking towards the dark, freezing car park of an industrial warehouse in crime-ridden Clapton, East London, were suited workers rubbernecking from their office chairs, curious about what was unravelling on the ground below them. They had been whiling away the last hours of their day, appearing to work but actually more distracted by the group of people and cameras pointing towards a rusty caravan that looked like it might collapse if someone sneezed on it. Their morbid curiosity may have led them to think that something sinister or even alien might have happened.

'No worries, man, I can do it,' said Arvy to me as he walked away holding the money that Steve handed him.

Inside the rickety old small 2-berth caravan were two bodies.

Amorous shenanigans were on the agenda between an Englishman and his fiery French girlfriend. I was caught in the intensity of the moment. I held my breath, and my heart was in my mouth but not from staring into the sparkling eyes of the beautiful French siren, but from staring at the film monitor that was set up metres away from the rusty caravan, waiting, hoping and praying for the best Money Shot in the world.
The characters in this crucial shot involved:
The neurotic film director, Carlos Revalos, played by Kyri Saphiris.
The fiery French actress Racquel, played by Denise Moreno.
The doting English boyfriend Oliver, played by Jack W. Carter.
The French cameraman, Jacques, played by Hadrien Mekki.
And the crucial man of the moment, Arvy'das Kizevicius, AKA Arvy,

MY EGO SCREWED MY ACTING CAREER

who was as reliable as a German car and a key member of our crew.

I called. *'Action.'*

A minute passed, and the frisky rumblings were happening between Racquel and Oliver within the caravan, but there was no sign of the rumble that I was expecting; there was no sign of the paid-for deal Steve and I made with Arvy. I called. *'Cut.'*

I walked around the back of the caravan to see why Arvy hadn't done anything. Arvy's spaced-out words floated towards my fire, which quickly fizzled when he said.

'Sorry man, I never heard you call Action. The battery died on my walkie-talkie.'

'Okay, okay, Arvy, forget the walkie-talkies. I'll yell Action!'

I checked in with the actors and camera operators in the caravan and ran back to my monitor and Steve.

I yelled. *'ACCCTIOOOONNNNN.'*

Another minute passed, and again, nothing happened. Frustrated, frazzled, and f@@ked off, I was just about to call CUT once again. BUT Suddenly, there it was! A giant 5-foot-tall purple, shiny, rubber-inflated Alien outside the caravan's PVC window, frightening the life out of Racquel and Oliver (the two actors inside the caravan). Then, the film's big scene...

BANG!!! BANG!!!, BOOM!!! 15 seconds later, Arvy's genius work championed making the caravan rock from side to side.

Oliver and Racquel, the two actors sitting by the PVC window, were not expecting the explosion's magnitude to be so powerful.

"So if we die, what happens, uh? Because I really don't think I'm going to come out of this film alive, you know," Racquel griped in a fiery Parisienne tone.

The film director, Carlos, barked.

"They buy a bloody blow-up doll, stick a sparkler up its arse, stick it onto a yellow remote control car and call it special effects."

"Merde, this is terrible, I quit!" Jacques yelled in a strong French accent.

I called. *'Cut.'*

Arvy appeared triumphantly from behind the caravan, bringing with him a mephistophelian laugh. His eyes shone like he was on top of the world, and I scooted over to make room for him.

'I told you I could blow it up, man; who needs special effects, huh. It was better than *Return of the Jedi?*'

The Money Shot scene outshone any special effects or AI. It was like a New Year's Eve celebration on the banks of the River Thames in

London with noisy trails of bright yellow and orange sparks. The booming, the crackle, the whooshes and the rumbles were created courtesy of Arvy, who had certainly delivered an explosive ending with the armful of November the 5th fireworks he got from a local shop in the bid to carry out the mission I asked him to do: Blow up the Alien.

Despite the dangerous shot, this was a spectacular scene which was nothing short of brilliant!

This was out-of-this-world acting and filmmaking. It was gritty, guerrilla, and chuffing GREAT!

'Make sure you get rid of all evidence of the explosion Arvy.'

'Will do, Jay, man.'

A trickle of a tear fell on my coral Outrage hoody, and I was blurry-eyed, partly from the toxic smoke of the explosion but mainly from the unexpected rapturous applause from the workers who had been watching from their office windows. The actors and crew turned to their audience, and all proudly took a bow, then turned round with applause just for me. It was a doozy moment, and my soul felt like warm apple pie.

Julian Lamoral-Roberts and Steve McAleavy both had my back, not just financially, but in every which way they could. They came on board as executive producers and championed the film with me. I, along with all the cast, crew, and all involved, bathed in the glory of the moment.

The following day, I got a call from Jacob, the landlord of the plot, where we filmed the caravan scenes. He asked if we'd used any explosives. The unexplained, melted, and ash-stained hole in the car park may have sparked his suspicion, but I denied it and made up a cock-and-bull tale.

However, this was no fairy tale; this was my sequel; this was *Le Sequel*.

A follow-on from my first feature film, *Le Fear*. *Le Sequel* symbolised the next stage of my journey in the world of filmmaking.

Making *Le Sequel* was unorthodox and, at times, chaotic, but for me, it was fucking beautifully chaotic.

LE SEQUEL movie poster by Kev Harper Scheme-comix.

Le Sequel had sparked and made its mark not only on the tarmac of the Clapton car park but also with the various film buffs and TV industry professionals who reviewed it:

'A very funny and cleverly thought-out comedy/horror film.' —*Road Rash Reviews*

'Other filmmakers will likely enjoy the journey of this film, which is amusing and oddly familiar!' *Meredith Byrd*

'This movie made my side split and is well worth the watch' ;] *yaddy33*

'The movie itself is like *Spinal Tap!* Shit just keeps going wrong...This thing is put together really well. It's really worth seeing!' — *Midnight Triple Feature*

'Surprisingly well acted and hilarious...It beautifully illustrates what an utter frustration it can be to try and make a film with no money.' *Hellmant*

'If you like mainstream polished movies, this might not be for you, but if you like quirky funny movies, check it out.' *Film buff*

'I love it when filmmakers take you on a surprise journey. You think you're going down the same storyline... but are you? Can't wait to see this filmmaker's next pic.' *Anonymous*

MY EGO SCREWED MY ACTING CAREER

'**Hilarious.**' — *Larry Charles, writer of the award-winning HBO sitcom Seinfeld, and director of Borat and Curb Your Enthusiasm.*

Courtesy of ShootingPeople.org

'**Orson Welles would be proud.**' — *Christopher Zisi, Zisi's Emporium for B-Movies.*

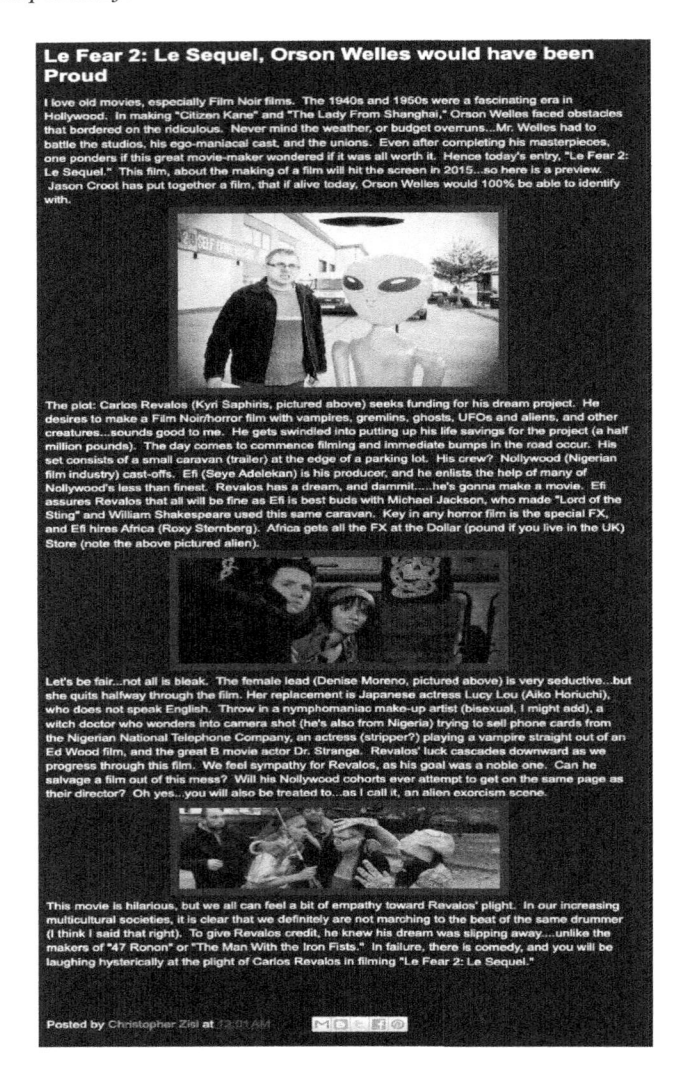

Le Fear 2: Le Sequel, Orson Welles would have been Proud

I love old movies, especially Film Noir films. The 1940s and 1950s were a fascinating era in Hollywood. In making "Citizen Kane" and "The Lady From Shanghai," Orson Welles faced obstacles that bordered on the ridiculous. Never mind the weather, or budget overruns...Mr. Welles had to battle the studios, his ego-maniacal cast, and the unions. Even after completing his masterpieces, one ponders if this great movie-maker wondered if it was all worth it. Hence today's entry, "Le Fear 2: Le Sequel." This film, about the making of a film will hit the screen in 2015...so here is a preview. Jason Croot has put together a film, that if alive today, Orson Welles would 100% be able to identify with.

The plot: Carlos Revalos (Kyri Saphiris, pictured above) seeks funding for his dream project. He desires to make a Film Noir/horror film with vampires, gremlins, ghosts, UFOs and aliens, and other creatures...sounds good to me. He gets swindled into putting up his life savings for the project (a half million pounds). The day comes to commence filming and immediate bumps in the road occur. His set consists of a small caravan (trailer) at the edge of a parking lot. His crew? Nollywood (Nigerian film industry) cast-offs. Efi (Seye Adelekan) is his producer, and he enlists the help of many of Nollywood's less than finest. Revalos has a dream, and dammit.....he's gonna make a movie. Efi assures Revalos that all will be fine as Efi is best buds with Michael Jackson, who made "Lord of the Sting" and William Shakespeare used this same caravan. Key in any horror film is the special FX, and Efi hires Africa (Roxy Sternberg). Africa gets all the FX at the Dollar (pound if you live in the UK) Store (note the above pictured alien).

Let's be fair...not all is bleak. The female lead (Denise Moreno, pictured above) is very seductive...but she quits halfway through the film. Her replacement is Japanese actress Lucy Lou (Aiko Horiuchi), who does not speak English. Throw in a nymphomaniac make-up artist (bisexual, I might add), a witch doctor who wonders into camera shot (he's also from Nigeria) trying to sell phone cards from the Nigerian National Telephone Company, an actress (stripper?) playing a vampire straight out of an Ed Wood film, and the great B movie actor Dr. Strange. Revalos' luck cascades downward as we progress through this film. We feel sympathy for Revalos, as his goal was a noble one. Can he salvage a film out of this mess? Will his Nollywood cohorts ever attempt to get on the same page as their director? Oh yes...you will also be treated to...as I call it, an alien exorcism scene.

This movie is hilarious, but we all can feel a bit of empathy toward Revalos' plight. In our increasing multicultural societies, it is clear that we definitely are not marching to the beat of the same drummer (I think I said that right). To give Revalos credit, he knew his dream was slipping away....unlike the makers of "47 Ronon" or "The Man With the Iron Fists." In failure, there is comedy, and you will be laughing hysterically at the plight of Carlos Revalos in filming "Le Fear 2: Le Sequel."

Posted by Christopher Zisi at 12:01 AM

MY EGO SCREWED MY ACTING CAREER

From Top right Kyri Saphiris. Hadrien Mekki, Kyri Saphiris, and Aiko Horiuchi, Alien on Car The Money Shot... Denise Moreno and Jack W. Carter, during the explosion. Writing the slate, with Shona McWilliams, Andrew Tiernan, the explosion. Denise Moreno...

Me and Arvy discussing The Money Shot on the Le Sequel set.

Julian Lamoral-Roberts, AKA Doctor Strange. RIP Julian. Photos courtesy of Steve McAleavy.

THAT'S A WRAP!

My feet are firmly on the ground, and my Ego WON'T screw my filmmaking career.
NOT
THE END.

ACKNOWLEDGMENT

First and foremost, I'm an actor at heart. Being a writer was never where I saw myself or my future, but I had had so many experiences that I wanted to get down somehow and share somehow, and as I did, somehow, this book was born.

From childhood to date, I've met so many wonderful people in so many different places, in person and online, and although I would've loved to have written about each and every person who has brought a piece of sunshine to my life, I couldn't quite get to grips with the fact that the book would turn into an encyclopedia that would never be finished. To all of the great people and furry friends who have come and gone, thank you, and I know that whether it is this small, quirky world or the next, we will all meet again one sunny day.

I have been blessed to have had these genuinely remarkable beings grace my world and place their own unique stamp on my heart. My life would not have been half as colourful as it has been if it hadn't been for the love, kindness, and passion they shared with me.

My Family played a big part in who I am today, and although I won't list all, they include:

Gan Gan William Banks R.I.P
Nana Eileen Banks R.I.P
Alice Croot
Dennis Croot R.I.P
Ellie Croot
Martin Croot
Lorelli Mojica
Brandon Mojica
Beulah (Donkey) R.I.P
Beulah (Dog) R.I.P
Toby (Dog) R.I.P

To get this book over the line, I needed the help of an editor to tow it over. I'd like to thank Kerin Freeman, who helped with my very first edit. I'd also like to thank the gifted writer Lorelli Mojica, who

has felt the brunt of my capricious moods whilst she spent months and months and months and months editing multiple versions, suggesting to me that I had to really tone parts down or jazz other parts up. For being the voice that reminded me that unless I wanted a lawsuit or two on my head, I couldn't write this-that-and-the-other. And above all of that, I'm grateful to her for trying her best not to murder me over being so damn stubborn.
Without her help, this book would not be released today.

My research into yesteryear led me back to old friends who sent me old emails and retro photos from back in the day, and it made me remember how great my school chums were in my early years.

A shout-out to one of the prettiest girls in our class, Justin Holiday, an old classmate who gave me some school information that I had long forgotten.

My smattering of different languages, as you've probably already established, is not the best, so to avoid having any sort of international bounty on my head from mistranslating something, I managed to get by with a little help from my friends:

Arabic; Amnah Alnami
French; JHUANG, Yi-Syuan 莊憶萱
Italian; Hayley Bianco
Japanese; Yasuyoshi Kindaichi
Mandarin;LU, I-Ching 呂怡青
Portuguese; Jairo Tronto
Spanish; Jairo Tronto

I also couldn't obtain permission for some photos to give my stories more provenance (so I didn't use those), but I needed to support some stories. And Open Sesame, my genies in bottles who granted me some of my wishes for the photo permissions I needed, included:

Cradle of Filth, Dani Filth and management
Madame Tussauds Amsterdam, Netherlands
Telegraph & Argus, Bradford
Dave Antonelli
Tom Tranter
NYFA
Stathis Athanasiou
Sachab
Caspa Codina, Gabriel Prokofiev
Steve McAleavy
Pete Hunt
Shooting People

MY EGO SCREWED MY ACTING CAREER

Christopher Zisi, Zisi's Emporium for B-Movies
Student Filmmakers
Slater King
Nick Kirk
Rich Allison
Martin Croot
Kev Harper, Scheme-comix

This book took me two years, night and day, to complete, so I've decided to write a second book... I won't announce the title just yet. But watch this space.

Thank you for reaching this part of my book.
- If you've enjoyed at least some of it (phew!) I'd appreciate an honest review.
- If you can spare me a photo of you with the book indoors or out and are able to add the photo to the review, I'd appreciate it even more.
- If you did enjoy the read, I'd appreciate it if you could tell your friends, family and the window cleaner about it.
- If you bought the physical book and don't intend to read it again. Please donate it to your local charity shop or second-hand book fair. Not only will the environment appreciate it, but so will I, knowing that this book will be doing more than gathering dust on just one bookshelf.

I'd like to end with a shameless plug of myself to:
- any writing agents who are more than welcome to contact me
- any acting agents or managers (if they like my showreels) can also get in touch
- any film directors who want a piece of the pie to get in touch while it is hot (joke)
- anybody who wants to add me on social media, I'm on pretty much all social media platforms

Our lives are just like books; we have many chapters, and we meet many characters, and we feel love and pain sometimes. Sometimes in life, those we meet may help bring us what we need in terms of passion, energy, intellect, harmony, strength, uniqueness, autonomy, and nirvana. For those who have done this and for those who have loved and supported me on my journey in life, I want to thank you all from the bottom of my heart.

Printed in Great Britain
by Amazon